# Tourism and Leisure Mobilities

This book reframes tourism, as well as leisure, within mobilities studies to challenge the limitations that dichotomous understandings of home/away, work/ leisure, and host/guest bring. A mobilities approach to tourism and leisure encourages us to think beyond the mobilities of tourists to ways in which tourism and leisure experiences bring other mobilities into sync, or disorder, and as a result re-conceptualises social theory. The anthology stretches across academic disciplines and fields of study to illustrate the advantages of multidisciplinary conversation, and in so doing it challenges how we approach studies of movement-based phenomena and the concept of scale. Part I examines the ways in which mobility informs and is informed by leisure, from everyday practices to leisure-inspired mobile lifestyles. Part II investigates individuals and communities that become entrepreneurial in the face of changing tourism contexts and reflects on the performance of work through multiple mobilities. Part III turns to issues of development, with attention to the cultural politics that frame development encounters in the context of tourism. The varied ways that people move into and out of development projects is mediated by geopolitical discourses that can both challenge and perpetuate geographic imaginations of tourism destinations.

**Jillian Rickly** is Assistant Professor of Tourism Marketing and Management in the Nottingham University Business School at the University of Nottingham, UK.

**Kevin Hannam** is Professor of Tourism at Edinburgh Napier University, UK, and a research affiliate at the University of Johannesburg, South Africa.

**Mary Mostafanezhad** is Assistant Professor in the Department of Geography at the University of Hawai'i at Manoa.

# Contemporary Geographies of Leisure, Tourism and Mobility

Series Editor: C. Michael Hall, Professor at the Department of Management

*College of Business and Economics, University of Canterbury, Christchurch, New Zealand*

The aim of this series is to explore and communicate the intersections and relationships between leisure, tourism and human mobility within the social sciences.

It will incorporate both traditional and new perspectives on leisure and tourism from contemporary geography, e.g. notions of identity, representation and culture, while also providing for perspectives from cognate areas such as anthropology, cultural studies, gastronomy and food studies, marketing, policy studies and political economy, regional and urban planning, and sociology, within the development of an integrated field of leisure and tourism studies.

Also, increasingly, tourism and leisure are regarded as steps in a continuum of human mobility. Inclusion of mobility in the series offers the prospect to examine the relationship between tourism and migration, the sojourner, educational travel, and second home and retirement travel phenomena.

*For a full list of titles in this series, please visit* www.routledge.com/series/SE0522

The series comprises two strands:

**Contemporary Geographies of Leisure, Tourism and Mobility** aims to address the needs of students and academics, and the titles will be published in hardback and paperback. Titles include:

**8. Understanding and Managing Tourism Impacts**
An integrated approach
*C. Michael Hall and Alan Lew*

**9. An Introduction to Visual Research Methods in Tourism**
*Edited by Tijana Rakic and Donna Chambers*

**10. Tourism and Climate Change**
Impacts, adaptation and mitigation
*C. Michael Hall, Stefan Gössling and Daniel Scott*

**11. Tourism and Citizenship**
*Raoul V. Bianchi and Marcus L. Stephenson*

**Routledge Studies in Contemporary Geographies of Leisure, Tourism and Mobility** is a forum for innovative new research intended for research students and academics, and the titles will be available in hardback only. Titles include:

**59. Political Ecology of Tourism**
Community, power and the environment
*Edited by Mary Mostafanezhad, Eric J. Shelton, Roger Norum and Anna Thompson-Carr*

**60. Managing and Interpreting D-Day's Sites of Memory**
Guardians of remembrance
*Edited by Geoffrey Bird, Sean Claxton and Keir Reeves*

**61. Protest and Resistance in the Tourist City**
*Edited by Claire Colomb and Johannes Novy*

**62. Tourism and Leisure Mobilities**
Politics, work, and play
*Edited by Jillian Rickly, Kevin Hannam, and Mary Mostafanezhad*

# Tourism and Leisure Mobilities

## Politics, work, and play

**Edited by Jillian Rickly, Kevin Hannam, and Mary Mostafanezhad**

**Routledge**
Taylor & Francis Group

LONDON AND NEW YORK

First published 2017
by Routledge

2 Park Square, Milton Park, Abingdon, Oxfordshire OX14 4RN
52 Vanderbilt Avenue, New York, NY 10017

*Routledge is an imprint of the Taylor & Francis Group, an informa business*

First issued in paperback 2020

*British Library Cataloguing in Publication Data*
A catalogue record for this book is available from the British Library

*Library of Congress Cataloging in Publication Data*
Names: Rickly, Jillian, editor. Hannam, Kevin, editor.
Mostafanezhad, Mary, editor.
Title: Tourism and leisure mobilities politics, work, and play edited by
Jillian Rickly, Kevin Hannam, and Mary Mostafanezhad.
Description: Abingdon, Oxon ; New York, NY Routledge is an imprint of
the Taylor & Francis Group, an Informa Business, [2017] Series
Contemporary geographies of leisure, tourism and mobility
Identifiers: LCCN 2016008439 ISBN 9781138921054 (hardback)
ISBN 9781315686660 (e-book)
Subjects: LCSH Tourism–Social aspects. Leisure–Social aspects.
Human geography.
Classification: LCC G155.A1 T589348695 2017 DDC 306.4812–dc23
LC record available at httpslccn.loc.gov2016008439

ISBN: 978-1-138-92105-4 (hbk)
ISBN: 978-0-367-66821-1 (pbk)

Typeset in Times New Roman
by Cenveo Publisher Services

# Contents

vi   *Contents*

**PART II**
**Work**                                                                     77

7  **Exploring tourism employment in the Perhentian Islands: mobilities of home and away**    79
JACQUELINE SALMOND

8  **The 'nextpat': towards an understanding of contemporary expatriate subjectivities**    91
ROGER NORUM

9  **Should I stay or should I go? Labour and lifestyle mobilities of Bulgarian migrants to the UK**    106
GERGINA PAVLOVA-HANNAM

10  **Workers on the move: global labour sourcing in the cruise industry**    121
WILLIAM TERRY

11  **Confronting economic precariousness through international retirement migration: Japan's old-age 'economic refugees' and Germany's 'exported grannies'**    134
MEGHANN ORMOND AND MIKA TOYOTA

12  **Home exchanging: a shift in the tourism marketplace**    147
ANTONIO PAOLO RUSSO AND ALAN QUAGLIERI DOMÍNGUEZ

**PART III**
**Development**    165

13  **Travelling beauty: diasporic development and transient service encounters at the salon**    167
LAUREN WAGNER

14  **Orphanage tourism and development in Cambodia: a mobilities approach**    178
TESS GUINEY

15  **Mobility for all through English-language voluntourism**    193
CORI JAKUBIAK

16  **When *pesos* come at the expense of tourism proximity and moorings**    208
MATILDE CÓRDOBA AZCÁRATE

# Figures

# Tables

Tables

# Contributors

**Mike Collier** is a lecturer, writer, curator, and artist. Much of his work is based around walking – through the city, the countryside, and urban Edgelands. His artwork, which is place-specific, integrates image and text, often drawing on the poetic qualities of colloquial names for places, plants and birds. In 2010 he co-founded WALK (Walking, Art, Landskip and Knowledge), a research centre at the University of Sunderland which looks at the way we creatively engage with the world as we walk through it. He has been responsible (as curator and artist) for a number of exhibitions and publications for WALK including co-curating *Walk On: From Richard Long to Janet Cardiff – Forty Years of Art Walking* in 2013/14 and *Wordsworth and Basho: Walking Poets at Dove Cottage in the Lake District* (2014). His most recent project, *Ghosts of the Restless Shore – Place, Space and Memory of the Sefton Coast*, is an exhibition and publication of new work based on a walk along the Sefton coast completed in 2015, a project he organised and curated with four other artists (a poet, a sound artist, an AV artist and a photographer). He is also a co-director of the publisher Art Editions North.

**Matilde Córdoba Azcárate** is a Lecturer in the Department of Communication and a Research Fellow at the Center for US–Mexican Studies at the University of California, San Diego. Her research uses a political economy approach to understand the relations between tourism, space production, and community development in Southern Mexico. She is currently conducting a multi-sited ethnography exploring how different tourism ventures, which have been promoted as sustainable development tools for impoverished Maya communities, have become integral in the contemporary reproduction of old uneven socio-cultural and spatial dynamics. Her research has been supported by the Fulbright Program, the Spanish National Research Plans, and more recently, the UC San Diego Non Senate Faculty Development Awards.

**Paula Danby** is a Lecturer in International Tourism and Hospitality Management at Queen Margaret University, Edinburgh, Scotland. Her research focuses on human–animal relationships within leisure and tourism environments, with a particular interest in equestrian tourism. Research interests include animal and wildlife tourism, rural tourism, ecotourism, adventure tourism, and also wellness tourism.

**Alan Quaglieri Domínguez** is currently a PhD candidate in Tourism and Leisure and member of the Research Group on Territorial Analysis and Tourism Studies (GRATET) of the Department of Geography of the Universitat Rovira i Virgili, Tarragona. He has a Master's degree in Tourism Management and Planning from the same university and a previous degree in Economics from the Università Commerciale Luigi Bocconi of Milan, Italy. He collaborated on several projects in the fields of tourism studies and cultural management both at academic level and for private institutions. His research interests concentrate on urban tourism, network hospitality, urban populations, and mobility.

**Bryan S. R. Grimwood** is an Assistant Professor in the Department of Recreation and Leisure Studies at the University of Waterloo, Canada. His research explores human–nature relationships and advocates social justice and sustainability in contexts of tourism, cultural livelihoods, and environmental learning and management. He is an engaged scholar and emerging specialist in participatory and Aboriginal research, northern landscapes, responsible tourism development, and experiential education. Recent and ongoing projects involve collaborations with Indigenous and tourist communities to document and dialogue culturally diverse relationships and responsibilities associated with a special and changing Canadian Arctic riverscape. As a parent and outdoor educator, Bryan is also interested in the 'nature stories' we tell ourselves and live, what these stories tell about our being human, and the extent to which they foster resilient children, communities and ecologies.

**Tess Guiney**, PhD, is a graduate of the Geography and Tourism Departments of the University of Otago, Dunedin, New Zealand. Her doctoral research adopted a critical geography approach to examine orphanage tourism in Cambodia and to unravel the complexities of popular humanitarianism. Her research focuses on untangling perceptions of place, the popularisation of particular humanitarian forms, impacts on host communities and within the international system, and resistance to these development trends.

**Kevin Hannam** is Professor of Tourism at Edinburgh Napier University, UK and a research affiliate at the University of Johannesburg, South Africa. Previously he was at Leeds Beckett University and the University of Sunderland, UK. He is founding co-editor of the journals *Mobilities* and *Applied Mobilities* (Routledge), co-author of the books *Understanding Tourism* (Sage) and *Tourism and India* (Routledge) and co-editor of the *Routledge Handbook of Mobilities Research* and *Moral Encounters in Tourism* (Ashgate). He has extensive research experience in South and South-East Asia. He has a PhD in geography from the University of Portsmouth, UK and is a Fellow of the Royal Geographical Society (FRGS), member of the Royal Anthropological Institute (RAI) and Vice-Chair of the Association for Tourism and Leisure Education and Research (ATLAS).

**Allison P. Holmes** has an Honours Bachelor of Arts in International Development from the University of Guelph, and a Master of Arts in Tourism Policy and

Planning from the University of Waterloo, Canada. She is currently a PhD student in Geography at the University of Ottawa where she is examining change and adaptation in Arctic Canada. Her research interests include tourism ethics, Indigenous research, climate change adaptation, and economic development.

**Cori Jakubiak** is an Assistant Professor of Education at Grinnell College in Grinnell, Iowa, USA. Her research focuses on English-language voluntourism, or short-term volunteer English language teaching in the Global South. She teaches courses in critical applied linguistics and educational foundations.

**Lauren J. King** is a PhD candidate in the Department of Environment and Resource Studies at the University of Waterloo, Canada. Her research and teaching interests include protected areas planning and management, co-governance, and Indigenous-led conservation. Her PhD dissertation research examines the negotiation of two co-governance agreements for a proposed national park reserve and territorial park through the lens of power.

**Jonas Larsen** is Professor in Mobility and Urban Studies at Roskilde University, Denmark. He has a long-standing interest in tourist photography, tourism, and mobility more broadly. More recently, he has written extensively about urban cycling and is now conducting research on running motilities and urban marathons. His latest books are the *Tourist Gaze 3.0* (2011, with John Urry) and *Digital Snaps: The New Face of Snapshot Photography* (2014, with Mette Sandbye).

**Lutsel K'e Dene First Nation** is situated on the East Arm of Great Slave Lake in the Northwest Territories, Canada. The Lutsel K'e Wildlife, Lands, and Environment Committee and its Manager are representatives designated by the Lutsel K'e Chief and Council to provide administrative and intellectual contributions to the Thelon River research reported in Chapter 18.

**Mary Mostafanezhad** is an Assistant Professor at the University of Hawai'i at Manoa. Mary's research interests lie at the intersection of critical geopolitics and cultural and development studies and explores market-based activism in tourism, fair trade, celebrity humanitarianism, and corporate social responsibility. Through this research she seeks to draw connections between popular culture, political economy, and geopolitical imaginaries. Mary is the author of *Volunteer Tourism: Popular Humanitarianism in Neoliberal Times* (Ashgate) and co-editor of *Cultural Encounters: Ethnographic Updates from Asia and the Pacific Islands* (University of Hawai'i Press), *Moral Encounters in Tourism* (Ashgate), *Political Ecology of Tourism: Communities, Power and the Environment* (Routledge) and *Event Mobilities: Politics, Place and Performance* (Routledge). Mary is a board member for the Association of American Geographers Recreation, Tourism, and Sport and Cultural and Political Ecology Specialty Groups, the co-founder of the Critical Tourism Studies Asia-Pacific Consortium, an affiliated faculty member in the Thai Studies Department at the University of Hawai'i at Manoa, and an affiliated researcher in the Research Network on Celebrity and North South Relations.

**Wairimū Ngarūiya Njambi** is Associate Professor of Women's Studies and Sociology at the Harriet L. Wilkes Honors College of Florida Atlantic University. Her research and teaching areas include science and technology studies, feminist theory, queer studies, feminist science studies, postcolonial studies, cultural studies, critical race, gender, class, and sexuality studies, and race, gender, and environmentalism. Her work has appeared in journals including *Feminist Theory*, *NWSA Journal*, *Meridians*, *Gender and Society*, *Critical Sociology*, *Journal of American Culture*, and *Australian Feminist Studies*.

**Roger Norum** is an anthropologist based at the University of Leeds and a researcher on the HERA-funded research project *Arctic Encounters: Contemporary Travel/Writing in the European High North*. His current research focuses on tourism, travel writing, and the environment in the European Arctic, drawing linkages between experiences of mobility, temporality, and sociality and examining everyday geopolitics among communities of transience and precarity. Roger read Near Eastern Studies Languages and Society (Arabic and Turkish) before working as a computer programmer, translator, and travel writer. His doctoral work explored how everyday experiences of spatio-temporal liminality serve as key influences on social exchange among Western expatriates in the Global South. He is the co-editor with Graham Huggan of 'The Postcolonial Arctic', a 2015 issue of *Moving Worlds: A Journal of Transcultural Writings*, and the co-author with Alejandro Reig of *Migraciones* (Ediciones Ekaré, 2016).

**William O'Brien** is Associate Professor of Environmental Studies at the Harriet L. Wilkes Honors College of Florida Atlantic University. He is the author of *Landscapes of Exclusion: State Parks and Jim Crow in the American South* (2016), published by the Library of American Landscape History and University of Massachusetts Press. His work at the intersection of environment and race has appeared in journals including *Historical Geography*, *Geographical Review*, *Human Ecology*, *Journal of Geography*, *Journal of American Culture*, and *Ethics, Place and Environment*.

**Meghann Ormond** is an Assistant Professor in Cultural Geography at Wageningen University in The Netherlands. A human geographer, her research is mainly focused on the intersections of transnational mobility, health, and care. She is the author of *Neoliberal Governance and International Medical Travel in Malaysia* (Routledge, 2013) and numerous journal articles and book chapters on 'medical tourism', migrant health, cross-border and intra-regional healthcare developments, personalised medicine, and international retirement migration. Her work has appeared in journals like *Social Science and Medicine*, *Health and Place*, *Globalization and Health*, and *Mobilities*.

**Gergina Pavlova-Hannam** is currently a doctoral student in the Faculty of Business and Law at the University of Sunderland, UK. Her PhD focuses on the mobility practices of Bulgarian students and migrants to the north-east of England, while her master's dissertation explored the experiences of volunteers at music festivals. She has previously worked extensively in the tourism, hospitality, and events sector.

**Jillian Rickly** is an Assistant Professor of Tourism Marketing and Management in the Nottingham University Business School at the University of Nottingham. She is a tourism geographer working in the areas of geohumanities and mobilities studies. Her work weaves together environmental perceptions, identity and bio-politics, and performance theories to consider the relations between travel motivation and experience. From this foundation, she has published widely on the concept of authenticity in tourism studies and has contributed a series of chapters to edited volumes regarding tourism mobilities as well as landscape perspectives for tourism studies. Dr Rickly is a co-author of *Tourism, Performance, and Place: A Geographic Perspective* (Ashgate) and a co-editor of *Event Mobilities: Politics, Place and Performance* (Routledge). She earned her PhD in Geography from Indiana University.

**Antonio Paolo Russo** is tenured assistant professor at the Faculty of Tourism and Geography, Universitat Rovira i Virgili, Tarragona, where he coordinates the Master in Tourism. He is a member of the research group 'Territorial Analysis and Tourism Studies' at the Department of Geography of URV. Previous appointments were with the Erasmus University Rotterdam (where he received his PhD in Economics in 2002), the Autonomous University of Barcelona, and IULM University Milan. His research interests range from tourism studies to cultural and urban economics. He is author of various publications on such topics in academic journals and books, among which *Cultural Resources for Tourism: Patterns, Processes and Policies* (NovaScience, 2008, with M. Jansen-Verbeke and G. Priestley) and *The Student City: Strategic Planning for Students' Communities in EU Cities* (Ashgate, 2004, with L. Van den Berg). He has been involved in EU research networks and other international programmes and as an independent expert advisor in various research projects in urban, regional, tourism, and cultural economy and management.

**Noel B. Salazar** is Research Professor in Anthropology at the University of Leuven, Belgium. He is editor of the *Worlds in Motion* (Berghahn) and *Anthropology of Tourism* (Lexington) book series, co-editor of various edited volumes and special issues, and author of numerous peer-reviewed articles and book chapters on mobility and travel. He is vice-president of the International Union of Anthropological and Ethnological Sciences, past president of the European Association of Social Anthropologists, and founder of ANTHROMOB, the EASA Anthropology and Mobility Network. In 2013, Salazar was elected as member of the Young Academy of Belgium.

**Jacqueline Salmond** received her PhD in Human Geography from the University of Kentucky in 2010. Her research focused on tourism development on the Perhentian Islands in Malaysia where she conducted a participatory action research project in collaboration with local residents. The project examined how tourism employment was understood and practised by island residents as a lifestyle choice. Her current research explores how tourism is situated within the lives of its participants and how tourism employment and entrepreneurship can be understood within a mobilities framework. She has presented at the American Association of Geographers and currently teaches within the Interdisciplinary Studies department at Florida Gulf Coast University.

**William Terry** is an Assistant Professor of Geography in the Department of History and Geography at Clemson University in South Carolina. He is an economic geographer whose research has often focused broadly on geographic aspects of tourism. He is an expert in the area of cruise ship research with past work that examined hiring practices and labour issues in the industry. His research has also combined his interests in food production with a recently concluded project examining the utility of volunteer tourism in organic agriculture through Worldwide Opportunities on Organic Farms (WWOOF). His most recent work involves evaluating the use of temporary migrant guest workers in the hospitality industries of the United States.

**Mika Toyota** is a Professor at the College of Tourism, Rikkyo University, Tokyo, Japan. Trained in social anthropology, sociology, and development studies, she has worked on ethnicity, migration, and tourism in South-East Asia (fieldwork was conducted in Thailand, Myanmar, Singapore, Malaysia, Indonesia and the Philippines). Her current research interests include transnational retirement migration, long-stay tourism, medical and health tourism. Before joining Rikkyo, she taught at the University of Hull, UK (2000–02) and worked at National University of Singapore (2002–12). Her recent publications include 'Ageing and transnational householding: Japanese retirees in Southeast Asia' in *International Development Planning Review* (2006, 28(4): 515–31), 'The emerging transnational "retirement industry" in Southeast Asia' (co-authored with Biao Xiang) in *International Journal of Sociology and Social Policy* (2012, 32(11/12): 708–19), and *Return: Nationalizing Transnational Mobility in Asia* (Duke University Press 2013, co-edited with Biao Xiang and Brenda Yeoh). She holds a PhD in Southeast Asian Studies from the University of Hull, UK, and before that she studied French and Sociology in Sophia University, Japan.

**Lauren Wagner** is an Assistant Professor in Globalisation and Development at Maastricht University. Her research focuses on issues of diaspora and belonging through microanalysis of everyday encounters, based both in linguistic recorded data as well as in observation of material atmospheres. More extended linguistic analyses are forthcoming in her 2016 book *Becoming Diasporic: Communication, Embodiment, and Categorisation* from Multilingual Matters.

# 1 Introduction

## 'New' tourism and leisure mobilities – what's new?

*Jillian Rickly, Kevin Hannam, and
Mary Mostafanezhad*

## The mobilities turn

We now, retrospectively, mark the mobilities turn in the social sciences as taking place in the early part of this century. Despite earlier claims about the conceptualisation of mobilities, this turn has proven to be far more than a cousin concept to globalisation (see Harvey 2006; Coles 2015). In particular, mobilities began to gain traction as a result of growing attention to increased opportunities for mobile interconnection and interaction through, for example, new communication, transportation, and media technologies. While researchers began to use the term mobility in new ways in the preceding years, the 2006 establishment of the journal *Mobilities* marked the solidification of a new field of social scientific inquiry. That same year, Sheller and Urry (2006) described the 'mobilities paradigm' as an approach that helped to frame the ways in which people's daily lives are spatially interconnected; this includes the politics that drive (and hinder) the movement of people as well as objects, information, and non-human things. In other words, the mobilities turn has been less about a new topic of study and more about innovative and holistic ways of examining what social science scholars have long been observing (cf. Salazar 2010). When mobility is thought of as constellations of movement, representation, and practice, we can think through a more finely developed politics of mobility, one that works with mobilities and immobilities so as to deduce particular facets, such as motive force, speed, rhythm, route, experience, and friction (Cresswell 2010a: 17). This framework provides new ways of thinking about the interconnectivity of mobilities. As Hannam (2009: 109) argues: 'Not only does a mobilities perspective lead us to discard our usual notions of spatiality and scale, but it also undermines existing linear assumptions about temporality and timing, which often assume that actors are able to do only one thing at a time, and that events follow each other in a linear order'.

### Newness

Concerns have been raised by scholars regarding the framing of this approach as 'new'. While Cresswell (2010a: 553; 2010b, 2012, 2014) advocates support for the mobilities turn, he is also hesitant to embrace its claims of 'newness':

> The focus on the new is definitely a potential pitfall for a self-identified 'new mobilities paradigm' and there is a danger of an incessant focus on

twenty-first-century high-tech hypermobility characterized by the car, the plane and mobile communications devices. There is also the danger of disconnecting new mobilities work from all the work on forms of mobility that geography has actually always been good at.

Indeed, an interest in movement, and more specifically the meaning of mobility, has long been a central concern of geographers, sociologists, and anthropologists, among others. If this is the case, why has the declaration of the mobilities turn been so widely adopted? Why does it resonate *anew* with so many researchers of movement-based phenomena? What does a 'new mobilities paradigm' mean for the social sciences, and for other areas of research (Sheller and Urry 2006)?

Perhaps it is best to start with the third, and broadest, of these questions. As Cohen and Cohen (2012, 2015a) observe, the mobilities turn has come about at a similar time to other interdisciplinary and postdisciplinary approaches, namely theories of performativity, non-representational theory and actor network theory. While each of these may be characterised by a distinct paradigm, they all inspire changes in perspective ranging from a move towards diachronic rather than synchronic analyses, a focus on fluid over fixed social patterns, and a widespread replacement of binary categories for the blurred boundaries of reality and virtuality (Cohen and Cohen 2012: 2180). Similarly, Salazar (2011: 576) notes that 'as a polymorphic concept, mobility invites us to renew our theorising, especially regarding conventional themes such as culture, identity, and transnational relationships'.

Shifts towards phenomena in process and the collapse of dichotomies instigated a generation of scholars seeking a more inclusive reading of tourist practice that attended not only to mobility but to the politics and embodied nature of the practice. Such trends, as Cresswell (2010b) observes, encourage postdisciplinary research, particularly between the social sciences and the humanities. In fact, there are numerous examples of mobilities studies bringing together mapping and meaning, modelling and experience, practicality and ethics (see Cresswell 1999; Merriman 2007; Bergman and Sager 2008; Cresswell and Martin 2012; as well as the *Routledge Handbook of Mobilities*, Adey *et al.* 2013). A mobilities approach not only affords but necessitates deeply rich accounts of movement. Yet, as Salazar (2011: 576) explains, 'mobility is a contested ideological construct involving so much more than mere movement'. Indeed, foundational works in this field by Kaufman (2002) and Urry (2000) mark this change in perspective by highlighting the ways in which notions of 'society', 'nation', and 'global' are being replaced by multi-scalar analysis that take into account the complex interweaving of scales of politics, bodies, objects, and movement. Research employing a mobilities approach has challenged these notions further, especially in the contexts of physical movement, representations of movement, and experienced and embodied practices and, in this way, 'mobility studies have begun to take the actual fact of movement seriously' (Cresswell 2010a: 18).

## Scale

By drawing attention to the interlacing of movements of bodies, objects, technologies, information, and politics, the mobilities turn has also brought renewed interest in the concept of scale. Cresswell (2010a: 552) notes that linking differ-ent scales of movement in our research has the effect of understanding the ways individual movements add up 'to more than the sum of the parts'. As Baerenholdt and Granas explain (2008: 2):

> We are thus in a state beyond the dichotomy of the good local, so-called 'internal', control versus the bad non-local, 'external' control. Connections and encounters crucial to people's lives are often much more complex and dynamic ... Contexts are thus not predetermined at any scalar level, but only emerge with the practices of making and becoming places and mobilities.

In this regard, it is unsurprising that scholars have developed new concepts to deal with the multi-scalar and multidimensional fluidity of their objects of study. Concepts such as assemblage (Cresswell and Martin 2012), conjuncture (Li 2014), and constellations of mobility (Cresswell 2010a) are increasingly making their way into our academic arsenal to describe the complexity of what can, inevitably, never be perfectly described. Such attention to scales of movement focuses not only on human movements (bodily movements, daily circulation, diasporas, etc.) but recognises how the world is additionally composed of diverse movements of objects and ideas.

As a result, the mobilities turn has also born an interest in developing new mobile methods. While many mobile methods serve to complement traditional methodologies, they also can have the power of changing the research perspec-tive in ways that illuminate previously unobserved processes (see Buscher and Urry 2009; Buscher et al. 2010; Merriman 2014). Methods that stem from geographical and anthropological material culture studies, such as research that 'follows the thing' (Cook 2004; Cook and Harrison 2007), illustrate the ways human and non-human mobilities intersect at various scales. Such approaches have even trended in popular culture, including the US National Public Radio programme *Planet Money*, which in 2012–13 aired a tracing of the economics of T-shirts, including where the design, fabrication, and distribution takes place. Other mobile methods, including mobile ethnographies, can both complement and complicate grounded ethnographies, as they change the focus of the research from a specific place and time to time-space produced in and through movement (see Germann Molz 2008, 2012; Vannini 2012).

Arguably, tourism studies has witnessed some of the greatest influence from the mobilities turn (Hannam 2009). Perhaps most importantly, approaching tour-ism from a mobilities perspective alongside other movement-based phenomena has provided a means to work past the dichotomies that have plagued traditional studies of tourism practice. Categorical, either/or ways of thinking of home/away, host/guest, work/leisure, among others, as well as strict notions of duration (more than 24 hours but less than one year) assigned by the UN World Tourism Organization, have become less important in defining tourism mobilities. As Cohen and Cohen (2012) observe, this transition from synchronistic to diachronic approaches has 'destabilised the modernist view of tourism as a discrete activity; separated from, and indeed contrasting everyday life' (2015a: 14; see also

Franklin and Crang 2001; Hannam 2009). In so doing, this approach denies much
of the extraordinariness of tourism by illuminating the ways tourism extends everyday life, albeit with reconfigured politics, work, and play for tourists, labourers and
communities. But to say that tourism is simply a particular form of mobility only
begins to hint at its relations, as different mobilities inform and are informed by
tourism (Sheller and Urry 2006).

## Where to turn next? New tourism and leisure mobilities

As a positive indicator of the fruitfulness of a mobilities approach, the previous
decade of academic engagement has brought more questions than answers. Nearly
a decade past the declarations of the 'new mobilities paradigm', mobilities studies
has become an interdisciplinary field of analysis in its own right. We can identify
specific academic programmes dedicated to the study of mobility (for example,
the Centre for Mobilities Research at Lancaster University in the UK, the Mobility
and Urban Studies Program at Aalborg University in Denmark, Drexel University's
Center for Mobilities Research and Policy in Philadelphia, and the Cultural
Mobilities Research Unit at the University of Leuven in Belgium). Indeed, mobilities studies has gradually moved from a scholarly turn to an institutionalised
approach to research and learning. But what does the institutionalisation of a
mobilities approach mean for training young scholars?

In particular, a mobilities approach to tourism and leisure encourages us to
think beyond the mobilities of tourists to ways in which tourism and leisure experiences bring other mobilities into sync, or disorder, and as a result re-conceptualises
social theory. In so doing, mobilities studies advances an agenda that thinks
relationally about the politics that hinder, encourage, regulate, and inform mobilities at various scales, from the microbiological to the bodily to the national, as
well as the mobility of information and non-human objects. Researching leisure
and tourism mobilities involves an understanding of complex combinations of
movement and stillness, realities and fantasies, play and work (Sheller and Urry
2004; Hannam *et al.* 2014). Studies of leisure and tourism mobilities have examined the experience of the different modes of travel that tourists undertake, seeing
these modes in part as forms of material and sociable dwelling-in-motion, dwelling-
in-tourism (Obrador Pons 2003), places of and for various activities. These
'activities' can include specific forms of leisure, work, or simply information
gathering, but almost always involve being connected, maintaining a moving
presence with others that holds the potential for many different convergences or
divergences of global and local physical presence (Hannam *et al.* 2006, 2014).

Recent research has uncovered multiple ways in which tourism mobilities
articulates overlapping yet distinct mobilities that call into question strict
disciplinary boundaries around traditional subjects of analysis in tourism studies:
lifestyle mobilities (Cohen *et al.* 2013; Duncan *et al.* 2014; Chapters 6, 7 and 8,
this volume), lifestyle migration (Benson and O'Reilly 2009a, 2009b; Benson
2011; Chapters 5 and 11, this volume), labour mobilities (Kesselring
2014; Chapters 9 and 10, this volume), development mobilities (Peters 2013;

Chapters 13, 14, 15 and 16, this volume), mobile hospitalities (Germann Molz and Gibson 2007; Chapter 12, this volume), post-humanistic mobilities (Obrador Pons 2003; Panelli 2010; Chapters 2, 3 and 4, this volume), postcolonial mobilities (Cohen and Cohen 2015b; Chapter 17 and 18, this volume), among many others. Breaking down tourism mobilities into mobilities that inform and are informed by tourism uncovers the multiplicity of objects and subjects in movement when tourism and leisure are enacted.

In this vein, this edited volume brings together research that challenges traditional conceptualisations of tourism and leisure but also pushes forward mobilities studies into new trans-disciplinary terrain. Throughout this collection, authors work at a number of scales of human sociality, from leisured bodies and labouring bodies to communities on the move and diasporas reaffirmed by mobility. Thus, a primary concept challenged and expanded in the following chapters is that of scale. By incorporating the mobilities of non-human bodies of leisure, corporations and international organisations, and tourism-oriented commodities into their investigations, the authors demonstrate the interlacing of tourism and leisure inspired mobilities by a variety of actors performing collectively. Indeed, these chapters exemplify changes in mobilities studies, as they are informed less by questions of what moves and to where, but rather why and how it moves.

The concept of scale is also reconsidered in the tourism and leisure mobilities research of this collection through the locations of research. While tourism research was once constrained by ideas of tourism as a spatially bounded, place-based activity, a mobilities approach attempts to capture the fluidity of movement of a variety of factors that together enact tourism and result from it. Thus the chapters on tourism-based development and work problematise the idea that tourism is made up of destinations and attractions; tourists and labourers alike are mobile and that mobility is necessary for tourism and work to take place. That is not to ignore the importance of immobility. Indeed, as Hall (2015: 8) notes, 'the reality is that tourism is an idealised commodity that is only accessible to some. Tourism is therefore part of a "mobility gap" in which the "hypermobile" or "kinetic elite" travel ever more frequently, while many do not travel far for leisure or business at all' (see also Gossling *et al.* 2009).

Finally, traditional tourism studies also privileged a Eurocentric bias, while ignoring much of the mobility gap inherent in the tourist/labourer dichotomy. In some ways, mobilities studies can be put to work to overcome some of the biases that plague Western theories of tourism encounters (see also Chapter 18). Looking beyond Western tourists jet-setting across the world, mobilities studies seeks to uncover the mobilities that course through tourism destinations. This includes the mobilities of tourists, labourers, corporations, transportation, goods, currency, legal rights, and so on. The authors in this book work at a diversity of locations, representing a global scope of tourism and leisure mobilities. By working across international contexts and mobilities, these chapters highlight the interlacing of such mobilities and in so doing unveil, engage, and challenge Eurocentric biases.

## Structure of the book

This book is organised into three broad themes: leisure, work, and development. While these themes offer a useful means to structure the text, most chapters address topics that extend across such categorical divisions and range in focus from the theoretical to the practical, as well as the methodological implications of mobilities research. Indeed, each chapter touches on the interplay of politics, work, and play in the performance of tourism and leisure mobilities. We see this diversity in topics and approaches as further demonstrating the malleability, openness, and conceptual richness of emerging work in mobilities studies.

Part I examines the ways in which mobility informs and is informed by leisure, from everyday practices to leisure-inspired lifestyle mobilities. While tourism was once defined in relation to leisure and recreation, current research in leisure mobilities challenges this relationship, as leisure is woven into and across our everyday as well as our travel practices. In Chapter 2, Mike Collier draws attention to the ways seemingly mundane mobilities, leisurely walking – in the form of meanderings – in particular, holds the promise of overlooked treasures and visual adventures. He demonstrates the ways moving *slowly* can affect the experience of place, allowing people 'to stop whenever and wherever they find something interesting to "explore"'. It is through this exploring via meandering that Collier has developed 'conversive wayfinding' as an artistically crafted means of 'fieldwork'. Leisured bodies are also central to Chapter 3, but here Paula Danby and Kevin Hannam interrogate the interconnectedness of human and equine mobilities. By employing a post-humanistic mobilities approach to human–equine interactions, the authors decentre the human subjects, blur the boundaries of human and horse actants, and uncover the material connections between motion and emotion co-constructed in entrainment practices.

As these chapters illustrate, leisure mobilities foreground the role of the body and embodied practices. Bodies perform leisure and leisure puts bodies into motion, and in so doing, the performance of leisure produces social relations that rarely distinguish work/leisure and home/away as mutually exclusive. The three following chapters each examine the politics of leisured bodies in quite different contexts, from bicycle mobilities to gendered automobilities to lifestyle rock climbing. Jonas Larsen's auto-ethnography of bicycling in Copenhagen, Amsterdam, London and New York City, in Chapter 4, illustrates the effects, and affects, that modes of transportation have on touristic experiences and being in places. He develops the 'bike gaze', exploring the ways touristic performances of cities varies in relation to this mode of transportation, as well as the social and political context of the cycling – the emotional and affective social relations of fellow riders and the 'bike-friendliness' of the city that presents certain affordances to bicycle tourists. Chapter 5 delves into the inherently political atmosphere that is automobilities in Saudi Arabia and the controversial affordances and limitations that gender presents to driving in the country. Next, Jillian Rickly's chapter concludes Part I by examining the politics of subcultural associations of leisure-inspired lifestyle mobilities – lifestyle rock climbing. In this chapter Rickly maps lifestyle rock climbing onto established categories of tourism and leisure mobilities. The end result demonstrates the distinctiveness of a mobilities approach, as it encourages working across and weaving together these categories in pursuit of greater representation of the complexity of lived and embodied leisure mobilities.

Part II addresses the theme of work mobilities, exploring ways that individuals and communities become entrepreneurial in the face of changing tourism contexts. Along with the binary of home/away, tourism definitions have also tended to dichotomise work/leisure and host/guest in ways not always articulated in the actual performance of tourism. Indeed, many long-term travellers find work along the way, while other tourists incorporate career opportunities (internships, volunteerism, etc.) into their travel itineraries. Similarly, local entrepreneurs respond to, and even foster, niche markets that develop out of tourism industries. Thus, this section reflects on the performance of work through multiple mobilities.

In Chapter 7, Jacqueline Salmond extends the scale of analysis of lifestyle mobilities to investigate a tourism community in the 'Global South'. She highlights the micro geographies of the Perhentian Islands, Malaysia, and the ways this tourism community is comprised of 'active participants in tourism, rather than passive recipients of tourism'. In particular, these workers challenge the binary association of home and away as they, instead, feel 'at home' in a particular island lifestyle that merges work, travel, and leisure activities. The non-binary, lived experience of the ways that work and leisure intersect with travel and lifestyle is further explored by Roger Norum in Chapter 8, as he considers the development of the concept of expatriatism. Grounding his research in Nepal, Norum weaves the historical threads of colonialism and the hippie revolution in the country with contemporary aid workers' neocolonialist geographic imaginaries of Nepal's exoticism. This new generation of expatriates, he suggests, fosters personal identities that thrive in this geographically remote place yet internationally diverse communities of hypermobile politically oriented labourers. In the following chapter, Gergina Pavlova-Hannam examines Bulgarian labour migrants in the UK and their ambivalences about staying in the country. While the educational and economic opportunities bring them to the UK, if even for the short term, the media representations and challenges regarding work regulations contribute to their feeling 'out of place'.

The hypermobility of cruise ship labour, coupled with the mobile nature of their work, is the focus of William Terry's research in Chapter 10. Cruise ships are perhaps the epitome of mobility. Not only are the ships continually moving passengers, who have travelled to the place of port to board the vessel, but the labour is internationally diverse, while also predominantly from 'Global South' countries, and the operations of the industry are majority transnational and multinational corporations with global capital flows. Yet, as Terry demonstrates, structural conditions that (re)produce cruise ship labour exhibit clear patterns of neocolonial power, investment capital, and neoliberal globalisation of business. Meghann Ormond and Mika Toyota work at the international scale of mobility in

Chapter 11, as they investigate transnational retirement mobilities. In particular, the authors focus on the shifting discourses around and practices of 'international retirement migration' (IRM) among the 'young old' and 'old old' Japanese and German, suggesting that economic precariousness is an overarching motivation for migration which is complicated with familial, social, economic and political nuances. Next, in Chapter 12, Antonio Paolo Russo and Alan Quaglieri Domínguez reconsider the host/guest dichotomy associated with travel by examining home exchanges. This accommodation practice challenges these rigid distinctions, at least in part through unequal participation in swapping schemes and offerings. This, the authors argue, is far beyond simply supply and demand, but is more related to layered, culturally significant ideas about standardisation and commercialisation of services.

Part III turns to issues of development from a mobilities perspective with attention to the cultural politics that frame development encounters in the context of tourism. The varied ways that people move into and out of development projects is mediated by geopolitical discourses that can both challenge and perpetuate geographic imaginaries of tourism destinations. Examples of the sometimes mobile and immobile actors operating within tourism development are highlighted in the chapters of this section, including the development-oriented tourist (e.g. the volunteer tourist), the local community member, and the NGO practitioner. Among others, these actors play a role in the broader reconfiguration of particular places through their connections with local, national, and transnational development discourse and practice. To begin this section, Lauren Wagner presents the case of the 'local but mobile' Moroccan diasporic visitor (DV) as challenging theories about diasporic communities' impacts on homeland development. Her investigation is based in the beauty salon where she interrogates the relations of embodied leisure and being on holiday to diasporic development. As one of the ways in which local residents and DVs encounter one another, salon visits also perpetuate the roles of consumer and service provider. In Chapter 14, Tess Guiney further explores the perpetuation of neoliberal ideals through tourism-based development with the case of volunteer tourism at orphanages in Cambodia. Rather than 'untangling' the concepts of tourism, poverty, volunteering, work, and migration in this iteration of development, she makes an argument for a mobilities perspective that sheds light on their necessary entanglements. Voluntourism is further explored in Chapter 15, as Cori Jakubiak examines the promises and consequences of English language voluntourism in a multi-sited study based in Costa Rica. Confronting the debates around the conceptualisation of whether English language skills are *for* development or assessed *as* development, Jakubiak advocates a mobilities perspective as crucial to understanding the ways scale, globalisation, and connectivity are at the heart of ideals about English language fluency.

Further exploring tourism development initiatives, in Chapter 16, Matilde Córdoba Azcárate grounds her work in the community of Celestun, Mexico, and its relationality to a nearby estuary preserve, a federally initiated conservation and ecotourism development project. In this chapter she outlines the ways community social power relations have been reorganised to monetise tours of the preserve, thus drawing particular attention to the (im)mobilities that locals employ in order to control access to the estuary. Also focused on the preservation of natural landscapes as tourism development agendas, William O'Brien and Wairimu Njambi in Chapter 17, re-examine the historical socio-political discourses that framed the establishment of the Maasai Mara National Reserve through a mobilities approach. In so doing, they challenge the notion of the Reserve as a 'nature island' and highlight the necessary mobilities (human, animal, viral, and technological) that coalesced in founding the Reserve, that perpetuate the ideology of the 'wild safari', and are required in the performance of the heterogeneous space today. Finally, in Chapter 18, a collaborative effort between researchers Bryan S. R. Grimwood, Lauren J. King and Allison P. Holmes and the Lutsel K'e Dene First Nation illustrates an attempt towards decolonising tourism research. Through their integration of mobilities studies and research design, the authors detail the process of co-developing a participatory, community-based, indigenous-driven research project – *Picturing the Thelon River*.

# References

Adey, P., Bissell, D., Merriman, P., Hannam, K. and Sheller, M. (eds) (2013) *The Routledge handbook of mobilities*. London: Routledge.
Baerenholdt, J. O. and Granas, B. (eds) (2008) *Mobility and place: Enacting Northern European peripheries*. Aldershot, UK: Ashgate.
Benson, M. (2011) 'The movement beyond (lifestyle) migration: Mobile practices and the constitution of a better way of life', *Mobilities*, 6(2): 221–35.
Benson, M. and O'Reilly, K. (2009a) 'Migration and the search for a better way of life: A critical exploration of lifestyle migration', *The Sociological Review*, 57(3): 608–25.
Benson, M. and O'Reilly, K. (2009b) *Lifestyle migration: Expectations, aspirations and experiences*. Burlington: Ashgate.
Bergman, M. and Sager, T. (2008) *The ethics of mobilities: Rethinking place, exclusion, freedom and environment*. Aldershot: Ashgate.
Buscher, M. and Urry, J. (2009) 'Mobile methods and the empirical', *European Journal of Social Theory*, 12(1): 99–116.
Buscher, M., Urry, J. and Witchger, K. (eds) (2010) *Mobile methods*. Abingdon: Routledge.
Cohen, E. and Cohen, S. A. (2012) 'Current sociological theories and issues in tourism', *Annals of Tourism Research*, 39(4): 2177–202.
Cohen, E. and Cohen, S. A. (2015a) 'A mobilities approach to tourism from emerging world regions', *Current Issues in Tourism*, 18(1): 11–43.
Cohen, E. and Cohen, S. A. (2015b) 'Beyond eurocentrism in tourism: A paradigm shift to mobilities', *Tourism Recreation Research*, 40(2): 157–68.
Cohen, S. A., Duncan, T. and Thulemark, M. (2013) 'Lifestyle mobilities: The crossroads of travel, leisure and migration', *Mobilities*, 10(1): 155–72.
Coles, T. (2015) 'Tourism mobilities: Still a current issue in tourism?', *Current Issues in Tourism*, 18(1): 62–7.
Cook, I. (2004) 'Follow the thing: Papaya', *Antipode*, 36(3): 642–64.
Cook, I. and Harrison, M. (2007) 'Follow the thing: West Indian hot pepper sauce', *Space and Culture*, 10(1): 40–63.

Cresswell, T. (1999) 'Embodiment, power and the politics of mobility: The case of female tramps and hobos', *Transactions of the Institute of British Geographers*, 24(2): 175–92.

Cresswell, T. (2010a) 'Towards a politics of mobility', *Environment and Planning D: Society and Space*, 28(1): 17–31.

Cresswell, T. (2010b) 'Mobilities I: Catching up', *Progress in Human Geography*, 35(4): 550–58.

Cresswell, T. (2012) 'Mobilities II: Still', *Progress in Human Geography*, 36(4): 645–53.

Cresswell, T. (2014) 'Mobilities III: Moving on', *Progress in Human Geography*, 38(5): 712–21.

Cresswell, T. and Martin, C. (2012) 'On turbulence: Entanglements of disorder and order on a Devon beach', *Tijdschrift voor economische en sociale geografie*, 105(3): 516–29.

Duncan, T., Cohen, S. A. and Thulemark, M. (eds) (2014) *Lifestyle mobilities and corporealities*. Aldershot: Ashgate.

Franklin, A. and Crang, M. (2001) 'The trouble with tourism and travel theory?', *Tourist Studies*, 1(1): 5–22.

Germann Molz, J. (2008) 'Global abode: Home and mobility in narratives of round-the-world travel', *Space and Culture*, 11(2): 325–42.

Germann Molz, J. (2012) *Travel connections: Tourism, technology and togetherness in a mobile world*. London: Routledge.

Germann Molz, J. and Gibson, S. (eds) (2007) *Mobilizing hospitality*. Aldershot: Ashgate.

Gossling, S., Ceron, J.-P., Dubios, G. and Hall, C. M. (2009) 'Hypermobile travelers', in S. Gossling and P. Upham (eds), *Climate change and aviation*. London: Earthscan, 131–49.

Hall, C. M. (2015) 'On the mobility of tourism mobilities', *Current Issues in Tourism*, 18(1): 7–10.

Hannam, K. (2009) 'The end of tourism? Nomadology and the mobilities paradigm', in J. Tribe (ed.), *Philosophical issues in tourism*. Bristol: Channel View, 101–13.

Hannam, K., Sheller, M. and Urry, J. (2006) 'Mobilities, immobilities and moorings', *Mobilities*, 1(1): 1–22.

Hannam, K., Butler, G. and Paris, C. (2014) 'Developments and key issues in tourism mobilities', *Annals of Tourism Research*, 44(1): 171–85.

Harvey, D. (2006) *Spaces of global capitalism: Towards a theory of uneven geographical development*. London: Verso.

Kaufmann, V. (2002) *Re-thinking mobility: Contemporary sociology*. Aldershot: Ashgate.

Kesselring, S. (2014) 'Corporate mobilities regimes: Mobility, power and the socio-geographical structurations of mobile work', *Mobilities*, ahead of print, 1–21. DOI:10.1080/17450101.2014.887249.

Li, T. M. (2014) *Land's end: Capitalist relations on an Indigenous frontier*. Durham, NC: Duke University Press.

Merriman, P. (2007) *Driving spaces: A cultural-historical geography of England's M1 Motorway*. Oxford: Blackwell.

Merriman, P. (2014) 'Rethinking mobile methods', *Mobilities*, 9(1): 167–87.

Obrador Pons, P. (2003) 'Being-on-holiday: Tourist dwelling, bodies and place', *Tourist Studies*, 3(1): 47–66.

Panelli, R. (2010) 'More-than-human social geographies: Post-human and other possibilities', *Progress in Human Geography*, 34(1): 79–87.

Salazar, N. B. (2010) 'Towards an anthropology of cultural mobilities', *Crossings: Journal of Migration & Culture*, 1(1): 53–68.

Salazar, N. B. (2011) 'The power of imagination in transnational mobilities', *Identities*, 18(6): 576–98.

Sheller, M. and Urry, J. (2006) 'The new mobilities paradigm', *Environment and Planning A*, 38(1): 207–26.

Urry, J. (2000) *Sociology beyond societies: Mobilities for the Twenty-First Century.* London: Routledge.

Vannini, P. (2012) 'In time, out of time: Rhythmanalyzing ferry mobilities', *Time & Society*, 21(2): 241–69.

Warne Peters, R. (2013) 'Development mobilities: Identity and authority in an Angolan development programme', *Journal of Ethnic and Migration Studies*, 39(2): 277–93.

# Part I
# Leisure

# 2 Meanders as mobile practices

*Street Flowers – Urban Survivors of the Privileged Land*

*Mike Collier*

## Introduction

In this chapter, I explore the way in which we relate to our environment and its often contested histories through the simple action of taking a *meander* through an 'edgeland' urban site (Farley and Symmons 2011) – a site local to me and the place where I work (Sunderland in the north-east of England). It is my contention that the action of moving *slowly* (or *meandering*) through our surroundings affects the experience of that place in ways that are not immediately apparent. Meandering allows the walker to stop whenever and wherever they find something interesting to 'explore'; and it allows them time to respond to the weather patterns and soundscapes of an environment. This creates an embodied experience which, when meandering in a group, seems to encourage the body and mind to co-respond by also *wandering* across a range of different areas of thought (Ingold 2010). In my artistic walking projects (for instance *In Temperley's Tread* (2013), *Walking Through the Sands of Time* (2014) or *Borderlands* (2015)), these have included discussions around natural history, social history, politics, and philosophy explored together in non-hierarchical and unstructured ways, ways which create new patterns of interdisciplinary and interconnected thinking.

As an artist, my work is based around my 'practice' of walking, or more properly, meandering. These meanders take a human and embodied approach to being in the landscape – what Robert Macfarlane calls 'landscape and the human heart' (Macfarlane 2012: xi) – and are shared with others. My approach is phenomenological and much influenced by the work of Wylie (2007) and Ingold (2010). The former stresses that 'direct, bodily contact with, and experience of, landscape' reveals 'how senses of self and landscape are together made and communicated, in and through lived experience' (Wylie 2007: 141). I am also cognisant of the wider tourism and leisure mobilities literature and how this can shape my artistic practice (Edensor 2000; Larsen 2001; Pinder 2001).

In her recent review, Jennie Middleton (2011) discusses how walking in the city has been conceptualised following de Certeau (1984) as a potentially emancipatory project which reflects a degree of romanticism about the everyday walker. Instead, she points out that much walking is subject to many constraints – from other forms of transport and, indeed, frequently other people. For many people, it can be acknowledged that walking is part of a job, a chore even (Hall and Smith 2013). Nevertheless, walking has become re-valued and artistic interventions have been an integral part of this political process. For example, Misha Myers (2011: 183) has highlighted how narrative walking practices, 'or modes of conversational activity set in motion by the conditions of wayfinding', offer a means of intervening in the politics of mobility. She discusses how the artwork 'way from home' provided an 'interventional methodology for eliciting and representing the transnational experiences, affects and significances of place for refugees and asylum seekers across the UK' (Myers 2011: 183).

In this chapter I present a different form of artistic intervention but one that similarly develops and uses the notion of conversive wayfinding. I focus particularly on the natural history of a place. This choice is the result of my interest in flora and fauna, which often have fascinating and complex stories to tell, that signpost and/or transcend social and political histories. Taking such an approach in urban wastelands that once supported thriving industries may be seen by some as irrelevant and indulgent. However, I intend to confront this perception, demonstrating that such *fieldwork* is embedded within a working-class culture (and not just the preserve of the leisured wealthy and middle classes), especially in the North of England – and to show why it is important to rescue this history. I will conclude the chapter by considering theories of *Slow Living*, making specific reference to the work of Parkins and Craig (2006). I suggest that, taken together, *meandering* and *fieldwork* can create a space to consider living and experiencing the world we are accustomed to differently, creating within each of us a sense of embodied identity that can help us to negotiate the *deterritorialisation* of culture (Parkins and Craig 2006).

## Method

In a recent essay about my working practice, the writer and historian, Carol McKay (2012), wrote:

> For Collier, the relationship between walking and artistic practice is a complex one, involving extensive collaboration, participation and conversational exchange. He *curates* walks that are inherently sociable, their meandering format inviting conversation and the sharing of knowledge even (or perhaps especially) among strangers. As process, the walking is ephemeral. It is repeatable, but never replicable, the vagaries of weather and seasonal patterns ensuring this … The shared experience, for Collier, generates new knowledge of species and plant-life encountered during the walk. This 'botanising' on the streets is married with the diverse individual perceptions and social observations that inevitably emerge as the conversations develop and the walk unfolds in its place-specific way. All of this serves as material for thought, layered intuitively into the fabric of the abstract paintings and drawings he constructs back in the studio. Text is important in the architecture of Collier's work, the familiar unfamiliarity of vernacular names, dialects of

birds and plants once known but fleetingly remembered, hinting back to the specificity of places and their ecological frameworks. Some of these art works return to the urban streets in the form of billboards, their visual poetry re-creating new encounters for by-passers; others find their location in the white walls of the gallery, where visitors again may walk, one foot after another and round again, in different but equally embodied experience.[1]

The two meanders of mine which are the focus of this chapter took place on 25 March and 29 May 2012, and are part of an ongoing series of walks that I call *Street Flowers – Urban Survivors of the Privileged Land*. They were selected for inclusion in the AV Festival (2012), an important event in the UK arts calendar. In the run-up to London 2012 with its motto of 'Faster, Higher, Stronger', AV Festival 12 presented an alternative, slower paced and relaxed rhythm to counter the accelerated speed of today. Titled after *ASLSP (As SLow aS Possible)*, by pioneering artist and avant-garde composer John Cage, the theme explored how artists have stretched, measured, and marked the passage of time.

*Figure 2.1* Mike Collier, *Street Flowers – Urban Survivors of the Privileged Land*, 2012 Billboard, St Mary's Way, Sunderland. From 'CIVIC', the first international exhibition of billboard art. Produced in collaboration with Tom Madge. (The colloquial names for four weeds encountered as we walked past this billboard: *Huggaback* – Tufted Vetch; *Twaddgers* – Bush Vetch; *Withywind* – Honeysuckle; *Bullister* – Blackthorn.)

The title of these meanders *Street Flowers – Urban Survivors of the Privileged Land* came from my reading of Richard Mabey's book *Street Flowers* in which he suggests that 'towns and cities aren't the kind of place in which we expect wild flowers to grow. Every imaginable obstacle seems to be in their way' (Mabey 1976: 9–10). Mabey's city weeds are itinerant survivors – rebels, insurgents, and anarchists: 'Where there is open ground, in parks and gardens, wild flowers are hunted down, weeded out and thrown away like litter' (Mabey 1976: 10–11). It's a surprise that any plants survive, he says. Mabey then goes on to explore some of the puzzles these survivors/immigrants/colonisers set us. How did they arrive here in the first place? How do they survive the harsh conditions of the city? Many arrived as stowaways on ships from around the globe; some thrive on the waste left behind from past industries that have long since disappeared; some moved in to colonise sites ravaged by the bombing of cities in World War Two, gaining a fragile foothold and then prospering. Each flower/weed has a tale to tell. But, Mabey concludes, street flowers have a wretched life. They're ignored, untended, trampled upon (the social simile here is clear, I think). But, he adds, 'they are amongst the very few wild, living things you will find in a city' (Mabey 1976: 11–13). Indeed, I would suggest that city edgelands represent some of the only truly wild places left in the UK (most of the countryside being extensively and intensively farmed and mechanised – either touristically or agriculturally – or, as is the case of national parks, both).

These meanders took place on the reclaimed banks of the River Wear in Sunderland, an area that just 60 years ago was the world's busiest centre for shipbuilding but is now an urban edgeland that is part wasteland, part parkland, part industrial site, part cycle route and part walkway. As well as broken glass, litter, and areas of closely mown grass, I and my colleague, the natural historian Keith Bowey,[2] have recorded over 160 different species of flora and fauna on our meanders through this place.

## The meander: field-notes

For the next part of this chapter I would like to take you, the reader, on this meander with me, stopping at various points to reflect on the histories of the river, exploring the thoughts and memories that some of the participants shared with me and each other and reflecting on the experience of walking through this edgeland *slowly*. To help us 'navigate' this route, I will introduce a series of waymarkers, or stopping-off points – points of interest, or places that for one reason or another triggered thoughts and memories within the two groups that walked with me. It is my contention that the activity of walking triggers thinking patterns that are different from those we might formally use when 'constructing' an essay, and so this part of my writing (compiled as series of ethnographic field-notes) will 'meander' in the same way that our walks meandered. In this I am developing a mobile methodology that I hope will be of use to both artistic and social sciences researchers alike.

As the first meander in March was fully booked, it was repeated two months later to accommodate those we had to turn away.[3] Both meanders began at dawn (at 7.30am on 25 March 2012, and at 5.30am on 29 May 2012) and followed roughly the same route. They were led at a pace of approximately one mile an hour along the banks of the River Wear, crossing the Wearmouth and Queen Alexandra Bridges before finishing back at the National Glass Centre four hours later for breakfast. These meanders allowed us to connect with our surroundings in a number of different ways, to view the route of our meander as a whole from the elevated viewpoint of the two bridges, as well as, from ground level, immersing ourselves in the surrounding environment by meandering through it. The field-notes below have been compiled and collated from information recorded on both meanders, and the grid references are taken from the OS (Ordnance Survey) map number 308 (Durham & Sunderland).

**Waymarker 1** (*GR 404577; 5.30am on 29 May 2012. Weather – still, with a chill in the air*). Before we walked anywhere, we stood motionless in the car park behind the National Glass Centre (an area of concrete and scrub), closed our eyes and listened without talking – for over five minutes. We had started early so as to catch the sounds of the dawn chorus and to experience the change in the texture of the local soundscape as Sunderland 'woke up'. We were encouraged by our 'guide' for the morning, Keith Bowey, to turn a full 180 degrees and to listen; attentively. Gradually, from out of the general background noise, we began to identify the song of Greenfinch, Goldfinch, Blackbird, Song Thrush, Jackdaw and Dunnock and the alarm call of Wren.

**Waymarker 2** (*GR 403577; 7.35am on 25 March 2012. Weather – an unseasonably warm morning*). As we walked away from the Glass Centre, I explained how the title of the meanders originated – discussing the ideas outlined by Mabey in his book *Street Flowers* (a copy of which I showed to the group at the end of the walk). A few people, however, wondered where the second part of the title, *The Privileged Land*, came from. I suggested that the derivation of Sunderland arose from the Old English, *sundor*, that is, land 'apart', or 'special'. This use of the term 'special', or 'privileged', may have related to the fact that the first mention of this area, which is situated at the mouth of the River Wear, was in the *Boldon Book* of 1183, when it was named as Bishop's or Monk's Wearmouth – and that perhaps it was the reference or association here to 'Bishops' and 'Monks' that 'made special' or 'privileged' the cluster of houses that later became known as Sunderland.

**Waymarker 3** (*GR 402576; 5.55am on 29 May 2012. Weather – moist, damp air*). A few yards further on, we stopped and found a number of interesting plants growing just a few yards from the footpath, including the exotic-looking Bee Orchid (Figure 2.2) and Squinancywort, a member of the bedstraw family. This is a small, prostrate, hairless plant with clusters of four pale-pink, petal-lobed flowers, more commonly found on the chalk downs of Southern England. Keith explained that its common name is derived from its former use as a medicinal herb said to cure quinsy (a streptococcal (bacterial) infection that develops as a

*Figure 2.2*  A Bee Orchid on the banks of the River Wear, 5.55am on 29 May 2012.

Source: Photo: Daniel Magill.

complication of an acute sore throat such as tonsillitis) and that potions of this waxy-flowered perennial would be made into an astringent gargle. It is possible that residue from old lime kilns (Figure 2.3) along the river may have provided an ideal habitat for the Squinancywort.

These kilns were constructed on the north bank of the Wear during the eighteenth and nineteenth centuries in order to process minerals from the adjacent Fulwell Limestone Quarry. The type of 'botanising' that our 'group' was now engaged in (and the discussions that followed, which ranged from social history to philosophy) mirrored the sort of activity introduced by the Field Clubs that sprang up in the industrial centres of northern towns and cities in England from the late eighteenth century onwards. These clubs, 'which concerned themselves largely or wholly with botany, were remarkable for the fact that all their members, without exception, were manual workers, most of them factory operatives or jobbing gardeners' (Elliston Allen 1976: 158). They organised field trips; walks that focused particularly on a 'keenness for botany – and, even more, for precise plant identification' (Elliston Allen 1976: 158). It is remarkable, says Elliston Allen, that this interest and activity 'should have persisted for so long and so strongly in such apparently inhospitable surroundings and often in the face of the most discouraging personal circumstances' (1976: 158).

**Waymarker 4** (*GR 398576; 8.00am on 25 March 2012. Weather – a warming and fresh light; three tall tower blocks appear on the horizon through the early morning mist, which gradually clears, revealing a clear, pale-blue sky*). Here we stopped to

*Figure 2.3* The River Wear at 8.15am on 25 March 2012. Very little remains of a once thriving shipbuilding industry.

Source: Photo: Adam Phillips.

look at *The Iron Tree*, which is part of a large riverside sculpture entitled 'Shadows in Another Light' by Craig Knowles, Colin Wilbourn and Karl Fischer (1998). It shows the metamorphosis of a shipyard crane into a tree. This sculpture prompted a number of participants to recall their own childhood memories of a river teeming with industrial activity, when many shipyards lined the banks of the Wear. A few remembered the names: A roll call of 'ghosts in the landscape' (Pinder 2001: 1): Swann, Hunter & Wigham Richardson Ltd; Sir J. Priestman; W Pickersgill & Sons Ltd; W. Gray; Short Brothers; W. Doxford and Sons Ltd; Sir James Laing & Sons Ltd; R. Thompson; S. P. Austin & Sons; J. Crown & Sons Ltd; J. L. Thompson & Sons Ltd; J. Blumer & Co; Sunderland Shipbuilding Co Ltd; Osbourne Graham; Bartram & Sons.

**Waymarker 5** (*GR 395575; 8.10am on 25 March 2012. Weather – sun breaking through; the river still; no wind*). A little further on, we came upon an area of scrub and wasteland with broken glass and concrete but brimming with weeds and insects. We stopped to look closely at this small patch of unloved land. Some of the group recalled memories from childhood, of exploring/walking through similar inner city sites in and around Sunderland. This barren area of 'abused' land was exactly the sort of area they, as children, used to love to explore. They were feral places; out of bounds, places they shouldn't be in. Areas like this are 'wilder' than many of the highly managed swathes of green in what we call in the

UK the countryside. The poet Paul Farley wrote about his similar memories in *Journey, NETHERLEY (Escaping the inner city)*.

> Somebody discovered a Victorian dump on the town side of Netherley, and digging into its black, oily earth littered with the broken clay pipes and Bovril jars and highly prised soda bottles from another age, I realised how this ground had once been deemed beyond the pale, a suitable site for the disposal of waste, out of sight, out of mind before the city had gradually caught up with its past. At that dump ... we learnt how to explore and find pleasure in our surroundings, and it feels to me now like the last moment when a generation of young lives could be lived largely outdoors.
>
> (Griffiths and Farley 2008: 165)

**Waymarker 6** (*GR 387584; 8.20am on 25 March 2012. Weather – bright and clear; no wind; the river flat calm*). The first meander in March had begun in a thick coastal haar, but as the morning progressed the sun burned this away and warmed the still air. We trained our binoculars across the river through the sharp northern light, looking at the bird life that punctuated the mudflats revealed by the low tide on the south bank of the River Wear at Deptford and Ayre's Quay. Keith 'named' a few birds, and we talked about their extraordinary migratory patterns as well as their habits and calls. I felt alive, subsumed within this environment; in it; part of it; of it. I began to wonder about the relationship between an embodied experience that is (necessarily) of the here and now to history, memory, and experience? Afterwards, I shared my thoughts with some of the group. We may not initially be able to articulate why we respond in the way we do to certain things, but it is more than likely embedded within a (personal) relationship to history. A number of people had very particular recollections of the past that seemed to form an alternative, individual story that ran parallel to the meta social and political histories we are taught; memories that were about their own (very personal) experiences of the world and how they relate to it – and how they engage with others.

Such reflection has led me, in my own studio work, to consider using words in their vernacular sense – words of things (birds, plants, animals, etc.) used and spoken locally. It is this combination of the local dialect and the spoken word that is of interest to me. When Merleau-Ponty (Kleinberg-Levin 2008) talks about how words (and poetry) are a way of 'singing the world', he is referring, I think, to the way that local words spoken have a rhythm and a 'gestural sense' that give meaning to the world. Merleau-Ponty proposes that the artist/poet can bridge the gap between our pre-reflective sense of the world and our reflective knowledge of it, and I am interested in the way he suggests that our experience of nature might be 'conceptualised in language' (Harney 2007: 144). Harney (2007: 144) argues that Merleau-Ponty did not intend to 'reduce nature to a human convention', but rather to 'ground language in the visible, audible world' – a world we experience by being in, and walking through, it.

Throughout our first meander we heard the call of Curlew (*Calloo*) and Redshank (often called the Sentinel of the Marshes as it is the first bird to cry out at the approach of potential danger). We saw Greenfinch (*Peasweep*), Goldfinch (*Flame of the Wood*), Blackbird (*Amsel*), Song Thrush (*Throstle*), and Dunnock (*Smokey*). We also caught sight of Kestrel (*Keelie* or *Wind Hover*), Stock Dove (*Cushat*), and Bullfinch (*Maup*) as well as newly arrived migratory birds from North Africa – Chiff Chaff (*Thummey*), Willow Warbler (*Fell Peggy*), and Garden Warbler (*Juggler*). The local derivation of these words reflects people's direct engagement with, and in, the world through which they walked during the course of their everyday lives. Colloquial names for flora and fauna are often expressive and poetic (see Wylie 2007).

**Waymarker 7** (*GR 385582; 7.00am on 29 May 2012. Weather – little change; still wearing coats and hats; sound carries well through the quietness of the listless atmosphere*). As we walked along the north bank of the river, our journey took us past a series of pigeon coops high above an outcrop of magnesium limestone, a habitat unique to the British Isles and home to plant communities not seen anywhere else in the UK. A few days after our second walk, I received (via email) a poem from one of the participants, which 'summarised' her experiences of the walk, focusing in particular on this one place.

**Waymarkers 8–9** (*GR 383575–GR 396575; 8.30am–9.30am on 25 March 2012. Weather – hats and coats off; walkers wearing T-shirts/short sleeves; a beautiful morning; warm and sunny*). I often find that on these meanders we spend longer in the first half of the walk identifying flora and fauna, but as the walk progresses and people become more comfortable in each other's company, conversations develop, and the pace marginally quickens. As we walk over the Queen Alexandra Bridge, I talk to a small group of folks about my own interest in walking and my early influences and 'heroes'. I am a Liverpudlian and my early walking took place in the landscapes of the Lake District and the Peak District. In this I was following in the footsteps of many northern working-class men and women (some perhaps friendly with my grandfather and great-grandfather – both miners). Howard Hill (1980: 13–17) described how an 'urbanised population, torn increasingly from its ancient roots in the soil by the industrial revolution ... sought to recapture the humanity they had lost in the factories and mines' by walking in the hills and dales of the north of England. 'Unlike the literary figures of the eighteenth and nineteenth centuries, the working class could neither desert the towns to live in the countryside nor spend weeks walking through it. But that did not mean that they needed or appreciated it less', and it was out of this need that the early ramblers' clubs were formed. However, once in the hills, the ramblers were often prevented from walking across large tracts of open fells fenced off by landowners who 'farmed' the land for grouse shooting – described by Ernest A. Baker in 1924 as a 'pastime for the idle rich' (Rothman 1982). And so walking also became a political activity, with walkers regularly trespassing deliberately on private land, land they believed they had a right to walk across. This trespassing came to a head when, on 24 April 1932, an organised 'mass trespass' tried to gain access to the tops of Kinder Scout in the Peak District.

The trespass was led by Benny Rothman, who was accompanied by over 300 ramblers from working class organisations in the North of England. They were attacked by gamekeepers, and a fight ensued, causing injury to a number of the trespassers, some of whom were subsequently arrested and jailed for their activities.

However, this direct action led, eventually, to the establishment of a network of rights of way across the UK and, recently, to the establishment of the 'Right to Roam' policy enshrined in *The Countryside and Rights of Way Act 2000*, which grants us much greater access to the countryside (see Kay and Moxham 1996). So, I see my interest in walking as more than just an escape from the vicissitudes of twenty-first-century living. Walking 'signifies the restlessness of the embodied mind' such that the mobility of the radical mind can become a powerful 'weapon of resistance' (Lewis 2001).

**Waymarker 10** (*GR 404476*). Our meanders ended where they began – at the National Glass Centre. We were ready for breakfast. Over tea, coffee, croissants, and bacon sandwiches, we talked about what we had just experienced. I handed out a print and talked about how my walking informed my studio work, explaining that I 'laid out' a series of colour swatches – colour-marks that I hope captured something of the depth, freshness, and vitality of our experience when meandering through these edgelands. Lime Green; Chartreuse; Powder Blue; Aqua Marine; Steel; Mauve; Soft Gold; Dark Yellow; Blue Haze; Etruscan Brown; Olive Green; Lilac; Common Blue. Intertwined within these intuitive marks of colour where the colloquial names of a selection of flora seen along the route we took; *Kattaklu* (Bird's Foot Trefoil); *Huggaback* (Tufted Vetch); *Claver* (White Clover); *Chaw* (Hawthorn); *Paigle* (Cowslip); *Snoxum* (Foxglove); *Golland* (Buttercup); *Twaddgers* (Bush Vetch); *Quillet* (Clover); *Okerdu* (Bugle); *Griggles* (Bluebell); *Hiskhead* (Self-heal); *Cammock* (Yarrow); *Cushycows* (Broad-leaved Dock); *Tassle* (Knapweed); *Swinnies* (Thistle); *Banathal* (Broom); *Scrogg* (Whitethorn); *Bullister* (Blackthorn). I laid out a series of books that informed my practice for people to read or refer to.

## Conclusions

Parkins and Craig (2006) situate the concept of 'slow living' within a larger cultural reaction to the time/space dislocations and the disjunctures of globalization. Slow living, they argue, can be understood as an attempt to 'individualise' and to challenge normative trajectories of global capitalism. It is 'fundamentally … an attempt to exercise agency over the pace of everyday life' (Parkins and Craig 2006: 67). They advance an argument that slow living is a potentially transformative paradigm because any attempt to slow down necessarily means engagement with all of the obstacles to slowing down. Parkins and Craig's optimistic assessment of slow living may raise the hackles of some who are sceptical of the romanticism and elitism that may be seen to go hand in hand with localised studies. Parkins and Craig confront these issues by arguing that it is counterproductive to want to get off the world – to escape the present and retreat into the past. We are where we are; and that is within, not outside, a global market economy which they articulate as a series of complex, interrelated local economies. If we are to successfully negotiate this apparent *deterritorialisation* of culture, we need to understand our post-humanistic sense of place and individuality (see Danby and Hannam, Chapter 3, this volume). To do this, we need to challenge dominant forms of contemporary thinking and at times to reinvent it. This requires us to confront hierarchical, normative ways of looking at the world. It also requires creative and syncretic thinking – something that often takes place in the spaces we find *between* our busy everyday lives. Meandering as a mobile method slows down the pace of everyday life and encourages creative thinking and social dialogue as well as the exchange of ideas, memories and reflections. This may allow us time to be ourselves and to develop a clearer sense of our own individuality as artists and researchers.

## Notes

1 Colour is a crucial component in my work. As the images in this chapter will be reproduced in black and white, I would refer the reader to my website (www.mikecollier. eu) for further reference.
2 Keith Bowey is a member of the Institute of Ecology and Environmental Management (MIEEM), a Fellow of the Royal Society for the Arts (FRSA). He is an environmental consultant and director of his own company, GEES (Glead Ecological & Environmental Services).
3 This second meander was part-funded by Comapp – a multi-platform media project to map the River Wear in sound, voice, and stories. Comapp is a University of Sunderland project funded by the EU (Education and Culture DG – Programme Lifelong Learning) and run by Caroline Mitchell and Mike Pinchin.

## References

de Certeau, M. (1984) *The practice of everyday life.* Berkeley: University of California Press.
Edensor, T. (2000) 'Walking in the British countryside: Reflexivity, embodied practices and ways to escape', *Body and Society*, 6(3–4): 81–106.
Elliston Allen, D. (1976) *The field club in The Naturalist in Britain: A social history.* London: Penguin.
Farley, P. and Symmons R. (2011) *Edgelands.* London: Jonathan Cape.
Griffiths, N. and Farley, P. (eds) (2008) Netherly in *GRANTA: The new nature writing (102).* London: Granta Books.
Hall, T. and Smith, R. J. (2013) 'Stop and go: A field study of pedestrian practice, immobility and urban outreach work', *Mobilities*, 8(2): 272–92.
Harney, M. (2007) 'Merleau-Ponty, ecology and biosemiotics', in S. L. Cataldi and W. S. Hamrick (eds), *Merleau-Ponty and environmental Philosophy: Dwelling on the landscape of thought.* Albany: SUNY, 133–46.
Hill, H. (1980) *Freedom to roam: The struggle for access to Britain's moors and mountains.* Ashbourne: Moorland Publishing.
Ingold, T. (2010) 'Ways of mind-walking: reading, writing, painting', *Visual Studies*, 25(1): 15–23.

Kay, G. and Moxham, N. (1996) 'Paths for whom? Countryside access for recreational walking', *Leisure Studies*, 15(3): 171–83.

Kleinberg-Levin, D. A. (2008) *Before the voice of reason: Echoes of responsibility in Merleau-Ponty's ecology and Levinas's ethics*. New York: SUNY.

Larsen, J. (2001) 'Tourism mobilities and the travel glance: Experiences on the move', *Scandinavian Journal of Hospitality and Tourism*, 1(2): 80–98.

Lewis, N. (2001) 'The climbing body', in P. MacNaughton and J. Urry (eds), *Bodies of nature*. London: Sage, 57–8.

Mabey, R. (1976) *Street flowers*. Harmondsworth: Penguin.

Macfarlane, R. (2012) *The old ways*. London: Hamish Hamilton.

McKay, C. (2012) 'Walking otherwise: one foot after another', paper presented to the AAH Conference, Milton Keynes, 29–31 March.

Middleton, J. (2011) 'Walking in the city: The geographies of everyday pedestrian practices', *Geography Compass*, 5(2): 90–105.

Myers, M. (2011) 'Walking again lively: Towards an ambulant and conversive methodology of performance and research', *Mobilities*, 6(2): 183–201.

Parkins, W. and Craig, G. (2006) *Slow living*. Oxford: Berg.

Pinder, D. (2001) 'Ghostly footsteps: Voices, memories and walks in the city', *Ecumene*, 8(1): 1–19.

Rothman, B. (1982) *The 1932 Kinder Trespass*. Altrincham: Willow Publishing.

Wylie, J. (2007) *Landscape*. London: Routledge.

# 3 Entrainment

## Human–equine leisure mobilities

*Paula Danby and Kevin Hannam*

## Introduction

Equestrianism provides a leisure opportunity for people to gain knowledge and skills associated with equine culture, to exhibit, and challenge their performances while also providing a stage for social interaction. It is easy to view a horse simply as a mode of mobility; however, a mobilities approach to equestrianism attempts to understand the fluidity of movements and interactions between humans and horses – what Löfgren (2008) has called, in the context of rail travel, the material connections between motion and emotion. Mobilities research develops a post-humanistic perspective, which allows more innovative and holistic research of human–equine interactions. Such research appreciates the lives and cultural dimensions surrounding horses by viewing them as key actants – playing active roles within human–equine relationships.

Mobilities research draws upon and develops post-humanistic theory in an attempt to create innovative ways of understanding the ways in which human subjects are decentred by the blurring of the boundaries between the human and non-human. This chapter thus reconceptualizes the human–equine divide in terms of the interrelations and interdependencies of humans and horses within their shared leisure spaces. In particular, we address the relative lack of research on human–equine relations from a mobilities perspective compared with other leisure pursuits such as cycling (see Larsen, Chapter 4, this volume).

Empirically, the chapter examines how equestrianism develops human–equine relationships through various performances and training methods. In particular, it explores the processes involved in the transfer of knowledge of horse culture to humans through the use of 'animal-friendly' training methods such as 'Natural Horsemanship' with regards to human–equine intercommunication, riding, and general horse welfare. We develop the argument that human–equine relationships involve the blurring of boundaries and an interconnectedness of human–horse bodies through riding and close sensuous emotional leisure encounters.

Understanding the ways in which humans, horses, and their surroundings are assembled together allows us to better comprehend what Crouch (2010) refers to as new ways of feeling, moving, and thinking. Humans and horses interact in a variety of spaces including familiar and unfamiliar environments as a result of various leisure and tourism activities. Within this chapter, we demonstrate how humans and horses bodies become combined and are 'enlivened into the landscape' (Crouch 2010: 5) through emotional processes of becoming together. Human–horse relations have the ability to provoke emotion and intimacy; a sense of 'oneness', 'togetherness', or what Hallberg (2008) calls 'entrainment' – the synchronisation of humans and horses to a particular emotional rhythm.

The chapter is organised as follows: we begin by developing the post-humanistic mobilities theoretical perspective. Second, the empirical qualitative methodology is described. This uses experiential interpretative narrative accounts of the complexities surrounding human–equine relations. Next, we analyse the experiences of leisure horse users and their training. We conclude by considering the possibilities for future work that examines leisure studies from a mobilities post-humanistic perspective. This may encourage further research with non-human actants who live in close proximity with humans as a result of increased leisure time.

## A post-humanistic mobilities approach towards human–equine relations

Non-representational theory, Thrift (1997: 126–7) argues, is about 'practices, mundane everyday practices, that shape the conduct of human beings toward others and themselves at particular sites'. It seeks to address the ways in which ordinary people incorporate 'the skills and knowledges they get from being embodied beings' (1997: 127). Drawing upon this insight, in tourism studies it has thus been frequently argued that we need to move beyond simply analysing the social construction of practices to develop a more informed theoretical analysis of the everyday embodiment and performances of tourism (Crouch *et al.* 2001; Coleman and Crang 2002; Franklin 2003). Much of this work has been centred on notions of tourists' agency (MacCannell 2001) and has in turn developed ideas concerned with the body in tourism (see Jokinen and Veijola 1994; Obrador Pons 2003). Jokinen and Veijola (1994) suggest that motivations for travel may emerge from a desire to immerse the body in contexts that have only previously been experienced through visual representations. This has subsequently led to a more in-depth discussion of the various sensuous and morally loaded encounters of hosts and guests sharing food, dancing, and other forms of hospitality as well as forming new relationships (see Crouch and Desforges 2003; Mostafanezhad and Hannam 2014).

Non-representational theory has, however, been criticised for its overemphasis on the embodied nature of tourism encounters. Hence, 'more than representational theory' has been put forward as a way of analysing the coupling of representations to the non-representational embodied practices discussed above through the notion of 'performativity' (Adey 2010). The concept of performativity is an attempt to 'find a more embodied way of rethinking the relationships between determining social structures and personal agency' (Nash 2000: 654). Nash (2000: 655) further argues that the notion of performativity is:

> concerned with practices through which we become 'subjects' decentered, affective, but embodied, relational, expressive, and involved with others and objects in a world continually in process. The emphasis is on practices that cannot adequately be spoken of, that words cannot capture, that texts cannot convey – on forms of experience and movement that are not only or never cognitive.

The notion of performativity is thus concerned with the ways in which people know the world without knowing it, the multi-sensual practices, and experiences of everyday life and is central to mobilities research. As Adey (2010: 149) notes: 'This is an approach which is not limited to representational thinking and feeling, but a different sort of thinking-feeling altogether. It is a recognition that mobilities such as dance involve various combinations of thought, action, feeling and articulation.' Adey (2010: 149) draws upon the work of Tim Ingold (2004) here, who proposes a rethinking of practices of walking as a combination of both 'thought and unthought'. In terms of examples, Spinney's (2006) work develops an understanding of the kinaesthetic and sensuous experiences surrounding the cyclist as fundamental in the rethinking of how people live, feel and create meaningful spatial relations with objects and Macpherson (2010: 1) emphasises the links between human bodies and the landscapes that they inhabit as being 'in a constant process of "becoming"'.

A post-humanistic mobilities approach thus aims to explore new modes of being and becoming in the contemporary world. In light of this, post-humanistic geographers have challenged the singular model of the human subject and have attempted to reconceptualise the blurring boundaries between humans and non-human things including animals (Castree and Nash 2006; Lorimer 2009). This arguably allows space for 'relationships' to be the focus of study rather than entities (Birke and Hockenhull 2012). Thus a post-humanistic mobilities approach to human–animal relations enables a fuller accommodation of the non-human by developing a more-than-human social research agenda that focuses on the living spaces and bodily entanglement between humans and non-humans (Panelli 2010). As Castree and Nash (2006: 501) argue: 'post-humanism names a contemporary context in which new scientific developments trouble the foundational figure of the human subject as distinct from other animal forms of life'.

Work from an Actor Network Theory (ANT) perspective has also inspired this approach, as it rejects the distinction between the human and animal, as the animal is more often than not an important actant in the human material world (Panelli 2010). Lorimer (2009) argues that this steps aside from debates around animal rights and seeks to grant a positive sense of existence to animals. Such an approach develops a non-anthropocentric perspective that emphasises how the social is populated and co-constituted by myriad non-humans through the particular assemblages they are engaged with (Lorimer 2009). Such a non-anthropocentric ontological perspective develops earlier work by Philo and Wilbert (2000), which attempted to reconceptualise the geographies of human–animal relations. They demonstrated the myriad ways in which animals have been historically incorporated into different societies and discussed how humans have placed various animals into specific categories according to notions of usefulness, domesticity, and wilderness.

Human–equine embodiment and performance from this perspective has been specifically explored by Game (2001) who argues that a pure horse or pure human does not exist. She proposes that we are always already part horse, and horses, part human: 'The human body is simply not human that through interconnectedness, through our participation in the life of the world, humans are always forever mixed and thus too have what could be described as a capacity for horse-ness' (2001: 1), such that the 'training of horses is based on sociality: in the absence of emotional support from the herd, horses look to humans' (2001: 3). Thus, Game argues that horses form an attachment to human-ness acknowledging that such a notion comes from a human-centred and individual connection between horse and human, while noting that when people are in a relation with a horse the issue is finding a way to coexist creatively: 'a forgetting of human self in a between-human-and-horse way of being' (Game 2001: 7–8).

Work by Evans and Franklin (2010: 173) has further developed the post-humanistic approach to research human–equine relations by examining the rhythms between horse and rider – what they describe as a 'floating harmony'. In their analysis of the discipline of dressage they note:

> Bodies disciplined in the nuances of stride, comportment and whole-body movement perform their rhythmical harmony in such a way that the training disappears, subsumed in the kinaesthetic union characterized by synchrony and synthesis. The performance is greater than the sum of its (training) parts, with transcendent moments composed out of the myriad rhythmical exercises which have been trained into their bodies. Between rider and horse, all these rhythms come into play and co-produce the composition 'Dressage horse/rider'.
>
> (2010: 174)

As such, 'isorhythmia' – a pattern of complex movements with a repeated rhythmic pattern – is achieved through the unity between horse and rider (Evans and Franklin 2010: 183). These aspects of emotional rhythms and connections are further explored empirically in the analysis below, after a brief discussion of our methodology.

## Methodology

An experiential narrative approach to the study of human–equine interactions required an innovative empirical focus, which was developed using a variety of methods. Data was collected through participant observation, in-depth interviews, and participant diaries from April 2009 until September 2010. The interview sample consisted of 21 participants, and the diary sample consisted of 15 completed diaries, all of whom interacted and participated in various equine-related activities on a regular basis, some with their own horses and others with a variety of shared horses. The personal diaries were kept by participants as a log of interactions, experiences, and emotions as a result of horse-riding activities and associated human–equine relations. Once the transcribed data from the interviews and diaries was prepared, coding enabled us to identify and explore significant human–equine motivations, interactions, and relations, as well as experiences and issues surrounding equine leisure and tourism.

## Human–equine embodied mobilities

Riders rely on their bodies as a site for transacting information, ideas, emotions, and knowledge to horses; therefore bodies act as a mobile communication mechanism; as horses and humans do not share a symbolic language, they both use their bodies as a basis for iconic transaction (Brandt 2004). Brandt (2004) bases the notion of an iconic transaction on the ways in which horses pick up sensations through their bodies to connect with humans, whether they are riding or working from the ground with the horse. Therefore close, harmonious human–equine relationships are of paramount importance in order for successful interaction and collaborative performances to occur (Evans and Franklin 2010).

### Encountering equine spaces

Horse-owners tend to feel totally focused and completely 'in the moment' when they are with their horses (Keaveney 2008). Riders encounter interconnectedness through a sense of being at 'one with the horse' both in heart and spirit (Keaveney 2008). What Keaveney (2008) is referring to here is a merging of the two species through connection, embodiment, and attachment regardless of any difference. As Game (2001: 8) argues, this requires relaxed concentration and a very focused and meditative state. Indeed, it requires a mindful embodied way of being and becoming for both humans and horses. According to Dutton (2012), the recognition of a kinship with another species based on inter-corporeality allows for a more integrative approach to negotiating species boundaries. She argues that becoming sensitive to the embodied nature of the relationship may deepen the understanding of the lived experience of other species, which assists in thinking about issues surrounding welfare (Dutton 2012).

Participants in this study revealed a distancing of themselves from their everyday lives when encountering equine spaces. They spoke of their altered sense of state when entering equine environments and how working with and being in the presence of horses enabled a sense of escape from the pressures of everyday life and routine, as we see in the case of Sharon, a 40-year-old horse-owner who argued:

> I run my own business so my brain is constantly on the go, working things out and dealing with people, which is mentally tiring. I come home from a

day's work here and I'm absolutely shattered but it's a good tired and it sounds ridiculous but I find it very relaxing because it's just you and the horses. You haven't really got to think about anything else and it's really lovely even in the winter when you are looking after and caring for them. A lot of it is dirty, horrible, menial work but it's very satisfying and it's very relaxing. If I'm having a bad time, you know, with a job I've got, it's going horribly wrong, I just come here and even if I go up the hill and I stand in the field with Chanel and just give her a couple of carrots, ten minutes and the problem's solved without even thinking about it. If you've had a bad day just half an hour with the horses and it's all forgotten. It is very hard to put into words ... it's just lovely ... you feel incredibly relaxed all over, tired but de-stressed.

Penelope, a horse-owner in her late fifties, also noted:

When I was working and riding, for me, they were a sort of therapy that I had because my work was therapeutic – I do therapeutic work so I needed something that lifted me out of ... umm ... that intense ... umm ... form of concentration and I found that the riding meant that I had to really focus upon what I was doing. I took it seriously and it meant that I couldn't think of anything else. For me it wasn't merely recreational, it had a real therapeutic value. I felt much calmer ... umm ... much more at ease with myself when I was riding and afterwards all my worries had gone so it had a real strong therapeutic value for me.

Jane, an instructor and horse-owner in her mid-fifties, further commented:

They're so big and strong and gentle and when you have a relationship with a horse they're so trusting. You just feel you're in a different world. You escape into this sort of world ... you just have a feeling of contentment and partnership. You're away from everything with this big, strong, trusting animal.

It becomes evident how the appeal of entering equine landscapes offers people an altered sense of consciousness, a forgetting of their 'human selves', and an emergence into 'another' world: a becoming other. People and horses are united in a moment of ekstasis as a result of high levels of body-to-body contact (Brandt 2006). The statements by our respondents illustrate that horse relations form part of a need to escape from the stresses of work commitments and general everyday life responsibilities. They acknowledge the fact that being with horses and spending time with them is therapeutic in that it alleviates stress and helps with their mental health. Engaging in human–equine interactions by entering the horse's own world for a period of time enables humans to become closer to horses in order to escape the everyday pressures of daily routine. They enter into a human–equine zone through which human and horse bodies experience the world by physically and spiritually interacting with their minds, personalities, sensations, and emotions while in motion. What they experience here is a mixing of emotions and senses through time and space, allowing more intuitive behaviour and associated interactions to form and become. This allows a feeling of transcendence where the human and non-human interact and merge within a particular environment (Keaveney 2008; Evans and Franklin 2010).

*Entrainment*

Watching riders and their horses perform at either professional or amateur level allows spectators to get close to and experience first-hand human–equine relations by witnessing human–equine entrainment through effective interactions. Participants in this study were conscious when watching these human–equine displays of how both rider and horse are mutually dependent upon each other in order to perform successfully. A strong element of trust between the two is essential in order to gain mutually positive experiences. Human–equine interactions are intimate and embedded with powerful emotions instilling a sense of togetherness, rhythm, and harmony (Evans and Franklin 2010). This was evident in the following statement by Penelope, a horse-owner in her late fifties:

> Well, he's a very easy-going … umm … laid-back horse who's got masses of potential and he loves jumping … so … umm … you know, if you can kind of get into the zone where he's concentrating on his task … umm … then there's a really kind of 'at oneness'. I don't have to worry about him not jumping something and he doesn't have to worry about me interfering with him we've got that kind of togetherness. I can feel when he's gonna go and I just let him go, so he takes over at that point and then I pull him back in so it's what I would call a synchrony about our relationship which has taken time for me to learn to trust him, and similarly, he trusts me. That's just a lovely feeling, you know, as we have that mutual trust and that's what I value the most about my relationship with him, is that he knows I never put him in a dangerous situation and I know that he won't put me in one either so we just trust one another.

This form of dual emotion, described above, is derived through an understanding and an appreciation of positive human–equine interconnectedness, interactions, and experiences, which are gained through successful human–equine performance at events. Game (2001) has similarly discussed that for humans and horses to coexist, humans need to forget themselves in order to form a state of 'between-human-and-horse' way of being and becoming, which is what Penelope describes here in her experience. In return, Penelope's horse looks towards her as a 'leader', where he trusts her commands and happily follows direction. At this point the horse acts out of guidance through bodily cues as a result of cross-species communication rather than of his own accord. As Brandt (2006) explains, horse-riders speak of a keen awareness of bodily sensations or 'feel' as a source to guide their interactions with horses. In this sense both the horse and rider share meanings, which is evident within Penelope's quote above. The appeal of being connected with her horse stems from the enhancement of bodily sensations while on the move and a mutual understanding during this leisure activity.

In Penelope's statement she describes her relationship with her horse as being at-oneness, or togetherness. She reinforces the element of mutual trust and respect in the human–equine relationship. Hallberg (2008) describes this experience as 'entrainment', a form of rhythmic synchronisation. Keaveney (2008) explains that when horse and rider together succeed in overcoming their fears, a unique bond develops. This is also evident in Penelope's statement, as when required the horse trusts her and equally she acknowledges the importance of trusting the horse in that he would not put her in a difficult situation, which reinforces the interdependencies. As Game (2001: 5) notes: 'What horse and rider entrain with is the relation, the rhythm between, the transporting flow, the riding'.

Participants had to adapt their own culture and way of being, however, in order for them to gain trust by the horse and to be accepted by them, which implies a shift of power with the relationship of the horse. Participants within the study regularly spoke of the educational function provided by equine events, enabling them to improve their own riding skills by watching other riders and their horses perform. They spoke of how their horses were able to teach them about their individual equine handling and riding skills as well as life in general. The boundaries and significant differences between humans and horses are then challenged by the fluidity and interconnectedness of both species through mobile embodied processes of knowledge exchange, companionship, and affection.

### Natural horsemanship

Animals have been widely recognised as useful vehicles for educating and entertaining adult humans as well as children, which include lessons on friendship, morality, and kindness (DeMello 2012). Participants in this study frequently spoke of the need and desire to attend equine workshops and training events to improve their human–equine relations. This is evident in the statements made by Megan and Laura below. Such equine workshops and training events portray animal-friendly messages to humans and encourage a willingness to connect with animals on their own turf and on their own terms (DeMello 2012). Many equine workshops and training events offer insights where the core focus is the horse's welfare and development. Such leisure events are held for humans to observe the horse as a significant actor and to learn about and understand the horse as an individual being that is valued for its own purpose.

'Natural horsemanship' training techniques are increasingly being promoted to assist with forming a successful human–equine bond. Such techniques, it is argued, allow humans to enter the minds of horses to understand what makes them think and behave in the way they do. The techniques have evolved through an understanding of horse evolution and instinct. These methods are seen as effective methods to improve relations between humans and horses that are mutually beneficial, as Megan, a horse-owner in her early forties, commented:

> There's a variety of events that … umm … do sort of equine teaching on your own horse you can go to. I wouldn't say no to that – taking Star somewhere else for them to show you how to do something in particular with him … it's natural aid techniques rather than you know using your whip.

Participants spoke of attending training events where they had the opportunity to take their horses to develop a particular discipline or handling skills to improve both the horse and rider. These types of training courses are usually held by renowned riders and skilled horsemen and women to train and improve riders' abilities using natural horsemanship techniques. Such techniques are 'horse-friendly' training methods more aligned towards a greater understanding and respect of horse culture and behaviour where humans use effective body language to communicate in a way the horse understands. The principles which underpin Parelli's (1993) 'natural horsemanship' techniques involve various stages that the trainer and horse undertake. The early stages develop a consistent relationship between the trainer and the horse based on the use of the body to reward or punish the horse for appropriate or unwanted behaviour (Mills and McDonnell 2005). Before humans can improve their relations with horses, however, a bond needs to be developed whereby humans and horses respect and trust one another. For a human to be able to work effectively with a horse, the horse needs to feel emotionally connected to the human by mutually respecting them as a partner in order to communicate effectively and safely.

The growing public interest in different forms of natural horsemanship reflects a shift in human attitudes towards non-human animals (Birke 2008). As a result, dramatic changes have occurred relating to how people understand and talk about animals that are close to them. Again this illustrates a post-humanistic development, in that humans are willing to engage in workshops and training events to look beyond themselves and to focus on their horses and to learn from them in order to gain a better understanding, which in turn improves their relations. Participants spoke of the willingness to travel to various parts of the country to engage in equine clinics and training events for educational purposes rather than purely for a leisurely day out, as Laura, an instructor and horse-owner in her early thirties, commented:

> I attend events quite regularly – well, I don't go to shows and events, more so clinics and demos, lesson-wise, you know, I'll go away and have lessons off various people. I have a lady who is my classical trainer. I arranged to have her come up to the yard yesterday and she did a clinic here so I'm more into that kind of thing. I'd rather go somewhere that I can learn something from it as opposed to just … I know it's good to watch other people doing it … umm … I mean the big shows … and what-not, you know they are good events to go and see, however, I think if it was a choice between that or go for a clinic … I would rather go and have a clinic …

Humans have a desire to invest in resources to learn more about equestrianism to benefit the horse as well as themselves. The educational role of equine events was seen as significant by participants and natural horsemanship methods of training were seen as fundamental for humans to understand and communicate more effectively with horses to provide mutual benefits in terms of welfare and positive relationship development.

## Conclusion

The post-humanistic mobilities lens has enabled us to explore human–equine relations by providing a new mode of enquiry into how humans and non-humans coexist within the contemporary world. This chapter provides an innovative exemplar to contextualise and enlighten the blurring boundaries between humans and horses within the leisure context. Deep connections with horses create an altered sense of human consciousness whereby humans are able to examine the world through the lens of a horse rather than only the human, reinforcing the post-humanistic argument of the importance of the non-human. Riding adds a level of mobile physicality and intimacy to the human–equine relationship where riding and embodiment intensifies the relationship (Brandt 2004). The rhythms and bodily movements performed through leisure and tourism configure spaces of connectivity between more-than-human life worlds (Whatmore 2002). This chapter illustrates how, when humans and horses become sensitive to the embodied nature of the relationship, it can deepen and heighten the awareness of cross-species communication through bodily signals, which create meaningful signs (Brandt 2004; Dutton 2012).

Equine leisure and related events provide spaces where human and horse bodies become entwined and united through which the boundaries between the two species become blurred and entangled. It became apparent within this study that the 'horse' has now become 'centre stage' in terms of performance and is the key actant within human–equine relationships. Equine events enable humans and horses to interact and to showcase their effective closely bonded relationships. The educational aspects of equine events were seen by participants as significant where the importance of natural horsemanship methods in training was viewed as fundamental for humans to understand and communicate more effectively with horses to provide mutual benefits in terms of welfare and positive relational development.

This chapter has shown that equine training and workshop events act as a mediator to enhance relations between humans and horses. Moreover it became evident within this study that, as Higgin (2012) has identified, the partnership between human and non-human develops with and through the particular capabilities of each partner. Human and non-human lives affect one another through emotionally intensive relations. Furthermore, it has been acknowledged how leisure and tourism facilitates spaces and experiences through which horses become embodied with humans and live their lives together by becoming entwined in processes of mobile becoming (Macpherson 2010).

The post-humanistic mode of thought and enquiry surrounding human–equine leisure mobilities thus provides innovative theoretical insights into the sharing of human–equine lifestyles entwined through leisure spaces and provides a platform in which to encourage mutual emotional, educational, and physical encounters between both humans and horses. Acknowledging the 'horse' as a sentient being within the human–equine relationship contributes towards a greater understanding of the complexities surrounding the lived and shared experiences of both humans and horses and assists us in thinking about issues surrounding human–equine welfare and development within leisure and tourism mobilities.

## References

Adey, P. (2010) *Mobility*. London: Routledge.

Birke, L. (2008) 'Talking about horses: Control and freedom in the world of natural horsemanship', *Society and Animals*, 16(1): 107–26.

Birke, L. and Hockenhull, J. (eds) (2012) *Crossing boundaries: Investigating human-animal relationships*. Leiden: Brill.

Brandt, K. (2004) 'A language of their own: An interactionist approach to human-horse communication', *Society and Animals*, 12(4): 229–316.

Brandt, K. (2006) 'Intelligent bodies: Embodied subjectivity human–horse communication', in P. Vannini and D. Waskul (eds), *Body/embodiment: Symbolic interaction and the sociology of the body*. Burlington, VT: Ashgate.

Castree, N. and Nash, C. (2006) 'Editorial: Post-human geographies', *Social & Cultural Geography*, 7(4): 501–4.

Coleman, S. and Crang, M. (eds) (2002) *Tourism: Between place and performance*. Oxford: Berghahn.

Crouch, D. (2010) 'Flirting with space: Thinking landscape relationally', *Cultural Geographies*, 17(1): 5–18.

Crouch, D. and Desforges, L. (2003) 'The sensuous in the tourist encounter', *Tourist Studies*, 3(1): 5–22.

Crouch, D., Aronsson, L. and Wahlstrom, L. (2001) 'Tourist encounters', *Tourist Studies*, 1(3): 252–70.

DeMello, M. (2012) *Animals and society: An introduction to human-animal studies*. New York: Columbia University Press.

Dutton, D. (2012) 'Being-with-animals: Modes of embodiment in human-animal encounters', In L. Birke and J. Hockenhull (eds), *Crossing boundaries: Investigating human-animal relationships*. Leiden: Brill, 91–111.

Evans, R. and Franklin, A. (2010) 'Equine beats: Unique rhythms (and floating harmony) of horses and riders', in T. Edensor (ed.), *Geographies of rhythm: Nature, place, mobilities and bodies*. Farnham: Ashgate, 173–88.

Franklin, A. (2003) *Tourism: An introduction*. London: Sage.

Game, A. (2001) 'Riding: Embodying the centaur', *Body and Society*, 7(4): 1–12.

Hallberg, L. (2008) *Walking the way of the horse: Exploring the power of the horse-human relationship*. New York: iUniverse Inc.

Higgin, M. (2012) 'Being guided by dogs', in L. Birke and J. Hockenhull (eds), *Crossing boundaries: Investigating human-animal relationships*. Leiden: Brill, 73–88.

Ingold, T. (2004) 'Culture on the ground – the world perceived through the feet', *Journal of Material Culture*, 9(2): 315–40.

Jokinen, E. and Veijola, S. (1994) 'The body in tourism', *Theory, Culture & Society*, 11(3): 125–51.

Keaveney, S. M. (2008) 'Equines and their human companions', *Journal of Business Research*, 61(5): 444–54.

Löfgren, O. (2008) 'Motion and emotion: Learning to be a railway traveller', *Mobilities*, 3(3): 331–51.

Lorimer, J. (2009) 'Post-humanism/Post-humanistic geographies', *International Encyclopedia of Human Geographies*, 344–54.

MacCannell, D. (2001) 'Tourist agency', *Tourist Studies*, 1(1): 23–37.

Macpherson, H. (2010) 'Non-representational approaches to body-landscape relations', *Geography Compass*, 4(1): 1–13.

Mills, D. and McDonnell, S. M. (2005) *The domestic horse: The evolution, development and management of its behaviour.* Cambridge: Cambridge University Press.

Mostafanezhad, M. and Hannam, K. (eds) (2014) *Moral encounters in tourism.* Farnham: Ashgate.

Nash, C. (2000) 'Performativity in practice: Some recent work in cultural geography', *Progress in Human Geography*, 24(4): 653–64.

Obrador, P. (2003) 'Being-on-holiday: Tourist dwelling, bodies and place', *Tourist Studies*, 3(1): 47–66.

Panelli, R. (2010) 'More-than-human social geographies: post-human and other possibilities', *Progress in Human Geography*, 34(1): 79–87.

Parelli, P. (1993) *Natural horsemanship.* Salt Lake City, UT: Publishers Press.

Philo, C. and Wilbert, C. (2000) 'Animal spaces, beastly places: An introduction', in C. Philo and C. Wilbert (eds), *Animal spaces, beastly places, new geographies of human-animal relations.* London: Routledge, 1–34.

Spinney, J. (2006) 'A place of sense: a kinaesthetic ethnography of cyclists on Mont Ventoux', *Environment and Planning D: Society and Space*, 24(3): 709–32.

Thrift, N. (1997) *Spatial Formations.* London: Sage.

Whatmore, S. (2002) *Hybrid geographies: Natures, cultures, spaces.* London: Sage.

# 4 Leisure, bicycle mobilities, and cities

*Jonas Larsen*

## Introduction

Modes of transport offer many affordances for the international transportation of tourists as well as their everyday micro-mobilities *within* tourism destinations. A key argument in the mobilities literature is that transport is more than displacement and arrival; it is an embodied, multi-sensuous experience and different modes of transport are said to produce different embodied geographies and affective experiences of places (Urry 2007). Yet the importance of mobility to the tourist *experience* has been trivialized in tourism studies, being understood as mere transportation: a boring necessity evil for *reaching* the desired destination (exceptions include Larsen 2001; Edensor and Holloway 2008; Butler and Hannam 2012). In my previous work, 'I have argued that transport is an integral part of the tourist *experience*'; 'touristic transportation is not *only* a trivial question of overcoming distances and reaching one's destination, it is also a way of being in, and experiencing landscapes' (Larsen 2001:81). In particular, I have shown how trains and cars are also technologies for visually experiencing or consuming those very places through mobile sightseeing and I have developed the notion of the 'travel glance' to capture what is characteristic of looking at fleeting landscapes through the window of the speeding car or train.

Yet cars are seldom used for *urban* exploration; congestion and lack of parking make it slow and expensive. Many urban tourists prefer to use public transport, walking, and as discussed in this chapter, bicycles. Indeed, many car-dominated cities around the world have invested in bicycle infrastructures to alleviate the pains of car dependency (e.g. Aldred 2013; Stehlin 2014; Larsen 2015b). This chapter explores how we can understand urban cycling within a tourism context. This is a novel approach. The existing literature on 'tourism cycling' tends to be concerned with cycling in rural areas (Pesses 2010), often along designated leisure routes (Cope *et al.* 1998; Meschik 2010). Other chapters deal with spectators to bike events such as the Tour de France (Berridge 2012) and amateur cyclists training to climb mountains on the Tour de France route (Spinney 2006) or participating in races (Bull 2006; Coghlan 2012). Some argue for the importance of making rigid definitions for what constitutes a proper 'cycling tourist' (Lamont 2009). In contrast, this chapter is concerned with tourists who use bikes on their vacations without necessarily considering themselves *bike* tourists. Few – if any – tourists travel to any city 'just to cycle' there, but many rent bikes, hire a rickshaw/cyclio, or participate on a guided bike tour at some stage to get around and experience the city. Tourism, mobilities, or bicycle scholars have not yet analysed urban tourism cycling; this explorative chapter attempts to fill this void.

The chapter consists of four ethnographic vignettes, from Copenhagen (my home town), Amsterdam, London, and New York City respectively. The Copenhagen case is based on 30 short interviews with groups or pairs of international 'cycling tourists' of varied ages, as well as observations around attractions. The interview guide covered motivations for – and the pleasures and pains of – cycling in Copenhagen, and how it compares to cycling at 'home'. The Amsterdam, London, and New York City cases are auto-ethnographically based on observations and my cycling (in some instances with my family) as a tourist/ethnographer in these places (on auto-ethnography and cycling, see Larsen 2014). Inspired by Spinney (2011), many of these rides were video- and sound-recorded with a helmet-mounted camera. The fieldwork took place between 2012 and 2014: it lasted one week in Amsterdam and four weeks in both London and New York City. This participatory and multi-sited perspective allows me to highlight differences between bike design and cycling in pro-cycling Copenhagen and Amsterdam and car-dominated – but bicycle-aspiring – New York City and London. My partner and son (who was 8–9 years old during the studies) participated partly on these trips and they occasionally joined me cycling. On those occasions, my bicycle performances changed; they became more social and meandering, but also cautious and anxiety-ridden at times.

Thus, I explore how (different) cities are corporeally performed, sensed, and experienced on bikes. What is unique to the 'bike gaze'? How does it connect with the other senses? What are the emotional and affective pains and pleasures of cycling in pro-cycling cities and low-cycling cities, respectively? What services, designs and 'place myths' (Shields 1991) afford (or hinder) cycling? In answering these questions, this chapter contributes to two different sets of literature: on 'tourism performances' (Edensor 1998; Haldrup and Larsen 2010; Urry and Larsen 2011) and 'embodied bicycle mobilities' (Jones 2005, 2012; Spinney 2006; Larsen 2014). Both 'literatures' are concerned with how people 'do' mobile performances and how objects, 'systems', and designed places present certain affordances and not others.

## Copenhagen

Copenhagen is famously known for being a green capital with myriads of cyclists on our endless miles of bike lanes so why not experience Copenhagen on a bike like a native?

(*Visit Copenhagen*[1])

If the thought of experiencing a capital city on two wheels scares you, Copenhagen will soon change your mind. The city is built for cyclists and you'll see more bikes than cars in the city centre ...

(*Visit Denmark*[2])

*I went for a long ride today around the tourist attractions. There is a new breed of cyclists in Copenhagen: tourists on hired bikes with hotel or rental shop logos, pottering about, leisurely. They increase in numbers as I make my way to Amalienborg and later The Little Mermaid. I think to myself: maybe our bike lanes and cycling culture are famous around the world, attractions even?*

(Diary notes, 30 August 2014)

Perhaps only rivalled by Amsterdam, Copenhagen is regarded as one of the world's best large cities for cycling (Buehler and Pucher 2012). Cycling is common and 'democratic', open to less skilled and able-bodied citizens, such as children and elderly people. Wide bike lanes make cycling easy and safe, with very few fatal injuries and casualties (Buehler and Pucher 2012; Larsen 2015b). This is in sharp contrast to most car-dominated Western capitals where bicycle infrastructures are few and far between, and the dangers for cyclists can be significant. In these cities, cycling requires physical skills and mental courage, or 'affective capacity': cycling is for the 'hardened few' (see below; Spinney 2010; Jones 2012).

Copenhagen Municipality and related tourism organisations use bicycling to brand and 'choreograph' the extraordinariness of Copenhagen as a tourist destination; cycling is inscribed as safe and authentic. Hotels and rental shops rent out bikes for a minimal fee. In 2013, Copenhagen Municipality launched a new bike-sharing programme, with commercials explicitly targeting tourists. Companies began offering guided bike tours that celebrate Copenhagen and cycling with equal enthusiasm. The company Cycling Copenhagen writes that they embed tourists into the local by offering tourists 'the chance to experience the city the same way as the Copenhageners' do. You will visit the major sights and hear a lot of funny anecdotes combined with facts from our local guides that all love Copenhagen and bikes.'[3]

'Mobilities', Urry (2007) argues, are organised in 'systems' that make them predictable, desirable, and do-able. A 'bike system' is in place in Copenhagen due to the bike infrastructure, the numerous cyclists, cheap bike rentals, guided tours, and globally circulating 'place myths' about Copenhagen as a 'cycling paradise'. As my diary above reveals, many tourists corporeally embrace and reproduce this 'system'. Based upon the research undertaken, I argue that a combination of 'elements' makes practices of cycling do-able and attractive to tourists, as I now discuss below.

First, cycling is said to be a practical and flexible way of touring cities, especially in a topographically flat and small capital such as Copenhagen. Moreover, as the Copenhagen Metro is still not fully built (with only a few operating lines), tourists have to use local buses and trains, and they are difficult to navigate, according to the interviewees. The 'mobilities literature' has portrayed cars as flexible and affording greater freedom than 'scheduled' public transport (Urry 2007). Yet in cities, the car's flexibility easily disintegrates into annoying, time-consuming traffic jams, and hunts for often pricey parking spaces (Hagnam 2006; Henderson 2009; Larsen 2015a). None of the interviewees envisaged cars as suitable for touring Copenhagen. But one compared cycling to driving – and flying: 'I think it is just kind of like driving. It's that freedom and you can really get by going quicker. And you can cut routes … if I wanna take a side road, I take a side road. It is sort of like flying, I guess' (man from London, in his thirties).

The alternative to cycling is walking and public transport. Bikes are superior to walking as they are faster and allow more places to be covered and seen in a quicker time, and they are said to be faster and easier than public transport because of their flexibility. Many of the interviewees were pleasantly surprised about how many places cycling had allowed them to see in such a little time. There was no need 'to figure out a schedule and waiting time' for public transport and 'walking just takes so long' (a couple from London). Cycling is time-effective and it does not prevent the pleasures of mobile sightseeing associated with walking. It allows intermittent stops for a quick photograph, window-shopping, refreshments, or a contemplative gaze, with bikes being conveniently parked anywhere on the pavement. Cyclists in Copenhagen seldom waste time in scouting for parking spaces (see Larsen 2015a). As a German couple said: 'you can draw your own route. You don't have to stick to the route of the bus. Or if you see something you can go there and say: oh, very nice. Or if you want a cup of coffee, then you are free to do so.' However, a minor inflexibility is that it is very difficult, if not impossible, to read maps while riding, so rhythms become staccato-like: riding, stopping, and way-finding. Rather than a semi-fast pace with a steady pulse, there is much speeding up and down (on rhythms of urban cycling more generally, see Spinney 2010; Larsen 2015b).

Second, tourists can embrace this 'flexibility' because they are aware of Copenhagen's reputation as a 'safe bike haven'. And once they start cycling, they vindicate the myth. The interviewees found it refreshingly easy to cycle here, not difficult and intimidating as 'at home'. Their experience tells them that the design of the city, and the numerous cyclists, make it safe and legitimate. As two couples from car-based societies said:

> I'm cycling here because the city invites you to do that. It's incredibly organ-ised. It's very respectful of bikers. You can feel safe and you can see much more of the city on bike than walking.
>
> (London couple, in their thirties)

> I've been very impressed with the way the city is built for bikes: the separate roads for bikes, the separate signals … This is the best town that I've seen for bicycle-friendly infrastructure.
>
> (US couple, late thirties/early forties)

In contrast, some 'locals' complain about crowded bike lanes and aggressive cyclists (Freudendal-Pedersen and Thorup 2014; Larsen 2015b). However, these tourists did not share these negative experiences. The fact that they experience Copenhageners as considerate, law-abiding, and mellow-paced cyclists, adds to the feeling of being safe. As one American couple said: 'The city is more biker-friendly … your bike lanes are much more developed. You ride slower here ... with more courtesy' (American couple, mid-fifties). Similarly, a German couple noted: 'People are really nice and they have rules. It is not like they are coming from every side. They really behave and they stop if it is a red traffic light.' The combination of supportive bike lanes and considerate cyclists empowers would-be bike tourists who are usually intimidated, or even completely put off by the idea of cycling in their home city. As one woman pointed out:

> Having that very biking-friendly infrastructure made me feel confident about renting a bike. Because I knew that I would be safe, as well as safe to others ... I didn't have to worry so much about getting run over. Or people moving in the way and hitting them and then being the ugly American that runs people over.
>
> (US woman, late thirties)

Third, some stress that cycling in Copenhagen is the most *authentic* way of experiencing a pro-cycling city where cycling is a socially acceptable and not deviant or stigmatised, as in many other cities (according to Aldred and Jungnickel 2013). In Copenhagen, the tourists take pleasure from the fact that they are 'in place' as cyclists: 'I think it's just nice that there are so many people that do it. It gets more acceptable, because there are not that many people that do it at home' (US woman, late twenties).

While cycling is perfectly ordinary for Copenhageners (Larsen 2015b), it is extraordinary – as well as authentic – for tourists intimidated from riding in their own car-based societies. While cycling in Copenhagen, tourists can feel safe, enchanted, and 'local'. The quest for 'authenticity' (MacCannell 1976) and 'extraordinariness' in other places are constitutive elements of tourism experiences (Urry and Larsen 2011), and this is why cycling in Copenhagen can be enjoyable and memorable, especially for tourists from car-based societies. Authenticity also stems from the fact that bikes make it easier to explore 'local' neighbourhoods. Bike lanes cover the length and breadth of Copenhagen and not just islands of (scenic) routes; even off the 'beaten track' tourists will be safe and guided all the way.

Fourth, cycling is also said to be sensuously stimulating, more so than 'underground travel'. The interviewees relish being outdoors, immersed in the 'weatherworld' (Ingold 2010), and actively moving about: 'You have the fresh air. It is better than sitting on public transport' (German man, mid-forties). In addition, cycling gives a much better-embodied feeling of a city's topography, physical layout, and road network. As another respondent commented: 'You get to appreciate the topography more than just going into the Metro in the ground' (Irish man, in his thirties). Metros are seen as boring, mere transport, a method of getting from A to B. Moreover, the safe environment affords time to unwind, relax, and 'tourist gazing', not just traffic gazing as in car-dominated cities. One interviewee suggested: 'It is easier than cycling in London, which is hectic, busy, and with angry motorists.' His partner added: 'It is a slow pace, which is nice when you are on holiday' (London couple, in their thirties). So, the relatively moderate pace of cycling in Copenhagen means that even inexperienced cyclists can potter about and enjoy the scenery – although some find walking slightly better suited, and paced, for gazing.

To sum up, cycling is central to how some independent tourists experience and memorise Copenhagen. It is perceived as inclusive, safe, time-effective, and sensuously pleasurable. The interviewees compare cycling in Copenhagen with cycling in Amsterdam, and yet maintain that cycling in car-dominated cities, such as those found in the UK or the USA, are Copenhagen's polar opposite. Hence, I now discuss other places, drawing on my own cycling and observations (with and without my family).

## Other places

### *Amsterdam*

There are many similarities between Copenhagen and Amsterdam's bike cultures. Amsterdam is another city where cycling is socially and spatially 'in place' (Buehler and Pucher 2012; Eyer and Ferreira 2015). Amsterdam, too, has extensive bike lanes, and people of all ages and from all walks of life ride in their everyday clothes on upright bikes, with moderate pace, sometimes with two or three people on one bike. The perceived safeness of biking in Amsterdam can be seen in relation to the fact that: '*no one wears helmets (even small children), that children are riding too, and that parents often ride with their kids on their bikes. Riding with a child without a helmet would be frowned upon in Copenhagen, these days*' (diary notes, 17 July 2013). So, we look ' *"out of place" – or touristic – my partner, son and I, on rented orange bikes and wearing our own helmets, embarrassing*' (diary notes, 17 July 2013). But we quickly feel 'at home' and at ease, even if we are cycling with a young child. In a mellow pace we 'potter about' and: '*when I later watch the video – that was produced by the Go-pro camera attached to my son's helmet – I realise that he has been humming most of the day. I take that as a sign that he enjoyed the day, too.*' However, as I was soon to discover, cycling in Copenhagen and Amsterdam was one thing, and cycling in London and New York was altogether another.

### *London*[4]

> *I'm about to 'do' London by bike. I hope that the bike will unlock London, its great beauty and geographical grandness, which the underground world of the Tube conceals.*
>
> (Diary notes 15 November 2012)

The speed and flexibility of bikes seems well suited for London. However, London is infamous for being a dangerous place to ride, and few people are brave (or stupid) enough to commute to work by bike (Spinney 2008; Aldred 2010;

Green *et al.* 2012). This situation is slowly changing as cycling has become a topic for politicians, especially the pro-bike Mayor of London, Boris Johnson, with many new bike lanes and a new public bike scheme (Green *et al.* 2012; Pucher *et al.* 2012). And yet, as I now discuss, my 'Copenhagenised' cycle body fell short and panicked in London. On departure, 'travel fever' kicked in:

> *But for the last couple of days the fear has outgrown the excitement. For the first time ever cycling scares me. I might be an experienced rider but my skills are nourished in a pro-cycling city and where I know the traffic rules ... I cannot help but to Google 'cycle death' in London ...*
>
> (Diary notes, 16 November 2012)

As a London friend – who has cycled in Copenhagen – texted to me:

> I'll try and give you a ring tomorrow. Address is ... There should be a quiet route along the river. Buy a decent map and be fucking careful – it's very different from CPH.

I'm instructed to be exceptionally cautious: this is not Copenhagen. I wonder: is biking turning London into a potentially lethal place, especially for a naive 'tourist'?

> *I enjoy the easiness of the Underground as I approach London. Walking out of the Tube I'm brutally overwhelmed by the traffic and there is no way I can see myself cycling here. I begin to doubt whether I'm actually a very skilful cyclist anyway. And they drive in the wrong direction too. Not sure that I have the stomach for this! At least I haven't brought my family along.*
>
> (Diary notes, 17 November 2012)

While London is normally perceived as a safe place, with numerous attractions, adventure tourism is not to be one of them. Or so it appears. Is seeing London by bike a form of adventure tourism where one puts one's own life in danger and the game, ultimately, is 'to cheat death'? If things go wrong, the consequences may indeed be fatal.

In *The Tourist Gaze 3.0* (see Urry and Larsen, 2011:220), we argued that tourism often involves combinations of pleasure and pain, risk and danger. Sometimes this is because tourist places are imagined as places of danger, crime, and terror. More central to this chapter, adventure tourism has developed distinctly active, dangerous, extreme performances such as bungee jumping, off-piste skiing, paragliding, skydiving, and white-water rafting. In such performances, tourists 'indulge their dreams of mastery over the earth, of being adventure heroes starring in their own movies' as they seek to cheat death (Bell and Lyall 2002: 22). I am not an adventure, daredevil-type person and have never exposed my body, nerves, or willpower to such adventures. And yet a part of me is excited about the sensory overload and risks involved in cycling in London.

The affective intensities of the noisy and compact traffic in London hit me like a hammer. With fear and adrenaline rushing through my body, I ventured into the morning rush hour the following day. I headed towards the city on one of the new, blue-painted Cycle Superhighways.[5] It felt like home, and yet I am constantly overtaken, unable to keep up with the pace – '*they are fast, these "lycra men on 'racerbikes'"*,' And: '*I am out of place in my black leather jacket and hired mountain bike*' (diary notes, 18 November 2012). Suddenly, the cycle lanes stop and I found myself engulfed by cars, buses, and lorries: '*This is why only two to three per cent of Londoners cycle to work, I think to myself*.' Here, my Copenhagen skills – of going slow, hugging the kerbs, and never crossing the lane into the traffic to make a turn – fall short. I witness in awe how cyclists change lanes and mingle with cars when they make turns or when kerb lanes turn left. No wonder that hardly any children cycle or get transported on their parents' bikes – so commonplace in Copenhagen and Amsterdam: *I was utterly frightened. Realising that cyclists have to drive like a car freaked me out as I do not know how to drive a car! Now I understand why cyclists in major UK cities are stigmatised as mad, according to Jones (2005)*' (diary notes, 17 November 2012). In London, where cyclists rub shoulders with and need to keep up with the speed of cars on busy streets, cycling requires physical abilities, a constant alertness and nerves of steel. This is what Jones (2012) and Spinney (2006) call 'affective capacity'.

During the first week, I experienced cycling in London as a form of extreme sport or adventure tourism, where the aim of the game is 'to cheat death' and have fun at the same time. London became one big racetrack with real thrills and dangers everywhere. In his discussion of adventure urban tourism, Beedie (2005) makes a distinction between 'perceived' and 'real' risks. He suggests that adventure risks are mostly 'perceived' as adventure tourism being commodified and controlled: they only give an illusion of risk, with objective risks being 'managed out'. Yet the risks of cycling in London are fatally real: cars and trucks killed six cyclists in the space of two weeks a year later (*Guardian*[6]). A part of me enjoyed the affective thrills of racing through London and being part of an affective 'neo-tribe' (Maffesoli 1996) of hardened cyclists. Another was petrified, 'sighing' with relief every time a ride was safely completed. On the second week my partner and son joined me, but we never seriously entertained idea of cycling together in London: there were hardly any cycling families on the road that could serve as role models, and London is not Amsterdam.

My ambition of visually consuming London through a 'mobile glance' (Larsen 2001) largely failed, as I had to focus my vision and attention on the traffic and the mobile space at hand – what is there now, and what is coming into being; there were few opportunities for letting the eyes and mind wander. With the exception of cycle paths along canals and parks, it is difficult to potter about and cycle two abreast, as in Copenhagen and Amsterdam. In London: 'To dither, or to travel aimlessly and deliberately inefficiently, or to travel in large communal groups, or to travel in order to maximise the opportunities for spectacle or interaction … (can) not be easily reconciled with cycling as it is currently constituted in practice' (Green *et al.* 2012: 286).

However, in this bike-hostile environment there are safe 'pockets', in parks and along canals, where tourists hire public bikes and participate in guided bike tours. Cycling tourists are visible around the major attractions and especially parks such as Hyde Park, Regents Park, and the royal parks where one can indeed dawdle about, enjoy the view, and cycle two abreast, with the affective capacity required being very low in comparison to the palpable risks just beyond the park gates. I participated on one specific tour – The Royal Tour – and the whole tour took place on bike lanes, at a *very* leisurely pace, within the royal parks. No longer were my eyes nervously fixed on the road-scape but simply enjoying the late autumn delights of a London park on a beautiful sunny day. On the few stretches where we were forced to ride on and cross streets for a minute or two, the guide almost 'took us by the hand'. We even walked the short stretch from the meeting point to the park. Such issues of the risks of cycling are also of paramount importance in New York City.

### New York City

Until recently, New York City was not designed for cycling. Very much like London, the streets were packed with cars, there were hardly any bike lanes, and cyclists were perceived as odd and reckless creatures not 'belonging' on the streets. The fearless, infamous bicycle messenger on brakeless fixies, moving at great speeds, and with a relaxed attitude towards red lights, was, and is, the emblematic icon of US urban cycling – including New York City (Culley 2001; Kidder 2005; Fincham 2006). Risks and edgy-urban-coolness are part of the thrill and aesthetics of cycling here, particularly in Brooklyn and Lower Manhattan where cyclists are style-conscious young adults who imitate the riding style and *look* of bicycle messengers, with their fixies, vintage bikes, tattoos, rackling keys, U-locks, and bike messenger rucksacks on display (Bike Snob 2010, 2013). This distinctly American bicycle culture is 'on the move', transported by magazines, films, and YouTube. Indeed, the New Yorker bicycle writer Bike Snob is bewildered when he comes across a New York City-inspired bike culture of fixed-gear bikes, bike messenger bags, U-locks, and Brooklyn caps, in Gothenburg, Sweden (2013: 80–1).

I am also fascinated by, and in awe of, the bike messenger culture. I thought:

> *If one is to get an 'authentic' taste of what cycling was all about before New York turns all pro-bike-lanes then one has to ride the busy streets and imitate – no matter how poorly – the bike messengers. And this, for sure, will turn New York – similar to London – into an adventure tourism site.*
>
> (Diary notes, 20 July 2013)

I did not have the stomach or skills for a 'fixie', so I purchased a cool second-hand vintage Schwinn racer with proper brakes and a relatively cool New York look (there is a vintage bike craze in New York City). Then I got hold of a bike map, indicating numerous bike lanes. Relieved, and reassured, I set out to explore Brooklyn. However, in reality the bike lanes:

> *do not offer much protection, being simple paint jobs (similar to London), often fading ones, sometimes to the extent that they are hardly recognisable. And the surface quality is poor, uneven, with nasty potholes. They are crying out for repair work. I jump-up-and-down; with the vibrations resonating throughout my entire body – while bouncing trucks and vans make an incredible noise.*
>
> (Diary notes, 21 July 2013)

Cars, trucks, and cabs weave in and out of the lanes when parking, loading, and dealing with customers; therefore being 'doored' is an ever present risk (Bike Snob 2010: 119), and something that one is constantly alerted to – as well as dangerous potholes. Still, one feels safer here than on the congested streets with all the tight-knit vehicles.

After a couple of days, I felt skilled and brave (or stupid) enough to take on Manhattan, in search of fellow bike tourists, to try the new Copenhagen-inspired bike lanes, and 'Bombin' Broadway'. Brooklyn Bridge is first:

> *the sheer number of (tattooed) cyclists blows me away. It is not light work to ascend it, not the job for an obese or unfit person. Everyone is pushing the pedals with determination; bodies that are standing or leaning slightly forward, sweating, and clenched faces reveal that work is required.*
>
> (Diary notes, 24 July 2013)

The reward is the 'visual thrill' at the top and then freewheeling down: a breath-taking panorama of Lower Manhattan's iconic glory unfolds before one's very eyes and tired legs. '*This is sublime sight-doing. I notice: that I'm not the only tourist here: now and then, cyclists stop, and snap, snap*' (Field-notes, 24 July 2013).

The intensity of London's streetscapes somewhat pales in comparison to what I first encounter in Manhattan. If I had not built up my 'affective capacity' in London, I would not have thrown myself into this cacophony and unpredictable sensory overload of cars, cabs, trucks, fumes, sirens, horns, speeding up-and-down, signs, and immense roads. I try to stick to the bike lanes but they always, suddenly, come to an abrupt end; back on the street my pulse is racing once again. All I care about is propelling myself forward while staying alive, not becoming the next 'ghost bike':

> *GHOST BIKES. One cannot help to notice some all-white painted bikes, so-called ghost bikes, erected by a pro-cycling organisation to honour, and raise awareness about, traffic-killed cyclists, at that very spot. In 2012, motorists killed 136 pedestrians and 19 cyclists across the city.*[7]
>
> (Field-notes, 24 July 2013)

I relish the fact that this 'survival game' is not part of my own everyday commute. I pity those that have to ride in such a 'disabling' environment. Yet there is also a part of me that is high on adrenaline and the New York smugness. This is *my* kind of adventure tourism and the *BIKENYC* guidebook persuades me to embark on the ultimate and most authentic bike messenger test in New York City: riding the iconic 13-mile Broadway from one end of Manhattan to the other:

> So you *wanna* be a bike messenger, huh? In Gotham, the Empire. For Couriers and fixed-gear riders, the ultimate no-brakes velodrome! Or maybe you just want to ride like one (Poser! Faker!), weaving in and out of gridlocked traffic … no other rush can compare.
>
> > (Blackman *et al.* 2011: 151)

Even as a genuine faker, this ride is affectively overwhelming, and its sensations beyond words. However, this trip – and subsequent ones – also revealed another picture: '*Wow! What a change. Approaching the commercial/touristic Times Square I ride along buffer zone bike lanes that separate bikes and cars: I sigh with relief*' (field-notes, 24 July 2013). New York City is on a mission to reduce the risks of cycling, to make it safe and legitimate, by installing new bike lanes, bike racks, and bike-sharing systems. There are currently 450 miles of cycling lanes in the city, with most having been built within recent years (Pucher *et al.* 2010; DOT New York City 2013[8]).

There is a distinctive geography of bike lanes and cycling in New York City. Despite the new investments, there is not yet an all-covering seamless bike lane network, so everyday users have to build up knowledge about safe and dangerous roads and routes, respectively, and how they can arrive quickly at their destination without compromising their safety. 'Bicycling tourism' in New York City, however, tends be located within small, isolated – although less so than in London – islands, at the most protective bike lanes, inside Hyde Park and up and down the west side of the Hudson River. Numerous (including some illegal[9]) on-street businesses and (some importunate) salesmen rent out bikes for short-term lets (as little as three hours). Renting is not cheap though: 35–40 dollars for a day! Many of the protective bike lanes where tourists congregate afford amazing views; they are 'tourist gaze machines', aesthetically framing the scenery. There is no worry about the traffic and one can calmly take in the sights. No wonder that they are popular with tourists as well as 'locals' – even families with children – enjoying a painless ride. '*It is, I think to myself, possible to cycle here with my partner and son*' (field-notes, 24 July 2013).

The following week my family arrived, and for the next two weeks we did all the protective touristic bike lanes as well as some more adventurous rides 'locally' in Brooklyn and to museums and attractions in Manhattan. We quickly became 'lay experts' in the whereabouts of the bike lanes and in spotting roads with little or heavy traffic. We always rode in a line with my son in the middle, to protect him, and he was instructed to ride on the sidewalks when the traffic became too intense (this is legal for children under 12 years of age). When out in the real traffic, I was relentlessly apprehensive about him, alerted to him, and the traffic around us, barking instructions. Now, in the company of my family, I often found cycling in New York stressful and nerve-wrecking, and: '*I lost the temper a few too many times when he or my partner did something "wrong" – he was not humming as much as in Amsterdam, instead telling me to relax*' (field-notes, 29 July 2013). The adventurous side of cycling became, frankly, too adventurous, too risky, in the company of my family. This reflects, more broadly, that gazing and performing depend upon one's co-travelling company; they are *relational* practices (Urry and Larsen 2011: 201). In some situations, tourists will feel safer and better protected in the company of co-travelling others. In others, there will be guilt about submitting one's loved ones – especially children – to real risks. The actual risks of cycling in New York City and the relationality of tourism performances explain why one study found that few (in this case, US) tourists consider the city attractive for 'bike sightseeing'[10] and the new-shared bike system – the Citi Bike – fails to attract nearly as many tourists as predicted,[11] despite the widespread claim that it has had negative consequences on independent bike rental companies and shops.[12]

## Conclusion

In this chapter I have suggested that systems and practices of cycling are increasingly central to how tourists move about and experience cities. This reflects that Western cities now build better infrastructures for bicycles in order to alleviate the apparent 'ills' of excessive automobilities. Infrastructures include bike lanes, shared bike systems, and a myriad smaller entrepreneurs that rent out bikes or organise sightseeing tours on bike.

I have argued that it is difficult to 'gaze' while cycling among cars in London and New York City, as one's vision and attention need to be on the traffic and the mobile space at hand; it is risky letting the eyes and mind wander for long. In contrast, bike lanes potentially afford a secure and less demanding space where one's gaze can often shift from reading the traffic to the wider environment, taking it in aesthetically, as a slow-moving panorama. This is particularly the case when bike lanes – especially in New York City – are designed along scenic routes. Here the bike lanes enable the 'tourist gaze'. However, congestion on bike lanes – so common in Copenhagen in rush hours – will force cyclists' attention back to the traffic.

I have shown that there are striking corporeal and sensuous differences between cycling in long-established pro-cycling cities, like Copenhagen and Amsterdam, and car-dominated cities, like London and New York City. In the latter, 'safe cycling' is restricted to scenic 'small islands' where one is largely out of harm's way. Outside these 'tourist enclaves', cycling is (too) risky. Here the pleasures of cycling resemble those of adventure tourism more than a stroll in the park. With regards to the former cities, I have shown that foreign tourists, with much joy and ease, use bicycles *throughout* the city, for transport *and* sightseeing. From a *tourist* perspective, cycling in Copenhagen is extraordinary and authentic.

Tourists from car-dominated societies appreciate that the environment is inclusive, that cyclists are considerate, and cycling is 'in place'. And on top of that, cycling in Copenhagen is seen as both convenient and fast.

## Notes

1 www.visitcopenhagen.com/search/editorial/global?keys=copenhagen%20bike%20 city.
2 www.visitdenmark.com/copenhagen/activities/copenhagen-two-wheels.
3 www.cycling-copenhagen.dk/about.
4 This section draws on material published in the article '(Auto)Ethnography and Cycling' (Larsen 2014).
5 www.tfl.gov.uk/roadusers/cycling/11901.aspx.
6 www.theguardian.com/uk-news/2013/nov/18/sixth-london-cyclist-killed-camberwell-lorry.
7 www.streetsblog.org/2013/01/31/nypd-15465-pedestrians-and-cyclists-injured-155-killed-in-traffic-in-2012/AS.
8 www.nyc.gov/html/dot/downloads/pdf/2013-nyc-cycling-in-the-city.pdf.
9 http://nypost.com/2014/05/27/scammers-duping-tourists-with-stolen-bikes-in-central-park/.
10 http://brokelyn.com/shocking-new-report-tourists-terrified-bike-nycs-streets/.
11 http://brokelyn.com/struggling-citi-bike-grasps-real-new-yorker-cred-blames-tourists-shortfall/.
12 http://observer.com/2013/07/citi-bike-cutting-into-central-parks-bike-rental-businesses/.

## References

Aldred, R. (2010) '"On the outside": Constructing cycling citizenship', *Social & Cultural Geography*, 11(1): 35–52.
Aldred, R. (2013) 'Incompetent or too competent? Negotiating everyday cycling identities in a motor dominated society', *Mobilities*, 8(2): 252–71.
Aldred, R. and Jungnickel, K. (2013) 'Matter in or out of place? Bicycle parking strategies and their effects on people, practices and places', *Social & Cultural Geography*, 14(6): 604–24.
Beedie, P. (2005) 'The adventure of urban tourism', *Journal of Travel & Tourism Marketing*, 18(3): 37–48.
Bell, C. and Lyall, J. (2002) *The accelerated sublime: Landscape, tourism, and identity*. London: Greenwood Publishing Group.
Berridge, G. (2012) 'The promotion of cycling in London: The impact of the 2007 Tour de France Grand Depart on the image and provision of cycling in the capital', *Journal of Sport & Tourism*, 17(1): 43–61.
Bike Snob, Eben Weis (2010) *Bike snob systematically & mercilessly realigning the world of cycling*. London: Hardie Grant.
Bike Snob, Eben Weis (2013) *Bike snob abroad*. London: Hardie Grant.
Blackman, M., Glazar, E. and Green, M. (2011) *BIKENYC: The cyclists' guide to New York City*. New York: Skyhorse Publishing.
Buehler, R. and Pucher, J. (2012) 'Big city cycling in Europe, North America, and Australia', in J. Pucher and R. Buehler (eds), *City Cycling*. London: MIT Press, 287–318.

Bull, C. (2006) 'Racing cyclists as sport tourists: The experiences and behaviours of a case study group of cyclists in East Kent, England', *Journal of Sport and Tourism*, 11(3/4): 259–74.

Butler, G. and Hannam, K. (2012) 'Independent tourist's automobilities in Norway', *Journal of Tourism and Cultural Change*, 10(4): 285–300.

Coghlan, A. (2012) 'An autoethnographic account of a cycling charity challenge event: Exploring manifest and latent aspects of the experience', *Journal of Sport & Tourism*, 17(2): 105–24.

Cope, A., Doxford, D. and Hill, T. (1998) 'Monitoring tourism on the UK's first long-distance cycle route', *Journal of Sustainable Tourism*, 6(3): 210–23.

Culley, T. H. (2001) *The immortal class: Bike messengers and the cult of human power*. Chicago: Villard Books.

DOT New York City (2013) '*Cycling in the city: An update on the NYC Cycling Counts*', New York: Department of Transport, New York City.

Edensor, T. (1998) *Tourists at the Taj: Performance and meaning at a symbolic site*. London: Routledge.

Edensor, T. and Holloway, J. (2008) 'Rhythmanalysing the coach tour: The Ring of Kerry, Ireland', *Transactions of the Institute of British Geographers*, 33(4): 483–501.

Eyer, A. and Ferreira, A. (2015) 'Taking the tyke on a bike: mothers' and childless women's space-time geographies in Amsterdam compared', *Environment and Planning A*, 47(3): 691–708.

Fincham, B. (2006) 'Bicycle messengers and the road to freedom', *Sociological Review*, 54(2): 208–22.

Freudendal-Pedersen, M. and Thorup, L. (2014) 'Cyklistens rytmer og kampen om pladsen i byen', *GRÄNSLØS NR 4*. Online at: http://journals.lub.lu.se/index.php/grl/issue/view/1899.

Green, J., Steinbach, R. and Datta, J. (2012) 'The travelling citizen: emergent discourses of moral mobility in a study of cycling in London', *Sociology*, 46(2): 272–89.

Hagnam, O. (2006) 'Morning queues and parking problems: On the broken promises of the automobile', *Mobilities*, 1(1): 63–74.

Haldrup, M. and Larsen, J. (2010) *Tourism, performance and the everyday: Consuming the Orient*. London: Routledge.

Henderson, J. (2009) 'The spaces of parking: Mapping the politics of mobility in San Francisco', *Antipode*, 41(1): 70–91.

Ingold, T. (2010) 'Footprints through the weather-world: Walking, breathing, knowing', *Journal of the Royal Anthropological Institute*, 16(1): 121–39.

Jones, P. (2005) 'Performing the city: A body and a bicycle take on Birmingham, UK', *Social & Cultural Geography*, 6(4): 813–30.

Jones, P. (2012) 'Sensory indiscipline and affect: A study of commuter cycling', *Social & Cultural Geography*, 13(3): 645–58.

Kidder, J. L. (2005) 'Style and action a decoding of bike messenger symbols', *Journal of Contemporary Ethnography*, 34(3): 344–67.

Lamont, M. (2009) 'Reinventing the wheel: A definitional discussion of bicycle tourism', *Journal of Sport & Tourism*, 14(1): 5–23.

Larsen, J. (2001) 'Tourism mobilities and the travel glance: Experiences of being on the move', *Scandinavian Journal of Hospitality and Tourism*, 1(2): 80–98.

Larsen, J. (2014) 'Autoethnography and cycling', *International Journal of Social Research Methodology*, 17(1): 59–71.

Larsen, J. (2015a) 'Bicycle parking and locking: Ethnography of designs and practices', *Mobilities*, ahead of print, 1–23.

Larsen, J. (2015b) 'Practices of urban bicycle mobilities: "Planning" and everyday cycling in Copenhagen', ms under review.

MacCannell, D. (1976) *The tourist: A new theory of the leisure class*. University of California Press: Chicago.

Maffesoli, M. (1996) *The time of the tribes*. London: Sage.

Meschik, M. (2010) 'Sustainable cycle tourism along the Danube Cycle Route in Austria', *Tourism Planning & Development*, 9(1): 41–56.

Pesses, W. M. (2010) 'Automobility, vélomobility, American mobility: An exploration of the bicycle tour', *Mobilities*, 5(1): 1–24.

Pucher, J., Thorwaldson, L., Buehler, R. and Klein, N. (2010) 'Cycling in New York: Innovative policies at the urban frontier', *World Transport Policy and Practice*, 161(1): 7–50.

Pucher, J., Lanversin, E., Takahiro, S. and Whitelegg, J. (2012) 'Cycling in megacities: London, Paris, New York, and Tokyo', in J. Pucher and R. Buehler (eds), *City Cycling*. Cambridge, MA: MIT, 319–46.

Shields, R. (1991) *Places on the margin: Alternative geographies of modernity*. London: Routledge.

Spinney, J. (2006) 'A place of sense: A kinaesthetic ethnography of cyclists on Mont Ventoux', *Environment and Planning D: Society and Space*, 24(3): 709–32.

Spinney, J. (2008) *Cycling the City: Movement, meaning & practice* (Doctoral dissertation). London: Royal Holloway, University of London.

Spinney, J. (2010) 'Improvising rhythms: Re-reading urban time and space through everyday practices of cycling', in T. Edensor (ed.), *Geographies of rhythm: Nature, place, mobilities and bodies*. Aldershot: Ashgate, 113–28.

Spinney, J. (2011) 'A chance to catch a breath: Using mobile video ethnography in cycling research', *Mobilities*, 6(2), 161–82.

Stehlin, J. (2014) 'Regulating inclusion: Spatial form, social process, and the normalization of cycling practice in the USA', *Mobilities*, 9(1): 21–41.

Urry, J. (2007) *Mobilities*. Cambridge: Polity.

Urry, J. and Larsen, J. (2011) *The tourist gaze 3.0*. London: Sage.

# 5 Gendered automobilities

## Female Pakistani migrants driving in Saudi Arabia

*Kevin Hannam*

## Introduction

Saudi Arabia is known around the world as the only country where women are not allowed to drive on public roads – they are allowed to own cars and drive them in their own courtyards but not publicly. In the weeks leading up to the 26 October 2013 campaign to allow women to be able to drive in Saudi Arabia, one Saudi cleric gave an interview in which he warned that Saudi women who drove risked damaging their ovaries (CNN 2013). A Saudi activist group, Women2Drive, started a campaign in 2011 utilising online social networks demanding women be allowed to drive (Agarwal *et al.* 2012). As of April 2013 women were allowed to ride bicycles and motorbikes; however, significantly, this new rule stipulates that women can only do so as a recreational activity as opposed to a mode of transportation. In December 2014, two Saudi women were arrested for attempting to drive across the border from the UAE into Saudi Arabia, and their status remains unknown. For Pakistani women living in Saudi Arabia who are accustomed to driving, the lack of access to automobility in all its senses remains a major obstacle, as these women must rely on their male relatives to drive them or hire a professional male driver (InterNations 2014).

One of the main reasons stipulated for mobility restrictions on women are due to 'Saudi society's strong belief in family honour. The pride and honour of a woman's family is directly related to her chastity, known as *ird*' (Baki 2004: 3). Sensitivity to *ird* is so great that Saudi society is structured in order to keep a woman within strictly defined limits (Mackey 2002; Baki 2004). Thus travel and the freedom to use both public and private means of transport for women within Saudi Arabia is highly constrained.

Automobility, in the purest sense, is the simultaneous achievement of autonomy and mobility, and in contemporary societies the chief purveyor of autonomous movements is the motorcar (Featherstone 2004). Indeed, geographers and social scientists have frequently portrayed the motorcar as the 'avatar of mobility' (Thrift 1996: 272), or the 'universal and incontestable' symbol of movement (Bohm *et al.* 2006: 5). The historical benefits of automobility have been well documented in academic literature, particularly from a Western vantage point in terms of driving being a leisure pursuit (Law 2014). A focus on automobility allows us to understand the often unproblematised discourses and practices of 'freedom' implied by driving a private motorcar for leisure (Freudendal-Pedersen 2009). As Sager (2006: 465) has written: 'Freedom as mobility is composed both of opportunities to travel when and where one pleases and of the feasibility of the choice not to travel.' The car's ability to provide both feelings of control and a sense of freedom have become dominant in most Western and Westernised societies (Freudendal-Pedersen 2009). After all, as Urry (2004: 28) suggests, 'cars extend where people can go to and hence what they are literally able to do'.

Cars offer a range of additional benefits to the driver. The car is seen to be a more reliable alternative to other modes of travel and provides flexibility as well as 24-hour availability (Urry 2004). Collin-Lange and Benediktsson's (2011) research on the automobilities of young Icelandic motorists noted that many selected cars over buses and trains due to the perception that public modes of transport were inefficient and unreliable. Thus, narratives extolling the automobility-sanctioning powers of the motorcar have frequently, and perhaps rather unfairly, juxtaposed them against other modes of transport to emphasise the driver's or passenger's acquisition of control and freedom. Larsen (2001) posited that although trains were responsible for the initial mobilisation of tourists, the car has now taken over this mantle as they provide sensations of unpredictability via the open road. This, of course, is in direct comparison to rigid and freedom-restricting rail tracks that ensure that detours and ad hoc stops can seldom be achieved by train passengers. In contrast to the car, then, public transportation is deemed to be both 'inflexible' and 'fragmented' (Urry 2004: 29). Moreover, Beckmann (2001: 598) has argued that cars can offer tourists access to 'car-only-sights' that exist in peripheral locations inaccessible to public transport.

Beckmann (2001: 598) suggests that society's increasing usage of motor vehicles has transformed roads to become 'grounds of battle', as space is increasingly contested. Thus, using cars may not only instigate feelings of freedom and adventure but instead promote a range of negative emotions such as fear, frustration, envy, anger, or distress (Sheller 2004). Indeed, the car's promise of freedom and adventure can be ironically hindered by other road users through the different and even dangerous driving techniques of other drivers (Butler and Hannam 2013). As Beckman (2001) and Featherstone (2004) have both argued, many drivers are now effectively 'captured', due to a reduction in the driver's ability to control their own freedom. Indeed, Beckmann (2001: 604) argues that automobilisation may have effectively 'turned against itself'. Similarly, Butler and Hannam (2013) have observed that although expatriate car users would often refer to their motor vehicles as being 'essential', 'must-haves', or even 'life-savers', many reported that their journeys frequently involved severe periods of immobility due to congestion.

Saudi Arabia, the focus of this chapter, thus provides a novel context to examine the different politics of automobilities and the various freedoms and constraints for people as they attempt to move around. Our research specifically focuses on the driving experiences of female Pakistani migrants living in Saudi Arabia. The number of Pakistanis in Saudi Arabia is estimated at over 1.5 million and constitutes the largest Pakistani expatriate population (Khan 2012). (According to the last census, Saudi Arabia's total population is just over 27 million including nearly 8.5 million non-nationals (*Saudi Gazette* 2010)). Increasing numbers of people from Pakistan emigrate both temporarily and permanently to find work in Saudi Arabia and recently this has included large numbers of trained male and female medical and oil and gas personnel (Kock and Sun 2011). Thus in this chapter we focus on the driving experiences of highly skilled female Pakistani migrants in Saudi Arabia. In the next section we review the literature on gender, mobilities, and automobilities.

## Gendered (auto)mobilities

Mobilities are fundamentally gendered. As Cresswell and Uteng (2008: 1) point out:

> Understanding the ways in which mobilities and gender intersect is undoubtedly complex given that both concepts are infused with meaning, power and contested understandings. The concept of gender does not operate in a 'binary' form. It is never given but constructed through performative reiteration. The resultant interpretations of gender are also historically, geographically, culturally and politically different, enabling a certain slippage between the different realms in terms of how genders are 'read'. This point is central to an analysis of how mobilities enables/disables/modifies gendered practices.

Gender, then, is considered as socially constructed in terms of dynamic different geographically and historically constituted discourses and practices that give rise to various dominant and subordinate meanings attached to masculinity and femininity through power relations (Connell 1987). The relations between and reproduction of gender, power, and mobilities can be understood in terms of how and why people move:

> The meanings given to mobility through narrative, discourse and representation have also been clearly differentiated by gender. Similarly, narratives of mobility and immobility play a central role in the constitution of gender as a social and cultural construct. Finally, mobilities are experienced and practised differently.
>
> (Cresswell and Uteng 2008: 2)

Indeed, feminist geographers have long recognised the significant differences of travel, transport, and mobility for men and women in different societies (Kinnaird and Hall 1994; Hanson and Pratt 1995; Law 1999). More recently, Hanson (2010: 8) has argued that the relations between gender and mobility should be focused on two related questions:

> In essence, one asks, 'How does movement shape gender?' and considers problems such as how processes of mobility/immobility shed light on the shifting power relations embedded in gender. The other line of research asks,

'How does gender shape movement?' and focuses on how gendered processes create, reinforce or change patterns of daily mobility.

In her research in Turkey, Akyelken (2013) has sought to reflect on the first of these questions by demonstrating how power relations underpin investments in transport infrastructure, which are frequently contradictory for women's needs. Porter (2011), meanwhile, examines the mobility constraints for women and female children in rural areas of sub-Saharan Africa in terms of accessibility to markets, education, and health care. However, in this chapter we focus more on the latter question that Hanson (2010) posits, on how gender shapes or rather constrains mobility and leads to social exclusion (Uteng 2009) for Pakistani women in Saudi Arabia.

Practices of driving are thus fundamentally gendered activities. This has been shown most evidently in advertisements for cars, where women are frequently represented negatively as being poor drivers and the car itself is represented as a masculine extension of power (Jain 2005; Paterson 2007). Scharff (1991) meanwhile has explored the history of women as drivers, the associations between masculinity and driving, and the difficulties women have faced when driving a car. Indeed, the historical connections between driving and masculinity have been shown to be aggressive and competitive (McShane 1994). For many women, however, driving can be a means by which they escape gender and generational constraints. Automobility also allows women, who are frequently the primary caregivers for children in many patriarchal societies, a degree of freedom to move with their children in a 'semi-private space' and relatively safe environment that allows the sharing of conversations and 'family-time' (see Dowling 1999; Bostock 2001; Sheller 2004; Murray 2008). As Murray (2008: 47) has noted:

> Within some white middle class cultures the car is a coping strategy, a way of overcoming risk and a symbol of good mothering. For others the only way to avoid risk is to remain relatively immobile, thus complying with local cultures of mothering predicated on risk aversion. There can be little doubt that mothering, along with other aspects of gender, is definitely shaped by mobility and its riskiness and in turn that changing intensities of mobility are determining what it is to be a mother.

Thus, based on research in Norway, Hjorthol (2008: 206) has argued that 'it is clear that women more than men see the car as merely a practical device, which suggests less ownership of cars among women than men'. In the Saudi Arabian context different cultures of automobilities and gendered constraints for Pakistani women are considered below, after a brief discussion of the methodology upon which this chapter is based.

## Methodology

At the outset the relative positionality of the author of this chapter should be recognised. The author is male, white, middle aged, of no religious faith, British nationality, and has visited Saudi Arabia for research purposes several times. The data collection process involved using a research assistant of British Pakistani origin, Muslim, female, middle aged, and who had also visited Saudi Arabia primarily for religious reasons. The data for this chapter consists of ten semi-structured interviews with female Pakistanis aged 18–30 who had previously lived in Saudi Arabia. Three interviews were conducted online using the Skype programme and the remaining seven were conducted face to face. The face-to-face interviews took place in Pakistan (three) and the UK (four). Two key themes were explored in these interviews. The first theme pertained to notions of home and identity. The second theme covered ideas of mobility – moving around Saudi Arabia for employment as well as for leisure, tourism, and pilgrimage, and moving between Pakistan and Saudi Arabia for familial obligations or visiting friends and relatives (VFR) tourism. All interviews were transcribed into English and sub-coded in terms of different types of mobility. All respondents were advised that their responses would only be used for the purposes of academic research and that their responses would be anonymised.

## Gendered freedom/unfreedom automobilities in Saudi Arabia

Mobility within Saudi Arabia is motivated by a number of considerations including work (commuting), religion (travel for prayer), pilgrimage (travel for respect), social ties (travel to visit relatives and friends), leisure (travel for shopping), tourism (travel as an escape from the relative constraints from the home compound), as well as travel for miscellaneous daily errands such as taking children to and from activities and picking up various goods (although most are delivered) (see Glasze 2006; Al-Saleh and Hannam 2010; Sattar *et al.* 2013; Al-Atawi and Saleh 2014). For women in Saudi Arabia, mobilities are highly constrained. Nevertheless, as we have seen above, travel experiences are highly governed by discourses of 'freedom' and the car, in particular, has been viewed as the key enabler of such freedom(s). Paradoxically, the freedoms afforded by the car also lead to what has been called 'unfreedom' (Bauman 1988; Freudendal-Pedersen 2009). Freudendal-Pedersen (2009) argues that 'unfreedom' becomes an *unintended* consequence of gaining more freedom. Having access to automobility may lead to many opportunities and subsequently obligations 'to be present in a variety of family, work, and leisure time events and situations' (Freudendal-Pedersen 2009: 80). However, in the case of Saudi Arabia 'unfreedom' is both an intended and unintended consequence of mobility. In what follows we discuss the problematics of freedom and mobility in Saudi Arabia as demonstrated by our female Pakistani interviewees. First, we reflect on issues pertaining to freedom, and second, we examine how these issues are gendered.

The first sub-theme with regard to driving in Saudi Arabia that was developed by the interviewees was in terms of economic motility – the relatively low price of petrol – (with Saudi Arabia holding an estimated 22 per cent of global oil reserves (Urry 2012)) and how this enabled a certain amount of freedom to travel (although not to travel alone):

> Yes, you have to have a car there in Riyadh. You can't travel very far without a car because there is no real public transport, you either walk, get a taxi, or you have to have some sort of car. I hired a car for six months.
>
> (Interviewee 4)

Here the respondent emphasises that using a car is a fundamental need in Riyadh. This was contrasted by the respondent's comment on the problems involved in using public transport:

> There were buses there, but to be honest with you, for one, they were dangerous! They were cheap enough but, erm, they weren't very frequent. There weren't any real bus routes. So it was just wherever you want to use one, you would flag it down and it would get off as close as to the place you need to go to, the nearest place they can take you. So there is no real bus route.
>
> (Interviewee 4)

The perceived lack of public transport infrastructure and the chaotic nature of their running reflect wider issues of automobility: 'Those who travel by car control, public transport users are controlled. Car users control and have power because, through their own personal choice, they decide when they want to do what. Public transport users, however, are forced to adapt' (Freudendal-Pedersen 2009: 81). Although it is debatable whether car users, in fact, have more control in reality as they need to plan their mobility (Beckmann 2001). Moreover, public transport use unfolds its own 'freedoms' – five minutes waiting for a bus is rarely equated with ten minutes waiting in congestion and it has been recognised that passengers using public transport may have more freedom to do other things while on the move such as reading and socialising. Nevertheless, cars symbolise a sense of private, personal space which public transport cannot afford the user.

This sense of personal space can be, however, frequently circumscribed by the behaviours of other road users. Many of our respondents were concerned about the relative lack of driving laws in Saudi Arabia and the extent to which these were actually enforced:

> Well, to be honest the roads weren't brilliant; there are no real laws there. If there are laws there no one follows there; there is no speed limit, everyone drives really fast, it can be dangerous, they go on the other side of the road and everything. To be honest it is a bit like Pakistan where there are very little rules and regulations that people follow. But we are really looking forward to going back [to Saudi Arabia].
>
> (Interviewee 6)

The respondent above notes the dangers of driving in Saudi Arabia (as much as in Pakistan) and as such this gives us a clear example of the unintended relative unfreedom that driving a car may afford the user. But she is also 'looking forward to going back' – there is a freedom to travel between Pakistan and Saudi Arabia, if not within Saudi Arabia itself.

The dangers of driving in Saudi Arabia were also linked to the development of a masculine culture of driving in Saudi Arabia that involves the illegal practice of 'drifting', defined as: 'when you get the car to slip and do skids and go in zigzags and a competition goes on. The police don't like this' (Interviewee 2). Another female respondent noted that:

> it is those people who do drive fast for leisure who pose a serious risk for the people who are driving to work. Because a lot of the time they get caught in the middle of these races weaving in and out of lanes when going to work. So, there are a lot of bad accidents because the people who drive for leisure really they do not understand that if they are weaving in a lane really fast and the driver is not expecting them to come and they have to slam on their emergency brakes there is no guarantee they are going to stop in time.
>
> (Interviewee 7)

Wells and Beynon (2011: 2492) have noted that 'Automobility cultures are … crucial to real-world death and injury rates', and, significantly here, we can see that driving in Saudi Arabia is not just a gender-segregated activity but also one that is highly masculinised – driving fast and not obeying the rules has been frequently associated with a masculine car culture, competitiveness and aggression (McShane 1994; Jorgensen 2008). The freedoms afforded a male driver for leisure in Saudi Arabia circumscribes the unintended and intended limitations on the freedom to travel for women. We discuss the intended limitations on gendered automobilities further below.

The second sub-theme suggested in the interviews concerned the intended constraints that driving in Saudi Arabia had for women and how these restrictions were felt to be the *Wahabist* Islamic 'rules' of Saudi Arabia (Baki 2004), in contrast to the freedom of what Muslim Pakistani women found elsewhere: 'My mother passed her driving in the courtyard … but she cannot drive out on the roads. It is very difficult, though, for women but these are the Islamic rules' (Interviewee 3). Another female Pakistani respondent reflected: 'It was frustrating, because you either had to have a driver to take you somewhere … all the time you don't really have the freedom to do what you want to do' (Interviewee 7). She had previously driven a car in the UK and was frustrated at the limits placed on her in Saudi Arabia. Bauman's (1988) comment on the freedom to travel leading to unintended unfreedom unravels somewhat here. In Saudi Arabia there are clear structural constraints on travel that are unknown elsewhere in the world.

However, other Pakistani women enjoyed the experience of not driving in Saudi Arabia as it made them feel closer to their spouses and more relaxed: 'It was absolutely fantastic. I did not feel restricted at all. Not driving was great – and it was really good because I would go with my husband and it made us closer' (Interviewee 6).

While there is a dominant Western ideology that connects ideas of freedom with mobility, this is clearly challenged in the above respondent's statement. There is a freedom identified in *not* driving and in the ways in which this may allow closer relationships. The private space of the car again allows this freedom even as it can be recognised as a perceived unfreedom in Western feminist accounts of driving practices.

## Conclusion

Freedom has been defined by Bauman (1988: 45) as 'to be allowed and to be able to keep others unfree'. Clearly, the religious as well as structural constraints in Saudi Arabia exemplify this statement more than in many other countries in terms of driving practices for women. The ideas of freedom and unfreedom refer to both the intended and unintended consequences of daily mobility (Freudendal-Pedersen 2009). The female Pakistani respondents interviewed for this study exemplified the profound mobility ambivalences that are experienced in Saudi Arabia. There are degrees of freedom found in different spaces. While the car remains a masculinised space of control and aggressive leisure, for others it is a space to reinforce relationships. There are frustrations in using both the car and public transport: both produce freedom and unfreedom in different ways as a result of the intended and unintended consequences of the structural constraints found in Saudi Arabia by the Pakistani migrants interviewed for this study.

## References

Agarwal, N., Lim, M. and Wigand, R. T. (2012) 'Online collective action and the role of social media in mobilizing opinions: A case study on Women's right-to-drive campaigns in Saudi Arabia', in C. G. Reddick and S. K. Aikins (eds), *Web 2.0 technologies and democratic governance: Public administration and information technology*. New York: Springer-Verlag, 99–123.

Akyelken, N. (2013) 'Development and gendered mobilities: Narratives from the women of Mardin, Turkey', *Mobilities*, 8(3): 424–39.

Al-Saleh, S. and Hannam, K. (2010) 'Shopping and domestic tourism in Saudi Arabia', in N. Scott and J. Jafari (eds), *Tourism in the Muslim world*. London: Emerald, 253–65.

Al-Atawi, A. and Saleh, W. (2014) 'Travel behaviour in Saudi Arabia and the role of social factors', *Transport*, 29(3): 269–77.

Baki, R. (2004) 'Gender-segregated education in Saudi Arabia: Its impact on social norms and the Saudi labor market', *Education Policy Analysis Archives*, 12(28):1–8.

Bauman, Z. (1988) *Freedom*. Berkeley, CA: Open University Press.

Beckmann, J. (2001) 'Automobility – a social problem and theoretical concept', *Environment and Planning D: Society and Space*, 19(5): 593–607.

Böhm, S., Jones, C., Land, C. and Paterson, M. (2006) 'Part one: Conceptualizing automobility: Introduction: Impossibilities of automobility', *The Sociological Review*, 54(1): 1–16.

Bostock, L. (2001) 'Pathways of disadvantage? Walking as a mode of transport among low income mothers', *Health and Social Care in the Community* 9(1): 11–18.

Butler, G. and Hannam, K. (2013) 'Performing expatriate automobilities in Kuala Lumpur', *Mobilities*, 9(1): 1–20.

CNN (2013) 2 'Saudi women detained for driving in ongoing bid to end ban', online at: www.cnn.com/2013/12/01/world/meast/saudi-arabia-female-drivers-detained/ (accessed 25 August 2015).

Collin-Lange, V. and Benediktsson, K. (2011) 'Entering the regime of automobility: Car ownership and use by novice drivers in Iceland', *Journal of Transport Geography*, 19(4): 851–8.

Connell, R. W. (1987) *Gender and power.* Cambridge: Polity Press.

Cresswell, T. and Uteng, T. (2008) 'Gendered mobilities: Towards an holistic understanding', in T. Uteng and T. Cresswell (eds), *Gendered mobilities.* London: Ashgate, 1–12.

Dowling, R. (1999) 'Cultures of mothering and car use in suburban Sydney: A preliminary investigation', *Geoforum*, 31(2): 345–53.

Edensor, T. (2007) 'Mundane mobilities, performances and spaces of tourism', *Social & Cultural Geography*, 8(2): 201–15.

Featherstone, M. (2004) 'Automobilities: An introduction', *Theory, Culture & Society*, 21(4–5): 1–24.

Freudendal-Pedersen, M. (2009) *Mobility in daily life: Between freedom and unfreedom.* Farnham: Ashgate.

Glasze, G. (2006) 'Segregation and seclusion: The case of compounds for western expatriates in Saudi Arabia', *GeoJournal* 66(1): 83–8.

Hannam, K., Sheller, M. and Urry, J. (2006) 'Editorial: Mobilities, immobilities and moorings', *Mobilities*, 1(1): 1–22.

Hanson, S. (2010) 'Gender and mobility: New approaches for informing sustainability', *Gender, Place and Culture*, 17(1): 5–23.

Hanson, S. and Pratt, G. J. (1995) *Gender, work and space.* London: Routledge.

Hjorthol, R. (2008) 'Daily mobility of men and women – a barometer of gender equality?', in T. Uteng and T. Cresswell (eds), *Gendered mobilities.* London: Ashgate, 193–212.

Huijbens, E. H. and Benediktsson, K. (2007) Practising Highland heterotopias: Automobility in the interior of Iceland', *Mobilities*, 2(1): 143–65.

InterNations (2014) 'Driving in Saudi Arabia', online at: www.internations.org/saudi-arabia-expats/guide/driving-in-saudi-arabia-16101 (accessed 25 August 2015).

Jain, S. (2005) 'Violent submission: Gendered automobility', *Cultural Critique*, 61(1): 186–214.

Jorgensen, A. (2008) 'The culture of automobility: How interacting drivers relate to legal standards and to each other in traffic', in T. Uteng and T. Cresswell (eds), *Gendered mobilities.* London: Ashgate, 99–114.

Khan, G. A. (2012) 'Number of Pakistani expats exceeds 1.5 m', *Arab News*, 29 August. Online at: www.arabnews.com/number-pakistani-expats-exceeds-15-m (accessed 25 August 2015).

Kinnaird, V. and Hall, D. (eds) (1994) *Tourism: A gender analysis.* Chichester: Wiley.

Kock, U. and Sun, Y. (2011) 'Remittances in Pakistan: Why have they gone up, and why aren't they coming down?', IMF Working Paper 11/200.

Larsen, J. (2001) 'Tourism mobilities and the travel glance: Experiences on the move', *Scandinavian Journal of Hospitality and Tourism*, 1(2): 80–98.

Larsen, J., Urry, J. and Axhausen, K. (2007) 'Networks and tourism: Mobile social life', *Annals of Tourism Research*, 34(1): 244–62.

Law, M. J. (2014) '"The flashy strings of neon lights unravelled": Motoring leisure and the potential for technological sublimity on the Great West Road', *London Journal*, 39(3): 281–94.

Law, R. (1999) 'Beyond "women and transport": Towards new geographies of gender and daily mobility', *Progress in Human Geography* 23(4): 567–88.

Mackey, S. (2002) *The Saudis: Inside the desert kingdom*. New York: Norton.

McShane, C. (1994) *Down the asphalt path: The automobile and the American city*. New York: Columbia University Press.

Murray, L. (2008) 'Motherhood, risk and everyday mobilities', in T. Uteng and T. Cresswell (eds), *Gendered mobilities*. London: Ashgate, 47–64.

Paterson, M. (2007) *Automobile politics: Ecology and cultural political economy*. Cambridge: Cambridge University Press.

Porter, G. (2011) '"I think a woman who travels a lot is befriending other men and that's why she travels": Mobility constraints and their implications for rural women and girls in sub-Saharan Africa', *Gender, Place and Culture*, 18(1): 65–81.

Rajan, S. C. (2006) 'Automobility and the Liberal Disposition', *The Sociological Review*, 54(1): 113–29.

Sager, T. (2006) 'Freedom as mobility: Implications of the distinction between actual and potential travelling', *Mobilities*, 1(3): 465–88.

Sattar, Z., Hannam, K. and Ali, N. (2013) 'Religious obligations to travel', *Journal of Tourism and Cultural Change*, 11(1–2): 61–72.

*Saudi Gazette* (2010) 'Census shows Kingdom's population at more than 27 million', online at: www.saudigazette.com.sa/index.cfm?method=home.regcon&contentID=201 0112487888&archiveissuedate=24/11/2010 (accessed 25 August 2015).

Scharff, V. (1991) *Taking the wheel: Women and the coming of the motor age*. New York: Free Press.

Sheller, M. (2004) 'Automotive emotions: Feeling the car', *Theory, Culture & Society*, 21(4–5): 221–42.

Sheller, M. and Urry, J. (eds) (2004) *Tourism mobilities: Places to play, places in play*. London: Routledge.

Thrift, N. (1996) *Spatial formations*. London: Sage.

Urry, J. (2004) 'The "system" of automobility', *Theory, Culture & Society*, 21(4–5): 25–39.

Urry, J. (2012) 'Do mobile lives have a future?', *Tijdschrift voor economische en sociale geografie*, 103(5): 566–76.

Uteng, T. (2009) 'Gender, ethnicity, and constrained mobility: Insights into the resultant social exclusion', *Environment and Planning A*, 41(5): 1055–71.

Wells, A. and Benyon, M. (2011) 'Corruption, automobility cultures, and road traffic deaths: The perfect storm in rapidly motorizing countries?', *Environment and Planning A*, 43(10): 2492–503.

# 6 What is a 'dirtbag'?
## Reconsidering tourist typologies and leisure mobilities through rock climbing subcultures

*Jillian Rickly*

## Introduction

The rock climbing community comprises numerous, overlapping subcultures that define themselves by a number of parameters, including dedication to the sport, style of climbing, and regional preferences, just to name a few. Of interest in this chapter is a type of lifestyle mobility that has come to be known as 'lifestyle rock climbing'. While this term is used to capture the diversity of full-time, non-professional, travelling, rock climbing livelihoods, the individuals who pursue this lifestyle, however, use several self-identifiers. 'Dirtbags' is the most common, with a historical lineage and ideology in the rock climbing community dating to the 1950s. The first full-time climbers camped in the Yosemite Valley for most of the year, then travelled along the West Coast in the off-season (Taylor 2010). Today, the dirtbag identity is alive and well in the climbing community, but the modes of travel and travel circuits have expanded and its everyday practices have changed with a greater integration of global communications technologies. In response to some of the negative connotations that the 'dirtbag' identity carries, some prefer to be identified as 'lifers' or 'full-timers', as a way to express their dedication to the sport, while others use 'vanner' in order to convey their minimalism and most common mobile abode. As such, dirtbags share commonalities with a number of travel and leisure typologies, including drifters, tramps, backpackers, pilgrims, adventure tourists, lifestyle sport subcultures, and lifestyle travel.

Despite claims that the categorical thinking that frames much research concerning tourist typologies misses the bigger picture of travel motivation, experience, and impact, scholars still make use of such categories. Typologies provide a starting point with clear boundaries from which to frame objects of study. However, for these same reasons such categories are limiting and rarely do our investigations of lived mobilities ever fully map onto these predetermined delineations. With that in mind, in this chapter I revisit one of the first questions that arose in my work with lifestyle rock climbers – what is a 'dirtbag'? This is a question that arose both on the online forums I analysed as well as in my own mind as I attempted to fit this travel mode into a tourism-based definition. Of course, this question asks very different things depending on the context in which it is posed. On the online forums of rockclimbing.com, climbers raised this question among themselves, as they were interested in the existential parameters of 'dirtbags' as an identity.

My wrestling with this question originally was an attempt to ground what I was observing in the tourism literature. Yet, mobilities studies inspired a shift in my analytical perspective. Rather, by rethinking my data from a mobilities framework, I learned that I was not asking the most pertinent questions. Rather than searching for the 'correct' box to check from the list of tourist and leisure typologies, I began to think relationally about the ways this lifestyle mobility brings together disparate mobilities resulting in significant individual experiences, community bonds, and senses of place beyond what a simple categorisation could account for. In other words, in analysing the everyday performance of dirtbagging, the boundaries between distinct tourist typologies crumble. Further, while the hypermobile subculture of interest in this chapter comes from the rock climbing community, it is important to note that this and similar forms of lifestyle mobilities have existed for some time with their constellations of mobility widely known in their respective lifestyle sports, such as surfing, mountain biking, kayaking, hiking, base jumping, and many others (see Chouinard 2006; Waeschle 2009; Taylor 2010; Thorpe 2014). As Cresswell (2010) has observed, while we may just be approaching the study of particular mobilities from an academic perspective, that does not mean that they do not have well-known rich histories for those familiar with their contexts. Dirtbags, as lifestyle rock climbers, are just such a case.

## Tourist and leisure typologies

Early theories of tourism sought to define the tourist and were informed particularly by psychological, sociological, and anthropological disciplines, and in relation to leisure and recreation studies. Psychological perspectives were used to comprehend tourist motivations. Maslow's (1943) hierarchy of needs model was a useful starting point, as it related tourism motivation to higher order needs, including notions of belonging, such as when travelling to visit family; aesthetic and cognitive needs, as travel allows one to explore and learn about new places and cultures; and, of course, tourism is increasingly considered a way to access self-actualisation, the highest order need. So while it became obvious that tourism is not a component of basic human needs, it does fulfil other human desires in more complex ways. Yet each tourist is an individual, with differing needs and thereby tourism preferences. As a result, tourism research towards classifying tourist types proliferated. Plog's (1974) psychological spectrum of psychocentric to allocentric personalities thus expanded potential for assessing the diversity of tourist motivations. This inspired a flurry of tourist typologies as Cohen (1979) identified five types: recreational, diversionary, experiential, experimental, and existential; Smith (1989) expanded this to seven: explorers, elite, off-beat, unusual, incipient, mass, and charter tourists, and Yiannakis and Gibson (1992) then more than doubled this number.

A result of the increased number of categories of tourists, however, was an (at least) equal number of exceptions that corresponded to multiple typologies or none at all. Thus, the late 1990s and early 2000s witnessed a shift to research at the margins of tourist typologies, so to speak. McCabe's (2005) article 'Who is a tourist?' is telling of the reflectivity of tourism scholars during this time, as well as the reflexivity of tourists themselves, as he argues that while typologies attempt to capture motivation and experience, they do not take into account the use of the term 'tourist' in everyday discourse. In other words, motivations for holiday are only part of the larger function of tourism, particularly in terms of the social and cultural capital of travel. This suggests that theories of leisure, such as Veblen's (1899) notion of conspicuous consumption, have much to offer post-modern touristic endeavours as well, as they reach beyond the tourism moment to other aspects of everyday life. Such has been the call of mobilities studies – tourism is not isolated from our everyday social, economic, and political practices but is an extension of them. In particular, Hannam (2009) advocates tourism be approached from a mobilities perspective, along with other movement-based phenomena (see also Sheller and Urry 2006).

The definitional boundaries of tourism, as set by the WTO, are far too limiting for research interested in the motivation, experience, and identity-processes of touristic behaviour. A mobilities perspective aims to understand the relationality of movement – not just why tourists move, but the ways tourist movements encourage (and are encouraged by) other movements and the ways touristic travel is put to use in, as well as extends to, other aspects of life. Indeed, Cohen, Duncan, and Thulemark (2013; see also Duncan *et al.* 2014), with their theory of lifestyle mobilities, illustrate the necessity of considering not categories of movement – travel, leisure and migration – but the various ways these inspire many mobilities. For example, whereas migration-like movements are prioritised for some mobilities with long-term durations (Benson and O'Reilly 2009; Benson 2011), leisure and hypermobility are favoured in others (see Duncan 2008; Thorpe 2012; 2014; Rickly 2016). Nevertheless, under the framework of lifestyle mobilities, each is considered in relation to the others as a means to dissolve distinct categories by recognising their fluidity.

## Methodology

This chapter is based on research concerning lifestyle rock climbing as a subculture of the larger climbing community, which focused on the differences in dedication to the sport in relation to travel motivation, behaviour, and experiences. Data collection extended from discourse analysis of climbing media and online forums, including rockclimbing.com and redriverclimbing.com, to grounded observation, surveys, and interviews in the Red River Gorge, Kentucky, USA. During the period of August to November 2011, a total of 148 surveys were solicited from the rock climbing community in The Red, most generally as a means of assessing intra-community differences in climbing and travel behaviour. Additionally, 21 semi-structured interviews were conducted with lifestyle climbers, specifically, so as to better capture individual motivations and experiences of full-time travelling rock climbers. Observation took place across The Red, including a number of crags, but it was particularly focused on Miguel's Pizza – the most popular camping site in the area, where climbers were more social, able to participate in interviews and conversation, and community dynamics and everyday practices could be directly observed.

The demographics of the 21 interview participants can be broken down as follows. A gender disparity of six females and 15 males is representative of the observed lifestyle climber population. While the age of participants ranged from 22 to 56 years, the time committed to climbing and travelling full time extended from beginners at just six months to veterans of 17 years. As reflected in the rock climbing population in general, interviewees were predominantly white (Erikson 2005). All but two were Americans, with the exception of one Canadian and one French; additionally, two respondents self-identified as gay and lesbian, respectively.

## Dirtbags: rock climbing and lifestyle mobilities

Although 'lifestyle climber' is an appropriately descriptive term for this endeavour, as it relates to the bodies of literature concerned with lifestyle mobilities (Cohen *et al.* 2013; Duncan *et al.* 2014), lifestyle travel (Cohen 2010, 2011), lifestyle sports (Wheaton 2004), and so on, this is not a phrase found within the rock climbing community itself. When the practice of full-time, non-sponsored, travelling rock climbing is described to a member of the climbing community, it is recognised is the 'dirtbag' identity. And why not – this was the derogatory epithet turned badge of honour that the earliest lifestyle climbers wore proudly. According to Taylor's (2010) history of rock climbing in Yosemite, dirtbags evolved out of a generation of 1950s Beatnik climbers who established the ideal of climbing as a lifestyle at Camp 4 in the Yosemite Valley. By the 1960s this lifestyle began to spread to other climbing areas, in the States predominantly. Among these early devotees arose legends in the rock climbing community who pushed beyond the limits of what was considered climbable. At the same time, the 'strategy' of dirtbagging was being perfected – dumpster diving, sneaking showers, bumming rides, and developing a travel circuit – all in an effort to maintain full-time rock climbing. Thus, Taylor writes, in these early years 'dirtbags were Brahmins and Untouchables all in one' (2010: 214). Their lifestyles of self-induced poverty pushed them to the margins of society, yet their climbing prowess gained them much cultural capital within the climbing community.

These earliest descriptions of the travel conditions of dirtbags most closely correspond to the tourist typologies described as drifters, tramps, and budget travellers. The longer time spans common to lifestyle climbing, usually years rather than weeks or months, accompanied by a minimalist lifestyle and highly flexible itinerary, is more akin to drifting (Cohen 1973, 1979; Theroux 1975; Riley 1988). Many drifters note social rebellion or political protest as a catalyst for their travelling (Cohen 1973, 1979), and likewise most dirtbags describe a disconnect between themselves and contemporary capitalist society, particularly the earliest lifestyle climbers who were inspired by the predecessor Beatnik climbers (see Rickly-Boyd 2014). Drifting and tramping are closely related travel modes in terms of travel patterns (Cohen 1973); however, with tramping, decisions to travel are most related to the need for work (Adler 1985; Cresswell 2001). Dirtbags, however, are driven to new destinations for a specific purpose – rock climbing. They do not wander aimlessly, even if their travel circuits remain flexible.

Despite their minimalist lifestyles, which includes tight budgets, strict food rationing (and dumpster diving to supplement), and few material possessions, it is worth pointing out that this is a choice – one that comes from a place of privilege. Their impoverishment is self-induced. In fact, the majority come from middle- and upper-class families and have given up significant educational and career opportunities to pursue rock climbing full time. For dirtbags, the less one manages to live on, the more cultural capital is gained within this subculture. Indeed, material sacrifice is the yardstick of dedication to the sport, by which one seems to be measured. As Stevens writes in his 'Confessions of a Dirtbag', 'the number of individuals taking favour to the idea of calling home wherever you decide to lay your head is growing'; dirtbagging, he asserts, 'is not based on a need to alienate oneself from society, but instead a passion to seek out new experiences that force us to live completely in the moment, and through that, achieve an entirely new level of appreciation for the simplest pleasures' (2010: 49). Thus, what is unspoken in many dirtbag weblogs, video-diaries, and online forum posts is the safety net that remains for them. The majority I spoke with, when pressed on the matter, conceded that if they encountered financial challenges they have family or friends they could turn to for support.

So while many similarities remain with the travel typology of the drifter, greater examination of the structural elements of this pursuit moves dirtbags outside the category of tramp. Moreover, as time has passed, it has also become more similar to backpacking culture. Drifters as a typology exhibit great variety, which reflects the individual's personal circumstances, whereas backpacking is more consistent in travel patterns, communication, and cultural practice. Indeed, as Cohen (2004) has shown, backpacking has become less spontaneous and more structured, with guidebooks aiming to cater to particular types of backpackers. The strong community networks, the presence of well-defined circuits of destinations, and the use of this identity as social capital suggest backpacking as a common typology to dirtbags (see Riley 1988; Shaffer 2004; O'Reilly 2006). As the lifestyle climber ideal has perpetuated in the rock climbing community, the Beatnik-inspired, drifter-esque dirtbags have evolved. With increased global communications, these travelling climbers have exploited mobile telecommunications and greater internet access to utilise online guidebooks and forums to maintain communication with fellow climbers, as well as to coordinate travel and keep up to date with the latest happenings at their preferred climbing areas. Yet, these changes have also brought about tension within the subculture, as some argue that the dirtbag is dying. As Iurato's article '*The death* of the dirtbag', in *Urban Climber*, explains:

> There was a time when living like a dirtbag was the only way for a climber ... Day in and day out they mastered moving over stone using all that was available to them, which wasn't much at all. It's not like that anymore. Today, thanks in part to the efforts of those very same dirtbagging lifers, the rest of us can push the boundaries of what's possible with more than just the bare essentials ... It goes to show that it's more fun to go with the right tools than to go without, especially in a sport where safety is the first concern. In a sense, the creations of the one-time dirtbaggers are pushing dirtbaggerkind to extinction.
>
> (2008: 16–17)

And echoed by this climber:

> I think dirtbags are dead. I don't think they exist any more. To be honest with you, I haven't eaten out of a dumpster lately. I ate out of a dumpster in like 96 or 97 in Squamish [British Columbia] 'cause I really had no money. So, I don't think it exists any more. I think there's opportunities and there's ways to make money in the sport now.
>
> (Male, mid-thirties, lifestyle climbing for 12 years)

However, Taylor's (2010) history of the Yosemite climbing community suggests such condescension is a clear part of the discursive history of dirtbagging. Just as the Beatnik climbers came to loathe the ideals of experientialists, Taylor (2010: 217) observes: 'dirtbags of the 1970s would grouse about dirtbags of the 1990s'. Whereas dirtbagging was originally an individual and highly exclusive identity, characterised by a strong dedication to both rock climbing and a life on the road, it grew in popularity in the 1980s–90s, signifying a collective, highly social community that maintains close connections despite its mobility (Taylor 2010). Increasing global communications technologies facilitate these changes, which are also illustrated by the growing presence of self-identified dirtbags on online community forums such as rockclimbing.com, as well as an increase in the number of personal weblogs. Yet, as with the evolution of backpackers' itineraries out of their predecessor drifters' travel routes, telecommunications is making a considerable impact on the ways climbers go about dirtbagging. As explained by this climber:

> It's all moving up in standard of living. So maybe, by my definition of dirtbag – that climbing is dictating your pace of life – that doesn't negate them as being dirtbags, the definition's just evolving and changing. There's less sitting around the campfire, talking about climbing and having a good time, and there's more time with your nose buried in your MacBook Pro trying to scam the nearest wireless.
>
> (Male, late twenties, lifestyle climbing for ten years)

The increasing prevalence of laptops and smartphones and use of social media is highly contested in this subculture. They help to maintain communication, as well as make life on the road easier through navigation and map services. Further, many now have internet-based jobs that support their full-time travel, including a writer, an illustrator, a copyeditor, a webpage designer, a graphic designer, a photographer, and a sales representative. However, for older generations of dirt-bags the use of such technologies indicates social dependency as well as a lack of self-sufficiency and dedication. This climber observed:

> It used to be, you didn't need to keep in touch. 'I'll see you when I see you, man.' … But now, to be honest, as lame as it is, this Facebook phenomenon is a wonderful thing. It consolidates everything right there.
>
> (Male, late twenties, lifestyle climbing for ten years)

This suggests the overall changes in this subculture. As newer members enter the community more accustomed to the integration of global communications technologies in their everyday lives, as well as the wide availability of internet services, their use will continue to grow and will likely become more accepted among the necessities of a minimalist lifestyle. So while the dirtbag identity continues, it is changing along with broader social movements to be less a life of sacrifice in order to maintain a mobile climbing lifestyle and more of a hypermobile lifestyle in which rock climbing is prioritised.

This discussion of the community's structure and networks highlights the similarity of dirtbags and backpackers, and even lifestyle travel. However, it does not shed light on the role of this embodied practice in this travel pursuit. Because the primary travel motivation is rock climbing and the experience of challenging physical limitations in dangerous yet managed conditions, dirtbags are related to adventure tourists. As one online user declares, 'you can take the dirtbag out of the climber, but you can't take the climber out of the dirtbag'. Indeed, like most rock climbers, dirtbags relish the thrill of the flow experienced when climbing at their limits (see Csikszentmihalyi 1990). However, dirtbags describe the role of rock climbing as more significant, as it extends beyond leisure mobility or a recreational pursuit to a deeply meaningful, embodied practice.

> Most of the dirtbags are out there because climbing means something to them, they believe in it and they believe it's going to do something to them … They know it, they've seen it make a change in their life and they keep pursuing that … They're not here for the social scene … they're here for the climbing. And all that other stuff exists as a by-product.
>
> (Male, late twenties, lifestyle climbing for ten years)

Because this high degree of reverence is upheld as of the greatest importance for acceptance as a lifestyle climber, this community exhibits a variety of national and regional origins, political viewpoints, religious affiliations, and education levels. That is, if one appreciates rock climbing enough to allow it to guide one's life choices and attitude, then one is accepted into the community. One climber explained that what bonds this subculture of the rock climbing community is a 'respect for other people's experience, and for the specialness of what it can be out there' (male, late twenties, lifestyle climbing seven years). Similarly, Varley's (2011) study of sea kayakers finds that the liminoid experiences of that sport form the basis for kayaking 'neo-tribes' (Maffesoli, 1996), or what are more akin to Dionysiac *thiasos*, he argues. 'Ritualistic, emotional, ecstatic communities (neo-tribes) are created as a response to the flatness of alienating and disenchanting life' (Varley 2011: 95; see also Cailly 2006).

Despite what on the surface seems a similarity, this is quite distinct from the spontaneous, short-lived *communitas* of pilgrimage (Turner 1973) and tourism (Wang 1999). Turner (1973) theorised pilgrim *communitas* as spontaneously generated, temporary communities in which individuals, stripped of socio-economic attributes, are treated as equals and joined by common belief and purpose. Wang (1999) adapted this for the tourism context, suggesting that when touring, individuals of similar touristic endeavours too group together and form temporary social bonds. Lifestyle climbers, while travelling in individual circuits that overlap in less than predictable ways, do form communities while in the same places of mooring. Yet the common bond of rock climbing dedication and shared social networks, and the social media and telecommunications connections that result, keep individuals in contact even when travelling in disparate directions. Thus, dirtbags are better understood as a lifestyle sport subculture than *communitas*. As Wheaton (2004: 4) argues, lifestyle sport subcultures are 'fundamentally about "doing it", about taking part' and participating in the appropriated subcultural spaces and practices. The factors of recurrent participation, trust, and social bonds result in lifelong relationships extending across generations. In fact, many recounted the mentor-based relationships that initiated their entrance into the dirtbag community. Mentorships not only pass down knowledge, skills, etiquette, and ethics, they are a form of gatekeepers and therefore strengthen community bonds by establishing multiple levels of trust.

Thus, we are once again pushing beyond categorical boundaries and reaching across several travel typologies in the analysis of dirtbagging, further illustrating the utility of a mobilities approach. This is much more than leisure or tourism mobility. In fact, Taylor (2010) terms these devotees 'pilgrims of the vertical', embracing the significance of what they pursue. Given that dirtbags emphasise their continuous journeys over individual destinations and the existential, even spiritual, experiences some have from climbing, this is not a far stretch of the term (Rickly-Boyd 2012). However, distinct from pilgrimage, this hypermobile pursuit does not take place outside of everyday work and family obligations, but mobility and rock climbing are integrated into their everyday practices. They are not touring away from home without intent to return, but they maintain a mobile home along the way (van or RV in most cases). Home is made on the road, dwelling becomes mobile, with mundane routines of domesticity performed in (and around) an abode that is mobile, which are filled with material objects of personal significance, and even houses non-human relations (usually in the form of a pet dog) (Rickly-Boyd *et al.* 2014). Indeed, they do stay only temporarily at each of the locations in which they moor, but their travel is extended for years, continually in the performance of climbing circuits, all of which is closer to the notion of lifestyle travel (see Cohen 2010, 2011). And, moreover, their mooring places are not superficial but embodied enactments of place (Rickly-Boyd 2012).

The fact that this rock climbing subculture is a lifestyle is of particular importance, as it suggests the depth of dirtbagging as a performative identity. As such, dirtbags have difficulty separating the travel and rock climbing aspects of their lives. They see and experience them as intertwined, informing one another, and thereby moving them along.

> I can't make a distinction between my life and climbing, I mean, it's like all together. It's been driving me all over the world.
> (Female, mid-thirties, lifestyle climbing for five years)

Lifestyle, Stebbens (1997) suggests, is best observed in everyday actions. It is through the mundane that dirtbags assert their subcultural identity and establish symbolic boundaries of belonging. One lifestyle climber who works as an outdoor recreation industry representative depends financially on the climbing community, generally. Yet, he sees a distinct difference between himself, as a dirtbag, and leisure climbers.

> It's their dream to be a dirtbag. Some people are like, 'I'm saving up. Yeah, I'm going to take four months off and dirtbag it four months.' And that's their vacation … But I'm not on vacation; I'm actually working.
> (Male, mid-thirties, lifestyle climbing 12 years)

Importantly, by noting that he is 'actually working', he is not referring to travelling as a sales representative but to rock climbing every day possible, training, and staying focused on his climbing goals. This is similar to the findings of Filho's (2010) analysis regarding the leisure/work relationship of lifestyle rafting guides in New Zealand for whom work and leisure are not separate but one and the same, and furthermore inform their subcultural identity. Thus, lifestyle climbers make a concerted effort to distinguish themselves from the general climbing community. So, just as lifestyle climbers lament misconceptions about what it means to be a dirtbag and to live one's life fully dedicated to rock climbing, they also work to define who does not belong among this social group. Novice climbers are teasingly referred to as 'gumbies' and 'chuffers' – novice climbers who take excessive risks, putting themselves and others in danger in an effort to display their climbing skills – are repeatedly made the punchlines of jokes by lifestyle climbers. Thus, dirtbags as a subculture continually negotiate the boundaries of this identity within the climbing community.

## Conclusion

Considering the everyday practices of dirtbags highlights the ways in which rock climbing and travel are intricately interwoven. Unable to be teased apart as mutually exclusive, each necessitates the other. This suggests that an analysis aimed at appropriating dirtbags into a tourist typology was perhaps flawed from the start. Nevertheless, the exercise offers strong evidence for the utility of a mobilities perspective. Thinking beyond the individual categories to the ways they are related uncovers a type of lifestyle unlike any others. For those who pursue lifestyle mobilities, identity is performed in the interlacing of full-time travel, a strong interest in leisure and/or recreation, notions of particular lifeways unique to the combination of these aspects, and intra-community distinctions. As such, a dirtbag shares much in common with drifters, tramps, backpackers, adventure tourists, lifestyle travellers, and even pilgrims, but stopping at these typologies leaves much unaccounted for. A leisure mobilities perspective, however, encourages searching beyond these boundaries to understand the motivations, experiences, and identity processes of this iteration of lifestyle mobility. Lifestyle rock climbing relates to many touristic typologies, but matches none. A mobilities perspective thus illuminates this not as a liability but as an asset. It suggests that in the actual performance of this mobility, and of most mobilities for that matter, categorical boundaries crumble and the complexity of the performance results in continually shifting relationality. In other words, a mobilities approach yields narratives of movement and meaning that better reflect lived experiences – as constellations of representation and practice (see Cresswell 2010).

This chapter has worked through one particular expression of lifestyle mobility – lifestyle rock climbing. In asking the question – what is a dirtbag? – the analysis has revealed the limits of tourist typologies as well as nuanced ways in which 'being a dirtbag' is not about rock climbing or travelling, but the ways each informs the other producing an identity that is necessarily mobile and embodied.

## References

Adler, J. (1985) 'Youth on the road: Reflections on the history of tramping', *Annals of Tourism Research*, 12(2): 335–54.

Benson, M. (2011) 'The movement beyond (lifestyle) migration: Mobile practices and the constitution of a better way of life', *Mobilities*, 6(1): 221–35.

Benson, M. and O'Reilly, K. (2009) *Lifestyle migration: Expectations, aspirations and experiences*. Burlington, VT: Ashgate.

Cailly, L. (2006) 'Climbing sites as counter-sites? Essay on neo-community forms and territorialisation processes at work in the practice of rock climbing', *Journal of Alpine Research*, 94(1): 35–44.

Chouinard, Y. (2006) *Let my people go surfing: The education of a reluctant businessman*. New York: Penguin.

Cohen, E. (1973) 'Nomads from affluence: Notes on the phenomenon of drifter-tourism', *International Journal of Comparative Sociology*, 14(1): 89–104.

Cohen, E. (1979) 'A phenomenology of tourist experience', in S. Williams (ed.), *Tourism: Critical concepts in the social sciences*. London: Routledge, 3–26.

Cohen, E. (2004) 'Backpacking: Diversity and change', in G. Richards and J. Wilson (eds), *The global nomad: Backpacker travel in theory and practice*. Clevedon: Channel View, 43–59.

Cohen, S. A. (2010) 'Chasing a myth? Searching for "self" through lifestyle travel', *Tourist Studies*, 10(1): 117–33.

Cohen, S. A. (2011) 'Lifestyle travellers: Backpacking as a way of life', *Annals of Tourism Research*, 38(4): 1535–55.

Cohen, S. A., Duncan, T. and Thulemark, M. (2013) 'Lifestyle mobilities: The crossroads of travel, leisure and migration', *Mobilities*, 10(1), 155–72.

Cresswell, T. (2001) *The Tramp in America*. London: Reaktion Books.

Cresswell, T. (2010) 'Towards a politics of mobility', *Environment and Planning D: Society and Space*, 28(1): 17–31.

Csikszentmihalyi, M. (1990) *Flow: The psychology of optimal experience*. New York: Harper Perennial.

Duncan, T. (2008) 'The internationalisation of tourism labour market: Working and playing in a ski resort', in C. M. Hall and T. Coles (eds), *International Business and Tourism*. London: Routledge, 181–94.

Duncan, T., Cohen, S. A. and Thulemark, M. (Eds) (2014) *Lifestyle Mobilities:Intersections of travel, leisure and migration*. Aldershot, Hampshire: Ashgate Publishers.

Erikson, B. (2005) 'Style matters: Explorations of bodies, whiteness, and identity in rock climbing', *Sociology of Sport Journal*, 22(2): 373–96.

Filho, S. C. (2010) 'Rafting guides: Leisure, work and lifestyle', *Annals of Leisure Research*, 13(2): 282–97.

Hannam, K. (2009) 'The end of tourism? Nomadology and the mobilities paradigm', in J. Tribe (ed.), *Philosophical issues in tourism*. Bristol: Channel View Publications, 101–13.

Iurato, J. (2008) 'The death of the dirtbag', *Urban Climber*, 16–17.

Maffesoli, M. (1996) *The time of the tribes: The decline of individualism in mass society*. London: Sage.

Maslow, A. H. (1943) 'A theory of human motivation', *Psychological Review*, 50(3): 370–96.

McCabe, S. (2005) '"Who is a tourist?": A critical review', *Tourist Studies*, 5(1): 85–106.

O'Reilly, C. C. (2006) 'From drifter to gap year tourist: Mainstreaming backpacker travel', *Annals of Tourism Research*, 33(3): 998–1017.

Plog, S. C. (1974) 'Why destination areas rise and fall in popularity', *Cornell Hotel and Restaurant Administration*, 14(1): 55–8.

Rickly, J. M. (2016) 'Lifestyle mobilities: A politics of lifestyle rock climbing', *Mobilities*, ahead of print.

Rickly-Boyd, J. M. (2012) 'Lifestyle climbers: Towards existential authenticity', *Journal of Sport & Tourism*, 17(1): 85–104.

Rickly-Boyd, J. M. (2014) '"Dirtbags": Mobility, community and rock climbing as performative of identity', in T. Duncan, S. A. Cohen and M. Thulemark (eds), *Lifestyle mobilities and corporealities*. Aldershot: Ashgate, 51–64.

Rickly-Boyd, J. M., Knudsen, D. C., Braverman, L. C. and Metro-Roland, M. M. (2014) *Tourism, performance, and place: A geographic perspective*. Aldershot: Ashgate.

Riley, P. J. (1988) 'Road culture of international long-term budget travelers', *Annals of Tourism Research*, 15(2): 313–28.

Shaffer, T. S. (2004) 'Performing backpacking: Constructing "authenticity" every step of the way', *Text and Performance Quarterly*, 24(1): 139–60.

Sheller, M. and J. Urry (2006) 'The new mobilities paradigm', *Environment and Planning A*, 38(2): 207–26.

Smith, V. (1989) *Hosts and guests: The anthropology of tourism*. Oxford: Blackwell.

Stebbens, R. A. (1997) 'Lifestyle as a generic concept in ethnographic research', *Quality & Quantity*, 31(3): 347–60.

Stevens, C. (2010) 'Confessions of a dirtbag', in *Dead Point Magazine*. Fayetteville, WV: Matt Stark, 46–9.

Taylor, J. E. (2010) *Pilgrims of the vertical: Yosemite rock climbers and nature at risk.* Cambridge, MA: Harvard University Press.

Theroux, P. (1975) *The Great Railway Bazaar.* Boston, MA: Houghton Mifflin.

Thorpe, H. (2012) 'Transnational mobilities in snowboarding culture: Travel, tourism and lifestyle migration', *Mobilities*, 7(2): 317–45.

Thorpe, H. (2014) *Transnational mobilities in action sport cultures.* Houndmills: Palgrave Macmillan.

Turner, V. (1973) 'The center out there: Pilgrim's goal', *History of Religions*, 12(2): 191–230.

Varley, P. (2011) 'Sea kayakers at the margins: The liminoid character of contemporary adventures', *Leisure Studies*, 30(1): 85–98.

Veblen, T. (1899) *The theory of the leisure class.* New York: New American Library.

Waeschle, A. (2009) *Chasing waves.* Seattle, WA: Mountaineers Books.

Wang, N. (1999) 'Rethinking authenticity in tourism experience', *Annals of Tourism Research*, 26(2): 349–70.

Wheaton, B. (2004) 'Introduction: Mapping the lifestyle sport-scape', in B. Wheaton (ed.), *Understanding lifestyle sports: Consumption, identity and difference.* London: Routledge, 1–28.

Yiannakis, A. and Gibson, H. (1992) 'Roles tourists play', *Annals of Tourism Research*, 19(2): 287–303.

# Part II
# Work

# 7 Exploring tourism employment in the Perhentian Islands

## Mobilities of home and away

*Jacqueline Salmond*

## Introduction

To contribute to our understandings of mobilities, this chapter will explore how those working within tourism communities understand and experience their engagement with tourism employment. How the self is understood through working in tourism can illustrate a more complex application of lifestyle mobilities, which serves to destabilise some of the binary concepts utilised within tourism studies. The mobilities literature occupies the spaces in-between structured disciplinary research and allows for a more nuanced understanding of how and why people move, both physically and conceptually (Sheller and Urry 2004). The ability to be mobile depends upon a particular set of social, physical, and economic conditions (Hall 2005; Cresswell 2010). As such, it is understandable that much of the existing mobilities literature focuses on those from wealthy regions; the Global North. However, lifestyle choices are not restricted to those from these backgrounds; there are many with less economic freedom that also choose to practise mobility for similar reasons to the more frequently researched groups engaged in lifestyle mobilities. When examined from this wider vantage point, it can be argued that a variety of peoples across the world are enacting lifestyle mobilities in the same way as those from more stable and privileged economic backgrounds. Extending this understanding of the mobilities literature to those from less wealthy backgrounds does not erase the differing levels of privilege experienced by some, nor the limits to mobility experienced by others, but it can serve to illustrate how some communities may be active *participants in tourism*, rather than passive *recipients of tourism*.

Other studies have highlighted how the lines between leisure and work are blurred, in examples of backpackers who work their way around locations (Diekmann and Hannam 2010; Cohen 2011), working tourists (Uriely and Reichel 2000), and workers within hospitality (Duncan *et al.* 2013). These studies have tended to be from the perspective of those from the Global North (elite) who are seeking a way to work and pursue their own dreams; it is my wish to highlight how this can apply to some workers in the Global South (non-elite) and highlight connections and similarities across groups.

Recent studies from a mobilities perspective have explored a more nuanced approach to tourism communities, highlighting connections between peoples and places. This research draws from recent literature examining the mobilities perspective as it intersects with more traditional tourism studies and applies the concepts to different groups, creating a more flexible and hybridised understanding of tourism communities. Similar theoretical pieces have destabilised these binary notions (such as White and White 2007; Cohen *et al.* 2015). My study combined theory and practice within participant research to explore how a tourism community as a whole could be situated within the mobilities perspective. This chapter thus examines a community engaged in tourism on the Perhentian Islands in Malaysia. The study explores how and why people choose to engage with employment in tourism and how this influences their understandings of self. How we are understood and defined by others can impact decisions made for communities, something which is particularly prevalent with tourism communities in the Global South.

## Staying at the stopover islands

The Perhentian Islands are an archipelago located in the South China Sea off the north-east coast of peninsular Malaysia, approximately 20 km from the mainland. The word 'perhentian' in Malaysian is translated as 'stopover', which is a fitting moniker for the islands given that most visitors stay an average of three to four days. Although there are several islands in the archipelago, only two have continuous habitation: Palau Kecil ('small island', approx. 1,294 acres) and Palau Besar ('big island', approx. 2,145 acres). These two islands make up the tourist focus for the destination and house the accommodations, restaurants, shops, and tour operators and are connected to the mainland and one another via small speedboat-style ferries (also known as taxi-boats). As there are no paved roads or vehicles on the islands, transport between the beaches is a choice of walking on tracks through the jungle or taxi-boat. The islands attract a variety of types of tourists, from backpackers to families and upscale customers. The islands receive a significant number of local tourists and tourists from neighbouring ASEAN countries, making the islands different from other regional destinations (such as Thailand), which have a predominantly international clientele. Most tourist activities on the islands revolve around the beaches and water activities (kayaking, snorkelling and scuba diving).

The tropical monsoon climate provides abundant sunshine and high temperatures during the tourist season (approximately February to November), with most resorts closed to tourists during the off-season. Few workers remain permanently on the islands, and during the off-season the majority return to the mainland. The physical geography consists of fringing coral reef, rocky sandy bays, and interior jungle, which remains largely intact. Some of the bays have been cleared of vegetation in order to build tourist structures, but the extent of this clearance varies across the islands and most of the smaller bays remain secluded, with no large-scale development. Palau Kecil has a small village of between 1,200 and

2,000 inhabitants (estimates vary) with a school, mosque, and a clinic with an emergency boat ambulance for transportation to the mainland. Prior to tourism on the islands, there were limited permanent habitations on other beaches and population was mostly confined to the village. Tourism began with local and regional tourists visiting the islands and small numbers of international backpackers (Cohen 2004) staying primarily with local families or camping on the beach. Tourism began slowly, with very small properties being built to take advantage of the growing interest in the islands and transport to the islands being negotiated via supply boats. At this time there was no electricity on the islands, lighting was by kerosene lamp, toilets were non-flush pit toilets, and washing would be mandi-style (water is scooped in a small container from a bucket or basin to wash). There were few places on the islands to buy food or supplies, so food needed to be brought from the mainland and water needed to be purified.

At the time of the study, the islands have a range of properties; although most of them remain simply built using mostly wood, there have been some recent developments which have used concrete. At the budget end, properties have around ten rooms, either in wooden longhouse style with shared dormitory rooms, or individual chalets with outside shared toilet and wash blocks. At the luxury end are properties which have around 100 rooms, 24-hour electricity, air-conditioning, hot showers, pool, and television (only one property). Although at the luxury end the accommodation is significantly different from the budget end, the facilities on the islands often do not match the 'luxury' tag as understood by most wealthy tourists, and remain at a lesser standard than what would be encountered on the mainland. The majority of properties fall somewhere in-between, with an average of 40 rooms covering a range of standards. The islands are frequently described in guidebooks as unspoilt, but on the cusp of overdevelopment.

As with many former colonial nations engaged in tourism (Hall and Tucker 2003), the Perhentian islands are imbued with the legacy of colonialism. Malaysia was colonised by the British in the nineteenth century, gaining independence in 1957. As with most postcolonial states, the years of colonisation have left a lasting impression on the country. One of the most obvious impacts of colonialism is seen in the multi-ethnicity within the country. The British encouraged Chinese merchants to relocate to Malaysia in order to facilitate the regional transfer of goods. In addition, the British imported Indian labourers to staff the rubber plantations established on the peninsular of Malaysia (Ongkili 1985). After Malaysia gained independence, these ethnic groups remained and form the current multi-ethnic society of Malaysia (Malay 58 per cent, Chinese 27 per cent, Indian 8 per cent, other ethnicities 7 per cent). The term *Malay* refers to the 'people of Malaysia'; the *bumiputera*, or 'son of the soil', is a descriptor specifically reserved for those who declare a historical and territorial claim to Malaysia as defined by birthright. There have been legal regulations established to protect the *bumiputera* and provide ethnic preference; one of these regulations limits ownership of land to *bumiputera* (Ong 2000). This complex multi-ethnic history influences the social relations of tourism on the islands.

## The tourism community

Tourism is the primary employment sector on the Perhentian Islands; even those not directly employed within tourism (such as fishermen or farmers) are impacted by tourism to the islands through supply networks or transportation. The presence of tourists can impact how a community chooses to develop infrastructure and change or structure social interactions. There is also a reflexive relationship in tourism communities, and tourists may be influenced by their interactions with tourism communities. As such, I consider the entire population of the islands as a 'tourism community', involving workers with both elite and non-elite social status as well as the consumers of the tourism product. My use of the term 'community' does not assume equality or similarity within or across groups, but is used as a tool to illustrate shared goals and motivations (Gibson-Graham 2006).

With a thriving tourist business the islands employ large numbers of workers to facilitate and support the industry. The majority of businesses are run by owner-operators who employ additional staff, with only a few businesses owned by individuals who do not live on the islands. Although some have lived on the islands for many years, there was a sense that these businesses were semi-permanent, with many businesses experiencing resale every three or four years. The island workers are mostly under 35 years of age, from European destinations, and local workers from across Malaysia. Many non-locals have lived on the islands for many years; some had families and had invested in property and businesses on the islands. Others were seasonal workers, such as those working in the scuba-diving community, who return to the Perhentian islands to work season after season. Both local and non-local workers were practising lifestyle mobilities; they were engaged in semi-permanent moves which incorporated daily activities (Cohen *et al.* 2015).

Given the diverse and changing nature of the island community, it is important for any representations to include as many voices as possible. As such, this research was designed as a participatory project where the process of research was a way for island residents to generate their own understandings of their community (Kobayashi 2001; Gibson-Graham 2006). The research utilised multiple techniques including in-depth individual interviews, message board discussions, surveys, focus group discussions, and participant observation. Focus groups participants were identified using a purposeful sampling technique (Bedford and Burgess 2001) and were both large (12 participants) and small (five participants); responses were audio-recorded, accompanied with contextual notes. In addition to structured research, while on the islands I worked in a dive shop and lived with the community, adopting the mobile lifestyle, so I was both insider and outsider, both home and away.

## Island workers: home and away

One of the key threads within mobilities literature is how individuals who travel for work and/or leisure understand concepts of home and away (White and White 2007).

Many who work away or travel for extended periods have shifting and complex understandings of their sense of place signalling new understandings of lifestyle mobilities and the reasons why individuals choose to be mobile (Gustafson 2001). They frequently identify with hybridised and complex identities for themselves and their locations, which bring into question binary notions of home and away. For many, 'home' is a mobile and flexible definition created from associations and actions that define the individual (Germann Molz 2008). In the context of those who travel to work in tourism, it is the social relations of the tourism community that create a particular sense of belonging for the individuals. In this way, it is less about creating approximations of 'home' in a particular place, or adopting particular homely behaviours, and more about redefining the self as different; as someone who feels more 'at home' in a particular lifestyle than a particular location.

This is illustrated on the Perhentian Islands where there are multiple layers of home and away which apply in flexible and changing ways. Since the expansion of tourism, the location has drawn a large number of workers from the Malaysian mainland and from across the world to work and live on the islands. As most workers return to the mainland during the off-season, the traditional understandings of fixed habitation become more complicated. A large number of workers return to the islands each year, but also spend time elsewhere, so they have a flexible definition of belonging, which illustrates a different lifestyle choice. Many of the workers are Malaysian nationals who migrate to the islands from very different places, such as Kuala Lumpur or distant states. For them the ethnic make-up as well as physical geography may be very different from their place of birth (for example, some individuals came from urban locations and some were Chinese Malaysians). However, when compared to tourists, they are perceived to be more at 'home' than those from, say, Europe, despite their own experiences of difference. These examples complicate binary concepts of host/guest and home/away as the individuals make their new home on the islands, but are not 'original' island dwellers. These populations describe their location in both terms – it is home and also away from home.

Workers who have come to the islands from outside Malaysia also experience shifting concepts of home and away. These individuals are geographically and socially further from their places of birth, but for many the lifestyle they have adopted through tourism work more closely defines their sense of self. For them, they feel more 'at home' on the islands or within their working network than in other locations. During focus group discussions, several of the workers who were originally from European destinations discussed how they felt that they no longer fitted in when they went back to Europe, and instead identified the Perhentian Islands, or more generally South-East Asia, as their home. For these individuals, the narratives used to describe belonging centred on a different lifestyle and the identification with a particular way of life and group of people.

Some individuals were incorporating a more mobile lifestyle along with longer periods of work in multiple locations. For example, the Perhentian Islands have a seasonal diving schedule; workers are employed for six or eight months, and many dive workers would frequently then return to locations elsewhere in South-East Asia that were on opposite monsoonal schedules. These individuals ranged in age from 18 to 42 years, and there was an even mix of men and women, education attained, and social status. The mobilities lifestyle was the link that connected them. They consider the islands their home and many individuals had returned to this particular location several seasons in a row, something they did not do for other locations. They would describe their return as 'coming home' or feeling 'good to be home', and their birth country would be described as 'going back' rather than going home. There were some individuals who planned to spend the off-season travelling rather than working, and in this context the Perhentian Islands became a temporary home for many in the backpacker and dive-shop community, and the secondary locations were experiential locations considered away.

Along with workers, many owner-operators experience changing identification with belonging and where they consider home. One owner-operator described her experience of the islands: 'When I first came here it was very different, I wanted to stay here for ever, but now things have changed ... (*pause*) I don't want to grow old in Malaysia.' She had lived on the islands for several years, and described the islands as her home (versus her birth country in Europe); although she was now seeking a new home, she did not consider returning to Europe. When asked why, she said she felt that South-East Asia better reflected her personality: '[birth country in Europe] is just not me'. She was clearly enacting a lifestyle mobility with semi-permanent residence on the islands and a view towards seeking new locations for settlement.

For those living and working on the Perhentian Islands, the idea of 'home' became more complex, with specific micro geographies at play. As each of the different beaches and bays have their own identity, individuals identify with a particular 'beach' that they consider to be their home. The identification with particular beaches parallels the attachment to particular neighbourhoods within large cites, and the location becomes part of the identity of the individual. Choosing to work on one beach signalled that you were a fun-loving party person, but working on a different beach indicated you were a 'hard-core' scuba diver. The individual identification with the character of a beach was illustrated through terminology used to describe the other beaches and they were often described in terms of difference; I don't like it 'over there' or the other beach is 'like that'.

Many who see their bay as home define other locations as markedly different and geographically separate. Visually there is very little difference between the bays on the islands; the main divide between the islands is the difference between Kecil and Besar, with 'long beach' on Kecil being described as the 'party beach'. These definitions serve to separate and reinscribe the different identities between locations on the islands. Travel between bays can be seen in much the same way city dwellers would travel uptown or downtown to specific locations for specific purposes. Partly due to the geography and the need to get a boat from one island to the next, travel between the islands is described and enacted as an outing. With a group of workers, a trip to the other island beach is always a planned affair and treated as an excursion. Island dwellers described the beaches in very different terms, and in a reflexive relationship, these beaches perform that identity. Therefore at the micro level, there was a reflexive relationship between the place and the individual, reinforcing particular behaviours (those at the party beach partied; those at the quieter beaches were more laid back, and so on). These identities are true for non-local as well as local workers. They are all enacting lifestyle mobilities; they are choosing to be in a specific location as a preferable place to work because of its identity.

Along with the island workers, the concepts of home and away were also more flexible for the tourists on the islands. There were significant contrasts to the tourism on the islands compared to tourism in other locations. A large percentage of tourists are Malaysian nationals, which establishes a particular relationship of home and away when placed alongside Western tourists. Many of the customs, foods, and languages are familiar to them, while being unusual to others, creating a greater sense of belonging and understanding different from those from elsewhere. There were also large groups who would return with great regularity to the islands (individuals and school team visits) and for them the locations became viewed as both home and away, illustrating that 'away' can still occur within the frame of the very familiar and 'home' surroundings. Of the Western tourists visiting, some were repeat visitors; one couple spoken to had been visiting the islands for 15 years and indicated that they felt this was 'like home to us'. Other visitors were staying on the islands for a week or more, which compared to the usual visitation of two to three days gave them a sense of belonging and familiarity that allowed them to feel that they could dispense advice from the position of understanding the place. Therefore they were performing 'home' while also being away.

To further collapse the binary between home and away for tourists, many local staff have their families with them, and the entire family is often involved in the workplace. The school is located in the village and children returning from school will be delivered by boat to the parent's place of work. Often children will join their parents at work or play on the beach partly supervised while the workers finish up their day; smaller children especially are frequently seen at work with parents and they will take priority over tourists. The tourist boats are also used to transport staff home at the end of their shift, which further fragments the sense of 'away' experienced by tourists. All these instances contradict the usual 'tourist bubble' where tourists are separated from workers and the tourist space is a protected and manicured enclave exclusively for their enjoyment.

There were frequent interactions throughout the day between staff and tourists, either sitting or sharing cigarettes, chatting, or playing volleyball together – such facilities were used more often by staff than tourists. At one resort I stayed at for a total of two months I never saw tourists playing volleyball alone; they would sometimes join in with staff, but never played alone. The volleyball court was effectively viewed as a staff space by tourists, which is very different from the rigidly defined worker and tourist spaces encountered in other locations. In contrast to experiences elsewhere, workers are not excluded from tourist spaces, thus suggesting that the categorisation that defined tourist space as something different, or other, does not apply here. This illustrates the flexibility with which the spaces of island tourism are maintained. Staff often performed tourist behaviours when off duty, such as snorkelling and swimming, playing volleyball, and using canoes. Through such negotiated behaviour the lines become blurred between staff and tourists and create a space different from the more traditional tourist spaces. As a worker, I was told to 'slow down, stop working, you're not in London now', so the concept of slow working and being casual was perceived as a benefit of the local working conditions.

In many situations when workers were off duty or on a break they would inhabit 'tourist space', such as sitting on hammocks or beach chairs, or relaxing in the restaurants. This helps collapse the binary between tourist and worker space, generating a sense that the workers could also experience moments of leisure usually reserved for the tourists. Similarly tourists would invade the space of staff, such as sitting on the wooden platforms and staff hammocks, and frequently coming to sit with staff after hours, whether invited or not. For many of the workers their time on the islands was blurred, with work and leisure collapsing into one; frequently workers would talk to and interact with tourists during their personal time. I asked a local staff member if he minded tourists talking to him or asking him questions when he was not working, and he suggested that he was never working: 'Look at it, how is this work? I get to spend time here in this beautiful place, this isn't work.' Another individual answered that this was part of the job: 'Well, it is what you have to do: you are here for people at all times,' although he didn't seem to be unhappy with this. Many others commented that they actively like to talk to the tourists, they joked about chatting to girls, and some said it is the best way to learn English; others said they like the tourists and like to learn about other places in the world.

There emerges a pattern of similarity between the motivations for tourism mobilities from local and non-local workers. The motivations from international workers are positioned within the backdrop of choice. Clearly, those from a higher socio-economic status at home are provided with more choices for work; the ability to fly around the world to pursue a particular sort of employment is a reflection of those freedoms. However, despite this difference in privilege, there remains a similarity across the two groups in terms of motivations to work in this particular industry. It is too simplistic to assume that the local workers are on the islands through a limited choice. Workers I spoke to discussed their interest and desire to work in this location based on choices; many of them could earn more money on the mainland doing office jobs or other careers. The work on the Perhentian Islands is seen as a 'non-work' space that encompasses idylls from films, tourist literature, and television. Many male workers spoke of the 'Hawaiian' or surfer-dude lifestyle they felt they were a part of and many wore clothing illustrating this lifestyle affiliation. Many indicated that they plan to continue in this type of employment; they are pursuing a mobilities lifestyle which allows them to perhaps change their own worldview and create a new future. Throughout conversations with local women workers, narratives of liberation and freedom illustrated that for them this mobility was a tool to change their social situation. Several women participants indicated that the islands allow them to live a 'different life' and they identified specific behaviours that would be expected of them in their family setting that they do not need to observe on the islands. This perception of lifestyle working choice carries over not just to the way in which the workers interact with tourists, but also in the way they defined the space they inhabit; despite difference in socio-economic status and backgrounds, there was a shared sense of pursuing lifestyle choices across members of the working community and tourists. Working on the islands is an opportunity to redefine themselves outside of their existing cultural confines, allowing them to be more outspoken or to escape some of the familial obligations that would be required of them in their home villages.

## Adopting a touristic lifestyle, collapsing binaries between work and leisure

Engaging with tourism work is a lifestyle pursuit illustrated by the behaviours adopted and personas enacted. These touristic behaviours preference leisure activities and a slower working pace, directly antithetical to the work ethic promoted elsewhere (on the mainland or in the home countries of the non-local workers). In the adoption of touristic behaviours the island workers perform two functions. First, they establish themselves within the same category as the tourists, adopting their lifestyles and creating fissures within the idea of hosts and guests. This in turn challenges the traditional tourism studies notions of tourism workers being subservient to tourists and reinscribes the workers as something other. Although they are at work while others are at leisure, adopting leisure practices while at work challenges the work/leisure binary. Their approach to the workplace prioritises different activities, such as interactions with tourists, relaxing within tourist spaces and posting images of activities to others on social media. Through this type of work they challenge their own social norms, confronting the established ideas of how they are expected to be and recreating subjectivities. Individuals assume different categorisations: they are not 'just' workers, but they are also not tourists. In this way they create a new social space in which they can perform different identities and become something other. These individuals, both local and non-local, are actively choosing which social criteria to prioritise, such as valuing free time, relaxing, and enjoyment. Therefore working in tourism in this context can be seen as an expression of agency and an active choice to adopt particular lifestyles.

For the Malaysian workers there was the sense that the behaviours adopted were choices constructed from a reasoned identification with desirable social activities. There did not seem to be any indication that the individuals are seeking activities attached to specifically Western or modern identities. The contrary appeared to be the case, with many identifying the value of the lifestyle chosen on the islands as a specific counter to associated modern or Western identities. Some identified the unpleasantness of cities, or the rushed pace of modern life, while others spoke of the wastefulness and distance from nature.

The positive aspects identified were those that centred on touristic behaviours, such as meeting new people, finding out about other places, and spending time in a beautiful location. What is then created is a type of hybrid identity which retains many of the traditional values of kampong society as discussed by Ong (1987) (such as not working too hard and enjoying free time) along with the 'modern' international identities of global citizens. As such, these individuals are adopting particular lifestyle choices that have been created and defined by particular and shifting social values. Workers from international destinations identified similar motivations for tourism work as Malaysian workers. Many suggested that they had come to the islands to experience different cultures and as part of a desire to travel, and working on the islands has made that affordable. Others suggested that they want to live a different life from the one they would have at home, describing their identity on the islands in contrast to that of their birth country.

By identifying these similarities, connections can be made between local and non-local workers, deconstructing the passive identity often extended to 'host' workers and communities. In addition to worker motivations, many of the owner-operators involved in island tourism described similar motivations based on lifestyle choices. This parallels the findings from other studies examining tourism entrepreneurs, which identify lifestyle choices as a motivator for engagement with tourism (Williams *et al.* 1989). Similarly, workers from both local and international sources identified motivations that were framed outside of economic gain or necessity and more closely related to experience and enjoyment. A number of aspects were frequently mentioned: many expressed an interest in meeting people from different cultures, making friends, sharing stories and undertaking leisure activities. The physical beauty of the location and the natural environment was also commonly mentioned as a draw for relocating to or remaining on the Perhentian Islands. In this way, the motivations for tourism work from local and non-local workers parallel desires for travel expressed by many tourists (Wickens 2002; Mowforth and Munt 2003). Many of the tourists on the islands identified the same criteria for choosing to travel in general and specifically for travel to the Perhentian Islands.

## Conclusion

By highlighting tourism work as a choice related to lifestyle mobilities for those from the Global South, new understandings of the connections within and between tourism communities can be explored. Connections can be identified that destabilise binary tourism concepts. This identifies the similarities between those who produce tourism and those who consume tourism, drawing into question the binary between host/guest and home/away. These connections between workers and tourists make it possible to identify a 'tourism community' that is made up from all members. Although this community is fleeting, changing, and imbued with power relations, acknowledging these similarities goes some way towards recognising the contingent and reflexive relationships between producers and consumers of tourism. This establishes a more nuanced understanding of tourism communities and how they are shaped by both social relations and our understandings of economic communities.

In traditional analyses of tourism communities, local and non-local workers are frequently treated as separate categories. However, this research found that there were numerous points of intersection and overlap between motivations for engagement in tourism work, which would suggest that separate categorisations do not fully represent the conditions that exist. Highlighting these similarities draws attention to how lifestyle mobilities are practised in different ways by different social groups. On the Perhentian Islands workers, both local and non-local, select tourism employment as a form of lifestyle mobility and see this as a route to recreate their identity. The adoption of touristic behaviours is not an act of resistance, but rather one of performing themselves differently. Employment in tourism for many is more than just wage labour, it has become part of the way in which individuals and groups define themselves and recreate their subjectivities along particular lines. The Perhentian Islands are not a unique space for this enactment of tourist/worker, but it is an example to support the theoretical applications of lifestyle mobilities.

## References

Bedford, T. and Burgess, J. (2001) 'The focus-group experience', in Limb, M. and Dwyer, C. (eds), *Qualitative methodologies for geographers: Issues and debates*. New York: Oxford University Press, 121–35.

Cohen, E. (2004) 'Backpacking: Diversity and change', in G. Richards and J. Wilson (eds), *The global nomad: Backpacker travel in theory and practice*. Clevedon: Channel View, 43–59.

Cohen, S. A. (2011) 'Lifestyle travellers: Backpacking as a way of life', *Annals of Tourism Research*, 38(4): 1535–55.

Cohen, S. A., Duncan, T. and Thulemark, M. (2015) 'Lifestyle mobilities: The crossroads of travel, leisure and migration', *Mobilities*, 10(1): 155–72.

Cresswell T. (2010) 'Towards a politics of mobility', *Environment and Planning D: Society and Space*, 28(1): 17–31.

Diekmann, A. and Hannam, K. (eds) (2010) *Beyond backpacker tourism: Mobilities and experiences*. New York: Channel View.

Duncan, T., Scott, D. and Baum, T. (2013) 'The mobilities of hospitality work: An exploration of issues and debates', *Annals of Tourism Research*, 41(1): 1–19.

Edensor, T. (2001) 'Performing tourism, staging tourism: (Re)Producing tourist space and practice', *Tourist Studies*, 1(1): 59–81.

Franklin, A. and Crang, M. (2001) 'The trouble with tourism and travel theory', *Tourist Studies*, 1(1): 5–22.

Germann Molz, J. (2008) 'Global abode: Home and mobility in narratives of round-the-world travel', *Space and Culture*, 11(4): 325–42.

Gibson-Graham, J. K. (2006) *A postcapitalist politics*. Minneapolis: University of Minnesota Press.

Gustafson, P. (2001) 'Roots and routes: Exploring the relationship between place attachment and mobility', *Environment and Behavior*, 33(5): 667–86.

Hall, C. (2005) 'Reconsidering the geography of tourism and contemporary mobility', *Geographical Research*, 43(2) 125–39.

Hall, C. and Tucker, H. (eds) (2003) *Tourism and post colonialism: Contested discourses, identities and representations*. London: Routledge.

Kobayashi, A. (2001) 'Negotiating the personal and the political in critical qualitative research', in M. Limb and C. Dwyer (eds), *Qualitative methodologies for geographers: Issues and Debates*. New York: Oxford University Press, 55–70.

Mowforth, M. and Munt, I. (2003) *Tourism and sustainability: Development and new tourism in the Third World*. London: Routledge.

Ong, A. (1987) *Spirits of resistance and capitalist discipline: Factory women in Malaysia*. Albany, NY: University of New York Press.

Ong, A. (2000) 'Graduated sovereignty in South-East Asia', *Theory Culture and Society*, 17(4): 55–75.

Ongkili, J. (1985) *Nation-building in Malaysia, 1946–1974*. Oxford: Oxford University Press.

Sheller, M. and Urry, J. (eds) (2004) *Tourism mobilities: Places to play; places in play*. London: Routledge.

Uriely, N. and Reichel, A. (2000) 'Working tourists and their attitudes to hosts', *Annals of Tourism Research*, 27(2): 267–83.

White, N. and White, P. (2007) 'Home and away: Tourists in a connected world', *Annals of Tourism Research*, 34(1): 88–104.

Wickens, E. (2002) 'The sacred and the profane: A tourist typology', *Annals of Tourism Research*, 29(3): 834–51.

Williams, A., Shaw, G. and Greenwood, J. (1989) 'From tourist to tourism entrepreneur, from consumption to production: Evidence from Cornwall, England', *Environment and Planning A*, 21(12): 1639–53.

# 8  The 'nextpat'

## Towards an understanding of contemporary expatriate subjectivities

*Roger Norum*

## Introduction

It is not uncommon among cocktail party etymologists these days to point out the historical linkages between the contemporary terms 'travel' and 'travail'. Occasionally, some make it beyond the lexically obvious fact that the former term derives from the latter, denoting burdensome, oppressive bodily or mental labour, or toil that brings about hardship and suffering. Romanic socio-linguistic scholars have traced both terms to the Vulgar Latin *trepālium*, a triple-staked torture device that became particularly prevalent during the Inquisition (Liberman 2007). Subjects of such torture would be tied to the trepalium, burned with fire, and occasionally impaled (Robinson 2007). The sense of the verb *trepāliāre*, then, was 'to put to torture, torment'; this later became the reflexive 'to vex, trouble, weary oneself', and the intransitive 'to toil, work hard, labour' (OED 2015). Some critics of late capitalism will no doubt be reassured to discover a modern global service industry that has emerged out of a third-century device that served as a source of agony and torture. With associations that originated perhaps as early as the third century, travellers were not simply tormented or doing unpleasant work in moving about. Rather, travel *was* torture. As Robert Cole (2009) has put it, 'Airline customer service never looked so good.'

In this chapter, I seek to question commonly held assumptions of a particularly loaded categorisation of mobile worker, the 'expatriate', to suggest that expatriatism is today (and perhaps has always been) articulated through a mobility that is as much about work, labour, and career as it is about lifestyle, leisure and travel (see Parkin 2000; Sarró 2009). As the introduction of this volume points out, there are multiple veiled links between travel, work, and other aspects of social life that mobility studies can help uncover. This chapter offers some theoretical reflections on why tourism and labour mobilities have been systematically decoupled, and then seeks to re-link them epistemologically and analytically, through a case study of Nepal, a region subsumed by specific (and perhaps contradictory) global imaginaries. I defamiliarise and draw attention to the narratives that help to produce experiences of mobile labour and tourism. In doing so, I show how these (often paradoxical) notions can be used to understand the ways in which imagined and lived practices of tourism, travel, and everyday life are experienced in expatriate contexts.

In considering the phenomenological aspects of mobilities that lie on the continuum of human movement between migration and tourism (Nagy and Korpela 2013), such research and analysis can shed light on the not disparate subjectivities of migrants, expatriates, tourists, and other mobile groups travelling to and living in radically different social and cultural contexts. Furthermore, in investigating the structures behind new movements of people and things, I stress the importance of avoiding simplification of otherwise complex forms of mobility. Studying up and across multiple social, cultural, economic, and geographic hierarchies, I consider specific trajectories of mobility that have thus far been largely elided or overlooked by anthropologists, geographers, and sociologists otherwise interested in transnationalism, globalisation, and the movement of peoples.[1]

Fieldwork for the research presented in this chapter was conducted over a period of 18 months from 2009 to 2011, primarily in Kathmandu, Nepal. Data was collected in a range of private and public spaces, which included workplaces, shared domestic spaces, tourism establishments, and the bars and restaurants of Kathmandu's night-time economy. During fieldwork, I worked from time to time as a freelance journalist and photographer, which provided me with inroads into the expatriate community beyond that of an ethnographer. I gathered extensive field-notes during participant observation and carried out conversational and semi-formal interviews, following up on these with more formalised interviews with people of interest. Using informal, snowball methods and not restricting myself to any one organisation, industry, or social circle allowed me to include a diverse range of both expatriates and tourists in my research.

## From migration to mobility

A recent UN estimate puts the number of international migrants at 232 million people, or 3.2 per cent of the world's population (UNDESA 2013). Though the accuracy of this figure is difficult to assess, it is clear that the vast majority of these migrants are people who move from the Global South to the Global North (UNPD 2002). Arguably more difficult to measure, though, is the number of people who voluntarily self-displace (often, though not always, in the other direction) from their countries of origin in order to advance their career, change their lifestyle, or travel the world – or all of these at the same time.

Scholarship on migration long neglected to include research on actors who had relative freedom of choice concerning the whens, wheres and hows of their migration. Over the past decade, the 'mobilities framework' (Urry 2007) has helped to challenge assumptions within the social sciences such as the static, bounded concepts of culture and society as a unit of analysis, the assumed centre-periphery nature of movement of peoples from developing to developed areas of the world, and the association of mobility with freedom (and immobility with oppression).[2] It has sought to overcome this sedentary bias implicit in the language of early migration scholarship by encouraging engagement with more robust considerations of human movement. Mobility lenses can lend other advantages, too. For example, as Hannam (2009: 109) has suggested, research that ignores considerations of mobility often presumes 'that actors are able to do only one thing at a time, and that events follow each other in a linear order'.

For these reasons, mobility as a framework is particularly useful to those doing research on unforced migration trajectories, such as business travel, volunteer tourism and expatriatism, which necessarily straddle a range of types of movement and motivations. Such a malleable and interdisciplinary analytical toolkit also allows for looking beyond disciplinary and theoretical boundaries. For example, while the literatures on migration and tourism have developed more or less in isolation from one another, these two spheres of movement are in fact very much interrelated – and are only becoming more so as the technologies and ways of life in which they are embedded continue to change. If the differentiation 'between permanent and temporary moves is no more than an artifact of statistical convenience', we can also be certain that distinctions between the two are nevertheless becoming 'increasingly blurred as a result of accelerating social, economic, and technological change' (Bell and Ward 2000: 104).

## Categorising life, work, and work-life

Within the field of mobility studies, economic and work-related aspects of society are often treated as distinct from other life practices, and theorised in different ways. However, in the wake of globalised capitalism and deliberate projects of transnational integration (e.g. the EU), many economic sectors and work/labour cultures are undergoing fundamental transformations (Caggese and Cunat 2008). In contrast to earlier industrial periods, when distinct spatial, temporal, and social separations existed between what constituted the domains of work and other spheres of life (such as family life or leisure), such boundaries are now becoming blurred. The changing parameters of working culture, characterised by increasing mobility, flexibility, and subjectification in how labour is provisioned, are becoming integrated with other life experiences, and once clear delineations between work and non-work are beginning to fade away. Such fluidity and flows between these various spheres of life are further enabled and encouraged by various ICTs that facilitate transgressing the once constraining boundaries of space and time.

While work is a central aspect of the chronologisation of the life course, the lived experiences of many contemporary occupations – e.g. the diplomatic corps, medicine, IT – transcend the times and spaces of so-called traditional work. As such, one's work can 'constitute more than an occupational identity, seeping into every aspect of the individual's life, and indeed that of their family' (Hockey and James 2002: 190). Such permeability is not just limited to the domain of those in immaterial professions. Across a range of fields and careers, then, seemingly contradictory activities such as work and travel may now be empirically and conceptually more alike than often imagined, and share common ground in ethnographic lived experiences, particularly when seen within the context of broader political economic structures of power and control (Büscher and Davidov 2013).

Whereas classical perspectives on work-related mobility and labour migration interpret everyday, private, and family life through the prism of economic demand, more fluid and less fixed perspectives allow for several advantages: (1) a wider perspective on motivations for and meanings of mobile lives; (2) the inclusion of atypical work and 'non-work' into the discussion; and (3) the examination of other life-spheres within each of these constellations. So, just as the experiences of many of the people we study break through these definitional boundaries, so are scholars slowly doing the same in order to better conceptualise these increasingly mobile subjects whose movements (geographic or otherwise) are harder to pin down using traditional ways of researching and analysing social worlds. Such an outlook encourages us to consider mobilities beyond strictly defined categories to 'think relationally about the politics that hinder, encourage, regulate and inform' such mobilities (Chapter 1, this volume).

## Studying the contemporary expatriate

There has been a lacuna in social science research concerning groups of people typically considered elite, privileged, and mobile; many scholars were simply long unwilling to investigate the lives of those similar to them. Despite repeated calls from scholars such as Nader (1972) and Hannerz (1998; see also Boyer 2014) to study up, sideways, or any which way other than down, ethnographic research into expatriate communities has only come forth over the last several years or so (see Walsh 2006; Fechter 2007, 2010; Coles and Fechter 2008; Coles and Walsh 2010; Farrer 2010; Hindman 2002, 2008; Hindman and Fechter 2011).[3] The phenomenon of Westerners who migrate, relocate, or travel for professional, personal, or lifestyle reasons hardly fits neatly with what was long a disciplinary fetish among many social scientists for the geographically rooted 'underdog' and a commitment to 'history from below'. Peter Redfield (2012: 358) explains that the involvement of expatriates in international aid programmes and business schemes represents 'the antithesis of ethnographic authenticity' to many anthropologists. It is specifically the professionalism, expertise, and access to social capital of such groups that has deterred engaged anthropological research on them.

My understanding of expatriatism builds on Mary Louise Pratt's (1992: 7) concept of 'contact zones', which she explains as 'an attempt to invoke the spatial and temporal copresence of subjects previously separated by geographic and historical disjunctures, and whose trajectories now intersect'. The notion of 'contacts', Pratt argues, reassigns emphasis to the ways in which subjects (e.g. colonisers and colonised, or travellers and 'travellees') are constituted through their relations to one another and 'in terms of copresence, interaction, interlocking understandings and practices, often within radically asymmetrical relations of power' (1992: 7).

Historically speaking, expatriatism had a far more complex meaning than its constituent parts (ex + patria, or outside the homeland) could express. The verb 'to expatriate' long carried with it a sense of banishment, applied to someone who had either been exiled from or renounced allegiance to their home country (Cohen 1977: 9). While it is not the purpose of this chapter to detail the distinctions between historical colonial and contemporary postcolonial societies in which expatriatism is popular, it should be mentioned that it is due to its colonial associations that the term expatriate continues to be heavily marked. The term still carries with it associations of luxury, leisure, and decadence, which conjure up 'images of colonial outposts, gin and tonics at the club and lavish benefits for pioneering men bringing enlightenment to far-flung corners of empire' (Harris 1999), as well as bohemian links to the project of modernism, during which American cultural figures lived out decadent fantasies in globalising cities such as Paris and Prague in the early twentieth century (Katz 2007).

The admittedly fuzzy contemporary usage of the term expatriate refers, broadly speaking, to voluntary temporary migrants, primarily from affluent countries, who for purposes of employment or leisure 'have chosen to live abroad for some period, and who know when they are there that they can go home when it suits them' (Cohen 1977: 6). Some scholars have argued that the '"morally-tainted" term expatriate may be falling out of use in favour of more all-encompassing terms such as "cosmopolitan" or "transnational",' both of which are 'now standard items in a postcolonial-cum-globalist "travelling-culture" lexicon that posits displacement, deracination and uprooting as "the way of the [contemporary] world"' (Alomes 1999: 270, cited in Huggan 2009: 51). Neha Vora has noted that although, generally speaking, '"expat" implies the foreign population of a country, it carries classed and raced meanings that privilege Western-educated, middle-class, English-speaking people' (Vora 2013: 790). This is, of course, precisely the reason many expatriates choose this term to describe themselves, and the term is indeed still in wide use. Many of my informants explicitly referred to themselves as expatriates and/or members of an expatriate community. In the section that follows, I explore some of the experiences and imaginations of these contemporary expatriates living and working in Kathmandu.

## Tourism and expatriatism in Nepal

> Uh, no, dude, I am not a tourist. I live here.
>
> (Thomas, 32, American expatriate in Kathmandu)

Nestled between India and China on the Tibetan Plateau, the tiny Himalayan nation of Nepal swiftly made its way onto the map as the birthplace of contemporary adventure tourism soon after Sir Edmund Hillary and Tenzing Norgay made their landmark ascent of Mount Everest in 1953. Within a decade, the country had become known as a quintessential unspoiled country whose vast mountainscapes and poor (but proud) people were thought to offer an antidote to the spoils of the industrialised West (Ferguson 1990; Liechty 2005, 2010). Indeed, unlike other modernising parts of Asia, Nepal's selling point was its very backwardness. The country became a popular destination for middle-class Western youth on the search for a spiritual meaning to life through travel, music, and drugs, abandoning normative societal ideals of a life working in a stable, respectable, and well-paid job. During the 1960s and 1970s, Nepal became 'probably the single biggest magnet in the world for the countercultural lifestyle', a period during which hundreds of thousands of European and American young people traversed the globe on shoestring trips towards the East (Ortner 2000: 182, 186). Anthropologist James Fisher, who did a stint at the Peace Corps in Nepal in the early 1960s, recalls being lured to the country by his imagination:

> I suppose what I was really searching for in Nepal … was Shangri-La and its benignly perfect people or at least a more equitable, less frenetically driven and materialistic society than the one I had just come from. Like many anthropologists, I was drawn to other cultures because I couldn't stand my own.
>
> (Fisher 1986: 2)

Indeed, Fisher's candour reminds us that such fascinated, exoticising projection was nothing new for Westerners of his race, education, and background. Relationships forged between privileged Euro-American and imagined exotic Eastern landscapes were the kindling that kept the fires of colonialism burning strong. Young European males fled the threat of humdrum domestic existences to live and work as colonial officers in faraway places, and the legendary literary figures (e.g. Burton, Lawrence) of the era only contributed to strengthening and propagating such mythologies. Even after the high colonial and hippie eras became relics of the past, popular travel narratives about Nepal continued to further exoticise the country and further establish it as a space paradigmatic of a certain type of travel.

Just as this diminutive Himalayan kingdom was beginning to open itself up to outsiders, the global travel industry was itself on the verge of immense changes on account of the rise in industrial affluence, growth of the middle class, and burgeoning of commercial jet travel – a synchronicity that one could argue was less than coincidental. By 2011, international tourist arrivals to Nepal had surged to nearly 740,000 visitors annually.

Around the same time the hippies were filing into their VW camper vans to speed east across the continent, Nepal was also becoming the poster child *sine qua non* for the international aid industry. The fictitious topos of 'remote Nepal' and its links between backwardness and exoticism, which inspired so much travel, also helped justify foreign aid intervention based on post-war (imperialist) theories of economic modernisation. By 2013, the Nepali government estimated some 700 separate foreign aid projects were being carried out inside the country. These are financed by as many as 50 multilateral donors, and are operated by more than 150 international NGOs and literally thousands of national and local NGOs. Planning, managing, realising, and supporting all these aid projects are several thousand Western expatriates based in the capital of Kathmandu, who work at various organisations directly and indirectly linked to the development industry. Their roles encompass a range of offices, including NGO employees, diplomatic and military representatives, private entrepreneurs, employees of multinational firms, doctors, teachers, academics, journalists, artists, volunteer tourists, and other itinerant so-called 'lifestyle migrants'.

Today, the Oriental history of Nepal, the mythologies of exotic travel and the neocolonial nature of aid industry patronage are visible across the capital. They have become inscribed in the spaces of everyday life in the city, seen across hundreds of city signposts, banners, and posters that brandish alterity and the foreign (Hindman 2002). Numerous neighbourhoods in Kathmandu – in particular Thamel, the 'tourist ghetto' (Mayhew and Bindloss 2006) where backpackers and expats often socialise – maintain survivals of Orientalist references and imagery. Walking down the street in Thamel, one passes exotically evocative marquees such as Nirvana Garden Hotel, Monumental Paradise, Shangri-La, and the Summit hotels, bars, and restaurants such as Funky Buddha, and businesses trading under romantic names such as Yeti Airlines and Dharma Adventures. The very presence of these establishments means that both local Nepalis and foreign visitors are regularly confronted with a prototypical Western imaginary of Nepal as exotic, Other, and Orient. There are other examples; many roads, while constructed almost exclusively by Nepali labour, are still often known in terms of the major donors on the projects (e.g. 'the Japanese Road', 'the Chinese Road'). Thus, the structures and paraphernalia of the foreign – past and present – inform the lives of every individual living in or visiting the city, whether they be a New Zealand-born aid worker, a Norwegian trekker, or a Nepali brick layer. Moreover, the geography of travel and adventure is visible on nearly every corner in Thamel (Figure 8.1); one can walk along the neighbourhood's streets for an hour or more and be confronted every few metres with reminders of exotic travel.

Imaginations and practices of travel are part of expatriates' everyday lives in other ways, too. While employment is the primary reason many expatriate informants moved abroad in the first place, the opportunity for further travel once there is an important factor in their decision to pick a position in Nepal over another country. Expatriates living in Kathmandu would typically venture off on a trek of some sort within a month or two of arriving to Nepal. The verdant areas around the Kathmandu Valley were popular among expatriates as day hikes or cycling trips, while longer trips to the northern Himalayan region (for trekking) and the southern Tarai region (for wildlife safaris) are also common holidays. A trek in Nepal is also effectively the sole reason many tourists come to the country. 'Doing Nepal', which generally refers to a trek to Everest Base Camp or along the Annapurna Circuit, is virtually a rite of passage for any tourist with a fondness for the great outdoors and a sense of adventure. As such, imagery of trekking is used across marketing brochures and websites of tour operators and adventure outfitters who organise trips to Nepal. It was also common for expatriates to take weekend trips to nearby international destinations; despite often being described as 'remote', Nepal is situated roughly a four-hour flight from other tourist destinations such as Dubai, Bangkok, Hong Kong and Bombay. A surfeit of disposable income and flexible work schedules mean that regularly taking time off to enjoy being in a part of the world was commonplace.[4]

One evening, an hour or so after arriving at a large going-away party for an American working at a legal NGO, I was asked by three UN expatriates I had just met if I wanted to join them on a weekend trip to Istanbul. The discount airline

*Figure 8.1* Thamel streetscape.

FlyDubai was offering 20 per cent off all their flights from Kathmandu; we could get return tickets for around £150, and we would stay on the roof of a hostel for £10 a night. 'Why shouldn't we all go?' one of them asked. A few minutes later, they asked a fourth person, a French woman at the party, if she wanted to join. 'I've always wanted to go to Istanbul,' she answered.

Various types of travel within Nepal were also common among expatriates. In Nepal, holidays such as trekking adventures become experiences through which the imagined, romanticised imagery of a pristine, untouched Shangri-La is lived out on the ground. Tourist fantasies and 'imaginative geographies' (Chard 1999: 32–33; Skinner and Theodossopoulos 2011: 22; Adams 2004: 295; Salazar 2012: 864) not only *affected* people's impressions of the country while there; they *effected* the types of experiences they sought out, and *how* they experienced them. The tourist imagination, as Kahn (2003) reminds us, does not merely *represent* what tourists come in search of; it *produces* it.

While expatriates' identities themselves have also developed around a self-identification that is explicitly distinct from tourists, travel is embedded in both the work and non-work lives of expatriates. Travelling as a mode of experience is important among many Westerners (as it is among those from other parts of the world) for the accumulation of cultural capital and cosmopolitan street credentials it affords (see for example Nyiri 2010). This was evident in the Facebook pages and blogs of numerous expatriates; one of them, Dominique, posted a photo with the caption: 'Two helicopter trips over the Himalayas before noon. This is the stuff status update dreams are made of.' This trip would for many back home be considered a once-in-a-lifetime journey. But her ironic, self-conscious caption suggests that superlative experiences such as a helicopter trip around Everest are sought and consumed in order for individuals to have something to post about to their peers.

And yet, despite the prevalence and fundamental importance of mobility in sustaining expatriates' lifestyles, certain types of travel are also often framed as superficial and inauthentic, while 'living somewhere' presupposes knowledge of and intimacy with the Other, its culture and language. That is to say, living in a place is more real than travelling there. As Lizabeth, an Australian, put it to me, there was cultural capital to be gained from being more than just a tourist: 'It's way cooler to say "When I lived in XYZ" rather than "When I travelled to ...",' as she put it.

It is clear, then, that the trope of travel – an exotic, Orientalising travel – is very much present in the geography and topography of Kathmandu. But there is a confluence of other factors in Nepal's expatriate society that forces leisure life into the mix with work life. Heather Hindman (2013) has described how new forms of precarious labour are now filling the gaps that are left as large national, international, and multinational bureaucratic organisations do away with long-term employment regimes in favour of more precarious forms of labour. The new expatriate worker, Hindman argues, is 'changing the social life of Expatria and the kind of work it is possible to do in Nepal, given a new class of experts and amateurs who are replacing the professional expatriate' (Hindman 2013: 207).

Such 'amateurs' tend to be younger, have fewer responsibilities, less tied down, and more given to being adventurous. Thus, the make-up of expatriate society in specific spaces can change, and often rather quickly.

And yet, many expatriates were well aware of how much their lives seemed, to outsiders, to privilege leisure over work. As May, an American in her early thirties working for an US-based research firm, put it:

> if you ask my mother she will call this my period of unemployment. She'd say, 'you don't have a real job, every time I talk to you you're playing tennis'. In some ways, though, she was right: it's like it wasn't quite a real job.

Lizabeth also expressed what was often a negative reaction to the various expectations and judgements peers back home had regarding her expatriate life(style):

> I get a bit snippy when friends at home say, 'Oh, when are you going to get a real job and stop travelling?' and granted, I do take holidays a lot more than them, and life can be kind of like a holiday at times, but maybe it's a bit of a backlash at that.

Lizabeth's statement says as much about the difference between 'non-traditional' expatriate and 'traditional' (e.g. corporate, material) career trajectories as it does about the fact that the ideas people have about these different lifestyles do not always change as quickly as the lifestyles themselves. Despite the invective from 32-year-old Thomas that began this section, expatriates are indeed very often tourists. While there were distinctions (and often hard boundaries formed) between Westerners in Nepal for work and leisure, many expatriates and tourists did congregate in the same spaces as well as engage in similar practices – and perhaps even have similar reasons for having come to Nepal. Work and leisure in expatriate contexts are mutually constitutive, since expatriate subjectivities introduce 'space into the equation in a way that entangles work in private realms in an unusual way', such that a 'small town feeling' develops in expatriate contexts that presupposes a cohort sharing common experiences of employment and mobility (Hindman 2013: 11).

## Conclusion

As this chapter has shown, the Nepal of the expatriate aid worker and the Nepal of the adventure tourist are both products of (neo)colonial moments and imaginary geographies.[5] Nepal, as I have suggested above, is a heavily imagined and mythologised space of exploration/adventure, remoteness, and (neo)colonialism, and the country has these imaginaries deeply embedded into the ways in which it is sold and consumed – as a destination for both tourism and expatriate employment positions. In the everyday experience of expatriatism, leisure is embedded in different ways into labour, just one of which being the countercultural search for spiritual meaning which so defined the East during the 1960s and 1970s.

Nepal also has the paradox of mobility and transience built into its very infra-structure: it is geographically remote and liminal, and yet it is a destination for global tourism and expatriate experience *because* it is so remote.[6]

In comparison to colonial officials of the previous centuries, contemporary expatriates tend to be much more transient and rarely follow career trajectories that are bound to a single host country – or, for that matter, a single occupation. The expatriate lifestyle supports and encourages short-term, mobile flexible labourers seeking out not just 'the good life' (Benson 2011). Nepal – among other destinations with sizeable expatriate populations – also draws high-risk adventure tourists on the hunt for authentic experience. Furthermore, the embedded, intermeshed nature of expatriate labour and expatriate lifestyle complicates what might otherwise seem to be a simple binary of work versus life, as recent scholar-ship on expatriate mobilities and material culture has shown (see Butler and Hannam 2013; Smirl 2015). It is not just that in Nepal these various actors often circulate in the same social spaces, however; rather, these individuals often share traits, practices and imaginaries. Nepal is a space that is now well known for being both the birthplace of adventure tourism and a space emblematic of the international aid and development industries; it continues to thrive as a destina-tion for practitioners of all of these lifestyles. And, as this chapter's case has shown, continuing to make the hard and fast distinctions between 'tourism' and 'work' makes it easy to ignore the similarities between the two.

The geographical work of 'following the thing', as Appadurai (1996) has suggested we do in order to trace globalised flows, is difficult when these things – whether they are things, people, or ideas – blur categories that we have long held to be seen as fixed. While contemporary tourism and work may not quite be analogous to the torture of yesteryear's *trepalium*, the conceptual linkages between the two suggest rethinking the categorising, binary boundaries facilitated by neat and clean scholarship that divides spheres of work from those of non-work, and leisure from non-leisure.[7] We have been bequeathed a global economy whose new structures of employment and of leisure have left little certainty as to when, in quotidian experience, one sphere of life begins and when it ends. In an era in which work, travel, and other aspects of life are now very much inter-twined, and in which the Gap Year has become the new Grand Tour, these are issues that social scientists would do well to take seriously.

## Acknowledgements

The author wishes to thank Raluca Nagy for her insightful comments on a previ-ous draft of this chapter.

## Notes

1 It is important to note that while recent scholarship from the field of mobility studies has centred on professional groups and social milieux moving under privileged circumstances (e.g. members of the so-called 'creative class', high-profile executives,

tourists) or within regulated transnational labour markets (e.g. seasonal workers in agriculture, mobile construction workers, fly-in/fly-out workers in resource extraction), freedom of movement is not necessarily available to everyone. For more on risk and precariousness among so-called 'privileged' mobile labourers, see Nagy and Korpela (2013).

2 A sedentary bias (Malkki 1995; Bakewell 2008) was long co-opted by European state institutions to argue that movement among the poor and disadvantaged – people who should otherwise 'stay home' – threatened the dominant public order. Such binaries between the mobile and the immobile, and the artificiality of the borders often drawn between them, date back to (at least) pre-Renaissance Europe (Anderson 2013).

3 The terms used to describe the subjects of this research (e.g. 'expatriate', 'tourist', 'Westerner') are not intended to be seen as creating homogenous (or mutually exclusive) groups of people sharing the same traits. Use of such terms can facilitate discussing the shared, 'partial connections' (Strathern 2005) between people who may have their own varying idiosyncrasies, while also helping to 'provide coherence and stability to identities that are historically situated, contextual and far from monolithic' (Moran 2004).

4 Whiteness and foreignness was often privileged in local development politics, enabling expatriates a level of purchase in society that would not exist back home. Foreigners thus were frequently imbued with 'professional' attributes, abilities, and a range of unspoken privileges. 'Western', as many scholars have noted, is often a stand-in for white (Fechter and Walsh 2010; see also Bonnett 2004; Knowles 2005).

5 Although Nepal was made a de facto British protectorate under the auspices of the East India Company in 1816, the country never experienced any official period of colonial or imperial rule, despite its geographic and cultural proximity to India. This historical 'oddity' of non-coloniality 'has ironically been used to create a highly orientalized image of exotic and backward Nepal', which has conveniently served both foreign and Nepali actors (Elmer 2013).

6 Memorably, some of my informants in Kathmandu were surprised to learn upon their arrival to Nepal that the capital was not situated high up in the mountains or near the summit of Mount Everest. These were well-educated people, too, often with masters degrees and occasionally doctorates, though evidently not in geography.

7 The preoccupation we have for such neat and discrete classification and categorisation makes sense, of course. Reflecting social groupings and linking the cultural, psychological and perceptual discontinuities of the concrete world, the assigning of constituent parts to categories is fundamental to all human societies (Durkheim and Mauss 1963[1903]). Yet it is important to realise when misinterpretations occur as a result of a 'classificatory fallacy' with the categories that social scientists use to order their data (Ellen 1996). This may be evident whenever ethnographers try to make sense of their data, be these relationship terminologies, plant taxonomies, or forms of movement. As Heather Hindman (2002: 99) has suggested, our methods of looking at various spheres of life often 'occlude a vision of the messy processes that occur in between'. We should be focusing on the experiences of those people who must live, work and breathe in the 'mess'. Our world is not neat and clean. Our research need not try to make it so.

# References

Ackers, L., Balch, A., Currie, S., Millard, D. and Scott, S. (2009) *The geographic dimension of labour mobility in the European Union*. Liverpool: University of Liverpool.

Adams, J. (2004) 'The imagination and social life', *Qualitative Sociology*, 27(3): 277–97.

Anderson, B. (2013) *Us and them? The dangerous politics of immigration control*. Oxford: Oxford University Press.

Appadurai, A. (1996) *Modernity at large: Cultural dimensions of globalization.* Minneapolis and London: University of Minnesota Press.

Bakewell, O. (2008) '"Keeping them in their place": The ambivalent relationship between development and migration in Africa', *Third World Quarterly*, 29(7): 1341–58.

Bell, M. and Ward, G. (2000) 'Comparing temporary mobility with permanent migration', *Tourism Geographies*, 2(1): 87–107.

Benson, M. (2011) *The British in rural France: Lifestyle migration and the ongoing quest for a better way of life.* Manchester: Manchester University Press.

Bonnett, A. (2004) *The idea of the West: Culture, politics and history.* Basingstoke: Palgrave.

Boyer, D. (2014) 'Reflexivity reloaded: From anthropology of intellectuals to critique of method to studying sideways', in T. H. Eriksen, C. Garsten and S. Randeria (eds), *Anthropology now and next: Essays in honor of Ulf Hannerz.* Oxford: Berghahn, 91–110.

Butler, G. and Hannam, K. (2013) 'Performing expatriate mobilities in Kuala Lumpur', *Mobilities*, 9(1): 1–20.

Büscher, B. and Davidov, V. (eds) (2013) *The ecotourism-extraction nexus: Political economies and rural realities of (un)comfortable bedfellows.* London: Routledge.

Caggese, A. and Cunat, V. (2008) 'Financing constraints and fixed-term employment contracts', *The Economic Journal*, 118: 2013–46.

Chard, C. (1999) *Pleasure and guilt on the grand tour: Travel writing and imaginative geography, 1600–1830.* Manchester: Manchester University Press.

Cohen, E. (1977) 'Expatriate communities', *Current Sociology*, 24(3): 5–90.

Cohen, R. L. (2010) 'Rethinking "mobile work": Boundaries of space, time and social relation in the working lives of mobile hairstylists', *Work, Employment & Society*, 24(1): 65–84.

Cole, R. (2009) 'Origin of the word "travel" (This explains so much ...)', *Rock Cheetah*, 12 August. Online at: http://rockcheetah.com/blog/humor/origin-of-the-word-travel-this-explains-so-much/ (accessed 15 May 2015).

Coles, A. and Fechter, A.-M. (2008) *Gender and family among transnational professionals: International studies of women and place.* New York and London: Routledge.

Coles, A. and Walsh, K. (2010) 'From "Trucial State" to "Postcolonial City"? The imaginative geographies of British expatriates in Dubai', *Journal of Ethnic and Migration Studies*, 36(8): 1317–33.

Craciun, A. (2009) 'The scramble for the Arctic', *Interventions*, 11: 103–14.

Durkheim, E. and Mauss, M. (1963[1903]) *Primitive classification.* Chicago: University of Chicago Press.

Ellen, R. (1996) 'Classification', in A. Barnard and J. Spencer (eds), *The Routledge encyclopedia of social and cultural anthropology.* London: Routledge, 103–6.

Elmer, S. (2013) '"Deprived of the civilizing achievements of colonialism": Non-colonialism and Nepal's development discourse', paper presented at Colonialism without Colonies, ETH Zurich, 15 June.

Farrer, J. (2010) '"New Shanghailanders" or "New Shanghainese": Western expatriates' narratives of emplacement in Shanghai', *Journal of Ethnic and Migration Studies*, 36(8): 1211–28.

Fechter, A.-M. (2007) *Transnational lives: Expatriates in Indonesia.* Aldershot: Ashgate.

Fechter, A.-M. (2010) 'Gender, empire, global capitalism: Colonial and corporate expatriate wives', *Journal of Ethnic and Migration Studies*, 36(8): 1279–97.

Fechter, A.-M. and Walsh, K. (2010) 'Examining "expatriate" continuities: Postcolonial approaches to mobile professionals', *Journal of Ethnic and Migration Studies*, 36(8): 1197–210.

Ferguson, J. (1990) *The anti-politics machine: Depoliticization and bureaucratic power in Lesotho*. Cambridge: Cambridge University Press.

Fisher, J. (1986) *Sherpas: Reflections on change in Himalayan Nepal*. Berkeley: University of California Press.

Gehring, J. S. (2013) 'Free movement for some: The treatment of the Roma after the European Union's eastern expansion', *European Journal of Migration and Law*, 15(1): 7–28.

Hannam, K. (2009) 'The end of tourism: Nomadology and the mobilities paradigm', in J. Tribe (ed.), *Philosophical issues in tourism*. Bristol: Channel View.

Hannerz, U. (1998) 'Other transnationals: Perspectives gained from studying sideways', *Paideuma*, 44: 109–23.

Harris, H. (1999) 'The changing world of the expatriate manager', *Management Focus*, 13.

Hindman, H. (2002) 'Everyday life of American development in Nepal', *Studies in Nepali History and Society*, 7(1): 99–136.

Hindman, H. (2008) 'Shopping for a hypernational home: How expatriate women in Kathmandu labour to assuage fear', in A. Coles and A.-M. Fechter (eds), *Gender and family among transnational professionals*. New York: Routledge.

Hindman, H. and Fechter, A.-M. (2011) *Inside the everyday lives of development workers: The challenges and futures of Aidland*. Sterling, VA: Kumarian.

Hindman, H. (2013) *Mediating the global: Expatria's forms and consequences in Kathmandu*. Stanford, CA: Stanford University Press.

Hockey, J. and James, A. (2002) *Social identities across the life course*. Basingstoke: Palgrave Macmillan.

Huggan, G. (2009) 'Globaloney and the Australian Writer', *The Journal of the European Association of Studies on Australia*, 1: 45–63.

Huggan, G. and Norum, R. (2015) 'Introduction: The postcolonial Arctic', *Moving Worlds*, 15(2).

Kahn, M. (2003) 'Tahiti: The ripples of a myth on the shores of the imagination', *History and Anthropology*, 14 (4): 307–26.

Katz, D. (2007) *American modernism's expatriate scene: The labour of translation*. Edinburgh: Edinburgh University Press.

Knowles, C. (2005) 'Making whiteness: Lifestyle migrants in Hong Kong', in C. E. Alexander and C. Knowles (eds), *Making race matter: Bodies, space and identity*. Basingstoke: Palgrave Macmillan, 90–110.

Liberman, M. (2007) 'Annals of exoticism', *Language Log*, 10 July.

Liechty, M. (2005) 'Building the road to Kathmandu: Notes on the history of tourism in Nepal', *Himalaya*, 25(1): 19–28.

Liechty, M. (2010) 'The key to an Oriental world: Boris Lissanevitch, Kathmandu's Royal Hotel and the "Golden Age" of tourism in Nepal', *Studies in Nepali History and Society*, 15(2): 253–95.

Malkki, L. (1995) 'Refugees and exile: From "Refugee Studies" to the National Order of Things', *Annual Review of Anthropology*, 24: 495–523.

Marchand, M. and Ruyan, A. S. (eds) (2000) *Gender and global restructuring: Sightings, sites and resistances*. London: Routledge.

Mayhew, B. and Bindloss, J. (2006) *Nepal*, 8th edn. London: Lonely Planet.

Moran, P. (2004) *Buddhism observed: Travelers, exiles and Tibetan Dharma in Kathmandu*. London and New York: Routledge Curzon.

Nader, L. (1972) 'Up the anthropologist: Perspectives gained from studying up', in D. Hymes (ed.), *Reinventing anthropology*. New York: Random House.

Nagy, R. and Korpela, M. (2013) 'Introduction: Limitations to temporary mobility', *International Review of Social Research*, 3(1): 1–6.

Nemeth, D. (1986) 'Service nomads: Interim masters of imperfect markets', *Nomadic Peoples*, 21/22: 135–51.

Nyíri, P. (2010) *Mobility and cultural authority in contemporary China*. Seattle: University of Washington Press.

OED (2015) Oxford University Press. Online at: www.oed.com/viewdictionaryentry/ Entry/11125 (accessed 4 July 2015).

Ortner, S. B. (2000) *Life and death on Mt Everest: Sherpas and Himalayan mountaineering*. London: Oxford University Press.

Parkin, D. (2000) 'Templates, evocations and the long-term fieldworker', in P. Dresch, W. James and D. J. Parkin (eds), *Anthropologists in a wider world: Essays on field research*. Oxford: Berghahn.

Pratt, M. L. (1992) *Imperial eyes: Travel writing and transculturation*. London: Routledge.

Rao, A. (ed.) (1987) *The other nomads: Peripatetic minorities in cross-cultural perspective*. Köln: Böhlau.

Redfield, P. (2012) 'The unbearable lightness of ex-pats: Double binds of humanitarian mobility', *Cultural Anthropology*, 27(2): 358–82.

Robinson, O. F. (2007) *Penal practice and penal policy in Ancient Rome*. London: Routledge.

Ryan, L. and Webster, W. (2008) *Gendering migration: Masculinity, femininity and ethnicity in post-war Britain*. Aldershot: Ashgate.

Salazar, N. B. (2012) 'Tourism imaginaries: A conceptual approach', *Annals of Tourism Research*, 39(2): 863–82.

Sarró, R. (2009) 'La aventura como categoría cultural: Apuntes simmelianos sobre la emigración Subsahariana', *Revista de Ciências Humanas*, 43(2): 501–21.

Sennett, R. (1998) *The corrosion of character: The personal consequences of work in the new capitalism*. New York: Norton.

Skinner, J. and Theodossopoulos, D. (2011) *Great expectations: Imagination and anticipation in tourism*. Oxford: Berghahn.

Smirl, L. (2015) *Spaces of aid: How cars, compounds and hotels shape humanitarianism*. London: Zed Books.

Smith, E. E. and Medin, D. L. (1981) *Categories and concepts*. Cambridge, MA: Harvard University Press.

Standing, G. (2011) *The precariat: The new dangerous class*. London: Bloomsbury Academic.

Strathern, M. (2005) *Partial connections*. London: Altamira Press.

UNDESA (2013) *Population facts*. United Nations Department of Economic and Social Affairs.

UNPD (2002) International migration report 2002at/Esa/Ser.A/220. New York: United Nations Population Division.

Urry, J. (2007) *Mobilities*. Cambridge: Polity Press.

van Baar, H. (2015) 'The perpetual mobile machine of forced mobility: Europe's Roma and the institutionalization of rootlessness', in Y. Jansen, R. Celikates and J. de Bloois (eds), *The irregularization of migration in contemporary Europe: Deportation, detention, drowning*. London: Rowman & Littlefield, 71–86.

Vora, N. (2013) *Impossible citizens: Dubai's Indian diaspora*. London: Duke University Press.

Walby, S. (2009) *Globalization and inequalities: Complexities and contested modernities*. London: Sage.

Walsh, K. (2006) 'British expatriate belongings: Mobile homes and transnational homing', *Home Cultures*, 3(2):123–44.

# 9 Should I stay or should I go?

## Labour and lifestyle mobilities of Bulgarian migrants to the UK

*Gergina Pavlova-Hannam*

## Introduction

> Frankly this is a topic on which I do not know if I ever will be able to decide
> what is right and what is not. Some time passes and we began to comment
> with my husband. England. Bulgaria. Bulgaria. England. Pros. Cons. Here
> and there.
>
> (Interview with M, Sunderland, 2014)

The above quotation sums up many of my respondents' feelings about being in
the north-east of England, to stay or to go back to Bulgaria; the many ambivalences of trying to make a new home in England and the ties with the old home
in Bulgaria. In terms of my research I have sought to analyse the difficulties of
gaining employment in the north-east of England, particularly due to media and
policy legislation. The UK media, particularly the tabloid newspapers, have
frequently portrayed migration from Bulgaria and Romania in negative terms
(Vicol and Allen 2014), while successive UK governments attempted to limit the
employment of Bulgarian and Romanian nationals through specific legislation
between 2007 and 2013.[1]

This chapter begins with a review of the existing literature pertaining to labour
migration and mobilities to argue that the mobilities paradigm offers more than a
nuanced understanding of migration, as it develops a critical perspective on
contemporary movement and lifestyle practices. Based upon empirical evidence
from interviews with Bulgarian students and migrants to the north-east of
England, the chapter focuses on the ambivalent mobilities of Bulgarians in terms
of their work experiences in the tourism and hospitality industries and how these
experiences have inspired further mobilities.

## Labour and lifestyle mobilities

In their report *A New European Agenda for Labour Mobility*, Larsson, Sforza,
and Turmann (2004) discuss the demographic changes due to labour mobility
within the European Union. They argue that labour mobility can be recognised as
a fundamental element of a competitive economy and that mobile employees

encourage the dissemination of knowledge and equilibrate for the shortage of skilled labour within member states. Furthermore Larsson *et al.* (2004) point out that the high mobility of workers between jobs and industries is an indicator of an efficient labour market, where labour proves to be adaptable to changes in the demand for skilled workers. Subsequently they suggest, 'the capacity problems of industrial production can be reduced by high mobility between jobs' (Larsson *et al.* 2004: 4) and that mobility reduces long-term unemployment as many job openings allow the unemployed to find new jobs. While this positive outlook is all very well, not all labour mobilities within the expanded Europe have been so smooth.

Focusing on the interrelationships between work and migration in the United Kingdom (UK), Jordan and Brown (2007) demonstrate how intertwined the migration and settlement experiences of new migrants are, and how this relates to mobility in the UK. By exploring the role of migrants in the UK division of labour, and how economic mobility is described, experienced, and managed by the migrants themselves, they are able to investigate how the formal framework for regulating labour migration reflects and refracts in the accounts given by a number of immigrants in the UK, including foreign workers, irregular workers, and jobseekers and permit holders. They argue that 'the rebuild of responsible citizenship to "independent", autonomous, self-realising, possessive individuals rely on mobility as an essential feature' (Jordan and Brown 2007: 256).

The mobilities of skilled workers have also been seen as a 'brain drain' which implies permanent loss of skilled labour. Increased mobility and connectivity have allowed more complex flows between more and less advanced areas within the European Union. Kale and Little (2007: 102) emphasise that the mobility of skilled workers is 'key to the improvement of capacity and capability of both recipient and donor countries, and constitutes a crucial dimension of cohesion within the European Union and beyond'. They point out as an example the migrants who return to their home and bring with them the new skills and ideas acquired abroad. According to them, that process has a positive impact on the development of these countries. They also underline the significance of labour dynamics and human mobility for industrial knowledge-building processes. They also note that processes of labour mobility within the European Union are subject to tensions both in areas receiving migration and in areas losing skilled workers.

Labour mobilities can also be analysed as 'a route to a better and more fulfilling way of life, especially in contrast to the one left behind' (O'Reilly and Benson 2009: 1). A new way of life for labour migrants could be different from the one searched for by other migrants, such as refugees or asylum-seekers. These particular lifestyle choices mostly refer to people from more developed countries. These individuals' labour mobilities are often an escapist intangible project, searching for a 'good life' (O'Reilly and Benson 2009). Such lifestyle mobility is the spatial mobility of relatively affluent individuals of all ages, moving either part time or full time to places that are meaningful because they offer the potential of a better quality of life.

Exploring lifestyle choices further, Cohen, Duncan, and Thulemark (2015: 156) demonstrate that 'voluntary on-going mobile lifestyles: (1) blur the boundaries between travel, leisure, and migration; (2) are exemplary of how a binary divide between work and leisure may be collapsed; (3) destabilise dichotomies of "home" and "away"; and (4) illustrate complexities of belonging and identity associated with sustained mobility'. More privileged citizens often see mobility as part of their everyday life, as familiar and taken for granted, rather than as a form of labour mobility that less privileged movers might. Former 'travellers' thus have the ability to be 'at home' in mobility, in the sense of being comfortable with their ability to relocate (Germann Molz 2008). Such mobility, however, still depends on access to economic conditions, power, technology, and networks that facilitate frequent movements across borders and cultures (Cresswell 2011). Recent research on highly skilled migrants addresses issues of transnationalism, global-local networks, citizenship, and belonging, from both economic and socio-cultural angles (Beaverstock 2005). The possession of Western country citizenship opens a range of opportunities including transnational mobility (Szewczyk 2014). McIntyre, Williams and McHugh (2006) claim that such mobilities raise the place-consciousness of migrants as it enables people to compare the qualities of different places.

For the rich, lifestyle mobilities may involve multiple 'homes', 'belongings', and sustained mobility throughout the life course. Indeed, such lifestyle mobilities differ from temporary mobilities in that 'it is sustained as an on-going fluid process, carrying on as everyday practice over time' (Cohen *et al.* 2015: 158). Moreover, unlike permanent migration, lifestyle mobilities do not presuppose that there is any intention to return, as the movement is on-going, 'a return to any identified "origin" cannot be presumed … Through lifestyle mobility, there is no "one" place to which to return, and through time, there may be multiple "homes" that one can return to and/or revisit' (Cohen *et al.* 2015: 159).

Migrants thus travel from and to many different places with a variety of motivations. They show various temporal and spatial modes of mobility; some of them go back every year whereas others migrate constantly (Cohen *et al.* 2015). They migrate to different places in their lifetimes and in various family situations; however, the personal stories of individual migrants in the pursuit of the 'good life' need to be contextualised within wider sociological structures (such as the governmental regulations restricting the employment of Bulgarians and Romanians noted above). O'Reilly and Benson (2009) also argue that the social construction of places and the way they are perceived often explains the desired destinations, but not always – as the case of the north-east of England will demonstrate. What is important is the role of the imagination in the decision to migrate. Lifestyle mobilities are about escape, escape from somewhere and something, while simultaneously an escape for a new life – a re-creation, restoration, or rediscovery of oneself, of personal potential, or of one's 'true' desires. Significantly, O'Reilly and Benson (2009: 5) argue that 'migration is thus aspirational, not only in the sense of what it holds in store for you, but also in terms of what you can become'. Furthermore they pay attention to the personal reasons for migration, the decision-making processes, and the consequences on migrant's lives and identities. According to them, all these matters reveal a broader rhetoric of self-realisation. Some migrants see themselves 'as pioneers, breaking new ground' (O'Reilly and Benson 2009: 5). This means that migrants perceive themselves as being somewhat different by engaging with their new lives and they possess this spirit of a pioneer, as they believe they are more courageous and adventurous than those who do not take these risks. Some migrants, however, also describe their migration as an unmediated individual choice 'through which they gain personal agency that was otherwise out of their reach' (O'Reilly and Benson 2009: 5). Such mobilities can also occur as an answer to a personal crisis, a turning point life event, or what O'Reilly and Benson (2009: 7) describe as 'a massive upheaval, bringing about many transformations in the migrants' lives'.

Another significant moment in migrants' lives is the feeling of ambivalence or liminality. This 'is not only the result of being caught between two cultures, but reflects the tension between reality and imagination' (O'Reilly and Benson 2009: 9). They suggest that after migration, everyday life eventuates into a permanent negotiation where migrants are looking to harmonise 'their experiences with their hopes and dreams' (O'Reilly and Benson 2009: 9). Some do not manage, despite protestations to the contrary, to release themselves from the perceived shackles of life before migration; structural difference and inequalities are reproduced rather than undermined. Indeed, as we shall see in my analysis, my respondents continually engaged in class-based processes of distinction when comparing their lives in the North East with the lives of their friends and families back in Bulgaria, lifestyle migrants in other destinations, and even their compatriots living locally.

The tension between reality and imagination has been termed by Eimermann (2014) as 'post-migration ambivalence', which he suggests is 'an everyday mismatch of post-migration experiences with pre-migration hopes and dreams' (Eimermann 2014: 2). Ambivalence is a significant issue for seemingly voluntary migration (Bærenholdt and Granås 2008). The role of pre-migration tourism imaginings as well as a 'wider sense of achievement through migration' is significant here in terms of motivations (Eimermann 2014: 3). This is also highlighted in Manolova's (2014) work on Bulgarian's imaginings of the UK. Migrants may benefit by gaining more subtle, complex, and dynamic understandings of their destination. Yet, on the other hand, the migrants who wish to return are often not able to find employment or affordable housing.

## Contemporary Eastern European mobilities

Recently there has been significant research interest in the mobilities of Eastern Europeans due to the accession of new member states to the EU. Burrell (2010) focuses mainly on Polish and Lithuanian migrants and explores their migration motivations and strategies, work, social networks, and local settlement. According to her, unemployment in the sending countries is one of the main reasons for migration. Migrants from Eastern Europe would like 'not necessarily to find a better life, but rather to live a "normal" life' (Burrell 2010: 298). This has led to a new cohort of younger migrants who want to engage with a new way of life, meet new people, and improve their English language skills. They would like to expose themselves 'to exciting new adventures' and to be able 'to live in a more "normal" environment and furnishing them with skills they will be able to use later in life in the UK or back home' (Burrell 2010: 299). Guereño-Omil, Brown and Hannam (2014) have also examined Polish networks and social ties in the north-east of England and have analysed the experiences, perception and mobilities of Polish migrants to better understand how they interact among each other, and whether their networks and ties with both their host and home regions and their mobility patterns are affecting their expectations for future mobility. They note that Polish migrants have been able to develop their own community support structures, which has enabled them to maintain a sense of Polishness.

The overall labour mobility process for Eastern Europeans has been dynamic, suggests Ciobanu (2014). She argues that the various mobility regimes in Europe have shaped the patterns of movement of Romanian citizens and recently allowed for their multiple migrations. She notes: 'While Romanians as EU citizens are entitled to travel within the EU, their access to labour markets is still limited, putting them in relative "slow lanes"' (Ciobanu 2014: 2). In the case of multiple mobilities, significantly, migrants may maintain ties to people from their former countries of destination – especially if they still have family there – but this is not always the rule.

> Migrants move from country A to country B, and later might decide to move on to country C. They might be in touch with friends and relatives from countries A and B, but might just as well have a reduced level of interaction which cannot develop into transnationalism or might even leave those ties beyond.
>
> (Ciobanu 2014: 3)

However, frequently they choose a destination where they can integrate into the labour market or in the educational system or if they have social connections in one country that can help them integrate. For example, another migrant can help someone to get an initial foot on the ladder or provide information about ways to access social benefits and the medical system. An extended family and weaker friendship ties settled in another country can also provide information on living costs and jobs' availability. However, she argues that in the Romanian case, 'highly skilled migrants searching for jobs at their level of education, they rarely follow family, but rather explore the best professional option. In the case of migrants who occupy lower skilled jobs, they mobilise all the addresses they can' (Ciobanu 2010: 10). Highly skilled Romanian women who work at their own skill level have migrated on their own, whereas Romanian women working in lower skills jobs or at a lower level than their studies migrated mostly with the family or based on social networks and their community of origin or religion are most relevant in getting a job. Other Romanian women, meanwhile, most often followed their husbands in the contexts of both the first and second migration experience. Social networks thus constitute one of the key variables in mitigating the propensity to migrate in general as well as the possibility to engage in multiple labour mobilities. Migration networks are important variables influencing the propensity to migrate and are associated with the reduction of migration costs and thus tend to contribute to increased levels of mobilities.

Recent research into EU mobilities has also focused on the new geographies of the EU border (Marcu 2014). On the one hand, EU borders can make human mobility difficult for some, as restrictions are placed on the movement of certain nationalities such as Bulgarians and Romanians, while on the other hand those from Eastern Europe also simultaneously learn about mobility and practise it as citizens of Europe. Marcu (2014) analyses the experiences of Eastern Europeans engaged in labour mobility in Spain, in order to understand how EU enlargement has influenced the mobilities of these citizens and the ways in which they interpret cross border practices. Importantly, she analyses whether borders can be seen as an 'instrument for learning mobility or as an obstacle to current human mobility' (Marcu 2014: 10). She further notes that for Romanians and Bulgarians circumstances have changed:

> migrants were gradually transformed into citizens who circulate. Upon arrival in Spain, they tended to settle themselves more easily into the receiving culture. Because of the ties that they maintain with their home countries and the ease of travel, they were able to create a kind of fluidity of movement.
>
> (Marcu 2014: 11)

This has allowed the creation of a transnational social space which, she argues, allows citizens to move and learn to live within and with borders. Romanians and Bulgarians have thus developed a culture of mobilities, facilitated by the use of the internet and mobile phone.

## Methodology

This research utilised a number of methods, including auto-ethnography, focus groups, and in-depth interviews. Auto-ethnography is an approach to research that seeks to systematically analyse the personal experiences of the researcher in order to understand wider cultural experiences. It is an approach that links auto-biographical writing with ethnographic observations (Ellis *et al.* 2011). An important issue to consider for any ethnographic approach is the positionality of the researcher, which allows the researcher to be aware of their own potential to influence the end results of the research (Rose 1997). As a migrant and member of the Bulgarian community in the North East, I recorded my experiences and encounters, because as Sanchez-Ayala (2012: 117) points out, 'it is very important to fully engage' in migrants' 'everyday life, and to capture the complexity of social relations embedded in their daily experiences'. Information was therefore collected with the use of a detailed research diary, which allowed me to reflect on my own experiences as a Bulgarian student and migrant as well as helping me to log the information from internet posts and media stories about Bulgarian migrants from social media sites. Since the data collection commenced, reflections have been logged in my diary on an almost daily basis from October 2012 to the present, with more details entered from January 2013 as data collection developed.

I initially organised one focus group, which included six participants – two males and four females. All of them were students and were identified through the snowballing sampling method of chain referral, whereby each student recruited others to participate in the study (Atkinson and Flint 2004). The focus group interview took place in April 2013 on a university campus. The first activity included watching a short movie called *Bulgaria – one of the poorest countries in Europe*. After that a discussion followed and the participants were asked what life was like in Bulgaria; what were the reasons for them to come to the north-east of England; whether they would like to work while they are here; whether they came to stay. The second activity included a discussion about tourist attractions in the area. The participants were asked to analyse and discuss visual materials. These consisted of brochures with tourist attractions in the north-east of England. The students were asked to take a look at the brochures and to speak about the places in area they had visited and about the ones they wanted to visit.

The first sets of interviews took place in April 2013 and involved nine Bulgarian student interviewees, of whom two were male and seven were female. Five of these initial interviews were taken with students, two of them with recent graduates, and two with Bulgarian migrants. All of these interviews took place on university premises, coffee shops, restaurants, and pubs or in the interviewees' homes, according to the preference of the interviewee, with each lasting 30–40 minutes. The second set of interviews took place in the period between September and November 2013. In that time 12 participants were interviewed, of whom ten were female and two were male; two of these were students from the University of Sunderland, seven were students from the University of Newcastle, one was a student from University of Durham, one was a now working graduate from University of Sunderland, and one was a lecturer in the University of Durham. Each lasted 30–40 minutes. All interviews again took place in university premises, coffee shops, restaurants, and pubs or in the interviewees' homes according to the preference of the interviewee. The third round of interviews took place from January 2014 to March 2015. The interviews in this period were only with migrants who live and work in the City of Sunderland.

## Discussion: should I stay or should I go?

The discussion below is organised into three themes: the ambivalences of staying or going, the impact of media representations, and the problems of working in the UK for Bulgarians in the tourism and hospitality industries and the ensuing further mobilities that this engenders.

### *The ambivalences of staying or going*

As discussed above, other studies of migration have highlighted the complex ambivalences of many migrants in different parts of the world in terms of their decision-making and reasoning for both migrating in the first place and for their returning home (Eimermann 2014). A key aspect of migrants' ambivalence is related to the strength of their pre-migration kinship, friendship and community ties (Ní Laoire 2007). Post-migration ambivalence implies a dissonance between post-migration experiences with pre-migration hopes and dreams (O'Reilly and Benson 2009). Some migrants reproduce rather than solve pre-migration concerns, which then become important for their post-migration identities (Benson 2010). In terms of pre-migration, many of my respondents had a touristic imaginary at work that pictured the UK as a place that they should visit rather than as one they would necessarily reside. For example:

> The UK is a destination that you must visit, but I would not recommend it for living. They care about their traditions, their pubs. Europe is modernising, but here they still keep the two separate taps.

Here the respondent reflects also on the differences in traditions and technologies found in the UK and how these simple things make it difficult to adapt and adjust. Conversely, other respondents reflected on how they needed to stay in order to confirm that they had made the right decision in the eyes of their peers back home:

> My family always thought that I would be here like a temporary military service and then come back, but I always thought that I will stay. Otherwise, how to tell if it is meaningless. In Bulgaria anyway you can get a higher education, but it seems here gives you a better start. Not necessarily to [stay for ever] in England. For example, it could be somewhere else in the world after.

Here the respondent makes a number of interesting points. First, there is the confirmation of staying, otherwise the attempt at migration is 'meaningless'. Second, higher education in the UK is seen as a particular attraction, giving you a 'better start' in life. Third, the respondent demonstrates that this migration may be a stepping stone to further migration elsewhere in the world, as other researchers have found such as in the case of Polish migrants to the UK (see Szewczyk 2014).

However, a minority of interviewees were content to stay in the UK and noted how their pre-migration ideas about staying for a year had changed into a commitment to settle in the UK because of the lifestyle they had developed:

> We came in [2006] and we were supposed to come only for one year but from then on it became one year, one year and a half, two years and so on. Initially our idea was to come here, to save money and buy an apartment in Bulgaria, and to go back and live there but we saw that life here is much easier, more settled, more relaxed and after three years we decided to stay. After three years we bought the house we live in now. The money we saved for the apartment in Bulgaria we used for the deposit for the house here [in Newcastle].

This links to broader work on lifestyle mobilities discussed above where the motivation for staying can be attributed to more intangible lifestyle characteristics rather than simple economic benefits.

### Reflections on media representations of Bulgarian migrants to the UK

Post-migration representations of Bulgaria and Bulgarian migrants in the UK media have played a key role in the development of the ambivalences noted above. Many of these representations in the leading UK newspapers portrayed Bulgarian migrants negatively.

Moreover, politically the issue of European migration, and particularly migration from Bulgaria and Romania, has raised significant concerns for all mainstream UK political parties with the rise of the UK Independence Party (UKIP). These concerns were parodied in the BBC TV series *The Thick of It*, which alluded that the issue of migration had become racist and xenophobic.

In turn, such concerns and parodies were also responded to on various social media platforms by Bulgarian migrants living in the UK who had found themselves the subject of such representations. For example, one respondent submitted a photo illustrating the hybridity of Bulgarian 'mackems' – a term used to describe people from Sunderland (see Figure 9.1).

*Figure 9.1* Bulgarian 'Mackems'.

Many of my interview respondents also reflected critically on the way the UK media portrayed them and how they themselves had to respond to the media representations in their place of work:

> I think it was a very far-fetched [the media]. It is always so in order for the government to cover up mistakes. Trying to refocus in another direction. It was bad because the more in the news they were talking about it, you see that even people who know you they become critical and it was bad. Even my colleagues who respect me very much and previously nothing had been said, but now they joked and said: 'Oh, now come your whole family is going to come like a flood, everyone will pour here. Are you waiting for them on the first of January?' And they continued. Dirty foreigners, filling our island which will overflow and will sink because it [migration] has become too much.

Another respondent reflected on the homogenising of Bulgarians in the UK media as if all Bulgarians were the same – a common trope in racist media:

> To some extent [the media] affect me because they put all the Bulgarians together, and not all of us are the same. We, as we came to England we haven't claimed even one pound in benefits. From the beginning we have worked. We arrived on the 6th and on the 8th we began work. And I know how much we have worked and we have always paid all our taxes. And I've always been annoyed when some people say: 'Where are you from? And why did you come here?'

The respondent above was clearly defensive about his status in the UK and how he was proud that he wasn't on social benefits like the Bulgarians described in the UK press. These issues then impacted on the problems of working legally in the UK, as noted below.

### Problems of working in the UK

Many respondents reflected on the problems they had in terms of obtaining the correct paperwork in order to be able to work as students in the UK. Many were angry at the way the process stigmatised them and deemed them to be 'second-class citizens of Europe'. The respondent below reacted by symbolically burning his 'yellow work permit card'. When asked why he burnt his yellow work permit, Ivan responded:

> Because I do not like such things. Yellow cards in Bulgaria are given to people with mental health problems. One night I was drunk and I thought, oh come on, fuck this yellow card ... It annoys me somehow – their funny cards and restrictions on students. I do not care about the stupid immigrants, but for the students it is really dumb. For some Asian ... they are getting off the

plane and they can do whatever they want. And it is not just a job, you go to the bank as a student to take a bankcard, and they give you a card that does not even have internet banking and which cannot even buy a ticket to go back to Bulgaria. For fuck's sake!

He also noted that he felt that Bulgarians were not given the same rights as non-European migrants and that the restrictions on employment made it difficult to live in the UK as everyday things such as making a bank account became problematic. Again, such difficulties post-migration engender ambivalences about staying in the UK as the respondent below noted:

Well, if it was not for all this discrimination against the Bulgarians about work, etc. I could and would have liked it a lot, but this changed my mind a lot and filled me with a lot of negative emotions towards England and made me see everything as negative, even if it is nice, simply because I am angry at England and see it as something that annoys me.

In terms of working in the tourism and hospitality industries themselves, many Bulgarian migrants wanted to obtain jobs in these industries but became frustrated at the lack of opportunities in the north-east of England compared to London. Gergana argued:

I came to study in the north-east of England with the idea that when I finish studying I will move south. Regarding that London is a great city and I thought there would be more job opportunities. And in general I was not especially fascinated by the northern part regarding the architecture of a place to stay to live in. I was suffocating, it was grim. I did not like the people, because there were still a lot of locals living there and I wasn't particularly fascinated by them. And just this greyness there [in the north] did not work well on my psyche, so I decided to move to London, as a larger, multicultural cosmopolitan city, etc. London is a big city that collected people from all over the world. For me, London is not England. There I barely meet any English people.

It is widely recognised that London is a global cosmopolitan magnet for migrants from around the world. However, some respondents returned to Bulgaria to gain more work experience before returning to the UK, as Polly notes:

In the beginning the first thing I started to do was working at the Lumiere festival in Durham as a volunteer. It was very interesting. The festival itself was amazing and it was very beautiful. I love Durham. My job was to hand out flyers and to provide help and information to the visitors. Then the summer after my first year in the university I went back in Bulgaria, because I could not get a job here in the North East due to lack of experience.

She further noted that she would not now remain in the UK even if she could find a job fitting her qualifications and experience:

> If I am not selected I will seek for a paid internship elsewhere. I do not intend to stay in England. I can remain only if I find an internship that I know will help me in the future, but otherwise I cannot stay here: I'll end up here all my life – I cannot. For me, three years are ample. I do not think to get back to Bulgaria either, I think of going anywhere else in Europe.

She used her experience in the UK as a stepping stone to elsewhere, amplifying her mobility patterns (Szewczyk 2014).

Other respondents also found temporary work in bars, which enabled them to travel further within Europe while resident in the UK due to the economic benefits this gave them. Silvia argued:

> I spent two years in this bar (a bar near Sunderland Marina), and I was able to afford a lot of things. For example, last year I visited five different countries. I was a full-time student with a part-time job. I visited Macedonia, Bulgaria, Hungary, Scotland, Morocco, and Germany. For example, if I was in Bulgaria and I was in the same position I will not be able to afford anything. It was hard here to combine studying and working, but even though I managed to afford some things.

Thus while some stay due to the economic benefits that arise, they use this to finance further travel mobilities within Europe. Other migrants, as we have seen, use their opportunities in the UK to plan their next stepped migration, while others attempt to stay because of the lifestyle they have developed in the UK. Working in the tourism and hospitality industries in the UK allows a great deal of flexibility in this regard, which was highly valued by the Bulgarian migrants interviewed in this study. Such industries, despite their long hours, were seen as attractive, as many respondents had previous work experiences in hotels in Bulgaria. The ambivalences of staying or going then are fractured by these different mobility factors, lifestyle, finance, travel, and work.

### Conclusion

The points raised above in the discussion highlight the fact that there is no perfect happiness for Bulgarian migrants – for most only continued mobilities. As Marcu (2014) has highlighted, mobilities have to be learned and the Bulgarian migrants in my study are still in the process of learning about both motility and mobilities. The existing literature on lifestyle mobilities has tended to overlook how lifestyles are still predicated upon a degree of work. As such this study has highlighted that education, work, leisure, and lifestyle are fundamentally entwined through the practices of mobility rather than being separate. Many respondents came to the UK as students, looked for work, gained work, and developed a lifestyle they could not have back in Bulgaria.

Other respondents, however, failed to realise the economic work opportunities in the UK and missed their more casual lifestyles back in Bulgaria. This, combined with negative media stereotypes, has led many to reconsider their migration and develop the 'post-migration ambivalence' that Eimermann (2014) has noted in his study. Consequently, most Bulgarian migrants, as my study shows, are highly ambivalent about staying, as the negative media representations, restrictions on work post-migration and strong pre-migration social ties all work against any settlement, to the extent that they feel 'out of place': 'Some time passes and we began to comment with my husband. England. Bulgaria. Bulgaria. England. Pros. Cons. Here and there' (interview with M, 2014).

## Note

1 Paragraph 2 of the 'Guidance for Nationals of Bulgaria and Romania on Obtaining Permission to Work in the United Kingdom' stated: 'As a Romanian or Bulgarian national you are able to move and live freely in any Member State of the European Union (EU). You do not need permission under our immigration rules to reside legally in the United Kingdom. You will have a right of residence in any EU Member State for the first 3 months of residence on an unrestricted basis and you can remain legally resident in that state as long as you wish, providing you are exercising a Treaty right as a student, a self-employed person, or if you are self-sufficient (and not economically active). You will not have an automatic right to reside as a worker in the United Kingdom (unless you are exempt from work authorisation requirements …)'. Those Bulgarians and Romanians who came to the UK to study could work provided they obtained a yellow coloured registration certificate commonly known as 'Yellow Card' from the government office based in Croyden, Surrey. After 12 months of continuous legal work they could then apply for residence under a so-called 'Blue Card' registration.

## References

Atkinson, R. and Flint, J. (2004) 'Snowball sampling', in T. Lewis-Beck, A. Bryman and T. Futing Liao (eds), *The Sage encyclopedia of social science research methods*. Online at: http://srmo.sagepub.com/view/the-sage-encyclopedia-of-social-science-research-methods/n931.xml (accessed 22 August 2015).
Bærenholdt, J. and Granås, B. (2008) *Mobility and place: Enacting Northern European peripheries*. London: Ashgate.
Beaverstock, J. (2005) 'Transnational elites in the city: British highly-skilled inter-company transferees in New York city's financial district', *Journal of Ethnic and Migration Studies*, 31(2): 245–68.
Benson, M. (2010) 'The context and trajectory of lifestyle migration', *European Societies*, 12: 45–64.
Burrell, K. (2010) 'Staying, returning, working and living: Key themes in current academic research undertaken in the UK on migration movements from Eastern Europe', *Social Identities*, 16(3): 297–308.
Canzler, W., Kaufmann, V. and Kesselring, S. (eds) (2008) *Tracing mobilities: Towards a cosmopolitan perspective*. London: Ashgate.

Chongarova, I. (2010) 'Bulgarian students in London: Migration patterns and educational strategies', National Science Fund: Ministry of education and science. Online at: http://files.slovo.uni-plovdiv.bg/clic/bulgarian-students-english-PRINT.pdf (accessed 16 November 2012).

Ciobanu, O. (2014) 'Multiple migration flows of Romanians', *Mobilities*, ahead of print, 1–20. DOI:10.1080/17450101.2013.863498.

Cohen, S., Duncan, T. and Thulemark, M. (2015) 'Lifestyle mobilities: The crossroads of travel, leisure and migration', *Mobilities*, 10(1): 155–72.

Cresswell, T. (2011) 'Mobilities I: Catching up', *Progress in Human Geography*, 35(4): 550–58.

Eimermann, M. (2014) 'Flying Dutchmen? Return reasoning among Dutch lifestyle migrants in Rural Sweden', *Mobilities*, ahead of print. DOI:10.1080/17450101.2014.980128.

Ellis, C., Adams, T. and Bochner, A. (2011) 'Autoethnography: An overview', *Forum: Qualitative Social Research*, 12(1): 10.

Germann Molz, J. (2008) 'Global abode: Home and mobility in narratives of round-the-world travel', *Space and Culture*, 11(4): 325–42.

Guereño Omil, B., Brown, R. and Hannam, K. (2014) 'Migrant geographies and social ties: Polish networks and mobilities in the North East of England', *Journal of Tourism and Human Mobility*, 2.

Hannam, K., Sheller, M. and Urry, J. (2006) 'Editorial: Mobilities, immobilities and moorings', *Mobilities*, 1(1): 1–32.

Jordan, B. and Brown, P. (2007) 'Migration and work in the United Kingdom: Mobility and the social order', *Mobilities*, 2(2): 255–76.

Kale, D. and Little, S. E. (2007) 'Flows and cohesion: Balancing capabilities across an expanded Union', *Mobilities*, 2(1): 99–108.

Larsson, A., Sforza, L. and Turmann, A. (2004) *A new European agenda for Labour mobility: Report of a CEPS-ECHR task force*. Brussels: Centre for European Policy Studies.

Manolova, P. (2014) 'Realities and imaginaries of Bulgarian migration to the UK and the Fatal Attraction of "the West"', paper presented at the International Conference on Migration, Sofia, Bulgaria.

Marcu, S. (2014) 'Learning mobility challenging borders: Cross-border experiences of eastern European Immigrants in Spain', *Mobilities*, ahead of print. DOI:10.1080/17450101.2014.934055.

McIntyre, N., Williams, D. and McHugh, K. (eds) (2006) *Multiple dwelling and tourism: Negotiating place, home and identity*. Wallingford: CABI.

Ní Laoire, C. (2007) 'The "green green grass of home"? Return migration to rural Ireland', *Journal of Rural Studies*, 23: 332–44.

O'Reilly, K. and Benson, M. (2009) 'Lifestyle migration: Escaping to the good life?', in M. Benson and K. O'Reilly (eds), *Lifestyle migration: Expectations, aspirations and experiences*. London: Ashgate, 1–13.

Rose, G. (1997) 'Situating knowledges: Positionality, reflexivities and other tactics', *Progress in Human Geography*, 21(3): 305–20.

Sanchez-Ayala, L. (2012) 'Interviewing techniques for migrant minority groups', in C. Vargas-Silva (ed.), *Handbook of research methods in migration*. London: Edward Elgar, 117–36.

Stenning, A. and Dawley, S. (2009) 'Poles to Newcastle: Grounding new migrant flows in peripheral regions', *European Urban and Regional Studies*, 16(3): 273–94.

Szewczyk, A. (2014) 'Polish graduates and British citizenship: Amplification of the potential mobility dynamics beyond Europe', *Mobilities*, ahead of print. DOI:10.1080/17450101.2014.969597.

Urry, J. (2007) *Mobilities*. Cambridge: Polity Press.

Vicol, D.-O. and Allen, W. (2014) *Bulgarians and Romanians in the British National Press: 1 Dec 2012–1 Dec 2013*. Migration Observatory report, COMPAS, University of Oxford.

# 10 Workers on the move

## Global labour sourcing in the cruise industry

*William Terry*

## Introduction

Few sectors in tourism are as highly globalised, capitalised, and as quickly growing as the cruise industry. The past several decades have witnessed a meteoric rise in worldwide demand for cruising and the industry continues to add capacity to match. Between 2003 and 2013 the number of passengers carried annually across the industry grew 77 per cent from just over 12 million passengers to over 21 million (CLIA 2014c). Demand is met with 410 ships in the global fleet, which include 29 new ships added between 2013 and 2014 (CLIA 2014a). Furthermore, this expansion is expected to continue over the next several years, with 28 new vessels currently contracted to be built by 2018 (CLIA 2014b). This growth has sparked a concurrent rise in demand for workers to operate the ships and serve the guests. In fact, the cruise business, like tourism as a whole, is particularly labour-intensive. Typically, ships employ one worker for every two to three passengers. On the largest vessels, such as Royal Caribbean's *Oasis of the Seas*, over 2,000 workers will live aboard and work to serve around 5,000 passengers. In 2005 when the last comprehensive survey of cruise employment was undertaken, at least 150,000 seafarers were required to staff the ships industry-wide (Wu 2005). That number is certain to have grown by close to 50,000 considering the substantial growth of the sector over the past decade.

Without some context, however, the growth of the industry and the size of its workforce might seem unremarkable. Yet the cruise industry is a special business with unique challenges in that it is entirely predicated on movement. Moving passengers from port to port is its *raison d'être*. As geographers have long noted, despite the mobility of capital, it must become rooted in place in order to enable profit (Harvey 1982). Despite some on-shore installations and offices that facilitate operations, the bulk of the investment in the industry lies in the ships themselves, that often cost close to half a billion dollars or more. But idle ships do not generate revenue, and therefore must constantly be in motion in order to bring a return on their investment. For this reason, ships are rarely in port for more than 12 hours at any given time; the rest of the time is spent at sea. Because seafarers must be present in order to enable this motion, they live about the ships for months at a time away from their home countries. In short, this is an industry that can only function due to the existence of a highly mobile workforce. Indeed, further context reveals that workers in the industry are sourced from all around the world, and as vessels return to their home port each week, they rotate on and off the ships in a constant cycle between ship and home country.

Such a large-scale movement of people for the purpose of keeping ships in the business of serving passengers is anything but simple or devoid of meaning. Indeed, the logistics of moving so many workers from dozens of countries to and from ships is daunting enough, but a deeper analysis begs the question of how workers come to be mobilised on a global scale in the first place. If, as Hannam, Butler, and Paris (2014: 172) remind us, tourism mobilities should be seen as 'integral to wider processes of economic and political development processes and even constitutive of everyday life', then we should recognise that the movement of cruise workers is part of a much larger constellation of forces shaping the world. Clearly in the twenty-first century, the movement of people around the world and the consequences of that mobility remain important factors in building knowledge and understanding of the world and how it operates. Furthermore, mobility is so interwoven with tourism that its import is beyond debate. Tourism at its root definition requires the mobility of tourists. Often forgotten, though, is that tourism can also involve the movement of workers (Baum 2007), and ignoring workers and their movement leaves a hole in our understanding of the spatial relationships structuring tourism and hospitality (Zampoukos and Ioannides 2011). The cruise industry provides the rare example where both tourists and workers are mobile at the same time, although this mobility is experienced in divergent ways and certainly for different reasons. Yet this unique example affords us an ideal laboratory for examining how the mobility of one group – tourists – hinges on the mobility (and immobility) of another – the workers. Furthermore, this case helps build on Ladkin's (2011: 1141) suggestion that 'if migrant labor is viewed as a form of mobility, migration for tourism employment could be an area that can develop in connection to mobility theory'. Developing these connections requires attention to Cresswell's (2010) conception of the 'politics of mobility', which suggests that mobilities are not only produced by social relations, but also serve to produce social relations. Accordingly, the task of this chapter is to take stock of the political-economic structures and cultural foundations (the social relations) of these mobilities and the inequalities associated with their creation.

## Workers on the move

Wrestling with worker mobilities requires attention to the social formations that make the movement of people to perform work both possible and necessary. Migration studies have long portrayed the motivation for workers to migrate in terms of push and pull factors (not unlike how tourism scholars have described the demand for tourists to leave their homes and travel to friendlier confines). At its heart, this effort is aimed at describing the forces that mobilise workers. While push factors are certainly diverse and are contingent on personal circumstances, labour migrants typically experience a dearth of local opportunities and therefore opt to leave for places where they do exist. This suggests that international labour migration often hinges on the geographically uneven nature of the global economy, especially as it pertains to the spread of global capitalism. To this point, Massey (1999) argues that social, economic, cultural, and political transformations associated with the penetration of capital into peripheral regions has served to displace people from longstanding customary livelihoods. These dislocations force people to choose between struggling to find work in a precarious local context or inserting themselves into labour markets that may take them far from home. The end result is the creation of a mobile workforce necessarily less attached to their home places that no longer provide opportunities for secure employment. While the reasons that people decide to migrate are personally variable, we must take into account the broad conditions that make labour mobility an indispensable feature of the global economy.

Recent mobilities scholarship has provided an important way forward for examining the relationships that structure human movement. Emergent in this body of work is the idea that mobility regimes are socially constructed through various socio-political processes that define 'how people, places and processes get connected and linked together' (Kesselring 2014: 3). It is in this way that the potential for mobility is often inscribed through ethnicity, race, class, and citizenship regimes, which are themselves tied to processes of economic globalisation and geopolitical engineering. The reality is that mobility regimes and spatial linkages between people and places are not always equal. Thus one theme that looms over mobilities research is the disparity between those who are mobile and immobile in society and how these differences are constituted through 'the unequal power relations which unevenly distribute motility, the potential for mobility' (Hannam *et al.* 2006: 14). Here we must pay close attention to the politics of mobile practice, wherein movement even between two same points on a map will be experienced and represented differently between people of distinct backgrounds and social classes (Cresswell 2010).

Yet, while it is clear that there are certainly differences in the level of mobility between people, importantly, it seems that mobility to some extent requires immobility. Thus, 'mobilities cannot be described without attention to the necessary spatial, infrastructural and institutional moorings that configure and enable motilities' (Hannam *et al.* 2006: 3). All people and things that are at movement must sometimes come to rest somewhere, where immobile people and things in place create motility; or, as Cresswell (2010: 29) suggests, 'even the seemingly frictionless world of global capital needs relative "permanences" in order to reproduce itself'. Ports are the textbook examples of these sort of immobile spaces that enable ships to practise movement. They are both the imaginative and literal 'moorings' envisioned in the mobilities literature, which showcase mobility and immobility as two sides of the same coin.

However, this perspective has not been without critique, especially the tendency of mobilities research to present a binary construction of mobile and immobile as oppositional poles, 'between those who possess mobility and those who don't' (Franquesa 2011: 1015). Recent scholarship on mobilities has been careful to recognise that mobility and immobility are intertwined and may even be co-existent in the same person at multiple scales. It seems then that the divide between those who are seen to possess mobility/power/agency and those who are immobile/passive/powerless is not as neat and tidy as is often assumed. Indeed, an examination of labour mobility in the cruise industry reveals not only the co-constitution of mobility and immobility, but also the notion that the two can be co-present in a single individual. As the experience of cruise-ship workers illustrates, 'people's mobility at one scale can co-exist with their immobility at another' (McMorran 2015). Viewed in relation to an average cruise passenger, a typical 'third world' cruise worker, while mobile for the purposes of work, is limited in how their mobility can be experienced. However, the same worker at the scale of their home country may represent the epitome of motility and be someone to emulate.

## Cruise workers on the move

Cruise work requires a high degree of mobility as a matter of vocation. Workers must be willing and able to leave their homes for long stretches of time. Those who choose to work on foreign vessels must also be ready to enter into an international working context in which they will be a member of polyglot crew; a single ship will typically host workers from dozens of countries across the globe. Cruise lines commonly tout their employment of a multi-ethnic crew as a sort of miniature version of the United Nations (Weaver 2005a). The reasons for this diversity are not altruistic, however, and instead lie in efforts to keep labour costs low and workers less inclined to organise (Garin 2005). Indeed, the vast majority come from low-wage countries. Despite a truly diverse range of represented ethnicities, certain countries tend to dominate labour supply. Most significantly, Filipinos comprise roughly 30 per cent of all cruise ship workers, outpacing all other nationalities by 25 percentage points. A few other nationalities do provide significant numbers as well: UK 6 per cent, Italy 6 per cent, Honduras 5 per cent, India 5 per cent, Indonesia 4 per cent, Germany 4 per cent (Wu 2005). Almost 30 per cent of all workers hail from the developed world and are predominantly found in officer and staff positions. These privileged positions grant them higher pay, better living quarters, and also shorter contracts, some as short as six weeks. This allows them more frequent 'vacation' periods to return home. The rest of the more labour-intensive positions are mostly staffed by workers from poorer countries who sign contracts that last anywhere from six months to a year without break. Typically, most return on a new contract after a two-month vacation, but not necessarily to the same ship.

A cross-section of employment in a typical vessel would show the lowest-paid workers, usually from South or East Asia, toiling below decks and managing the operation of the ship away from the gaze from passengers. Asians, alongside Central Americans and Eastern Europeans, are also often found labouring in other areas of the ship such as the kitchen, dining rooms, and in the many staterooms as cabin stewards. Not represented are some of the poorest countries, such as sub-Saharan African states, which would seemingly provide the cheapest possible labour. This suggests that while keeping labour costs at a minimum is obviously important, cruise lines still must hire qualified workers, especially those with experience, proper training, and the ability to speak English (Terry 2011). Whether they work in an engine room or in service positions on a cruise ship, all workers are required to display a high level of skill and many, such as those in marine departments, require minimum safety training certification. These skills are not found in any one place, but across the globe in pockets where labour costs are low but educational systems are in place to create acceptably cheap but effective workers. It is due to these hiring practices that the cruise labour market is well known for being highly segmented and reliant upon mobile yet relatively low-paid workers.

### Flags of convenience

In practice, the cruise industry maintains one of the few true examples of a global labour market. The polyglot crews found aboard ships is a special consequence of the open registry or flags of convenience (FOC) system. FOCs first emerged in the first half of the twentieth century, between the two World Wars, when American shipping companies began to register ships in Panama in order to avoid what were seen as burdensome crewing regulations pertaining to US flagged vessels (Langewiesche 2004; Bloor *et al.* 2014). Since that time the system of open registries has expanded to allow shipping companies a variety of choices as to under which flag to operate their vessels. Many of these new flags arose from non-traditional seafaring states, which utilised ship registries as a form of revenue. This process, also known as 'flagging out', gives owners the ability to choose a balance of regulations that best suit their operations (Lillie 2004; DeSombre 2006). In the twenty-first century, FOCs provide the backbone of the international shipping industry, with almost 73 per cent of all Dead Weight Tonnage now represented by a foreign flag (UNCTAD 2014).

FOCs facilitate mobility by creating demand for labour from around the world. They essentially provide a ship owner with strategic flexibility by eliminating restrictions on crew and owner citizenship and reducing other forms of regulation such as safety, environmental, and labour controls. Non-FOC registries typically require crews to be citizens of the flag country and to be paid on a par with standard national salaries and protected by normal labour laws, all of which make flagging ships in wealthy countries more expensive. Since each ship owner is required to abide by the regulatory statutes associated with the ship's country of registration, jurisdictionally known as 'flag state control', despite their mobility, ships are not without some official oversight (Bloor *et al.* 2014). Each flag state provides different rules and regulations governing labour and environmental policies. For example, the Bahamas and Liberia are countries that have adopted relatively few ILO labour agreements. It is no surprise that the labour-intensive cruise industry would overwhelmingly decide to register their ships in those two countries.

The Bahamian registry in particular displays a rather poor record of worker protection and as a result has become a niche for shipping companies that prioritise undercutting labour costs. It is no accident that roughly 40 per cent of all cruise ships fly the Bahamian flag (DeSombre 2006). In this way, despite the fact that ship owners typically hail from OECD countries, by flagging out they are able to maintain a legal fiction that allows them to operate from low-wage countries with associated standards. Not surprisingly, some have described the impacts of the FOC system as a race to the bottom for environmental, safety, and labour standards (Bloor *et al.* 2014). In essence, open registries effectively allow shipping companies a maritime (and ironic) form of offshoring.

### *(Re)producing mobile workers*

If FOCs play a large role in shaping the demand for a globally mobile workforce, other forces are in play that facilitate worker movement. A persuasive argument can be made that states are possibly the single most important agents that attempt to influence international migration flows (Bauder 2006). For example, demographic shifts in many European countries have created a shrinking workforce that has led governments to adopt immigration platforms that embrace foreign workers. Other states have found that their populations give them a comparative advantage in global labour markets, and thus take steps to invest in and promote their human capital through deliberately constructed emigration regimes. Perhaps no other country displays the latter as well as the Philippines, which has managed to develop a socio-political society that revolves around labour migration. The fact that Filipino seafarers dominate the global labour market is neither a mistake nor a natural occurrence. Certainly Filipinos possess many important cultural traits that make them attractive to the industry, paramount among them being a high level of English-speaking ability. However, their abundance in the labour market is in large part orchestrated by the Philippine state.

Since the 1970s, when the Philippine economy stalled under the weight of the kleptocratic Marcos regime, the Philippines has relied on emigration for the purposes of reducing unemployment, improving living conditions, and family income, and introducing valuable foreign exchange to the country in the form of remittances. In order to promote this labour migration-as-development strategy, the state has maintained a massive emigration regime, currently embodied in the Philippine Overseas Employment Agency (POEA), which is charged with the purpose of facilitating overseas employment and protecting workers as they go abroad. Aside from serving as a clearing house for documentation of workers, recruiting agencies, and employers, it also serves a marketing role by positioning Filipinos as a professional, mobile, and relatively inexpensive body of workers.

The result of these many years of fostering overseas work has been the development of a culture of migration in the Philippines. Much has been written about this, from the sense of obligation felt by family members to work abroad (McKay 2007) to the state marketing efforts that discursively make Filipinos into migrants (Tyner 2004). Indeed, in the realm of seafaring, Filipinos maintain a special place as industry-speak constructs them as the embodiment of the 'perfect worker' that cruise lines could hope to employ (Terry 2014). In essence, they are seen to be naturally suited to the particular demands of the industry.

In the Philippines, the labels applied to Filipinos who go abroad reflect the high social standing of those who leave to work and send money home. 'Balikbayan' (nation returnee) was a term coined in 1974 by the government to recognise returning overseas workers and confer them special privileges, such as being allowed to bring back up to two 'balikbayan boxes' loaded with duty-free goods. 'Bagong Bayani' is a separate title coined in the late 1980s and heavily used by Corazon Aquino to describe overseas Filipinos as 'new heroes' of the republic in recognition of their sacrifice for country and family. The normalisation of labour emigration is on full display in the cultural landscape of the Philippines where labour recruitment agencies, training academies, and advertisements for various migration associated services are ubiquitous around urban hubs like Manila, and the impacts of remittances are often conspicuous (see Figure 10.1).

*Figure 10.1* Private bus in Manila, Philippines. Artwork of Carnival *Ecstasy* suggests that the bus was most likely purchased with money earned while aboard a cruise ship and continues to be part of their identity.

The sum total of the Philippine state's efforts to promote labour emigration might be read from the perspective Scott (1998) establishes with his theory regarding the relationship between states and society. He argues that countries attempt to more effectively govern and control people by making citizens increasingly 'legible' to the state, requiring registration and documentation about their lives. Similarly, we can see that the multiple ways that the Philippines, documents, markets, regulates, and entices its overseas foreign workers effectively makes Filipinos 'legible': in other words, ready made for international labour markets.

The POEA provides an important example of this process with the implementation of a standard seafarer contract, which governs the relationship between shipping companies and Filipino maritime workers. This document codifies every facet of working life, including compensation, termination, working hours, grievance, and injury settlement. It is notable that both salary and the amounts awarded to workers or their families in the case of death is relatively low compared to what would be expected in developed countries (Terry 2009). Ultimately, the standard seafarer contract provides predictability for those who wish to hire Filipino seafarers. With this document, the state, alongside other non-state actors like recruiting agents, creates a simplified process that regularises the experience of hiring Filipinos. This 'legibility' to labour markets is one among many factors in play that shape Filipino motility. In contrast, by viewing other nationalities without a significant presence in the cruise labour market we might argue the reverse: workers who cannot be made legible to markets will remain immobilised due to the perceived risks of hiring them. In this way, entire ethnicities can be effectively blocked from entrance to global labour markets. Thus, what happens at the level of the state has a profound impact on the sort of global outcomes associated with labour migration. This is a lesson that some states seem to be incorporating, and are acting accordingly in order to facilitate their workers' mobility.

Nigeria provides an interesting example of a country that has recently begun efforts to emulate the many Asian countries with long records of providing significant numbers of mariners to the global labour market. Despite its abundance of low-paid workers, the country sends a relatively small number of people into the global seafaring labour force. Indeed, Africa in general, aside from South Africa, has not been viewed as a relevant recruiting ground for cruise workers, particularly because it is seen as a place that lacks the human capital necessary for the industry (Terry 2011). Those Africans who typically have the sort of labour skills required for jobs at sea are most likely working domestically in other areas that require them. Thus the challenge of establishing a seafaring labour force in a place like Nigeria is not simply in developing a migration system that facilitates workers going abroad, but in developing an educational system that can deliver people with the right set of skills and certifications required in the industry. This is a project that Nigeria began in 2009 with the creation of the Nigerian Seafarers Development Programme (NSDP). The goal of this effort is to send up to 5,000 Nigerians abroad to be trained in seafaring academies in other countries, including Romania, the Philippines, the United Kingdom, the United States of America, India, and Egypt. Tuition and other costs under the programme, possibly up to $150 million, are shared by the various Nigerian states and the Nigerian Maritime Administration and Safety Agency (NIMASA) (Chikere 2014). These efforts are in place despite the presence of the Maritime Academy of Nigeria (MAN), which has been educating cadets for several decades, but lacks a training vessel to allow students to complete their training locally. Incidentally, lack of any training ship also plagues Kenya, where the Kenya Maritime Authority in 2014 resorted to sending 170 trainees abroad for their sea trials (Mghenyi 2014).

At its heart, the Nigerian state has created a plan to develop a mobile seafaring force, by first mobilising several thousand students to gain the necessary training. The current plan also establishes a new academy, the Nigerian Maritime University, alongside MAN, in addition to new programmes at existing universities. The outcome of these efforts will only be known in the future; however, it seems fairly certain that without state intervention, the development of a significant Nigerian seafaring labour force would have little chance to grow in any sort of timely or orderly manner. It should be noted that these efforts are mostly directed at workers in marine functions on ships rather than the hotel/service side. For Nigeria to emerge as a true contender for cruise positions, it would also need to develop programmes aimed at cultivating service skills for the more numerous hospitality positions.

### *Immobilities*

The irony of mobility is that while cruise workers are mobile at the scale of the global economy, they are relatively immobile while actually at work on board ships. Obviously, passengers and workers are both contained inside the vessels, but workers experience this to a much higher degree. With crew and passenger spaces clearly demarcated, much of the ship is off limits, and workers are restricted to those areas that serve their work functions (Weaver 2005b). Enforcement of these policies involves some elements of surveillance, like security cameras at doorways that transition from crew to passenger spaces. But more important is a sort of social regulation based on the fear of reprimand or outright dismissal. Furthermore, most seafarers simply do not have the time for personal mobility as they typically work 10–14 hours per day, seven days a week. The occasional day off in port allows for enough time to quickly shop or enjoy a location, but only for a few hours as the ship always looms awaiting their return. Indeed, for foreign crewmembers movement is highly restricted. Those on board ships that port in the United States hold the C1/D visa, which is required to allow workers to access the ships. This visa system restricts workers only to movement in times and spaces that allow them transit to the ships and experience a few hours of shore leave. Any movement outside these parameters is considered unlawful. In this way, mobility is an illusion of sorts for crewmembers as their nationality remains the ultimate arbiter of the type of movements they can make in society.

While cruise workers become mobile in the global marketplace, they are ultimately tied to home, tethered to places. Much as a cruise ship must return to port every week in order to replenish supplies and passengers, workers must return home periodically between contracts. During this (unpaid) vacation, usually last-ing two months, the international mobility of a cruise worker from a developing country is temporarily curtailed. Yet even when mobility is restored, as workers return to their lives aboard the ship, they remain attached to home due to social obligations of various types, most notably in the form of remittances. In many cases, others remain 'moored' in place in order to enable the worker's mobility. For example, as young parents go abroad to support their children, other extended family members remain in place to provide care for those who stay behind. The Philippine state even maintains policies to make sure overseas workers remain tethered to home, by requiring that 80 per cent of seafarers' wages must be remit-ted to bank accounts in the Philippines. The state thus solidifies this connection and ensures that 'family becomes the site for the regulation of migrants' remit-tances' (Rodriguez 2010: 86).

But mobility also comes with costs for workers and their families. Transnational families necessarily suffer from separation, which can take an enormous emotional toll. This is especially true for children suffering feelings of neglect when their parents, especially mothers, are abroad (Parreñas 2005a, 2005b). Families are often strained by the distance and effort required to maintain trans-national kinship ties, especially when 'left-behind' members harbour resentments towards those who have gone abroad or expect a measure of reciprocity for help-ing to mobilise their family members to emigrate (Reynolds 2011). The mobili-ties approach has been criticised for too often focusing on the mobility of individuals (Holdsworth 2013), but the experience of cruise workers with fami-lies displays how various forms of human immobility are inextricably linked to the mobility.

Interestingly, and perhaps ironically, the immobilities that enable mobility are also responsible for providing a means of protecting the very workers who are vulnerable due to their status as mobile migrant labourers. The hypermobilities engendered by the FOC system has certainly made the task of protecting seafarers especially challenging. However, it is possible because of the ways in which shipping is tied to ports, where ships must literally be moored. The International Transport Workers Federation (ITF) has long waged an anti-FOC campaign aimed at combatting the mistreatment of workers who go to sea amid an ocean of mixed-up rules and regulations associated with the various flag states, going so far as to label cruise vessels 'sweatships' (Mather 2002). It is through the threat of action in ports by ITF affiliate longshoremen that maritime labour unions have been able to collectively bargain with many shipping companies even in a deterritorialised industry (Lillie 2004). Similarly, it is through the mechanism of Port State Control that the recently enforced Maritime Labour Convention (ILO-MLC) is being implemented to ensure that all ships meet minimum ILO requirements for seafarer treatment. In this way, whenever a cruise ship is moored and worker abuses noted, it can be inspected and the owners fined. Because the MLC is so new, it is difficult to know what its impacts will be, but it certainly has the potential to be a transformative tool in the global effort to protect seafarers.

## Conclusion

Taking stock of all of the forces that create or constrain motility in the world of cruise ship work forces us to recognise the layers of mobility and immobility that can exist in a single body. The example of a typical cruise worker from the developing world shows that they are mobile because they are both disadvantaged and underpaid on a global scale. At a local scale, they are mobile because they have the qualifications and skills to make them a competitive hire, and therefore experience a level of mobility out of reach to most people. While global inequalities actually help produce the mobility that allows some workers from poor countries to go abroad, most local workers remain immobile due to lack of skill, connections, or luck. Many of those afforded the chance to leave have important skills that allow them to access the global labour market. The poorest in these societies typically do not possess the kind of skills that will make them mobile in a global workforce. Certainly this is the case for the cruise industry, which is able to cherry-pick the best workers. In short, the 'third world' workers on cruise ships are typically not the poorest from their countries, and most are very well educated/trained for their jobs.

However, this is not to suggest that all forms of mobility are equal. Ultimately there is a qualitative difference in the mobilities between the passengers on a cruise ship and the typical worker. Passengers are effectively mobilised by choice and more importantly have the privilege to make that choice. Ironically, cruise vacations are accessible for middle-class passengers because the cruise industry keeps costs affordable by employing a mobile, inexpensive multi-ethnic crew. A Filipino, Indian, Malaysian, or other worker from the 'third world', while certainly not without agency, is mobilised as a worker due to the great inequalities that exist and the immense social formations in place that facilitate their movement to do work. Without these they would likely remain immobilised, locked out of the global labour market. And even in the labour market as a global labourer with mobility, a worker is forced along a path, their movements authorised through visa systems and work contracts. In short, if cruise workers can teach us anything about mobility, it is that our nationality is inescapable; the social world continues to keep people tethered to places, and we are only as mobile as our governments and economies allow us to be.

## References

Bauder, H. (2006) *Labor movement: How migration regulates labor markets*. New York: Oxford University Press.

Baum, T. (2007) 'Human resources in tourism: Still waiting for change', *Progress in Tourism Management*, 28(6): 1383–99.

Bloor, M., Sampson, H. and Gekara, V. (2014) 'Global governance of training standards in an outsourced labor force: The training double bind in seafarer license and certification assessments', *Regulation & Governance*, 8(4): 455–71.

Chikere, C. (2014) 'Remodeling Nigeria's seafarer development programme', *Daily Independent*, October. Online at: http://dailyindependentnig.com/2014/10/remodelling-nigerias-seafarers-development-programme/.

CLIA (2014a) *2014 state of the cruise industry report.* Fort Lauderdale, FL: Cruise Lines International Association.

CLIA (2014b) *Five year cruise industry capacity outlook.* Fort Lauderdale, FL: Cruise Lines International Association.

CLIA (2014c) *The global economic contribution of cruise tourism 2013.* Fort Lauderdale, FL: Cruise Lines International Association.

Cresswell, T. (2010) 'Towards a politics of mobility', *Environment and planning D: Society and space,* 28(1): 17.

DeSombre, E. R. (2006) *Flagging standards: Globalization and environmental, safety, and labor regulations at sea.* Cambridge, MA: MIT Press.

Franquesa, J. (2011) 'We've lost our bearings: Place, tourism, and the limits of the mobility turn', *Antipode,* 43(4): 1012–33.

Garin, K. A. (2005) *Devils on the deep blue sea: The dreams, schemes, and showdowns that built America's cruise ship empires.* New York: Viking.

Hannam, K., Sheller, M. and Urry, J. (2006) 'Editorial: Mobilities, immobilities and moorings', *Mobilities,* 1(1): 1–22.

Hannam, K., Butler, G. and Paris, C. M. (2014) 'Developments and key issues in tourism mobilities', *Annals of Tourism Research,* 44(1): 171–85.

Harvey, D. (1982) *The limits to capital.* Oxford: Blackwell.

Holdsworth, C. (2013) *Family and intimate mobilities.* Basingstoke: Palgrave Macmillan.

Kesselring, S. (2014) 'Mobility, power and the emerging new mobilities regimes', *Sociologica,* 1(1): 1–29.

Ladkin, A. (2011) 'Exploring tourism labor', *Annals of Tourism Research,* 38(3): 1135–55.

Langewiesche, W. (2004) *The outlaw sea: A world of freedom, chaos, and crime.* New York: North Point Press.

Lillie, N. (2004) 'Global collective bargaining on flag of convenience shipping', *British Journal of Industrial Relations,* 42(1): 47–67.

Massey, D. S. (1999) 'International migration at the dawn of the twenty-first century: The role of the state', *Population and Development Review,* 25(2): 303–22.

Mather, C. (2002) *Sweatships: What it's really like to work on board cruise ships.* London: International Transport Worker's Federation.

McKay, D. (2007) 'Sending dollars shows feeling: Emotions and economies in Filipino migration', *Mobilities,* 2(2): 175–94.

McMorran, C. (2015) 'Mobilities amid the production of fixities: Labor in a Japanese inn', *Mobilities,* 10(1): 83–99.

Mghenyi, C. (2014) 'Egypt: Mariners sail to Egypt over Kenya's lack of training ship', *All Africa,* 24 October. Online at: http://allafrica.com/stories/201410241149.html.

Parreñas, R. (2005a) *Children of global migration: Transnational families and gendered woes.* Stanford, CA: Stanford University Press.

Parreñas, R. (2005b) 'Long distance intimacy: Class, gender and intergenerational relations between mothers and children in Filipino transnational families', *Global Networks,* 5(4): 317–36.

Reynolds, T. (2011) 'Caribbean second-generation return migration: Transnational family relationships with "left-behind" kin in Britain', *Mobilities,* 6(4): 535–51.

Rodriguez, R. M. (2010) *Migrants for export: How the Philippine state brokers labor to the world.* Minneapolis: University of Minnesota Press.

Scott, J. C. (1998) *Seeing like a state: How certain schemes to improve the human condition have failed.* New Haven, CT: Yale University Press.

Terry, W. C. (2009) 'Working on the water: On legal space and seafarer protection in the cruise industry', *Economic Geography*, 85(4): 463–82.

Terry, W. C. (2011) 'Geographic limits to global labor market flexibility: The human resources paradox of the cruise industry', *Geoforum*, 42(6): 660–70.

Terry, W. C. (2014) 'The perfect worker: Discursive makings of Filipinos in the workplace hierarchy of the globalized cruise industry', *Social & Cultural Geography*, 15(1): 73–93.

Tyner, J. A. (2004) *Made in the Philippines: Gendered discourses and the making of migrants*. New York: Routledge.

UNCTAD (2014) *Review of marine transport*. New York: United Nations Conference on Trade and Development. Online at: http://unctad.org/en/pages/PublicationWebflyer. aspx?publicationid=1068.

Weaver, A. (2005a) 'Representation and obfuscation: Cruise travel and the mystification of production', *Tourism Culture & Communication*, 5(3): 165–76.

Weaver, A. (2005b) 'Spaces of containment and revenue capture: "Super-sized" cruise ships as mobile tourism enclaves', *Tourism Geographies*, 7(2): 165–84.

Wu, B. (2005) *The world cruise industry: A profile of the global labour market*. Cardiff: Seafarers International Research Centre (SIRC). Online at: www.sirc.cf.ac.uk/pdf/ WorldCruiseIndustry.pdf.

Zampoukos, K. and Ioannides, D. (2011) 'The tourism labour conundrum: Agenda for new research in the geography of hospitality workers', *Hospitality & Society*, 1(1): 25–45.

# 11 Confronting economic precariousness through international retirement migration

## Japan's old-age 'economic refugees' and Germany's 'exported grannies'

*Meghann Ormond and Mika Toyota*

### Introduction

Many of the world's demographically oldest countries are increasingly 'outsourcing' care from abroad for their elderly. Indeed, seniors wishing to age in place in countries like Germany and Singapore are making – and in some cases, as in Japan, beginning to explore how to make – use of at-home help, frequently provided by female migrant care workers (see e.g. Lutz and Palenga-Mollenbeck 2010; Lopez 2012; Huang *et al.* 2012). However, as with the 2011 film *The Best Exotic Marigold Hotel*, premised on budget-conscious British pensioners opting to spend the rest of their lives in India, more seniors are also relocating abroad for more affordable long-term domestic or institutional living and care arrangements (Toyota 2006; Ormond 2014). Compared with traditional accounts of 'international retirement migration' (IRM), which take as their prime subjects a pool of relatively autonomous, mobile, affluent, healthy 'young old' (King *et al.* 2000), this relatively novel type of relocation draws attention to the significance of economic precariousness and its attendant embodied socio-spatial dependencies, vulnerabilities, and 'stuckness' (Cresswell 2012) underlying this form of transnational mobility for many older people living abroad.

Economic motivations – involving the pursuit of safe, friendly, comfortable places in which one's savings and pension will stretch further for longer – have certainly long been central to IRM relocations. Warm climates, tax advantages, and the comforting prospect of returning to one's country of origin when one's health declines seem to go hand in hand. However, in recent years, and especially with the global economic crisis, IRM numbers have dropped in traditional destinations, with people opting to stay in or return to their home countries, or to move on to alternative climes perceived to be more stable, with immigration and tax regimes favourable to them and (what remains of) their assets (Oxlade 2013; Rainey 2014). Others are limited by unfortunate property investments and waning pensions and welfare benefits, with some consequently entering into old-age poverty in their IRM destinations with limited prospects of returning to their home countries (Betty and Hall 2013).

In this chapter, we look at how IRM discourses and practices are shifting and growing more complex by focusing on 'young old' and 'old old' Japanese and

German pensioners who have resettled abroad. Japan is home to the highest proportion of seniors in the world, with 23.1 per cent over the age of 65 in 2010. The percentage is expected to steadily increase to 30 per cent by 2030 and to 40 per cent by 2055. In terms of absolute numbers, 29.44 million were 65 and older in 2010, of which 14.22 million (10 per cent of Japan's population) were 75 and older (Toyota 2013). In Germany, meanwhile, people aged 75 and older constituted 7 per cent of the population in 2010, a figure expected to rise to over 10 per cent by 2020 and 15 per cent by 2050 – making it among the countries with the oldest populations in the world, alongside Japan, South Korea, and Italy (Dallinger and Eichler 2010). By 2050, Germans aged 60 and over will make up more than half of the population, second oldest after Japan (de Pommereau 2013).

German insurers cover healthcare and long-term care services beyond their national borders, and while Japan's national health insurance coverage is reserved for those who pay tax and maintain an address in Japan, it is possible to maintain this entitlement even while living abroad. Coverage like this has helped to enable the growing economically driven and care-motivated transnational mobility of both 'young old' and 'old old' pensioners from Japan and Germany. With the Japanese case below, we examine the shift between two waves of Japanese IRM. The first wave, starting in the late 1980s, constituted a luxurious option for better-off 'young old' Japanese pensioners in pursuit of conditions supportive of active ageing. The second wave, which began in the 2000s and was triggered by various demographic and social changes within Japan, reflected a coping strategy for both 'young old' and 'old old' pensioners struggling with financial and physical difficulties in Japan. The two waves differ from each other in terms of the destinations and patterns of migration and mobility. We then go on to the German case to examine the popular and political reaction within Germany to the '*oma export*' ('granny export') or '*greisen export*' ('senior export') phenomenon. 'Young old' German pensioners have long been seasonally and more permanently relocating to southern European countries, like Spain and Portugal. The recent '*oma export*' phenomenon, however, profiled a very different (if small) group of German seniors, most of whom in their 'old old' age moved either on their own or were moved as a result of their adult children's wishes to a growing number of residential care homes abroad catering specifically to the needs of German-speaking seniors.

With ageing people being cast as burdens to current and future generations of taxpayers and family members and becoming what Cresswell (2013) calls 'shadow citizens' in their home countries, what is the transformative potential – both individual and collective – of long-term economically driven and care-motivated migration among 'young old' and 'old old' seniors within, between, and beyond IRM source and destination countries? As we will see, the Japanese and German IRM flows examined here reflect broader ethico-political debates on social citizenship and solidarity in the face of rapid population ageing unfolding not only within these migrants' countries of origin but also throughout a growing number of sending and destination countries across the globe.

## Japan's old-age 'economic refugees'

Japanese seniors who move overseas after retirement are generally doing so in pursuit of new lifestyles, care, and livelihood security. Some 10 per cent of people aged 60–69 travel abroad at least once per year (Japanese Statistics Bureau 2006) (see Table 11.1). As a result of tourism and/or previous work experience with Japanese companies abroad, retirees frequently become retirement migrants in destinations with which they are already somewhat familiar. This type of post-retirement mobility can be placed within the context of a wider spectrum of activities that encompasses both tourism and migration (Williams and Hall 2000).

Japanese IRM can be traced back to the Silver Columbia Plan put in place in 1986 by the then Ministry of International Trade and Industry (now the Ministry of Economy, Trade and Industry). Japan was already experiencing rapid ageing at that time, and senior welfare entered the agenda as a public concern. Taking advantage of the appreciating value of the Japanese Yen following the 1985 Plaza Accord, the plan encouraged Japanese seniors to live overseas for a period of time. It was projected as an alternative trade policy, enabling seniors to consume non-importable goods (e.g. climate, land, natural resources, beef, and fruit). More focused on encouraging active ageing than on seeking solutions for senior care shortages, the Silver Columbia Plan sought to encourage seniors to explore new continents as if they were a silver-haired Christopher Columbus. Meanwhile, 'a society for the study of leisure in the form of staying abroad' was inaugurated in 1987, and in 1989 the 'Long Stay Plan 90' was announced. The Long Stay Foundation, a public-service corporation, was then established in 1992 as an extra-departmental body authorised by the Ministry of Economy, Trade and Industry. Japanese construction industries wasted no time in constructing 'Japanese overseas villages' in popular destinations such as Spain and Australia.

Most of the Japanese seniors taking part in this first wave of IRM were finan-cially well off. These 'wealthy, healthy, older people' – sometimes referred to as 'whoopies' (Mowforth and Munt 1998: 131) – were interested in investing in their 'second life'. Thanks to Japan's remarkable past economic growth and its well-developed welfare system, seniors over 50 years old comprise 42.7 per cent of Japan's population but hold 75 per cent of all individual wealth (Japan Cabinet Office 2008). Consequently, high levels of Japanese investment triggered strong

*Table 11.1* Japanese seniors travelling abroad (2008)

| Age group | Numbers |
| --- | --- |
| 50–54 | 1,357,514 |
| 55–59 | 1,490,023 |
| 60–64 | 1,318,517 |
| 65–69 | 824,878 |
| 70+ | 683,745 |
| All senior age groups | 5,674,677 |

Source: Japanese Ministry of Justice 2009

opposition in their IRM destination countries, especially in Australia, where housing prices grew out of reach for locals.

Japan's sustained ageing and the economic stagnation it has faced since the 1990s turned IRM from a luxurious option into a survival strategy for some. Anxiety about the sustainability of Japan's national pension scheme has worsened in recent years with concerns about a very high age dependency ratio and social welfare policies for seniors. While their pensions remain limited, individuals' medical expenses are on the rise. The government's White Paper on the Ageing Society reported that 37.8 per cent of Japanese seniors over 65 feel financially insecure and about 60 per cent of elderly households earn less than JPY 3,000,000 annually (Japan Cabinet Office 2008). More households depend on state welfare than ever before. This sense of insecurity – compounded by other factors, such as the lack of care providers and changing family structures leading to a steady increase in the number of seniors living alone and of households with multiple generations of seniors under one roof – has propelled many to seek solutions abroad.

In this context, two interrelated changes have occurred with regard to IRM. First, IRM destination countries have grown more diverse. South-East Asia emerged as an alternative to Australia, Spain and the USA, soon becoming Japanese seniors' main IRM destination. Thailand, Malaysia, and the Philippines in particular initiated IRM programmes specially targeting Japanese. The three host countries introduced a special visa category for those with sufficient savings or pensions, provided they do not seek employment in these countries. The Philippines took the lead, setting up the Philippine Leisure and Retirement Authority in 1985. They were followed by the Malaysian government with its Silver Hair Programme (later renamed Malaysia My Second Home (MM2H)) in 1996, and the Thai Ministry of Commerce with its Long-Stay and Health Care Project in 1998. In 2006, Taiwan extended a special multiple-entry, long-stay (up to 180 days at one time) visa to Japanese retirees. Indonesia, meanwhile, has attracted a sizeable Japanese senior population, especially in Bali, and Laos and Cambodia are emerging IRM destinations due to low living costs and recent economic and infrastructural improvements. While it is difficult to estimate the exact number of Japanese seniors who have relocated for long periods to South-East Asia, the population is sizeable and clearly increasing. Malaysia and Thailand, for example, currently annually attract 20,000 foreign retirees entering on various types of visas for long stays, and Japanese constitute a significant proportion of this group (Gulane 2006). Table 11.2 shows the slow but steady increase in Japanese seniors in the MM2H programme, which provides foreigners with entitlements comparable to those of Malaysian citizens on the condition that they purchase property and deposit a certain amount of money in designated banks.

Second, Japanese retirement migrants' profiles have grown more diverse. Due to Japan's long period of economic stagnation, careworker shortage, and lack of confidence in the sustainability of the national welfare system, fewer pensioners can be classified as 'whoopies', and more migrate out of necessity. Indeed, with the economic gap between Japanese seniors widening (Japan Cabinet Office

*Table 11.2* MM2H participants

| Year | 2004 | 2005 | 2006 | 2007 | 2008 | 2009 | 2010 | 2011 | 2012 | 2013 |
|---|---|---|---|---|---|---|---|---|---|---|
| Japanese | 42 | 87 | 157 | 198 | 210 | 169 | 195 | 423 | 816 | 739 |
| Total | 1,917 | 2,615 | 1,729 | 1,503 | 1,512 | 1,578 | 1,499 | 2,387 | 3,227 | 3,675 |
| % Japanese | 2% | 3% | 9% | 13% | 14% | 11% | 13% | 18% | 25% | 20% |

Source: Ministry of Tourism Malaysia 2014

2008), those in old-age poverty constitute a new social group in Japan. Japanese retirees driven away from Japan have been dubbed by our informants as 'economic and care refugees'. Japan's economic recession hit people in their fifties – one generation younger than the baby boomers – particularly hard. Some, having lost their jobs before retirement age, have had to manage long-term unemployment until reaching the legal age to begin collecting a pension. The following experience of a 58-year-old Japanese man living in Chiang Mai, Thailand vividly illustrates how socially and economically marginalised 'young old' seniors have had to migrate:

> I lost my job before retirement … It's really hard to find a new job in Japan if you are a male in your fifties. Young people or females are preferred as part-time employees in the service sector; nobody wants to employ a bald man with limited sociability, you know? I lost face among neighbours and relatives. My wife was deeply ashamed of the situation. In order to preserve our household's honour, my wife asked me to leave the house instead of lying around the whole day. She can then tell others that I got a job working overseas. I somehow need to eke out a living with limited savings until I start receiving my pension. I came here because the cost of living is low and I can stretch my limited savings.

Men like him, with little regular income, often rent small rooms in local neighbourhoods. Some enter Thailand without a visa (no visa is required for Japanese staying less than 30 days); others enter with 60-day tourist visas. They may extend their stay by exiting Thailand every 30 days on short 'visa run' trips across nearby borders with Malaysia, Laos, or Myanmar, regularly repeating the runs over several years. The Japanese consulate in Cebu, the Philippines, informed us that some very poor Japanese seniors are even without sufficient funds to take the ferry or bus to the consulate to renew their passports. The number of elderly 'economic refugees' has become so sizeable that a number of South-East Asian governments have recently begun to place new restrictions on IRM, seeking to attract 'higher quality' (read 'wealthy') retirees and to stem the inflow of poorer, less mobile – and thus less desirable – 'denizen' retirees (Toyota and Xiang 2012; Cresswell 2013; Ormond 2014).

Subtle changes in Japanese public perception of IRM can be discerned over the last 30 years. While the government initiatives of the late 1980s encouraging 'whoopies' to move abroad raised concern at the time that the Japanese government was 'exporting' its elderly, the current wave of Japanese senior outmigration has attracted notably less public criticism, primarily because this wave has resulted from 'individual' initiative. Numerous books and blogs have been published by Japanese seniors living in South-East Asia which describe their lifestyles and care arrangements. Some promote South-East Asian countries as a 'care paradise' because of the easily available and affordable domestic workers. In fieldwork interviews, it emerged that some 'young old' couples in their late sixties moved to Malaysia, Thailand, and the Philippines, together with their 'old old' parents who were in need of intensive long-term care. These countries' low wages for carework enabled the Japanese retirement migrants to afford the costs associated with live-in foreign domestic workers caring for their elderly parents. Recently, the Long Stay Foundation website began to describe affordable care provision in South-East Asian countries as a benefit of living for long periods abroad. However, such practices do not seem to trigger any public criticism in Japan.

## Germany's 'exported grannies'

As in many high-income countries, policy in Germany has shifted away from institutionalised care towards home care, away from public provision towards private or mixed services subsidised by cash transfers, and towards complementing – rather than replacing – informal care (Bettio and Verashchagina 2012). Indeed, though Germany has nationally mandated long-term care insurance, economic crises, and welfare reforms are putting increased pressure on families to assume responsibility for caring for their dependent seniors by insourcing and/or outsourcing such care. This is partly attributable to the careworker shortages it faces, which is expected to worsen with time. Shortages are not only caused by rapidly ageing populations but also result from the poor societal recognition of care as a profession, unattractive wage levels, families' limited capacity to pay, and the care sector's disproportionate feminisation (Bettio and Verashchagina 2012: 19).

The predominant focus on 'ageing in place' in Germany today means that elder care largely happens within private households. As such, long-term care insurance (*Pflegeversicherung*) established by the German state in 1995–96 pays EUR 1550 a month, serving as a cash benefit/payment to domestic caregivers, be they family members or hired help. Bettio and Verashchagina (2012: 11, 17) found that selective cash transfers facilitating at-home care such as this were associated with increasing irregular markets for unskilled, mobile, and migrant careworkers; tax evasion; risks for lower health standards; and the overall development of an untrained and underequipped workforce. At the same time, the move away from public institutional care has led to the growth of private residential care facilities and home care agencies in Germany. For many, however, residential care in Germany is unaffordable. The amount of government mandated long-term care coverage does not reflect the actual amounts charged for such care. As such, working-class people with smaller pensions, in particular, end up unable to fully

140   *Meghann Ormond and Mika Toyota*

cover care costs on top of their normal living costs. Indeed, a recent Federal Statistical Office report found that 400,000 within Germany were unable to afford care (Keller 2012).

A crop of private residential care facilities catering specifically to ageing German-speakers has begun to sprout outside of Germany. Some are geographically closer to home, like SeniorCare on the Hungarian Lake Balaton and those in the Polish ski resort of Szklarska Poreba. Others, though further afield, like Haus Koroneos north of Athens, Greece, and Baan Tschuai Duu Laa in Phuket, Thailand, are located in familiar international holiday destinations well serviced by low-cost airlines. These facilities provide permanent residents with a spectrum of care-intensity options as well as more temporary options for 'old old' seniors with a range of physical and mental care needs, with some specialising in dementia. In addition to long-term residential care, they often include formal care-centred 'serviced holidays' for dependent seniors, giving temporary respite to their family and friends providing informal at-home care so as to avoid caregiver burnout. These facilities' prices coincide with German, Austrian, and Swiss care coverage limits, factoring in average pensions. Indeed, while the average monthly cost of residential care within Germany is EUR 3,250 a month, equivalent care can be had in Poland for approximately EUR 1,200 a month (Buchdahl 2013) (see Table 11.3). Currently the German government pays EUR 700 a month for nursing costs outside of Germany; when joined with one's pension, residential care becomes far more comfortably within reach for middle- and lower-income individuals and families.

Such alternatives heighten conventional IRM concerns with stretching one's pension, bringing to light not only the increasing personal costs of long-term residential and at-home care within Germany but also the societal costs and implications (*Der Spiegel* 2012). Media coverage of the '*oma export*' phenomenon recounts personal experiences with or concerns about the poor quality of elder care within Germany (Buchdahl 2013). These are linked to the expected worsening of the current nursing and caregiver shortages within a rapidly ageing Germany as well as to circulating stories of caregivers abusing or neglecting their wards in Germany (*Der Spiegel* 2012).

*Table 11.3* Cost comparison

| Countries of settlement | Number of German pensioners (2011) | Average cost per month (EUR) for private residential care homes catering to German pensioners |
| --- | --- | --- |
| Germany | 17,000,000 *(2012)* | 2,900–3,400 (of which 1,023–1,750 is subsidised) |
| Czech Republic | >3,000 | 1,050–1,550 |
| Hungary | 7,146 | 1,500–2,100 |
| Polandn | n/a | 1,250–1,300 |
| Slovakia | 600 | 1,100 |

Source: Bettio and Verashchagina 2010: 165; Dowideit 2012; Keller 2012; Buchdahl 2013; Kresge 2013

By contrast, residential care facilities catering to Germans in other countries are depicted in media accounts in glowing terms. Residences located in Polish, Czech, and Hungarian resort areas can offer significantly lower care costs, due to comparatively lower wages within these countries. Many possess German-speaking staff, offer greater and more personalised attention than a resident would receive in Germany, and provide a diverse range of activities (e.g. fine dining, singing German folk songs together, manicures, etc.): 'One home in the Polish town of Zabelkow in Silesia has German-speaking nurses, lift announcements, and emergency call systems in German and shows German Bundesliga football on fancy flat-screen TVs' (Buchdahl 2013).

Some popular websites, like Wohnen-im-Alter (2011), began posting profiles of residential facilities abroad, organised by country, as well as preparatory checklists to help seniors and their relatives with their decision-making process. Readers were encouraged to consider not only what facility may be economically feasible but also what it is that 'old old' seniors themselves want and need. What type/level of skilled support do they need? Will they encounter linguistic barriers? How often do they wish to see their families and friends? What sort of location do they desire and what sort of landscapes do they believe will have a positive impact on their overall health (e.g. mountains, coast, etc.)?

Yet the prospects of '*oma export*' are clearly more appealing to some than to others. Unsurprisingly, perhaps, insurers have been among those at the forefront of the phenomenon. European Union law forbids German insurance funds from establishing deals with nursing homes abroad because they cannot reliably certify quality (de Pommereau 2013). However, Connolly (2012a) notes that the 'statutory insurers that make up Germany's state insurance system are openly discussing how to make care in foreign retirement homes into a long-term workable financial model'. German insurers like AOK (the largest of the country's 180 statutory health insurance funds) and Barmer GEK have requested that the government permit care funds to cover residential care facilities abroad (*Der Spiegel* 2012).

Such requests follow in the footsteps of German insurers like Techniker Krankassen (TK), which has already contracted out the services of dozens of clinics and health facilities in both Western and Eastern European countries to fulfil Germans' healthcare needs abroad. Indeed, people insured under the German statutory health insurance system have had medical treatment in other EU countries recognised and covered since the 2004 Healthcare Modernisation Act (Wagner and Verheyen 2009). Yet, this type of cross-border care pursuit (Glinos *et al.* 2010; Gatrell 2011) has not provoked as much alarm as the prospect of pursuing more easily accessible long-term care abroad, as with the '*oma export*' phenomenon. If the German state is seen to condone and enable such mobility by funding long-term care abroad, then it is thought to risk both voter backlash and outcry from those within the domestic care industry (Connolly 2012a).

Ensuring universal access and standards of care for an ageing population *within* Germany, therefore, is a politically charged and morally sensitive issue. Much of the sting in the '*oma export*' phenomenon derives from the perception that people are not going abroad of their own will, as they might have done when engaging in conventional IRM. While individuals going abroad were pitied, relatives encouraging such moves, as well as insurers and the state, were targets of harsh critique. A 2013 study by the German polling company TNS Emid found that 85 per cent of Germans polled would refuse to consider sending an infirm older relative to an Eastern European care home (Wendl 2013). Indeed, few commentators have explicitly defended the positive potential of such cross-border care outsourcing, and political figures have been quick to condemn. One prominent commentator, Heribert Prantl, for example, framed the phenomenon as 'gerontological colonialism', accusing complicit Germans of 'dumping' their sick and elderly 'rubbish' in cheaper places abroad instead of taking care of them (in Buchdahl 2013; see Ormond 2014 on parallel discourse in Asia). While this response reflects a broader unwillingness within Germany to send relatives to residential care homes even *within* Germany (Wendl 2013), it also has raised the uneasy spectre of Nazi-era deportations of the old and infirm.

The extended geography of outsourced elder care beyond Germany (Prantl's 'gerontological colonialism') was further decried as a way of ensuring the welfare of younger people in Germany at the expense of unjustly impacting other parts of the world. Such sentiment is described in a newspaper commentary as an 'equality' between young and old in Germany 'whose direct consequence is likely to mean even more "residences" in low-wage countries. Today Poland and Hungary, Bulgaria, or Romania tomorrow, the day after the Philippines or the Congo' (Posener 2014). There was even concern that outsourcing elder care to Eastern European countries would take employment opportunities away from the estimated 100,000 Eastern European migrant women currently involved in at-home care giving in Germany (Wendl 2013).

Some, however, did call on German society to reassess its ill-judgement of those sending their relatives abroad as 'stingy' or 'heartless' (Keller 2013) by taking into consideration the difficulties increasingly personally faced in supporting and caring for their older relatives in Germany. '*Oma export*' seemed to reflect the condition of the modern Western family and state, characterised by fragmented families, increasingly unstable jobs, growing rates of old-age poverty, 'young old' pensioners taking care of their 'old old' parents, and underappreciated and undercompensated caregiving professions. Western families – especially those in the USA, where sending relatives to care homes was deemed to be far more common – were contrasted with those from Asia, Africa, or Latin America, where families were thought to care for their own 'no matter what' (Godwin-Jones 2012).

Yet how many people are believed to be engaging in long-term care-motivated migration? German pension statistics suggest that a mere 10,000 people drawing a German pension live in Eastern Europe (Keller 2012). However, the less regulated freedom of movement within the European Union (EU) and increasingly around the world – along with a growing number of special programmes set up by countries to promote IRM – means that it is difficult to precisely calculate how many are moving and settling abroad to access care options and for how long.

Still, a 2013 study of German health and care insurers managed to halt much of the moralistic hand-wringing around '*oma export*', revealing it to be largely hyperbolic. Journalists, it turns out, had blown the phenomenon out of proportion. The 2013 study found that, compared with the 770,000 applications made within Germany in the same time period, only 5,000 people with German insurance coverage requested long-term care coverage in other EU countries, and a mere 1,164 applications were made for care insurance outside of the EU (Mihm 2013). The study further suggested that many of these 1,164 applications could be attributed to retired migrant workers who had left Germany and returned to their non-EU countries of origin for retirement.

## Conclusion

This chapter has sought to draw mobilities scholars' attention to intergenerational and age-related political economy of care issues and the much overlooked significance of how these are translated in transnational mobility practices. In profiling recent concerns and debates around growing flows of Japanese and German seniors who leave their home countries as 'economic and care refugees', we have sought to complicate the ways in which international retirement migration (IRM) has been conventionally understood. For an ever larger number retirees, IRM is not a luxury but rather a necessity. While the magnitude of these flows from Japan and Germany is limited, they are likely to increase because they are driven by careworker shortages and pensioners' declining purchasing power – long-term trends unlikely to be easily reversed. This emerging form of IRM reflects the further commoditisation of care and inculcation of neoliberal self-responsibility that embraces transnational mobility as a panacea for care deficits 'back home' (Ormond and Sothern 2012). Indeed, the phenomena outlined here are embedded in many contemporary ethico-political questions about the limits to personal, familial, societal, civic, and governmental responsibilities to ageing and other vulnerable population groups amid the dissolution, de-territorialisation, and reformulation of state, civic, community, religious, and family structures and relationships both within and beyond the container of the nation-state. Such questions merit serious consideration in future studies, not only of IRM but also of other forms of transnational mobility, like 'medical tourism' and trans-border living (Löfgren 2008; Terlouw 2012), where discussions of practices linked to ageing are all but absent.

## References

Bettio, F. and Verashchagina, A. (2012) *Long-term care for the elderly: Provisions and providers in 33 European countries*. Fondazione G. Brodolini, Nov. Luxemburg: Publications Office of the European Union. Online at: http://ec.europa.eu/justice/gender-equality/files/elderly_care_en.pdf.

Betty, C. and Hall, K. (2013) 'Returning from Spain: The experiences of older British people who return to the UK', Good Life in Practice/Practicing the Good Life Conference, Univ. Nova de Lisboa, Lisbon, 18 October.

Breuer, T. (2005) 'Retirement migration or rather second-home tourism: German senior citizens on the Canary Islands', *Die Erde*, 136: 313–33.

Buchdahl, E. (2013) 'Germans sending parents to nursing homes in Poland because it is cheaper, with one in five planning to do it', *Daily Mail*, 17 September. Online at: www. dailymail.co.uk/news/article-2423559/Grandma-export-Germans-sending-parents-nursing-homes-Poland-cheaper.html.

Connolly, K. (2012a) 'Germany "exporting" old and sick to foreign care homes', *The Guardian*, 26 December. Online at: www.theguardian.com/world/2012/dec/26/german-elderly-foreign-care-homes.

Connolly, K. (2012b) 'Germany's far-flung pensioners living in care around the world', *The Guardian*, 28 December. Online at: www.theguardian.com/world/2012/dec/28/germany-pensioners-living-care-world.

Cresswell, T. (2012) 'Mobilities II: Still', *Progress in Human Geography*, 36(5): 645–53.

Cresswell, T. (2013) 'Citizenship in worlds of mobility', in O. Soderstrom and D. Ruedin (eds), *Critical mobilities*. London: Routledge, 105–24.

Dallinger, U. and Eichler, A. (2010) 'Der graue Markt für Altenpflege – institutionelle Voraussetzungen und Ambivalenzen transnationaler Pflege', in H. G. Soeffner (ed.), *Unsichere Zeiten. Herausforderungen gesellschaftlicher Transformation*. Wiesbaden: VS-Verlag, 169–82.

Dowideit, A. (2012) 'Granny lives in Slovakia now', *VoxEurop*, 31 October. Online at: www.voxeurop.eu/en/content/article/2976711-granny-lives-slovakia-now.

Gatrell, A. C. (2011) *Mobilities and health*. London: Ashgate.

Glinos, I. A., Baeten, R., Helble, M. and Maarse, H. (2010) 'A typology of cross-border patient mobility', *Health and Place*, 16(6): 1145–55.

Godwin-Jones, R. (2012) 'Oma export': Communicating across cultures (blog), 31 December. Online at: http://acrosscultureweb.com/wp/?p=222.

Gulane, J. T. (2006) 'Retirement sector now a flagship program for Arroyo government', *Business World*, 31 May.

Huang, S., Yeoh, B. S. A. and Toyota, M. (2012) 'Caring for the elderly: The embodied labour of migrant care workers in Singapore', *Global Networks*, 12(2): 195–215.

Japan Cabinet Office (2008) 'White paper on the ageing society'. Heisei 20. Online at: www8.cao.go.jp/kourei/whitepaper/w-2008/zenbun/20index.html.

Japanese Ministry of Justice (2009) *Annual statistical report of exit and entry*.

Japanese Statistics Bureau (2006) *Heisei 18th Basic Survey on Social Life 2006* (平成18年度 社会生活基本調査 2006), Director-General for Policy Planning and Statistical Research and Training Institute of the Ministry of Internal Affairs and Communications. Online at: www.stat.go.jp/data/shakai/2006/index.htm.

Keller, A. (2012) 'Werden Alte ins Ausland abgeschoben?', *Wohnen im Alter*, November. Online at: http://news.wohnen-im-alter.de/2012/11/werden-alte-ins-ausland-abgeschoben-2/

Keller, A. (2013) 'ZDF Beitrag zur Pflege im Ausland', *Wohnen-im-Alter*, 25 January. Online at: http://news.wohnen-im-alter.de/2013/01/zdf-beitrag-zur-pflege-im-ausland/.

King, R., Warnes, T. and Williams, A. M. (2000) *Sunset lives: British retirement migration to the Mediterranean*. Oxford: Berg.

Kresge, N. (2013) 'Deutsche exportieren Omas nach Polen – Geschichte einer Familie', *Die Welt*, 20 September. Online at: www.welt.de/newsticker/bloomberg/article120205478/Deutsche-exportieren-Omas-nach-Polen-Geschichte-einer-Familie.html.

Löfgren, O. (2008) 'Regionauts: The transformation of cross-border regions in Scandinavia', *European Urban and Regional Studies*, 15(3): 195–209.

Long Stay Foundation (n.d.) www.longstay.or.jp.

Lopez, M. (2012) 'Reconstituting the affective labour of Filipinos as care workers in Japan', *Global Networks*, 12(2): 252–68.

Lutz, H. and Palenga-Mollenbeck, E. (2010) 'Care work migration in Germany: Semi-compliance and complicity', *Social Policy and Society*, 9(3): 419–30.

Mihm, A. (2013) 'Kein "Oma-Export" nach Osteuropa Der Deutsche lässt nur ungern im Ausland pflegen', *Frankfurter Allgemeine Zeitung*, 21 January. Online at: www.faz.net/aktuell/wirtschaft/menschen-wirtschaft/kein-oma-export-nach-osteuropa-der-deutsche-laesst-nur-ungern-im-ausland-pflegen-12031697.html?printPagedArticle=true#pageIndex_2.

Ministry of Tourism Malaysia (2014) 'Malaysia my second home programme statistics', personal communication.

Mowforth, M. and Munt, I. (1998) *Tourism and sustainability: New tourism in the Third World*. Abingdon: Routledge.

Ormond, M. (2014) 'Resorting to plan J: Popular perceptions of Singaporean retirement migration to Johor, Malaysia', *Asian and Pacific Migration Journal*, 23(1): 1–26.

Ormond, M. and Sothern, M. (2012) 'You, too, can be an international medical traveler: Reading medical travel guidebooks', *Health and Place*, 18(5): 935–41.

Oxlade, A. (2013) 'Why tomorrow's expats should choose Germany over Spain', *The Telegraph*, 28 June. Online at: www.telegraph.co.uk/finance/personalfinance/comment/10148585/Why-tomorrows-expats-should-choose-Germany-over-Spain.html.

de Pommereau, I. (2013) 'Exporting Grandma? Some German elderly head abroad for nursing care', *Christian Science Monitor*, 10 March. Online at: www.csmonitor.com/World/Europe/2013/0310/Exporting-Grandma-Some-German-elderly-head-abroad-for-nursing-care.

Posener, A. (2014) 'Deutschland wird Weltmeister im Oma-Export', *Die Welt*, 24 October. Online at: www.welt.de/kultur/article133590183/Deutschland-wird-Weltmeister-im-Oma-Export.html.

Prantl, H. (2012) 'Pflegeheime im Ausland Die verrückte Idee vom Greisen-Export', *Süddeutsche Zeitung*, 2 November. Online at: www.sueddeutsche.de/politik/pflegeheime-im-ausland-die-verrueckte-idee-vom-greisen-export-1.1512615.

Rainey, S. (2014) 'Has the sun set on the expat dream in Spain?', *The Telegraph*, 23 April. Online at: www.telegraph.co.uk/news/features/10782662/Has-the-sun-set-on-the-expat-dream-in-Spain.html.

Der Spiegel (2012) 'Teure Pflege: 400.000 Senioren können Altenheim nicht mehr zahlen', *Der Spiegel Online*, 27 October. Online at: www.spiegel.de/wirtschaft/soziales/hunderttausende-senioren-koennen-ihre-altenpflege-nicht-mehr-zahlen-a-863822.html.

Terlouw, K. (2012) 'Border surfers and Euroregions: Unplanned cross-border behaviour and planned territorial structures of cross-border governance', *Planning Practice and Research*, 27(3): 351–66.

Toyota, M. (2006) 'Ageing and transnational householding: Japanese retirees in Southeast Asia', *International Development Planning Review*, 28(4): 515–31.

Toyota, M. (2013) 'Japan: Elderly care in a transnational context', in Y. Li (ed.), *Global aging issues and policies: Understanding the importance of comprehending and studying the aging process*. Highland Heights, KY: Charles C. Thomas, 91–108.

Toyota, M. and Xiang B. (2012) 'The emerging transitional "retirement industry" in Southeast Asia', *International Journal of Sociology and Social Policy* 32(11/12): 708–19.

Wagner, C. and Verheyen, F. (2009) *TK in Europe: German patients en route to Europe*. Hamburg: Techniker Krankenkasse. Online at: www.tk.de/centaurus/servlet/contentblob/220638/Datei/2028/Europe-Survey-2009.pdf.

Wargas, R. (2012) 'Elderly Germans must move abroad to avoid high cost of living', *PJ Media*, 28 December. Online at: .http://pjmedia.com/tatler/author/robertwargas/.

Wendl, L. (2013) '"Oma-export" oder letzter Ausweg', *Senioren Zeitscrift*, 3: 53. Online at: www.senioren-zeitschrift-frankfurt.de/hintergruende/pflege-im-ausland/oma-export-oder-letzter-ausweg.html.

Williams, A. M. and Hall, C. M. (2000) 'Tourism and migration: New relationships between production and consumption', *Tourism Geographies*, 2(1): 5–27.

*Wohnen-im-Alter* (2011) 'Altenheime in Polen: Eine gunstige Alternative fur deutsche Senioren?' *Wohnen-im-Alter*, 25 September. Online at: http://news.wohnen-im-alter.de/2011/09/altenheime-in-polen-eine-gunstige-alternative-fur-deutsche-senioren/#sthash.wh3kZIYe.dpuf.

# 12 Home exchanging

## A shift in the tourism marketplace

*Antonio Paolo Russo and Alan Quaglieri Domínguez*

## Introduction

Exchanging homes has become a model of hospitality that represents an alternative to stays in commercial establishments for a steadily increasing number of tourists in the last decade. In a wider sense, though, it could be defined as a whole new concept at the crossroads of alternative tourism and the emerging paradigm of 'collaborative consumerism' (Botsman and Rogers 2010) or 'sharing economy' (Gold 2004), which has been triggered by the evolution of social networking and user-produced content in the 2.0 internet generation. It is also a phenomenon that sits well in the emerging research agendas on mobilities (Urry 2007) and on tourism as a form of mobilisation of places through the transience and negotiation of different populations.

Home exchange is not a new thing altogether: it emerged in the 1950s as a practice between friends and families especially in the UK and the USA, and has been growing significantly in the 1990s thanks to the appearance of the internet (Forno and Garibaldi 2011). However, it has been given little attention in research as an economic and social phenomenon, only to gain recent visibility in the wake of the increasing concern of the academy for the sharing economy. Thus, Forno and Garibaldi (2011) analysed the profiles and motivations of Italian swappers from a marketing perspective, while Andriotis and Agiomirgianakis (2013) proposed a conceptualisation of its economic nature. This chapter is concerned with the geography of home exchanging. Our main thesis is that this 'new' hospitality model is reconfiguring processes of attraction, place-making, and tourism practices at various scales. In the first place, it is bound to produce a shift from an industry-centred model of place-making, largely estranged from the host communities and germane to the development of dual tourism spaces *à la* Urry (1990), towards an alternative, unmediated community-centred model which offers greater opportunities for negotiation between hosts and guests. Second, the geographies of mobility implied by the house swapping model – by which suppliers and demanders are part of a peer community and all types of places are mobilised in both directions – implies a rupture in traditional core-periphery patterns of tourism.

This chapter is organised as follows. The next section proceeds to frame the growing popularity of home exchange practices into the broader wave of alternative hospitality models whose dynamics and organisation are founded on online social networking and global consumerism. It then sets out to discuss, at a conceptual level, the transformations of tourism mobilities brought about by the rise of house swapping, and formulates a number of working hypotheses that we then go on to test empirically. The third section presents the results of a statistical analysis of a large sample of listings in the www.homeexchange.com website, analysing the main trends in supply and demand of house swaps, as well as the principal patterns of 'matching' established within the swapping community. The chapter then discusses these results through the introduction of a schematic model that conceptualises peer-to-peer hospitality, of which house swapping represents the 'purest' case, as a 'marketplace' with shifting dimensions and agencies with respect to commercial tourism. Finally, we conclude by elaborating on the concept of house swapping as a potential catalyst of a new platform for mobility distinctively different from commercial tourism.

## Home exchange and network hospitality

The boom of peer-to-peer online platforms such as HomeExchange, CouchSurfing, and Airbnb has arguably led alternative models of hospitality to gain some centrality in the debate on current tourism trends. In this sense, it could be claimed that one of the main aspects is related to the opportunities enabled by the emergence of the Web 2.0 in terms of its capacity to disrupt the conventional hospitality supply chain. Drawing on the concept of 'network sociality', Germann Molz (2011) introduced the term 'network hospitality' to describe the advent of online networking systems for searching and/or offering accommodations, while Steylaerts and O'Dubhghaill (2011) refer to 'web-based hospitality exchange networks'. Both terms highlight the reticulate nature of the systems enabling the access to or the exchange of accommodation. The network evokes the multiplicity of players and the relations between them as alternatives to the more linear and mediated encounter between demand and supply proposed by the conventional hotel industry.

Home swapping web pages represent a community of peers interacting in order to temporarily exchange their houses without any third party mediation, or 'surrogate parents' (travel agents, couriers, hotel managers) that relieve them of responsibility and protect participants from the 'harsh reality' (Urry 1990: 7) and 'dangers and uncertainties' (Minca 1996: 126) entailed by the encounter with otherness. Given the transactional and symmetrical nature of exchange and the uniqueness of the item (the home of the hosts), negotiation is a central issue in home swapping. The simultaneous role of each member as host and guest entails a certain degree of flexibility in the time and (especially) spatial scale of the exchange.

If the operability of the Web 2.0 explains the emergence of home exchanging from a technical point of view (facilitating ubiquitous accessibility to digital platforms and the interactions between members), it could be argued that the boom of network hospitality is significantly related to motivational issues on the demand side. Thus, besides the practical aspect of saving on the costs of hospitality, the growth of the home-swapping phenomenon can be framed in a general reaction to the homogenising effect of globalisation on mobility landscapes, reflected in particular by the conventional hotel model (Germann Molz 2011; Steylaerts and O'Dubhghaill 2011).

For an increasing number of travellers, staying at another member's home is seen as the opportunity for experiencing domesticity 'away from home' and as an alternative to the impersonal and highly predictable settings of commercial facilities. In other words, swapping and other home-stay hospitality models would offer access to allegedly more 'authentic' (Steylaerts and O'Dubhghaill 2011) and personalised experiences. Unlike CouchSurfing and (in part) Airbnb, home exchange does not offer the opportunity for offline encounters with the local host member during the stay. Nevertheless, the embedding of the swapping experience in an everyday life environment is (and branded) to provide meaningful interactions with other representatives of the local community, such as next-door neighbours and local commerce, or the materiality of a 'lived environment' such as a home. Home swapping, it could be said, is thus not just about accommodation. Temporary living in a stranger's home could arguably imply a differential cognitive process of 'discovery' of a destination, and thus stimulate patterns of activity of the visitor at destinations that shift away from 'mainstream' tourism.

The largest swappers' website, HomeExchange, was established in 1992 out of the founders' 'belief in home swap as a comfortable alternative to high priced hotels and typical tourist vacations, and towards a way to experience an area as a local, not a tourists' (HomeExchange.com). It currently hosts more than 65,000 listings but has hosted throughout its period of activity more than 230,000. For a moderate annual fee, subscribers can upload information and pictures about their property, mostly first homes but also second homes or sections of a larger property. The information in the listings includes the location, type, size, sleeping capacity, and facilities of the houses, plus the main features of the areas or neighbourhoods where they are located. Cars and other transport means (bikes, boats, etc.) may also be offered or swapped together with homes. Members may indicate their list of 'wanted' swaps, which can include a specific place and/or period, a more generic indication of a region or city and the season, a type of property; or, as frequently happens, leave all that open to any proposals.

Visitors can scroll through large columns of listings in a given region or city (and even at neighbourhood level in big cities) to seek for the best matches, but the advanced search utility of the website also allows the user to filter for the various property features. Most exchanges are simultaneous, but if second homes are involved there is more flexibility with dates. The next section provides details on the swaps that are effectively concluded, but it is intuitive that whoever can offer attractive properties in the most desirable and upscale places gets the most propositions from which to select. Eventually the laws of supply and demand produce a sort of 'evening out' of property levels by which swaps are approximately in the same quality range, although properties in top destinations are more likely to swap with those of a higher standard in less attractive places, and vice versa. This pushes up the supply from popular destinations, as residents there may expect to have relatively high chances to swap on very good conditions.

In our research, we wish to test the hypothesis that home exchanging makes a difference in the way that tourists approach and select destinations. We assume that the practice of house swapping involves a switch away from a narrative focusing on the 'exceptionality' of tourist places towards one that hints at the attractiveness of mundane landscapes (Maitland 2008) built on negotiation between hosts and guests, of which the trust involved in swapping is possibly the most evident trait. From this point of view we could characterise swappers as a category of tourists that partake in the livelihoods of other groups of citizens – mostly 'mobile' cosmopolitan middle classes – with distinct patterns of spatial activity and place performance, as nuanced in Russo and Quaglieri Domínguez (2012). We also wish to test another hypothesis, brought in by a geographical perspective on house swapping. Traditional conceptions of the tourist space are built on duality, between cores and peripheries. This duality can be defined in purely spatial terms (Miossec 1976), but also in terms of economic, political, and even cultural power (Minca 2007). These perspectives differentiate between a powerful, 'travelling' northern and western world and destinations in the southern and the eastern 'pleasure peripheries': warm, welcoming, but needful, 'weak', and fictionalised though agency: a pattern that has been variously used in postcolonial critiques of global tourism but could easily apply within national systems in Italy, France, US, etc. Contrasting with this 'asymmetrical' world, the geographies of mobility supposedly involved in the house-swapping model – by which suppliers and demanders are part of a peer community, and all types of places are mobilised in both senses – may well imply a rupture in such traditional core-periphery patterns, both at the wider global scale and at the finer scale of the spatial organisation and specialisation of space within destination regions.

## The mobilities of home exchanging

In this section we look into the data on home swaps collected through the analysis and classification of information in 1,041 listings published (in May–June 2012) on the www.homeexchange.com website: 2.8 per cent of the total at the time at which this survey was carried out. This sample has been selected randomly, with the constraint that the breakdown by region of origin (location of the offering party) is similar enough so as to allow statistical inferences by regions based on the sample without the need of adjustment. For every listing, we collected and codified the information included in the sample as shown in Table 12.1.

The macro-regions by which we have subdivided the offer and the number of listings overall and in our sample are shown in Table 12.2. Thus, approximately half of the published listings (49.9 per cent) are located in European regions and concentrated to a very large extent in Western Europe. Europe is followed by North America, with 37.2 per cent of the listings (the US West and Pacific region alone counting for 16.4 per cent of the listings), and by Oceania, counting for

*Table 12.1* Variables collected and measured from the sampling of listings in www. homeexchange.com

| Variable | Data and classes considered |
|---|---|
| Location of offering party/ property | Coded by regions and macro-regions (as in Table 12.2) |
| Class of place | City centre; Suburban / resort town; Small city / town / village; Isolated / rural |
| Class of location | Coast / lake; Inland; Mountain; Island |
| Available sleeping capacity | 1; 2; 3-4; >4 |
| Prior exchanges | N. |
| Size of offering travelling party | 1; 2; 3-4; >4 |
| Auto offered | yes/no |
| Private pool available | yes/no |
| Exchange open to groups with children | yes/no |
| Demanded destination (places) x (x: 1...4) | Region and macro-regions coded as in supply locations |
| Demanded destination (class) x | Large city / national capital; Heritage city; Seaside resort town / island; Rural; Mountain |
| Demanded period or season 1 | High season / Low Season / Long duration |

*Table 12.2* Breakdown of listings published in sample and universe by regions and macro-regions.

| | Sample | | Total homeexchange.com | |
|---|---|---|---|---|
| | Frequency | Percent | Frequency | Percent |
| Northern Europe | 57 | 5.5% | 2.192 | 5.9% |
| Eastern Europe | 10 | 1.0% | 230 | 0.6% |
| South Eastern Europe | 8 | 0.8% | 191 | 0.5% |
| West-Central Europe | 279 | 26.8% | 10.336 | 27.9% |
| South Western Europe | 158 | 15.2% | 5.562 | 15.0% |
| TOTAL EUROPE | 512 | 49.2% | 18.511 | 49.9% |
| US Northeast | 70 | 6.7% | 2.292 | 6.2% |
| US Midwest | 9 | 0.9% | 333 | 0.9% |
| US South | 70 | 6.7% | 2.591 | 7.0% |
| US West & Pacific | 171 | 16.4% | 6.066 | 16.4% |
| Canada | 70 | 6.7% | 2.516 | 6.8% |
| TOTAL NORTH AMERICA | 390 | 37.5% | 13.798 | 37.2% |
| Central America (insular Caribbean) | 10 | 1.0% | 337 | 0.9% |
| Central America (non insular) | 17 | 1.6% | 647 | 1.7% |
| TOTAL CENTRAL AMERICA | 27 | 2.6% | 984 | 2.7% |
| South America | 15 | 1.4% | 573 | 1.5% |
| TOTAL SOUTH AMERICA | 15 | 1.4% | 573 | 1.5% |
| Africa North (Maghreb countries) | 4 | 0.4% | 72 | 0.2% |
| Rep. South Africa | 4 | 0.4% | 167 | 0.5% |
| South Eastern insular Africa | 4 | 0.4% | 64 | 0.2% |
| Sub-Saharan Africa & other African countries | 1 | 0.1% | 26 | 0.1% |
| TOTAL AFRICA | 13 | 1.3% | 329 | 0.9% |

*(continued)*

*Table 12.2* Breakdown of listings published in sample and universe by regions and macro-regions (Continued).

| | Sample | | Total homeexchange.com | |
|---|---|---|---|---|
| | Frequency | Percent | Frequency | Percent |
| Middle Orient | 4 | 0.4% | 142 | 0.4% |
| Indian peninsula | 1 | 0.1% | 27 | 0.1% |
| Central Asia | 1 | 0.1% | 1 | 0.0% |
| South Eastern Asia | 7 | 0.7% | 282 | 0.8% |
| China and neighbouring countries | 4 | 0.4% | 133 | 0.4% |
| Japan & South Korea | 1 | 0.1% | 15 | 0.0% |
| TOTAL ASIA | 17 | 1.6% | 600 | 1.6% |
| Australia | 53 | 5.1% | 1.906 | 5.1% |
| New Zealand | 11 | 1.1% | 335 | 0.9% |
| Oceania other countries | 2 | 0.2% | 56 | 0.2% |
| TOTAL OCEANIA | 66 | 6.3% | 2.297 | 6.2% |
| **TOTAL GENERAL** | **1.041** | **100.0%** | **37.092** | **100.0%** |

Source: Our elaboration of information published in www.homeexchange.com, last accessed 15 June 2012.

6.2 per cent. A first question that arises from this table is the degree of similarity of the homeexchange.com 'supply side' with the regional structure of the international tourism system, represented by the actual distribution of commercial accommodation, as illustrated in Table 12.3.

These differences hint at an important first fact in our analysis. Commercial accommodation is especially available in 'destination regions'. Rather than a tautology, this should be seen as the result of a process by which specific regions go through a process of discovery and infrastructure development, responding to a market opportunity determined by both demand pressure (with important

*Table 12.3* Supply of bed-places in macro-regions of origin.

| | Offered bed-places in homeexchange.com sample | | Available tourist bed-places as recorded in UNWTO statistics[a] | |
|---|---|---|---|---|
| | Estimated number | Percentage | Estimated number | Percentage |
| **Europe** | 2.443 | 48.5% | 14,762,651 | 35.9% |
| **North America** | 1.896 | 37.7% | 9,603,780 | 23.4% |
| **Central America** | 132 | 2.6% | 1,903,164 | 4.6% |
| **South America** | 78 | 1.5% | 3,908,103 | 9.5% |
| **Africa** | 68 | 1.4% | 1,500,525 | 3.6% |
| **Asia** | 89 | 1.8% | 8,695,786 | 21.1% |
| **Oceania** | 329 | 6.5% | 752,974 | 1.8% |
| **TOTAL** | 5.035 | | 41,126,983 | |

[a]Most recent available data. Missing data for 75 countries among which: Hong Kong, Japan, Malaysia, Montenegro, Republic of Korea, Singapore, Taiwan, Macedonia, United Arab Emirates, Tanzania, Vietnam

Source: Our elaboration of information published in www.homeexchange.com, last accessed 15 June 2012, and UNWTO (2012a).

variations determined by agency in the tourist industry) and political and entre-preneurial initiative. Yet in the case of the house-swapping system the parties demanding and offering accommodation are part of the same community and there is no commercial intermediation involved. This means that the localisation of supply represents by and large the spatial distribution of the community of swappers rather than portraying places where people want to go or that are fash-ioned as tourist destinations. This tends to over-represent the most populated places, and places where the cultural attitude towards swapping is more open, whereas it may under-represent 'tourist places': unlike accounts of the tourism infrastructure, it is a picture of demand rather than of supply.

It can be seen how Europe, North America, and Oceania offer a relatively wider supply of swaps than commercial beds, whereas destination regions like Latin America, Africa, and Asia are under-represented in the swapping community in relation to their commercial supply. In this sense, the Asian case is arguably exemplary. In fact, this continent has one-fifth of the global commercial supply, mainly in the two economic powers and regional tourism giants, Japan and China, while their representation in the homeexchange.com network is very limited. The cultural element also seems to matter: newcomers in the tourism market and places and societies where the sense of home and privacy imply a certain 'cultural resistance' (Forno and Garibaldi 2011) to swapping with strangers.

A glance at destinations that swappers query in their listings returns another important element, as illustrated in Table 12.4. It appears that the geographical distribution of 'wants' adheres to a higher degree to the distribution of commercial accommodation capacity. Within the community of swappers, the most solicited destinations are Europe, and within Europe especially Western Central Europe including countries like France and the UK, followed by North America, where the lion's share is represented by the Pacific West US and California in particular. These are followed by Oceania (with Australia getting the largest share), while South and Central America, Asia, and Africa get only a small share of preferences.

A more finely grained analysis addresses the main trends in the associations between destinations (available supply) and wishes (queried destinations). Concretely, for the sake of statistical reliability we focused on the eight countries with the highest numbers of homexchange.com members, namely the United States, France, Canada, Spain, Italy, Australia, the Netherlands, and the United Kingdom. We used 2010 outbound data from the UNWTO Compendium of Tourism Statistics (UNWTO 2012a) database for each of these countries expressed in terms of arrivals of residents to countries of destination. The latter were aggregated into our macro-regions and compared with the preferences expressed by swappers in our sample. It is important to note that the UNWTO data registers 'real' trips while the destinations mentioned by the swappers are just preferences for future possible exchanges. We deemed it useful to consider all queried destinations (a maximum of four for each user) and compare these with the actual flows in order to point out at least the most outstanding mismatches.

One of these is the significant appeal of Australia among swappers from several countries. This country is frequently mentioned among the destinations

Table 12.4 Solicited destinations in www.homeexhange.com and inbound tourism movement

| | Destinations indicated at least once in desiderata | | Total number of indications | | UNWTO Tourism movement dataa | |
|---|---|---|---|---|---|---|
| | Frequency | Percentage | Frequency | Percentage | Inbound visitors 2010 | Percentage |
| Northern Europe | 55 | 3.17% | 64 | 2.85% | 26.538 | 2.34% |
| Eastern Europe | 17 | 0.98% | 21 | 0.93% | 156.397 | 13.77% |
| South Eastern Europe | 31 | 1.79% | 32 | 1.42% | 78.918 | 6.95% |
| West-central Europe | 432 | 24.93% | 619 | 27.56% | 189.884 | 16.72% |
| South Western Europe | 345 | 19.91% | 522 | 23.24% | 108.819 | 9.58% |
| TOTAL EUROPE | 880 | 50.78% | 1.258 | 56.01% | 560.556 | 49.37% |
| US Northeast | 134 | 7.73% | 149 | 6.63% | | |
| US Midwest | 14 | 0.81% | 15 | 0.67% | 59.793 | 5.27% |
| US South | 70 | 4.04% | 91 | 4.05% | | |
| US West & Pacific | 150 | 8.66% | 207 | 9.22% | | |
| Canada | 70 | 4.04% | 78 | 3.47% | 16.095 | 1.42% |
| Non spec. North America | 68 | 3.92% | 68 | 3.03% | | 0.00% |
| TOTAL N.AMERICA | 506 | 29.20% | 608 | 27.07% | 75.888 | 6.68% |
| Central America (insular Caribbean) | 36 | 2.08% | 42 | 1.87% | 19.694 | 1.73% |
| Central America (inland) | 44 | 2.54% | 48 | 2.14% | 30.697 | 2.70% |
| TOTAL C.AMERICA | 80 | 4.62% | 90 | 4.01% | 50.391 | 4.44% |
| South America | 49 | 2.83% | 52 | 2.32% | 22.616 | 1.99% |
| TOTAL S.AMERICA | 49 | 2.83% | 52 | 2.32% | 22.616 | 1.99% |

| | | | | | | |
|---|---|---|---|---|---|---|
| North Africa (Maghreb countries) | 14 | 0.81% | 14 | 0.62% | 32.991 | 2.91% |
| Republic of South Africa | 16 | 0.92% | 16 | 0.71% | 8.073 | 0.71% |
| South Eastern insular Africa | 4 | 0.23% | 4 | 0.18% | 1.74 | 0.15% |
| Sub-Saharan Africa & other African countries | 3 | 0.17% | 3 | 0.13% | 22.354 | 1.97% |
| TOTAL AFRICA | 37 | 2.14% | 37 | 1.65% | 65.158 | 5.74% |
| Middle Orient | 8 | 0.46% | 10 | 0.45% | 42.046 | 3.70% |
| Indian peninsula | 6 | 0.35% | 6 | 0.27% | 8.707 | 0.77% |
| Central Asia | – | 0.00% | – | 0.00% | 7.62 | 0.67% |
| South Eastern Asia | 30 | 1.73% | 39 | 1.74% | 73.203 | 6.45% |
| China and neighbouring countries | 9 | 0.52% | 9 | 0.40% | 200.323 | 17.64% |
| Japan & South Korea | 20 | 1.15% | 20 | 0.89% | 17.41 | 1.53% |
| TOTAL ASIA | 73 | 4.21% | 84 | 3.74% | 349.309 | 30.76% |
| Australia | 67 | 3.87% | 75 | 3.34% | 5.885 | 0.52% |
| New Zealand | 31 | 1.79% | 31 | 1.38% | 2.512 | 0.22% |
| Oceania other countries | 10 | 0.58% | 11 | 0.49% | 3.102 | 0.27% |
| TOTAL OCEANIA | 108 | 6.23% | 117 | 5.21% | 11.499 | 1.01% |
| **TOTAL number of indications** | **1.733** | **88.2%** | **2.246** | **90.7%** | **1,135,416** | |
| **Open to any destinations** | **231** | **11.8%** | **231** | **9.3%** | | |

aMost recent available data. Missing data for 27 countries

Source: Own elaboration of data from sampling of listings in homeexchange.com and UNWTO, 2012b.

sought by members from the Netherlands (15 per cent), Canada (12 per cent), United States (7.4 per cent), and United Kingdom (7.4 per cent); the actual arrivals of residents from these countries to Australia, however, represents respectively 0.18 per cent, 0.4 per cent, 0.63 per cent, and 1.2 per cent of the total outbound trips. The United States and Canada also score high in swappers' queries, with a significant increase over the destinations chosen by Europeans in commercial tourism. For instance, more than one-third of the users from France (38.6 per cent), Italy (35.0 per cent), and Spain (38.1 per cent) express an interest for swapping in the US, while just a little over the 3 per cent of the outbound trips from these countries have the US as destination. Instead, 7.4 per cent of the British residents travelled there in 2010, while more than half of the swappers from the UK expressed a wish for exchanging homes with the US. About a half of users from the US (45.9 per cent), Canada (53.4 per cent), and Australia (50.0 per cent) quote at least one destination belonging to the Central-West European macro-region, but these shares respectively shrink to 38.9 per cent, 34.5 per cent, and 27.3 per cent of users in relation to queries for swaps in the South-Western European region.

That does not necessarily mean that closer destinations are neglected. For instance, the Central-Western and the South-Western European macro-regions are rather popular among European swappers. As these regions record the highest demand among the whole swapping community, this trend is likely to be influenced more by the attractiveness of the region itself than by geographical proximity. Nevertheless, the comparison of the two indicators considered in this analysis hints at a higher significance of three main intercontinental flow axes in home exchanging, namely those connecting Central-Western and South-Western Europe with North America and Australia, and those between the latter regions, while popular but closer destinations in the rest of the Mediterranean or in Asia are relatively under-considered. Figures 12.1 and 12.2 compare graphically the main (potential) flows of swappers and those related with all the outbound tourists from two countries concentrating the highest number of users and representing two specific cultural landscapes of the Western world: the US (Figure 12.1) and France (Figure 12.2).

To refine the analysis of the patterns of 'matching' we have considered the demand for a given location showcased in a listing in terms of the number of exchanges concluded in the past. *A priori*, this indicator would depend upon the quality characteristics of the property (both in terms of its features and amenities and in terms of location in a specific destination) and upon the relative 'scarcity' of properties on offer with those same characteristics. All other things being equal, however, it would proxy the 'realised attractiveness' of places (as opposed to an ideal, *a priori* attractiveness as expressed by users' declared preferences with respect to destinations). The results confirm the strength of the main destinations detected through the analysis of the swappers' preferences, although some differences concerning their ranking can be singled out. Western-Central Europe confirms its primacy: indeed, this is the area where the largest number of swaps took place (27 per cent of all prior exchanges considered). It is followed by South-Western Europe (16.3 per cent) and the West-Pacific area of the United

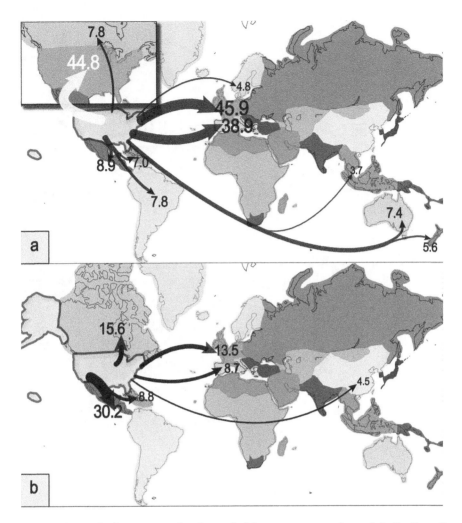

*Figure 12.1* Main flow patterns by share of visitors to macro-regions of destination of (a) house swappers from the US (declared preferences) and (b) registered outbound tourists from the US.

Source: Own elaboration of data from sampling of listings in homeexchange.com (retrieved 15 June 2012) and UNWTO (2012a)

States (10.8 per cent). After that, the North-Eastern US region – the fourth area most frequently mentioned among the preferred destinations – is surpassed, with 4.2 per cent of the swaps concluded by the Southern US region (9.6 per cent), Oceania (7.2 per cent), Northern Europe (5.4 per cent), and Canada (4.3 per cent).

At the country level, the United States (26.2 per cent) and France (18.2 per cent) confirm their leadership as tourism destinations (respectively second and

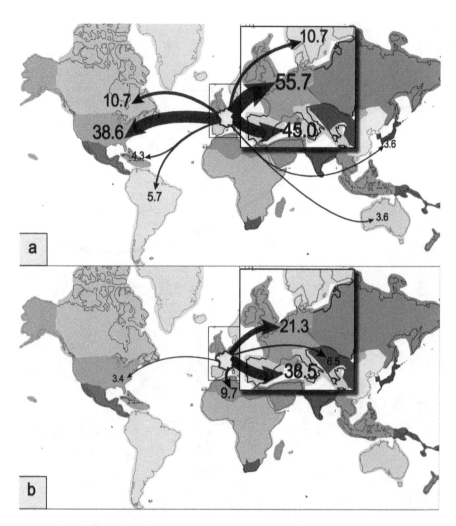

*Figure 12.2* Main flow patterns by share of tourists to macro-regions of destination of (a) house swappers from France (declared preferences) and (b) registered outbound tourists from France.

Source: Own elaboration of data from sampling of listings in homeexchange.com (retrieved 15 June 2012) and UNWTO (2012a).

first in world destinations in terms of international arrivals as noted by the UNWTO 2012a). Particularly significant is the popularity of Australia where 1 in 20 exchanges (5.2 per cent) takes place, while the country is not even among the top 40 destinations according to the UNWTO international arrivals ranking. Instead, China, third in that ranking, confirms its marginal role in the swapping community. Besides, we have seen that if the data from UNWTO shows in several cases higher travel rates to closer destinations, as is to be expected, the analysis of preferred swapping destinations highlights a comparatively high demand for faraway destinations. This is not necessarily an outstanding fact in tourism: people long for exotic and iconic places, but not everybody has the resources or the time to actually travel there. The significant fact is that home exchanging, to some degree, allows people to realise their dreams, because of the saving in accommodation costs that it implies. As a matter of fact, being fully aware that expressing a desire for a destination does not necessarily turn into a real trip, we can state that intercontinental destinations are relatively more valued among the specific community of swappers than the actual distribution of 'commercial' trips may suggest, and among these, some clear origin-destination patterns emerge.

There are various possible explanations to this. One might be the cultural proximity and flows that relate countries like France and UK with their overseas territories or former colonies, which to some extent the home exchange system facilitates, establishing a dialogue between parties who may share a common linguistic or cultural domain. Other reasons (especially for the stratification of origin–destination flows) may relate to the characteristics of the exchanges that are proposed. While the features of properties offered and of the offering party do not vary sensibly across the sample, cross-analysing origins with the type and location of places offered yields some useful insights. Hence, unsurprisingly, the large majority of properties on offer are located in metropolitan areas (65 per cent of the sample). A very similar concentration is obvious looking at demand data in terms of prior exchanges (64.9 per cent). Within macro-regions, 'urban' properties are more frequent in Western and Northern Europe, as well as in the US North-East, and Canada, whereas South-Eastern Europe, the US South, and Pacific West are more frequently featuring coastal and suburban developments.

Interesting matches in flows can be observed between types of places exchanged (offered and requested). In this case we do not have to pay too much attention to the merely 'potential' nature of desiderata, as the data indicates a general trend: if somebody wants to stay in a seaside resort and cannot find a perfect match in terms of location, they are likely to conclude a swap in a similar type of destination elsewhere. Thus, we note that swappers offering (and mostly residing in) central city locations are consistently (also in a statistical sense, with a Pearson test indicating a 1 per cent significance value) looking for other urban destinations, whether in large urban areas, national capitals or heritage cities. Offers in suburban communities and resort destinations are more likely to seek exchanges in coastal and island resorts. Similarly, swappers offering rural, island, or isolated settings are more likely to be looking for similarly non-urban locations. This, again, is not a banal finding. Traditional sociological theory indicates that the need or the desire to 'escape' represents a central push factor for holidaying (Edensor 2001; Cohen 2010) also in term of locations chosen as destinations. A 'break in the routine' for urbanites means vacation in coastal resorts or rural settings, whereas people with properties in such settings are expected to long for an experience of life in the city.

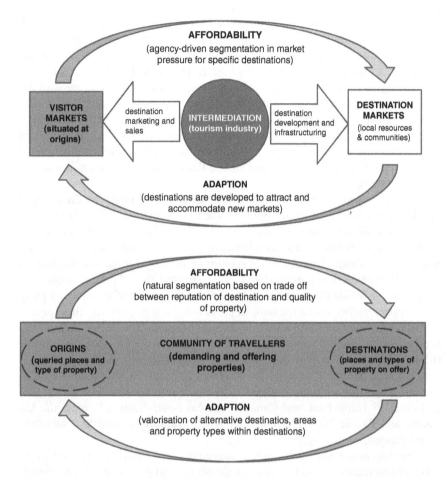

*Figure 12.3* Alternative models of the home exchange marketplace and its dynamics: commercial tourism (above) and home exchanges (below).

In our community of home exchangers, however, experiences of place and tourism cultures seem to be pushing in the opposite direction.

We can make sense of these results when we nuance how the home exchange 'marketplace' actually works, based on previous conceptual knowledge on tourism drivers and effects, but also on the most relevant insights from this research, as illustrated in this section. We consider both the structure – the characterising elements that constitute demand and supply and their transactional logics and channels – and the evolutionary dynamics of the marketplace: that is, how, faced with a constant evolution of demand and supply (in terms of socio-demographic trends, technology, etc.), the agencies of tourism develop new opportunities for such matching. Thus commercial tourism (see Figure 12.3) abides to a 'mainstream' model by which the key components of the marketplace are demand – constituted of pools of actual or potential travellers – and supply, which can be understood either in terms of places to be visited or in terms of the infrastructure that makes them an actual destination. The tourism industry intermediates this marketplace, first by ensuring that places are equipped to receive tourists on profitable conditions, and second by developing distribution chains that connect demand markets and supply. However, demand and supply structures shift continuously. The agency of the tourism industry fosters those changes to unearth new opportunities for business. It does so through marketing destinations in ways that select markets according to their capacity to pay, the result of which is that more 'elitist' destinations are offered to markets that can afford those higher costs. On the other side, the industry 'makes space' for increasing numbers of visitors through physical and symbolic development of incumbent and novel spaces which are fashioned up as tourist destinations. Thus, destination development is the result of a constant dynamic adaptation between affordabilities and growth; the 'soft' agency of marketing and the 'hard' agency of construction ensure that opportunities for tourism are always available and commercialised to all existing and potential demand markets.

The marketplace of home exchanges – the purest model of peer-to-peer hospitality – functions in an altogether different way, illustrated in the lower part of Figure 12.3. First, its structure is constrained by community. There is no 'supply' and 'demand', or at least they cannot be ontologically separated: a party can be a supplier only if it is simultaneously a customer. Moreover, 'demand' and 'supply' agents cannot be separated from the places in which they live – there is only a degree of flexibility in cases where second homes are exchanged. Thus we have, ontologically, only a separation between places offered for swaps and places that accept swaps. The agents that produce a matching and a transaction are, however, remarkably different, because such a transaction is not of an economic nature – it does not become 'business'. When destinations achieve high occupancy rates for the properties offered there, there is no new development: markets get segmented and transactions regulated on the base of property qualities – either inherent or contextual ones – but also, as we have seen in our study, on the basis of elements of cultural proximity between exchanging parties. On the other side, adaptation does not mean new development but rather that new places are popularised as 'alternative' locations – both destination regions and sites that can offer attractive features to exchangers (profiled above as 'expert' cultural explorers) and new places within destinations that provide the type of properties and amenities sought by such collectives, which are typically residential.

These two forces mean that home exchange develops as a force that remaps tourist places, from the centre to the periphery, in all senses. As we have seen in our research, what is now substantially a 'Western affair' is bound to mobilise cosmopolitan middle classes across the globe in a condition of parity: the most popular places can be increasingly visited only if the 'periphery' is also visited, both locally and globally. The impacts of home exchanging at destinations have been explored by Russo and Quaglieri Domínguez (2014), exclusively in terms of the activation of alternative areas within two emblematic tourist cities

(Barcelona and Paris). Further research is needed to make sense of such shifts also in relation to other network hospitality models (Airbnb, CouchSurfing, etc.).

## Conclusion

In this chapter, we have presented a glimpse of an alternative tourism model that could be characterised as a 'dream world', where networking and collaborative consumption are strongly reducing the agency of mediation, and tourism development is almost exclusively driven by existing opportunities and untradeables. The main results of our analysis can be summarised in the following points. The users' location and the main flow patterns identified suggest that the swapping phenomenon is very much a 'Western affair', for the time being. Cultural aspects seem to matter in this regard, in terms of the conception of home and the degree of tourism 'maturity'. At the same time, Western countries appear more suitable and accessible – for Western swappers at least – for experiencing individually a destination without the mediation support and the 'safety net' of the tourism industry; in other words, 'like a local'. In this regard, it could be argued that Western societies have been more deeply affected by the spread of global patterns of consumption and standardised everyday spaces and landscapes. Therefore, it seems that this process, described by some as McDonaldisation (Ritzer 1993), produces both the premises and the conditions for home swapping. On the one hand, it would push experienced tourists to claim for non-standardised accommodation and more personalised experience of the territory; on the other hand, increasing numbers of travellers seem able and willing to approach these destinations autonomously. This is thanks to the proliferation of familiar 'moorings' (Hannam *et al.* 2006) that make destinations – even out of tourist precincts – 'legible' to a global audience and reduces the perceived riskiness and unpredictability of the territory.

Another point we discussed based on the available data is that property availability to some extent 'forces' swappers towards regions with a high concentration of other swappers, so origin–destination flows take place mostly within the Western world. Moreover, the comparative analysis of users' preferences in terms of destinations and outbound tourism for the main countries has shown that in general swappers are much more inclined to long-range travel as compared to the global demand. Particularly significant are the flows between Western Europe and North America and from these two macro-regions to Australia and New Zealand: expensive trips, especially for large travelling parties; but economising on accommodation costs can make such travel much more affordable.

Our final remarks regard the degree of 'desirability' of home exchanges over commercial tourism, and the possible insights on the foreseeable evolution of tourism models in the future. In our study we suggested that home exchanges may be activating alternative places and area types as tourist spaces, which is one of the mantras of tourism policy and planning in mature tourist destinations. Moreover, the 'non-intermediated' nature of home exchanges is certainly welcome to the extent that it reduces the agency of commercial actors and capital in general in the restructuring of places, their meanings and collective identities. Authors who have studied the construction of tourist places (for instance, Judd and Fainstein 1999; Gill 2000) claim that this process of 'harmonisation' is not without its consequences for destinations, both in terms of new opportunities for – and unwanted effects on – socio-economic development, and in terms of how change makes places more or less attractive at subsequent stages of development, as in life-cycle theories (Agarwal 2002). It may then be argued that in a 'home-exchanging world' that does not involve the industrial intervention of the tourism industry in filling this need gap, places could be more resilient to the externalities and impacts provoked by tourism development.

The non-monetary nature of house-swapping 'transactions', indeed, is a central point of this argument. The absence of profit excludes the intervention of commercial actors and the processes of 'standardisation' of the urban landscape that generally drive large-scale operations – thus its alleged loss of authenticity (see Ponzini *et al.* 2016). It must be noted that the emergence of alternative strategies of tourism development and new actors are not alien to such processes, as demonstrated in relation to the operation of Airbnb by Arias Sans and Quaglieri Domínguez (2016). However, in the case of a 'pure' peer-to-peer model, it is not likely that house swaps alone fulfil the demand to visit specific places. Thus to some extent the mainstream and the alternative hospitality systems should be seen as complementary, with the latter possibly leading to a slower-paced and perhaps more sustainable process of place development, more genuinely 'negotiated' between communities. In the future, we may expect the home-exchanging system to keep growing, but also to become more specialised in terms of involving specific audiences and their peculiar needs, for instance on a regional or cultural basis.

## References

Agarwal, S. (2002) 'Restructuring seaside tourism: The resort lifecycle' *Annals of Tourism Research*, 29(1): 25–55.

Andriotis, K., and Agiomirgianakis, G. (2013) 'Market escape through exchange: Home swap as a form of non-commercial hospitality' *Current Issues in Tourism*, 17(7): 576–91.

Arente, H. and Kiiski, V. (2005) 'Tourist identity expression through postmodern consumption: A focus on the home-exchange phenomenon' unpublished dissertation. Göteborg University, Göteborg.

Arias Sans, A. and Quaglieri Domínguez, A. (2016) 'Placing network hospitality in urban destinations: The case of Airbnb Barcelona' in A. P. Russo and G. Richards (eds), *Reinventing the local in tourism*. Clevedon: Channel View.

Botsman R. and Rogers, R. (2010) *What's mine is yours: The rise of collaborative consumption*. New York: Harper Collins.

Cohen, S. (2010) 'Searching for escape, authenticity and identity: Experiences of "lifestyle travellers"' in M. Morgan, P. Lugosi and J. R. B. Ritchie (eds), *The tourism and leisure experience: Consumer and managerial perspectives*. Bristol: Channel View, 27–42.

Edensor, T. (2001) 'Performing tourism, staging tourism: (Re)producing tourist space and practice' *Tourist Studies*, 1(1): 59–81.

Forno, F. and Garibaldi, R. (2011) 'Andare in vacanza scambiando la casa. Una casa del profilo e delle motivazioni di un segmento crescente di turisti' *Rivista di Scienze del Turismo*, 2(2): 87–112.

Germann Molz, J. (2011) 'CouchSurfing and network hospitality: "It's not just about the furniture"' *Hospitality and Society*, 1(3): 215–25.

Gill, A. (2000) 'From growth machine to growth management: The dynamics of resort development in Whistler, British Columbia' *Environment and Planning A*, 32(6): 1083–104.

Gold, L. (2004) *The sharing economy: Solidarity networks transforming globalisation*. Aldershot: Ashgate.

Grit, A. (2008) 'An analysis of the development of home exchange organizations' paper presented at the 26th EuroCHRIE conference, 6–9 October 2014, Dubai.

Hannam, K., Sheller, M. and Urry, J. (2006) 'Editorial: Mobilities, immobilities and moorings' *Mobilities*, 1(1): 1–22.

Homeexchange.com (2015) *About HomeExchange.com™, the World's #1 Home Exchange Site*. Online at: www.homeexchange.com/en/about/ (accessed 12 March 2015).

Judd, D. R. and Fainstein, S. S. (1999) *The tourist city*. New Haven, CT: Yale University Press.

Maitland, R. (2008) 'Conviviality and everyday life: The appeal of new areas of London for visitors' *International Journal of Tourism Research*, 10(1): 15–25.

Minca, C. (1996) 'Lo Spazio turistico postmoderno'. In VV.AA. Il Viaggio – dal grand tour al turismo post-industriale, Atti del Convegno Internazionale – Roma 5–6 dicembre 1996. Naples: Magma, pp. 123–33.

Minca, C. (2007) 'The tourist landscape paradox' *Social and Cultural Geography*, 8(3): 433–53.

Miossec, J. M. (1976) *Elements pour une theorie de l'espace touristique*. Centre des Hautes Études Touristiques, Aix-en-Provence. Serie C, n. 36.

Ponzini, D., Fotev, S. and Maravacchio, F. (2016) 'Place-making or place-faking? The paradoxical effects of transnational circulation of architectural and urban development projects' in A. P. Russo and G. Richards (eds), *Reinventing the local in tourism*. Clevedon: Channel View (forthcoming).

Ritzer, G. (1993) *The McDonaldization of Society*. Thousand Oaks, CA: Pine Forge Press.

Russo, A. P. and Quaglieri Domínguez, A. (2012) 'From the dual tourist city to the creative melting pot: The liquid geographies of global cultural consumerism' in M. Smith and G. Richards (eds), *Routledge handbook of cultural tourism*. London: Routledge, 324–31.

Russo, A. P. and Quaglieri Domínguez, A. (2014) 'La lógica espacial del intercambio de casas: una aproximación a las nuevas geografías de lo cotidiano en el turismo contemporáneo' *Scripta Nova* XVIII(483). Online at: www.ub.es/geocrit/sn/sn-483.htm.

Steylaerts, V. and O'Dubhghaill, S. (2012) 'CouchSurfing and authenticity: Notes towards an understanding of an emerging phenomenon' *Hospitality and Society* 1(3): 261–78.

UNWTO (2012a) *Compendium of tourism statistics, data 2006–2010*. Online at: www.e-unwto.org (accessed 20 May 2012).

UNWTO (2012b) *Tourism highlights, 2012 edition*. Online at: http://mkt.unwto.org (accessed 15 June 2012).

Urry, J. (1990) *The tourist gaze*. London: Sage.

Urry, J. (2007) *Mobilities*. Cambridge: Polity.

# Part III
# Development

# 13 Travelling beauty

## Diasporic development and transient service encounters at the salon

*Lauren Wagner*

### Introduction: diasporic transience as 'development'

For post-migrant generation Moroccans from Europe, the annual summer holiday in Morocco might be discursively characterised as a 'return' visit to a 'homeland' – more specifically, to the homes and localities of extended family there. Other researchers have approached what individuals from similar family histories of migration do during visits to a homeland as 'diasporic tourism' (Coles and Timothy 2004; Basu 2007; Reed 2014), focusing on activities of cultural or heritage consumption and how 'the Diaspora' participates in 'Development'. While many examples describe configurations of diasporic-ness in various homelands that become instrumental in purposeful, directed Development (cf. Markowitz and Stefansson 2004; Scheyvens 2007; see also Berriane 1992; Stafford *et al.* 1996; Berriane and Popp 1999 on Morocco), participants in my research only seldom pursued such explicitly 'cultural' activities referred to in this directed heritage 'Development'. Rather, they were often pursuing leisure consumption of everyday facilities – in many ways 'dwelling-in-mobility' in this second-home environment (Haldrup 2004; Veijola and Falin 2014) – that focused more on restful, embodied leisure than cultural consumption.

For these individuals – whose parents or grandparents migrated from Morocco to France, Belgium, or the Netherlands, and who were born and/or raised in that European 'homeland' – visiting Morocco is indisputably a 'return' to somewhere familiar to them, as they generally 'returned' annually throughout their childhoods. Their access to these leisure activities often intersected with, and were facilitated by, their 'diasporic-ness' – as in, their capacities and attributes as repeat, diasporic visitors in Morocco, who can speak 'local' languages and understand some 'local' forms of lifestyle consumption (Wagner 2011, 2015). Yet, like many diasporic community members worldwide, that form of 'return' is effectively as a familiar visitor, which I call 'diasporic visitor' (DV), and involves travel and tourism mobilities beyond those precipitated by migratory flows. They were often acting both as 'locals' and as 'tourists': visiting as ('Moroccan') 'locals' in some ways, they bring along with them ('European') 'non-local' habits of doing and being, and are continually negotiating how to do 'being local but mobile' in their interactions with each other, with local residents, and with non-Moroccan visitors.

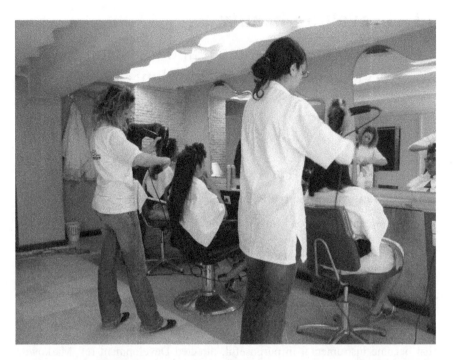

*Figure 13.1* Three women getting their hair blow-dried before going back to the Netherlands, 27 May 2008, Marrakech.

This chapter explores one context where these negotiations are repeatedly enacted by DV women: the beauty salon. By focusing on visits to the salon, I want to open space for thinking about diasporic development that is not cultural consumption or purposeful interventions for 'development', but nevertheless constitutes 'development' precipitated on diasporic connection, enacted through transient presence, and with potentially important economic and social impacts. I argue that this development happens through a combination of the repeated cyclical presence, ordinary leisure consumption, and specific configurations of belonging relevant to this mass of Moroccan diasporic visitors. This combination emerges in service encounters – like those in salons – that tend to perpetuate geographically inflected inequalities between Morocco and Europe through positionings between 'local', 'immobile' service provider and 'mobile', 'elite' diasporic consumer. These service encounters are both a boon to an economy that focuses on tourism as a source for development (in a space that is not widely available to tourists who may not know how to find it), and also possibly a source of negative effects experienced by providers of emotional labour, whose value becomes comparatively less as a trusted expert and more that of an interchangeable service provider.

To interrogate these dynamics of complexly diasporic development, I will discuss various ways in which salons have the potential to create space for community, through ethnographic analyses about their specific iterations in Morocco – first from Susan Ossman's (2002) theorisations on salons as part of their situated and globally connected neighbourhoods, then from my own descriptions of diasporic visitors. Next, I outline how the practices of DV women seeking beauty treatments at salons take place as a negotiation of geographically inflected attributes of mobility, balancing the value created by the skill of individual stylists against the comparative price value of generic services between homelands. Together, these sections evoke how the dynamics of the activity 'going to a salon in Morocco' are specifically iterated for many DV women who choose to do so, and indicate some ways that these dynamics might impact the potential for diasporic development through socio-economic relationships.

## Salons: beauty services and encounters

In her book *Three Faces of Beauty* (2002), Susan Ossman compares beauty salons in Paris, Casablanca, and Cairo to explore how stylists and clients locally enact beautification with reference to other places as much as to the immediate surroundings. The salons she describes in Casablanca become sources for beauty knowledge and advice – sites where clients can find the latest magazines as well as trained professionals replicating the styles seen in them – and a continuously recombining community where women from a neighbourhood might see and interact with each other semi-regularly. The beauty professional of the salon becomes a trusted adviser over time and repeated visits, as someone whose skills in creating beauty are priced at a value related to her ability to attract clients over repeat visits. Taking salons as a context of both interaction and consumption, we can recognise how they are spaces of cooperative transformation and (ideologically) beautification of clients' bodies, as well as spaces of encounter between persons involved directly or peripherally in that transformation.

In terms of creating valuable beauty, salons are complex, dynamic, and primary actors in creating consumption through the body by converting economic capital to physical capital (Shilling 2004). The labour they house – of transforming clients into something beautiful along their perceived standards – may be considered a necessity as much as it might be a luxury or indulgent pleasure. This physical capital, as an 'improvement' of the body, becomes more than tangible as a commodity service: it is both visually perceivable as beauty that stays temporarily on the body, and affectively sense-able through the experience of being touched and caressed in the process of beautification and the concomitant production of a state of relaxation and 'improvement'. The creation of capital that can command a price, in this case, relies on the service encounter interaction between actors, where, despite its intangibility, the affective state as commodity can be immensely important to its continued value (Kang 2003; Wharton 2009).

Ossman's work also reflects the important parallel functions of spaces where beauty is produced in the Muslim world as spaces of encounter between women, construing possible intimacies outside of the home. Specifically, these spaces involve exposing parts of the body that may be subject to other regulations of gendered gazes (Llewelyn-Davies 1977; Fernea 1988), and are often socially and materially organised to facilitate this intimate space outside of the home. In Morocco, salons for women, like *hammams* (communal baths) for both genders, tend to be enclosed from public view and staffed by members of the same gender as their clients. Women entering them are therefore able to expose aspects of their bodies – their hair, their arms and legs, or in the case of *hammams* their entire bodies down to underwear – with the understanding that these time-spaces are only accessible to other women. They become 'safe' spaces where women can share, gossip, and develop friendships beyond their immediate social networks of families or neighbours.

Framing salons in parallel to *hammams* as sites for semi-regular and semi-familiar interaction between women while consuming beauty as a commodity contrasts how spaces of beauty and wellness are commodified for the temporary visitor. In line with seeking cosmetic surgery or other elective medical procedures – or, indeed, other forms of 'transformational' encounter found through long-distance travel (Reisinger 2013) – spa and wellness services are increasingly a motivation to visit certain places. These services and practices can be ideologically typified as 'local' commodities, produced and embedded within specific regions or lifestyles. This type of consumption is not at all uncommon in Morocco, particularly in Marrakech (Williams 2010), where many hotels provide *hammams* as an extra service for guests; and increasing numbers of *hammams* are opening city-wide that provide a mediated, tourist-friendly experience of 'local' customs for communal bathing. Of course, these businesses translate the 'local' practice into something more easily practised by 'non-local' bodies – without the presence of any 'local' customers, and often charging more than ten times the 'local' price. Implicitly, also, these spaces for non-local consumption are not sites where one might encounter others repeatedly, on one's 'regular day' to go to the *hammam* or standing appointment for beauty services; rather, each client might be expected to come once in her lifetime, or perhaps regularly on a much longer cyclical timescale, in line with her long-distance travel habits.

As such, the salon practices of participants in this project deviate significantly from the dynamics of salons as Ossman portrays them. They may still be sites of expertise on beauty, but they are arguably more similar for DVs to a generic 'salon' than a stylist–client relationship: each salon is more or less interchangeable, as a service provider of the commodity of 'beauty', embodied as transportable physical capital that women can feel during the experience and take with them when they exit. Exchanging economic capital for physical capital becomes both a way of spending one's time in leisure pursuits and a kind of souvenir-gathering in preparation for return to the real world.

## Going to a salon at 'home'

The salons I visited with DV women were parallel sites to those Ossman describes; the encounters between participants, however, illustrate different influences. This section presents some observations from a larger project using multi-sited, 'follow the people' ethnography as a method, in which I had different durations and intimacies of contact with approximately 100 DV participants, both during and in-between their summer holidays. Many of the more intimate and longer duration contacts were with groups of women, especially through the three main families (A, B and C) involved in the project (see Wagner 2011 for further details about the participants).

The day after arriving by car from Belgium to their home in Tangier, the women I travelled with in family B – Malika, my main contact, and her sister Souad, along with myself – sought out a salon:

*The next day, today, we woke slowly and without [husband] again ... Souad [wife] had expressed an interest in getting her hair done and Malika also wanted to get a pedicure (as did I). Malika suggested that she and I go out alone, so that then we could watch the kids while S went alone later, but Souad suggested we all go together and take the kids (which meant, in the absence of the car, 2 taxis). It was 11 before we were all dressed and out the door, and [husband] arrived back at that moment. He drove us to the street where Malika knew a salon and took the kids on a ride while we all went for services.*

*The hair salon didn't have a nail person, and we had a half-hour wait until the stylist was finished. Souad took a couple of pictures of us waiting there – a behaviour I thought at the time seemed like something only a person on holiday would do, take a picture at the hair salon, before remembering that I did it too. After looking at magazines a while, I suggested that Souad and I go to the other salon the stylist knew down the road to do our pedicures. It was the first time she did one. The first price they gave us was 70 Dh (7 euro), which I complained was too expensive, then she (greeter?) suggested we could have it done by students, using a word that neither Souad nor I got exactly until she translated with 'stagiare', for only 30 Dh (3 euro). We both preferred that, so we headed downstairs to the school part of the salon.*

*The students were young, maybe 16, 18, but not so much younger than other women I've seen doing this work. We didn't chat with them, but chatted to each other in English mostly. Souad's girl was wearing a skin mask and asked another student to help her so she could finish more quickly. The three, plus another sitting in the room, were chatting intermittently about what they needed to do in the afternoon, which Souad listened to but I didn't.*

*I finished first, and discovered Malika upstairs waiting. She hadn't been let downstairs because it was too late to do hers, but came down with me after I paid for me and Souad. By that time, our appointed meeting with [husband] was coming close, so Souad and I rushed to the other salon so she could do her hair, and I went back to the patisserie meeting place to tell [husband] to come back later. He told me to come to his parents' house after.*

*I went back with his daughter, who hung around while her mom was getting blow-dried. Malika had told her this morning, you mustn't speak in Dutch, you must speak Arabic or they will raise the prices. She didn't say much in the shop.*

*When we went back to find Malika, she had made an appointment with one
of her students for a full massage the next day.*

(Field-notes, 16 July 2008)

This account indicates several key aspects to the activity of 'going to a salon' that
are part of what makes it a relevant, and possibly important, site to examine for DVs:

1    It involves choosing and prioritising the leisure of certain family or group
    members over others; in this case, Souad and Malika were balancing their
    roles as caretakers of children with their desire to enjoy their own embodied
    leisure.
2    It is desirable enough to pursue despite logistical barriers, like the problem
    of finding transportation that was solved above by the husband's return.
3    Being in a salon involves a significant investment of time (30 minutes to sev-
    eral hours), and along with that many potential social interactions between
    co-present individuals, from within a group of friends to the stylists and
    salon employees to other customers waiting for or receiving services. These
    interactions inevitably require linguistic and cultural skills on the part of
    DVs, in order to be adequately and appropriately friendly and polite in rela-
    tion to the context. The length of time spent there further raises the stakes for
    maintaining 'correct' salon behaviour, as a 'Moroccan' interlocutor.
4    It requires the 'local knowledge' of the 'right' price – this may be achieved
    through repetition of these visits over the years, or asking a friend what she
    paid for the same service, but can often be confusing because the pricing
    level is radically different between Europe and Morocco.
5    Finally, the salon visit takes place at certain times during the holiday – upon
    arrival or before leaving – indicating that it engages a mobile form of physi-
    cal capital that is to be displayed in the next location. That is, one invests
    time, effort, and money into going to the salon in order to look and feel good
    for the immediately following days and activities, whether in Morocco or in
    Europe.

My field-notes are dotted with visits to salons throughout the summer, in different
locations and with different women, that I witnessed or were recounted to me
after the fact, that reiterate these points:

*17 March, Marrakech: Last minute before leaving, Yasmine, Saliha, and
their Algerian friend stop at a salon on the way back to the hotel and on to
the airport. Yasmine gets a blow-dry and the other two get manicures; the
stylist has to call a friend in to help with the volume of customers.*

*27 May, Marrakech: After finishing the interview, I go with Fouzia and two
of her friends to have their hair blow-dried before they depart for the airport. Fouzia complains because her stylist repeatedly interrupts to answer
his phone, and they are in a hurry (Figure 13.1 above).*

*2 June, Marrakech: During their week-long visit Yasmine takes her French friend to the salon for epilation, then returns after her friend leaves for a blow-dry.*

*14 June, Marrakech: Rabia apparently spent four hours at a salon the day before, getting her hair coloured, shampooed, and cut, also manicure (and pedicure?) and epilation. Two years ago this cost 400 (€40), now it was 1040 (€104). They have separate prices for each individual service and tally them up at the end.*

*22 July, Al Hoceima: During my visit with (veiled) Amina, we stop in to have her hair blow-dried, which becomes a communication task, as none of the women in the busy salon seem to speak Tarifit and she is struggling with Derija.*

*7 August, Marrakech: Sanae and I stop by the salon around 9pm one night for services, shortly before her return to Belgium.*

The repetition of this practice, across many DV participants, demonstrates how 'going to the salon' is an ordinary activity that DV women may choose to do on holiday – whether they were on family trips to their home towns (Tangier or Al Hoceima), or on more explicitly leisure trips with friends (generally in Marrakech). These visits frequently occurred immediately before returning to Europe, and were often characterised by participants as being motivated by the impending departure – like a task that needed to be done before leaving. They were also often sites of negotiation – about the value of speeds and prices of services and of linguistic engagements between the diasporically resident European-Moroccans and the locally resident salon professionals.

Choosing this activity over all other possibilities for using one's precious hours of summer vacation indicates how it has developed a specific niche for DV women visiting Morocco. Broadly, it is an activity that intersects with general ideas about 'being on holiday' and consuming embodied leisure or wellness (Smith and Kelly 2006; Reisinger 2013), as well as boosting one's physical capital as a distinctive consumer (Shilling 2004) by consuming comparatively cheap embodied services. This consumption is not unlike the 'body capital' acquired through cross-border cosmetic surgery (cf. Viladrich and Baron-Faust 2014) – which is carried as embodied, 'beautified' wellness back to Europe. More specifically to this case, the preponderance of this activity speaks to how DVs negotiate 'doing being Moroccan from Europe', as individuals who can both move through 'local' environments with some knowledge about languages and practices of interaction and consume those environments like 'tourists' who have access to higher incomes abroad.

## Value in geography: cheap, 'Moroccan' services

In thinking about how diasporic visiting might contribute to development in a place like Morocco, these practices indicate how service domains and the possibilities for face-to-face engagement they create can have a profound influence on how locally and diasporically resident individuals engage with each other, and how those engagements come to characterise their mutual recognition. While these women are prioritising the accumulation of physical capital at the salon as a holiday activity, the way they do it is strikingly different from the long-term relationship that Ossman describes of residents visiting these same salons. DVs, as mobile consumers, create a new demand for services that differs from resident women: they may not be as interested in creating relationships as in the monetary and physical value of specific salon labour tasks that are interchangeable across geographically inflected providers. In other words, one motivation for DV consumers is the geographical location of these salons across a cost-of-living border that they are able to cross relatively easily through their diasporic mobilities. Unlike other visitors, they have the capacities necessary to locate these 'local price' services; unlike many resident Moroccans, they can afford to pay for more services because they are comparatively cheap.

DVs' ability to access these salons relates both to their practised ability to read how businesses are semiotically indicated in a 'Moroccan' landscape and to their potential preferences for enclosure in beauty practices. While only one of the women I accompanied to the salon was veiled, and would therefore be specifically sensitive to a gender-enclosed environment for cutting her hair, all of them knew how to recognise the storefront for a salon on the street. As an enclosed space, Moroccan salons for women never have transparent glass shopfronts, and are often located on the upper floors of a building, where their inner rooms are certainly not visible by passers-by. Looking for a service activity that is purposefully hidden means being able to read the semiotics of signposting on the street and to have some awareness of where to look for those signs. This semiotic familiarity might be a barrier for other visitors, like a 'tourist' who would be equally interested in inexpensive beauty; it is one of the ways that the *'hammam'* experience is mediated for tourists in the simple gesture of advertising where and how to find it.

Beyond that first requirement of being able to access this service time-space, there is the important geographical value in mobility between Morocco and Europe. These women were also very explicitly motivated, as they explained to me, by price differential between services across geographical locations. The entire range of services available in these salons is priced between a quarter and a half of what is paid for the same service in Europe. The comment by Rabia (see the 14 June example above) about the price she paid for the full gamut of services in Marrakech speaks to her own expectations – about 40 euro for everything she had on her last visit, instead of the 104 euro she paid this time – and to the way prices are rising dramatically in Morocco. Still, she is willing to pay for those services on her Moroccan holiday: over her week-long stay with her husband and young son, it was part of her dedicated leisure time to visit the salon for a few hours.

The geographical value of the stylist diverges from Ossman's description, particularly in that for these clients these professionals are not 'experts' as much

*Figure 13.2* 'Mouna', one of the more heavily signposted salons I saw, was located on a main
           street in Marrakech. While the signs attempt to draw your attention, you would
           have to look up to notice it, and also search on the side street to find the entrance.

as interchangeable service providers. In the example above, Fouzia was annoyed
by her stylist because he answered his phone during her blow-dry, causing her
delay. She expressed her annoyance, particularly because her friends were both
finished ahead of her, and they were all due to catch a bus to the airport soon after –
bound by time constraints related to her position as 'traveller'. Having her hair
blow-dried was evidently both a commodity she was taking home from her travels and a human-powered service she expected to conform to her schedule. That
hierarchical prioritising of client over provider might shift if Fouzia was engaged
in a long-term repetitive relationship with this stylist, to accommodate more
mixture between professional performance and personal needs (Kang 2003). In
light of the fact that this was her first and most probably last visit to this salon – it
was her first exceptional visit to Marrakech, and she was unlikely to return soon –
her priorities are to accomplish the activity in a limited amount of time, rather
than build familiarity and a rapport with the stylist as a person.

These discourses and encounters indicate a central ideology of 'cheapness' in
services that pervades this practice. Although these DV women do not seem to
intentionally demonstrate their economic capital in this kind of consumption, it is
inevitably on display: because they see these services as bargain-priced, their
consumption is extravagant, while for most locally resident Moroccan women
such intensive consumption would be economically difficult. They take on roles
as itinerant consumers, seeking only the service rendered and not investing in a
relationship beyond that. DVs can then become inadvertently one-dimensional to
the locally based salon workers, as 'upper-class' consumers who show off their

wealth in their careless spending, then disappear only to (perhaps) return a year later. These kinds of socio-economic encounters can, as demonstrated by Kang (2003), perpetuate relationships that devalue labour and perpetuate stereotyping and distinctions between groups on either side of the service encounter. Particularly in light of the descriptions by Ossman (2002), Llewelyn-Davies (1977), and Fernea (1988) of the centrality of relationships created in beauty spaces in Morocco, the potential for these encounters to perpetuate the distance between stylist – who themselves are generally 'ordinary' residents – and DV women may contribute to broader social distinction between residents and diasporic community members.

The way that these encounters play out reflects the geographical time and space dimensions of value that make them work. To the extent that DV women are 'Moroccan', they can appreciate the specificities of finding and going to a salon as it is practised in Moroccan space. They might choose to go to a non-local-oriented salon, but can also find the 'local' salon if desired. Their geographical mobility often means that they do seek the 'local' salon, simply because services there are cheaper than they would find at home. That geographical mobility, however, does seem to create specific ripples on how the encounter between client and stylist plays out, as being one that can potentially build over regular visits, or one that, given the uncertainty of future visits to that city, may never be repeated.

### Transient service encounters: diasporic development?

Collectively, the above vignettes describe some of the aspects of 'going to a salon' that makes it part of the diasporic holiday. Friends on holiday together make it one of the activities on their itinerary, as an embodied sign of the leisure capital they can acquire before returning home. Busy mothers entrust fathers with childcare so they can spend a larger block of time on self-indulgent beauty. Overall, this practice can be framed as a leisure service encounter, where DV women spend their discretionary capital on embodied beauty that is significantly cheaper in Morocco than in Europe. In this light, the practice comes to parallel other forms of wellness and transformational tourism, as a means to acquire affective states and embodied quality of life through travel.

Yet, because of the specific geographical and migratory contexts involved, this practice is also implicated in questions of how the 'Moroccan diaspora' from Europe, who continue to visit Morocco year after year, participate in developing this 'homeland'. As a behaviour motivated by a search for 'cheap' value, as well as one that involves face-to-face interaction with a professional (whose skill level may or may not be verifiable), going to the salon perpetuates roles between diasporic visitors and local residents as consumer and service provider. Simultaneously, it perturbs the presumed 'local' relationship that might develop if this service was a regular and repeated interaction. These visits to a salon, while they might be characterised as incidental or last-minute activities, are one of the central ways in which DVs and local residents encounter each other, and need to be considered as one substantial site where diasporic development happens.

# References

Basu, P. (2007) *Highland homecomings: Genealogy and heritage tourism in the Scottish Diaspora.* London and New York: Routledge.

Berriane, M. (1992) 'Tourisme national et migrations de loisirs au Maroc (étude géographique)', Rabat: la faculté des lettres et des sciences humaines.

Berriane, M. and Popp, H. (eds) (1999) *Le tourisme au Maghreb: Diversification du produit et développement local et régional,* Tanger: la Faculté des Lettres et des Sciences Humaines – Rabat.

Coles, T. and Timothy, D. J. (eds) (2004) *Tourism, diasporas and space.* London and New York: Routledge.

Fernea, E. W. (1988) *A street in Marrakech: A personal view of urban women in Morocco.* Long Grove, IL: Waveland Press.

Haldrup, M. (2004) 'Laid-back mobilities: Second-home holidays in time and space', *Tourism Geographies,* 6(4): 434–54.

Kang, M. (2003) 'The managed hand: The commercialization of bodies and emotions in Korean immigrant-owned nail salons', *Gender & Society,* 17(6): 820–39.

Llewelyn-Davies, M. (1977) 'Some Women of Marrakesh.' Film. *Disappearing world.* Royal Anthropological Institute: ITV.

Markowitz, F. and Stefansson, A. H. (eds) (2004) *Homecomings: Unsettling paths of return.* Lanham, MD: Lexington Books.

Ossman, S. (2002) *Three faces of beauty.* Durham, NC: Duke University Press.

Reed, A. (2014) *Pilgrimage tourism of diaspora Africans to Ghana.* New York: Routledge.

Reisinger, Y. (ed.) (2013) *Transformational tourism: Tourist perspectives.* Wallingford: CABI.

Scheyvens, R. (2007) 'Poor cousins no more: Valuing the development potential of domestic and diaspora tourism', *Progress in Development Studies,* 7(4): 307–25.

Shilling, C. (2004) 'Physical capital and situated action: A new direction for corporeal sociology', *British Journal of Sociology of Education,* 25(3): 473–87.

Smith, M. and Kelly, C. (2006) 'Wellness tourism', *Tourism Recreation Research,* 31(1): 1–4. doi:10.1080/02508281.2006.11081241.

Stafford, J., Bélanger, C. E. S. and Sarrasin, B. (1996) *Développement et tourisme au Maroc.* Montréal: Harmattan.

Veijola, S. and Falin, P. (2014) 'Mobile neighbouring', *Mobilities,* ahead of print. DOI:1 0.1080/17450101.2014.936715.

Viladrich, A. and Baron-Faust, R. (2014) 'Medical tourism in tango paradise: The internet branding of cosmetic surgery in Argentina', *Annals of Tourism Research,* 45(1): 116–31.

Wagner, L. (2011) *Negotiating diasporic mobilities and becomings: Interactions and practices of Europeans of Moroccan descent on holiday in Morocco.* Doctoral thesis, London: University College London. Online at: http://discovery.ucl.ac.uk/1317815/.

Wagner, L. (2015) 'Shopping for diasporic belonging: Being "local" or being "mobile" as a VFR visitor in the ancestral homeland', *Population, Space and Place,* ahead of print. doi:10.1002/psp.1919.

Wharton, A. S. (2009) 'The sociology of emotional labor', *Annual Review of Sociology,* 35(1): 147–65.

Williams, G. (2010) 'The 31 Places to Go in 2010: #16. Marrakesh', *New York Times,* 7 January, Travel section. Online at: http://travel.nytimes.com/2010/01/10/travel/10places.html?pagewanted=all.

# 14 Orphanage tourism and development in Cambodia

## A mobilities approach

*Tess Guiney*

## Introduction

It is perhaps more true than ever that contemporary society is a 'society on the move' (Lash and Urry 1994). Globalisation has increased movement between regions and nations in unprecedented numbers and international tourism is now a common practice. The 1990s are described as the beginning of the mobility 'turn' in social sciences. Since then, there has been a rapid development in literature concerned with the importance that mobility has upon individuals and society (Adey 2006; Urry 2008; Cresswell 2010a; Duncan 2012; Cohen and Cohen 2015; Coles 2015; Thulemark *et al.* 2014). As Sheller and Urry describe, there has traditionally been a tendency within social science to ignore, trivialise, or uncritically investigate 'the importance of the systematic movements of people for work and family life, for leisure and pleasure, and for politics and protest' (2006: 208). Mobilities literature, in contrast, argues that mobility and movement are 'at the center of constellations of power, the creation of identities and the microgeographies of everyday life' (Cresswell 2010a: 551). Tourism is increasingly seen as interwoven within 'everyday life' (Franklin 2006; Edensor 2007; Hannam 2008), or what can be considered within lifestyle mobility (Duncan 2012).

Development is a dynamic field that has gone through major transition within recent decades (Potter *et al.* 2008; Willis 2011). Although there is a long history of development work in the Global South, development was initially conceptualised in the wake of World War Two. It has become an important aspect of modern society, with aid campaigns and development iconography a common fixture (Manzo 2008; McGregor 2008; Potter *et al.* 2008; Nathanson 2013). However, more recently development is becoming a phenomenon of the untrained, short-term, often young tourists, within society (Telfer and Sharpley 2008; Palacios 2010; Baillie Smith and Laurie 2011; Vrasti 2013; Mostafanezhad 2014). This shift in development mobilities from organisations trained in such practices towards a burgeoning tourism phenomenon has encouraged unprecedented numbers to travel to the Global South in the name of development. Through Cresswell's (2010b) description of the significance of mobilities within everyday life, this mobility within tourism development can be seen as having a profound impact upon both the communities they act within and the tourists themselves. Framed within the lens of tourism development mobilities, this chapter presents findings from four months of fieldwork on orphanage tourism in Cambodia. Highlighting the importance of individual actors within development trajectories through orphanage tourism, I examine how the data gathered illustrates development tourism within a niche environment and is indicative of a burgeoning field in international mobility. The explosion of 'new' tourism, especially volunteer tourism, illustrates this desire to give back while on holiday, which has its roots in ideas of development. As Sheller and Urry (2004: 5) explain:

> There are not two separate entities, 'tourism' and 'mobilities', bearing some external connection with each other. Rather they are part and parcel of the same set of complex and interconnected systems, each producing the other. There is a proliferation of countless discourses, forms, and embodiments of tourist places and tourist performances.

By only considering such practices within the field of tourism, the importance of notions of development are often ignored. These practices are often based on dual motivations, incompatible in many ways, of tourism (principally enjoyment) and development (conceptualised here as helping others/communities or for sustainability projects). There has been recognition of the diverse range of activities that different forms of tourism can include, even when considering a specific aspect or age range (Heath 2007; Duncan 2014). Within tourism literature it has been common to consider distinct cohorts or practices as separate. However, here I draw from Cresswell's arguments that mobility is 'particular patterns of movement, representations of movements, and ways of practising movement that make sense together' (2010b: 18) to consider tourism development mobility in a more cohesive way. What may seem like distinct tourism trends (e.g. gap years, volunteer tourism, poverty tourism), can be considered within a framework of development mobilities to and with the Global South. In addition, a mobilities lens enables an examination of the fluid identities within tourism development, outlining the shift between tourist, volunteer of staff member that many experience.

## The growth of mobility

Mobilities has garnered significant attention in recent decades within the social sciences, although as Cresswell and Merriman explain, 'geographers are not coming to mobilities anew but are revisiting an old friend' (2011: 4). They point to Crowe's 1938 call for geographers to study 'men and moving things', but indicate how this call did not garner significant attention except from within spatial science and their focus on costs, with migration and transport geography also important considerations (Cresswell 2010a). The 'new mobilities paradigm' is concerned with a range of movements, at all scales, from the everyday spaces and practices of walking, to themes such as migration, tourism, and refugees (Cresswell 2010a; Cresswell and Merriman 2011). Canzler, Kaufmann, and Kesselring (2008: 2) argue that although the 'new mobilities paradigm' has been heavily criticised, it 'emphasizes the changing constellations and configurations of mobile and stable elements in modern socio-material contexts. It is a paradigm of mobilities and immobilities, fluidities and stabilities.' For example, within tourism, it has been argued that mobility is not experienced equally by all and there is an inequality as to who can move (Cresswell 2010b; Duncan 2014; Thulemark 2014). Nevertheless, mobility has dramatically increased and has become a common experience for many (Edensor 2007; Hannam 2008).

Mobility is underpinned by globalisation, which has allowed certain forms of mobility to flourish for certain people, such as tourists from the Global North, but it is also constituted with ideas of place-making (Duncan 2012). Flows have increased dramatically as transport has increased; however, by simply looking at flows the motivations that prompt them are not revealed: 'Most notably, they do not tell us to what extent these flows are the result of a social system of opportunities and constraints that are more open than in the past' (Canzler *et al.* 2008: 5). Cadman argues that tourism is not 'simply personal, individual, or local' (2009: 459); rather, tourism reflects a wider network of practices that are produced within society and are thus fluid and constantly changing (Cresswell 2012).

The tourism development agenda incorporates a range of tourism practices, with volunteer tourism, the fastest-growing niche tourism form, at the forefront of this agenda (Brown and Morrison 2003; Harlow and Pomfret 2007; McIntosh and Zahra 2007). It is seen as an altruistic, sustainable, and mutually beneficial form of tourism by many (Wearing 2001; Lyons and Wearing 2008; Hitchcock *et al.* 2009). As Duncan argues, 'tourism, whether seen as temporary mobility, a privileged form of mobility or as part of the everyday, cannot be separated from larger social, political, economic and cultural processes' (2012: 115). Mobility is about more than just movement, it is about movement being meaningful both socially and culturally, and is linked to social change (Urry 2007; Oakes and Price 2008; Cresswell 2010b). Sheller and Urry explain: 'Tourism is not some "pure" leisure activity only conducted within Mickey Mouse's special kingdom' (2004: 6); 'new' tourism is emblematic of an even more pronounced shift away from ideas of 'pure' leisure. Tourism development is intimately tied to wider processes within society, and research has reflected the neoliberalised nature of tourism development mobilities (Baillie Smith and Laurie 2011; Georgeou 2012; Vrasti 2013; Mostafanezhad 2014). Mostafanezhad explains that this 'expansion of volunteer tourism is more than the latest trend in alternative travel; it is a cultural commentary on the appropriate response to global economic inequality' (2014: 2).

From this perspective, it becomes clear that orphanage tourism is not a spontaneous development, but rather one steeped in moral and cultural notions of what it means to be an active and moral global citizen (Vrasti 2013; Vrasti and Montsion 2014; Mostafanezhad 2014). Tourism development, Hannam argues, has created professionalisation and institutionalisation of power-knowledge relationships: 'this has allowed the state to "remove from the political realm problems which would otherwise be political" (Escobar 1984: 387–88), and then to recast them into the apparently more neutral realm of tourism management for "experts" to consider' (2002: 231). The privatisation and moralisation of development has created a perception that to be a responsible global citizen one needs to volunteer (Baillie Smith and Laurie 2011; Baillie Smith *et al.* 2013; Lyons *et al.* 2012).

## A case study of development through orphanage tourism

This chapter utilises primary data collected at 53 orphanages in Cambodia. Tourism development within orphanages is illustrative of the burgeoning trend of tourism within development projects internationally (Tomazos and Butler 2010, 2012; Reas 2013a, 2013b, 2015; Proyrungroj 2014). Study participants worked for, managed, or volunteered at orphanages in a range of Cambodian cities and towns including Phnom Penh, Battambang, Siem Reap, Takeo, Kampong Cham, Banteay Meanchey, Kampong Speu, and the wider Kandal province. Individual or pair interviews were conducted, utilising a semi-structured interview format to foster fluidity (Coll and Chapman 2000; Adams 2012; Stewart-Withers *et al.* 2014). The research is based upon the perspectives of 86 participants. Participants included 43 orphanage staff members (including founders, managers, directors, and volunteer/communication liaisons), 36 international volunteer tourists, and two representatives from NGOs providing education to orphans within a community. From three organisations that oppose orphanage tourism, seven staff members were interviewed. To protect the anonymity of research participants, all names in the chapter are pseudonyms.

All volunteers who participated in interviews were from so-called Western nations (Australia, New Zealand, Austria, Germany, England, Ireland, Scotland, America, Sweden, and France). There were no specific criteria for participation in the study for volunteers, rather convenience sampling (Patton 2002) provided the most representative means of recruitment in a field where spontaneous volunteering is common, and often this is done through direct contact with orphanages rather than sending organisations. Volunteer participants were located on-site within orphanages, either while conducting participant observations at orphanage performances or when interviews with orphanage directors were conducted at orphanages. The exclusively Western citizenship of volunteers is illustrative of their dominance in South-East Asia (Conran 2011), and indeed within voluntary travel more generally (Sheller and Urry 2004). Some orphanage representatives who were too busy to conduct interviews also put me in contact with long-term volunteers who were now considered staff members, illustrating the fluid and often blurred definitions of volunteers versus staff members (discussed later in this chapter). There were six such volunteers/orphanage employees. Volunteer length ranged considerably, from two or three days to those mentioned above who were now considered staff members.

## Tourism development as dynamic mobility: tourist, volunteer, staff?

At its heart, development is a field concerned with the advancement of society in some way, or implies goodwill activities, where 'individuals offer their services to change some aspect of society for the better' (Callanan and Thomas 2005: 184). Such ideas have held currency for an extended period, with there being a traditional belief that the nobility had a duty towards the weak and unprivileged (Tomazos and Butler 2008). However, more prominent forms of volunteerism have been present since World War Two and the destruction that it created. In 1960 then Senator John Kennedy encouraged University of Michigan students to live and work in poor, remote nations throughout the world to serve their nation, with the Peace Corps being created as a result. Peace Corps is an especially prominent example of this push towards volunteering on an international scale and has seen nearly 220,000 American volunteers sent to 140 countries since 1961, with operations continuing in 64 nations (Coverdell 2014).

Development theory has altered considerably since its first articulation in the 1950s and the theory of modernisation and top-down development approaches, which focused on overall economic growth and often led to greater inequality (Potter *et al.* 2008). Tourism development can be seen as closely aligned with ideas about development as those who participate – organisations and volunteers – perceive that improvements can be achieved via this mechanism. Nevertheless, the incompatibility between such leisure-based mobility and development has been questioned. When discussing gap year experiences in developing countries, Simpson (2004) describes how organisations construct an image that values the 'get on with it' attitude to development. This is in stark contrast to the shift in development theory that values strategic project planning and has recently shifted to more participatory approaches to development. As Hannam suggests, 'both tourism development and tourism development research could be perceived as not necessarily strategies that solve underdevelopment; rather they combine in creating a subdomain of development that is politically, economically, culturally and environmentally manageable for a variety of agencies and structures' (2002: 232). Volunteer tourism, gap years, those who initially volunteer and then become quasi-staff members, and budget travellers who include some form of 'giving back' while on holiday can be considered within the frame of tourism development. Often considered an 'alternative' tourism form, such mobility is interwoven with ideas of morality and ethical travel (Butcher 2003, 2009; Mustonen 2007; Barnett *et al.* 2010; Duncan 2014).

Traditionally tourism and development have often been conceptualised and explained as distinct practices or hybrid subjects and therefore literature has often reflected this separation, with discussions of tourism and development then drawing upon both (Hannam 2002). Hannam argues that there is a growing need for tourism to be increasingly theorised, which has arguably been significantly addressed (Tomazos and Butler 2008; Vodopivec and Jaffe 2011; Vrasti 2013; Mostafanezhad 2014). Nevertheless, currently there still exists much disconnect between ideas of volunteer tourism and development and therefore of a general tourism development theorisation. There is significant literature on volunteer tourism (Wearing 2001; Guttentag 2011; Vrasti 2013; Mostafanezhad 2014) and the overlap between this and development is evident (Simpson 2004). For tourism development, it is important to understand the dynamic nature of the phenomenon and therefore to adopt a flexible approach when considering what constitutes tourism. A good example of this is the edited volume by Sheller and Urry (2004) and the usefulness of mobilities when conceptualising what is tourism. As Sheller and Urry explain: 'Tourism mobilities involve complex combinations of movement and stillness, realities and fantasies, play and work' (2004: 1). Because mobilities literature incorporates ideas from a range of fields (anthropology, geography, economics, cultural studies, migration studies, tourism, sciences and communication, transport studies) the usefulness of it for examining tourism development is that it is possible to illustrate the crossover between tourism, development, and tourism development, which are often considered separately. As Cresswell explains: 'Mobility has a wide theoretical purchase because of its centrality to what it is to be in the world. This fact connects forms of movement across scales and within research fields that have often been held apart' (2010a: 551).

Volunteer tourism at orphanages, as with all projects, cannot be thought of as a cohesive group. Not only does the type of activity differ, but duration of project varies, and skill level and age requirements also change. A significant target market for charities in developing countries is 'gappers', that is, gap-year participants, usually taking a break after school or university (Callanan and Thomas 2005; Hopkins 2010). Tourism development is commonly practised particularly often by those aged between 18 and 25 (Vrasti 2013) or under 30 (Heath 2007). Indeed, within my own research 58 per cent were 18–25 years of age, with 83 per cent between 18 and 35. Once considered a marginal activity, a gap year is now considered a rite of passage, although one necessarily for the relatively privileged (Jones 2004; Simpson 2004; O'Reilly 2006; Lyons *et al.* 2012; Heath 2007; Ansell 2008). Such excursions commonly go into developing nations, most often for between three and 12 months (Simpson 2004; Ansell 2008; Hopkins 2010). Gap years are often organised through sending organisations and the increasing number of these is illustrative of this burgeoning mobility form. However, in Cambodia there is a tendency to avoid sending organisations as they charge participants large sums of money, while little is received by the local orphanage. Many volunteers become disillusioned with this. Amanda, a 23-year-old volunteer from the US on her second trip to the same Cambodian orphanage, initially volunteered through a sending organisation but decided to return to Cambodia under her own steam the following year because the majority of the money does not reach the local organisation, and sending organisations often provide very little once the volunteer is in country. When asked about her experience with the sending organisation, Amanda stated, 'it's like $2,500 for the first two weeks and then like about $500 after that per week. And so I mean I paid like $5,000 for my stay here and [the orphanage] got $100 a week of that.'

Nevertheless, tourism development includes a far greater range than what would be considered gap years or young travellers. Development tourists can be middle aged or retired and either volunteer as part of a holiday or specifically travel to a location in order to volunteer at a particular organisation or for a particular cause. Within my own research there were notable exceptions; a number of volunteers were retired or semi-retired, while some still worked in their origin nations but visited Cambodia several times a year in the hopes of contributing to a specific organisation. Several volunteers were unhappy in their current employment, or had experienced a significant upheaval in their life, and were volunteering as a break or in-between a career change. For many younger volunteers this was also not their first time at the orphanage: three were on their second trip, while another three were on their third visit; this disrupts some common assumptions about gap-year tourists and their extremely transient nature. Indeed, Amanda, quoted above, was so positive about the orphanage she volunteered at as part of an organised project that she returned for six months the following year on her own. Other volunteers were extremely dedicated to ideas of development, and unlike gap years did not treat volunteering at a Cambodian orphanage as a temporary opportunity, but rather as a stepping stone into development work, either at the centre they were working at or elsewhere.

Not all mobility can be considered fixed; transnationalism of the privileged (in contrast to precarious migrants with limited resources) is becoming more frequent and contradicts previously taken-for-granted assumptions about tourists, migration, citizens, and belonging (Smith 2001; Jackson *et al.* 2004; Hannam 2008). Duncan discusses this with reference to backpacker tourists, who often hold multiple identities while travelling: 'these individuals' working and travelling experiences allow them to explore both the personal and professional possibilities that are bound up in the broader social networks associated with contemporary practices of mobility' (Duncan 2012: 116). Although principally discussing tourists to developed countries, tourism development contains similarly fluid mobility. By conceptualising different forms of mobility within distinct disciplines (Cresswell 2010a), such as tourism or migration, there is a failure to reflect the often fluid nature of movement and the dynamic and sometimes spontaneous progression within it (Duncan 2012). This fluidity operates over multiple levels as well. For example, gap years have been identified as a diverse group, from planned trips to those identified as drifters: 'the drifter ideal is one of little or no advance planning, allowing word of mouth and serendipity to influence the itinerary' (O'Reilly 2006: 1001). For some, visiting an orphanage was not a consideration before arriving in Cambodia; others, although they intended to volunteer at an orphanage, often stay far longer than initially envisioned, sometimes becoming permanent staff. When asked how long they had been in Cambodia, and how long they planned to stay, many participants' answers reflected the fluidity within tourism development mobility, as this exchange between Angela (from Australia) and Alice (from New Zealand), in their early to mid-twenties, illustrates:

*Angela*: Been here nine months. Yeah, I'll stay until they fire me. Until they ask me to leave. But yeah, I really do like [the organisation] so there's no reason why I need to go back. I did a Bachelor of Art and I majored in Human Geography and the Environment and International Affairs. So it's what I wanted to do and before I came here I worked in Thailand at a woman's shelter …

*Alice*: I've been here for six months already. Just came here under my own steam with the arrangement that I would do a three-month trial and then after I'd been here for a couple of weeks I was asked if I wanted to stay for a year and I said 'yup', but I want to stay for longer than a year so I'll basically just keep working here until for some reason I have to go.

Examples such as the experiences of Angela and Alice created confusion around who was a volunteer and who was a staff member, which appears important in volunteer tourism literature where categorisation is common (Guttentag 2009; Callanan and Thomas 2005).

My own research began with the intention to investigate orphanage tourism in Cambodia by talking to orphanage directors or staff members and then with volunteers. Once in the field, however, distinctions about who fits within these categories were challenged. Individuals who perhaps came to Cambodia as a volunteer tourist, or indeed just a tourist, often remain far longer than expected or have become deeply enmeshed within organisations, confronting the distinction between temporary, semi-permanent, and permanent mobility. As Anna, a 43-year-old volunteer stated, 'I am [here] indefinitely. This is my home now. So as long as it works.' Within strict considerations of tourism development, Anna (and indeed Angela and Alice above) would not be considered tourists. In contrast, by considering them within the frame of tourism development mobility, the fluid and changing nature of the trend is highlighted. Orphanages and other NGOs throughout Cambodia are often founded by people who initially came to Cambodia as tourists or within the tourist development movement; however, by remaining they confront this perception of temporary mobility and are difficult to categorise simply within a specific category. Guttentag (2009), for example, categorises volunteer tourists as those staying less than a year, and therefore excludes Peace Corps, etc. However, what about Volunteer Service Abroad's university programme, for example, which offer programmes of less than a year? By using a mobilities framework it becomes less important to distinguish concretely between these distinctions, rather focusing on the embodied, lived, and meaningful experiences of this mobility (Cresswell 2010a; Duncan 2012, 2014).

As Jakubiak (2014) describes, there is significant overlap between what is considered development and what is seen as too inconsequential for such a term (also see Jakubiak, Chapter 15, this volume). When considering English language teaching in Costa Rica as/for development, many volunteers explained that they did not consider what they were doing to be development (Jakubiak 2014). Nevertheless, ideas of giving back and helping are deeply embedded within ideas of tourism development and volunteer tourism, so where one ends and the other begins is complicated. Yet, the variation that exists within tourism development that is examined in this chapter can also be seen as potentially undermining the potential of the trend to enact change. Length of stay can range from a day to over a year. This can have a significant influence on the outcome of the venture. For example, Callanan and Thomas (2005) categorise participants into either 'shallow' or 'deep' volunteer tourists. This distinction is made upon the basis of duration, importance of destination, focus of experience, skills of the participant, the level of participation, and finally the level of contribution. This variety of participation implies perhaps that criticisms of volunteer tourism only relate to specific project or participant types, rather than to the entire practice. There is a need to consider tourism development as part of a wider commentary on mobility to the Global South, and examine the variation that exists within rather than have a blanket condemnation of it.

It has been noted elsewhere that orphanage tourism in Cambodia is becoming heavily criticised (Guiney and Mostafanezhad 2015). The rapid increase in tourism development mobility outlined here is emblematic of an expanding phenomenon, but one that is not always closely considered, as the spontaneity within the trend illustrates. Tourism development mobility to orphanages in particular is being increasingly criticised and several organisations have created resistance movements opposing it (Friends International 2011; UNICEF 2011; Cambodian National Police and SISHA 2013; Orphanages.No 2014; ConCERT n.d.). Figure 14.1 shows an image of Friends International's campaign flyer warning tourists against orphanage tourism in Cambodia. These resistance movements are particularly opposed to short-term touristic engagement within orphanages, although they often criticise the entire phenomenon and the existence of orphanages at all. Friends International (2011), for example, are particularly concerned about the naivety within orphanage tourism, as tourists fail to critically evaluate the whole practice, but also the centres themselves, with corruption a common concern (Lefevre 2012;

*Figure 14.1* Friends International campaign flyer.

Ruhfus 2012). As the flyer illustrates, they consider orphanage tourism to be potentially voyeuristic and exploitative. Anti-orphanage tourism organisations are actively trying to limit mobility and tourism within these spaces, with UNICEF and SISHA seeking to impose regulation; Friends International has focused their attention on the tourists themselves and are seeking to limit the flow of tourists to these spaces. Although founded on ideas of development, tourism development mobility in this form is seen as inadequate and potentially extremely damaging (UNICEF 2011; Guiney and Mostafanezhad 2015).

## Conclusion

Tourism development is now a firmly established tourism trend that is taking advantage of the increasingly mobile nature of society in the hopes of addressing inequality and achieving development. Nevertheless, to date it has been conceptualised within distinct fields of inquiry – from tourism, geography, and development studies. As a result, phenomena such as orphanage tourism are often considered as a more singular trend than they are in reality. Adopting a mobilities lens for such an examination enables the dynamic and fluid nature of tourism development to be untangled (Cresswell 2012; Duncan 2012). To date, orphanage tourism is repeatedly conceptualised as a short-term phenomenon, especially as it relates to volunteer tourism (Tomazos and Butler 2010, 2012; Reas 2013a, 2013b, 2015; Proyrungroj, 2014). However, orphanage tourism is a particular form of tourism development mobility, and is illustrative of the dynamic nature of concepts of tourism, volunteering, work, and migration, as many participants illustrated the often chaotic and fluid progression between these different forms of mobility. Orphanage tourism is extremely complex and dynamic, and incorporates qualities of poverty tourism, volunteer tourism, and charity within a singular trend. Such mobility is not necessarily planned, unidirectional, or always compatible with simplistic definitions of motivations or length. Rather, tourists often hold multiple identities while partaking in tourism development, and these can change throughout the process as their intentions and positions change. What is often a spur-of-the-moment activity for tourists can turn into long-term engagement with Cambodian organisations, with many returning repeatedly to the same organisation or raising money in their home country. Some even permanently move to Cambodia. Those who plan to visit long-term are often both tourists and volunteers, depending on the activity they are participating in at the time. The overlap between considerations of who is a staff member, who is a tourist and who is a volunteer are important concerns that have been relatively unexplored within tourism, and geography literature, which has focused either on short-term volunteers, principally tourists, or on development as practised by those employed longer term by organisations.

Greater attention to the fluidity and difference within orphanage tourism, and tourism development more widely, is important for encouraging increased understanding of its impacts. By considering such trends within distinct academic fields, and as distinct groups such as gap years, a comprehensive picture of tourism development is impossible, and criticisms will remain all-encompassing. Critiques of Cambodian orphanage tourism, for example, are increasingly pronounced, yet perhaps a more all-inclusive analysis of the range of orphanage tourism experiences within the trend will ensure beneficial steps towards best practice, rather than focusing exclusively upon a complete abandonment of experiences such as orphanage tourism. By considering orphanage tourism, and indeed tourism development, within the frame of mobility, it is possible to understand these conflicting and transitional experiences, which are often considered as distinct and unrelated trends. Orphanage tourism, for example, is often solely considered a volunteer tourism trend (Tomazos and Butler 2010; Voelkl 2012; Reas 2013a, 2013b, 2015; Proyrungroj 2014; Verstraete 2014). By considering it as a component of mobility, aspects of volunteer tourism, poverty tourism, and donations can be considered at the same time, allowing for a more cohesive analysis. This encourages greater understanding of a still relatively underexplored phenomenon, one that to date has not been considered as an aspect of tourism development mobilities.

## References

Adams, K. M. (2012) 'Ethnographic methods', in L. Dwyer, A. Gill and N. Seetaram (eds), *Handbook of research methods in tourism: Quantitative and qualitative approaches.* Cheltenham, UK: Edward Elgar, 340–51.

Adey, P. (2006) 'If mobility is everything then it is nothing: Towards a relational politics of (im)mobilities', *Mobilities*, 1(1): 75–94.

Ansell, N. (2008) 'Third World gap year projects: youth transitions and the mediation of risk', *Environment and Planning D: Society and Space*, 26: 218–40.

Baillie Smith, M. and Laurie, N. (2011) 'International volunteering and development: Global citizenship and neoliberal professionalisation today', *Transactions of the Institute of British Geographers*, 36(4): 545–59.

Baillie Smith, M., Laurie, N., Hopkins, P. and Olson, E. (2013) 'International volunteering, faith and subjectivity: Negotiating cosmopolitanism, citizenship and development', *Geoforum*, 45(1): 126–35.

Barnett, C., Cloke, P., Clarke, N. and Malpass, A. (2010) *Globalizing responsibility: The political rationalities of ethical consumption.* West Sussex: John Wiley.

Brown, S. and Morrison, A. (2003) 'Expanding volunteer vacation participation: An exploratory study on the mini-mission concept, *Tourism Recreation Research*, 28(3): 73–82.

Butcher, J. (2003) *The moralisation of tourism: Sun, sand ... and saving the world?* London: Routledge.

Butcher, J. (2009) 'Against "ethical tourism"', in J. Tribe (ed.), *Philosophical issues in tourism.* Bristol and New York: Channel View, 244–60.

Cadman, L. (2009) 'Nonrepresentational theory/nonrepresentational geographies', in R. Kitchin and N. Thrift (eds), *International encyclopaedia of human geography.* Oxford: Elsevier, 456–63.

Callanan, M. and Thomas, S. (2005) 'Volunteer tourism: Deconstructing volunteer activities within a dynamic environment', in M. Novelli (ed.), *Niche tourism: Contemporary issues, trends and cases.* Oxford: Elsevier, 183–200.

Cambodian National Police and SISHA (2013) 'Official press release: Cambodian National Police and SISHA'. Online at: www.sisha.org/news/136-officialpressreleasec ambodiannationalpolicesisha/ (accessed 30 March 2013).

Canzler, W., Kaufmann, V. and Kesselring, S. (2008) 'Tracing mobilities – an introduction', in W. Canzler, V. Kaufmann and S. Kesselring (eds), *Tracing mobilities: Towards a cosmopolitan perspective*. Burlington: Ashgate, 1–10.

Cohen, E. and Cohen, S. A. (2015) 'A mobilities approach to tourism from emerging world regions', *Current Issues in Tourism*, 18(1): 11–43.

Coles, T. (2015) 'Tourism mobilities: Still a current issue in tourism?', *Current Issues in Tourism*, 18(1): 62–7.

Coll, R. K. and Chapman, R. (2000) 'Choices of methodology for cooperative education researchers', *Asia-Pacific Journal of Cooperative Education*, 1(1): 1–8.

ConCERT (n.d.) *ConCERT: Helping you to help*. Online at: www.concertcambodia.org/ default.html (accessed 11 December 2012).

Conran, M. (2011) 'They really love me! Intimacy in volunteer tourism', *Annals of Tourism Research*, 38(4):1454–73.

Coverdell, P. D. (2014) *Peace Corps fact sheet*. Online at: http://files.peacecorps.gov/ multimedia/pdf/about/pc_facts.pdf (accessed 10 July 2015).

Cresswell, T. (2010a) 'Mobilities I: Catching up', *Progress in Human Geography*, 35(4): 550–8.

Cresswell, T. (2010b) 'Towards a politics of mobility', *Environment and Planning D: Society and Space*, 28(1): 17–31.

Cresswell, T. (2012) 'Mobilities II: Still', *Progress in Human Geography*, 36(5): 645–53.

Cresswell, T. and Merriman, P. (2011) *Geographies of mobilities: Practices, spaces, subjects*, Surrey: Ashgate.

Duncan, T. (2012) 'The "mobilities turn" and the geography of tourism', in J. Wilson (ed.), *The Routledge handbook of tourism geographies*. Abingdon and New York: Routledge, 113–19.

Duncan, T. (2014) 'What's the "use" of young budget travel?', in K. Hannam and M. Mostafanezhad (eds), *Moral encounters in tourism*. Surrey: Ashgate, 209–19.

Edensor, T. (2007) 'Mundane mobilities, performances and spaces of tourism', *Social & Cultural Geography*, 8(2): 199–215.

Franklin, A. (2006) 'Tourism', in C. Rojek, S. M. Shaw and A. J. Veal (eds), *A handbook of leisure studies*. New York: Palgrave Macmillan, 386–403.

Friends International (2011) *Children are not tourist attractions. Think Child Safe*. Online at: www.thinkchildsafe.org/thinkbeforevisiting/index.html (accessed 20 January 2012).

Georgeou, N. (2012) *Neoliberalism, development and aid volunteering*. New York: Routledge.

Guiney, T. and Mostafanezhad, M. (2015) 'The political economy of orphanage tourism in Cambodia', *Tourist Studies*, 15(2): 132–55.

Guttentag, D. (2009) 'The possible negative impacts of volunteer tourism', *International Journal of Tourism Research*, 11(6): 537–51.

Guttentag, D. (2011) 'Volunteer tourism: As good as it seems?', *Tourism Recreation Research*, 36(1): 69–74.

Hannam, K. (2002) 'Tourism and development, I: Globalization and power', *Progress in Development Studies*, 2(3): 227–34.

Hannam, K. (2008) 'Tourism geographies, tourist studies and the turn towards mobilities', *Geography Compass*, 2(1): 127–39.

Harlow, S. and Pomfret, G. (2007) 'Evolving environmental tourism experiences in Zambia', *Journal of Ecotourism*, 6(3): 184–209.

Heath, S. (2007) 'Widening the gap: Pre-university gap years and the "economy of experience"', *British Journal of Sociology of Education*, 28: 89–103.

Hitchcock, M., King, V. T. and Parnwell, M. (2009) 'Introduction: Tourism in Southeast Asia revisited', in M. Hitchcock, V. T. King and M. Parnwell (eds), *Tourism in Southeast Asia: Challenges and new directions*. Honolulu: University of Hawaii Press, 1–42.

Hopkins, P. E. (2010) *Young people, place and identity*. Abingdon and New York: Routledge.

Jackson, P., Crang, P. and Dwyer, C. (2004) 'Introduction: The spaces of transnationality', in P. Jackson, P. Crang and C. Dwyer (eds), *Transnational spaces*. London: Routledge, 1–23.

Jakubiak, C. (2014) 'Moral ambivalence in English language voluntourism', in K. Hannam and M. Mostafanezhad (eds), *Moral encounters in tourism*. Surrey: Ashgate, 93–106.

Jones, A. (2004) *Review of gap year provision*. London: Department for Education and Skills.

Lash, S. and Urry, J. (1994) *Economies of signs and space*. London: Sage.

Lefevre, N. (2012) 'Orphanage tourism in Cambodia means big business', *Ethical Traveler*. Online at: www.ethicaltraveler.org/2012/06/orphanage-tourism-in-cambodia-means-big-business/ (accessed 20 March 2013).

Lyons, K., Hanley, J., Wearing, S. and Neil, J. (2012) 'Gap year volunteer tourism: Myths of global citizenship?', *Annals of Tourism Research*, 39(1): 361–78.

Lyons, K. D. and Wearing, S. (2008) *Journeys of discovery in volunteer tourism: International case study perspectives*, Cambridge: CABI.

Manzo, K. (2008) 'Imaging humanitarianism: NGO identity and the iconography of childhood', *Antipode*, 40(4): 632–57.

McGregor, A. (2008) *Southeast Asian development*. New York: Routledge.

McIntosh, A. J. and Zahra, A. (2007) 'A cultural encounter through volunteer tourism: Towards the ideals of sustainable tourism?', *Journal of Sustainable Tourism*, 15(5): 541–56.

Mostafanezhad, M. (2014) *Volunteer tourism: Popular humanitarianism in neoliberal times*, Farnham: Ashgate.

Mustonen, P. (2007) 'Volunteer tourism: Altruism or mere tourism?', *Anatolia*, 18(1): 97–115.

Nathanson, J. (2013) 'The pornography of poverty: Reframing the discourse of international aid's representations of starving children', *Canadian Journal of Communication*, 38(1): 103–20.

O'Reilly, C. C. (2006) 'From drifter to gap year tourist: Mainstreaming backpacker travel', *Annals of Tourism Research*, 33(4): 998–1017.

Oakes, T. and Price, P. L. (2008) *The cultural geography reader*. Routledge.

Orphanages.No (2014) *Orphanages not the solution*. Online at: www.orphanages.no/ (accessed: 20 April 2014).

Palacios, C. M. (2010) 'Volunteer tourism, development and education in a postcolonial world: Conceiving global connections beyond aid', *Journal of Sustainable Tourism*, 18(7): 861–78.

Patton, M. Q. (2002) *Qualitative research and evaluation methods*, 3rd edn. Thousand Oaks, CA: Sage.

Potter, R., Binns, T., Elliot, J. A. and Smith, D. (2008) *Geographies of development: An introduction to development studies*, 2nd edn. Harlow: Pearson Prentice Hall.

Proyrungroj, R. (2014) 'Orphan volunteer tourism in Thailand: Volunteer tourists' motivations and on-site experiences', *Journal of Hospitality & Tourism Research*, 1096348014525639.

Reas, J. (2013a) '"Boy, have we got a vacation for you": Orphanage tourism in Cambodia and the commodification and objectification of the orphaned child', *Thammasat Review*, 16: 121–39.

Reas, P. J. (2013b) 'The "must-have" tourist experience: An exploration of the motivations, expectations, experience and outcomes of volunteer tourists in Siem Reap, Cambodia', unpublished PhD thesis, University of Leeds.

Reas, P. J. (2015) '"So, child protection, I'll make a quick point of it now": Broadening the notion of child abuse in volunteering vacations in Siem Reap, Cambodia', *Tourism Review International*, 18(4): 295–309.

Ruhfus, J. (2012) 'Cambodia's orphan business', *People and Power*, documentary, Aljazeera. Online at: www.aljazeera.com/programmes/peopleandpower/2012/05/201252243030438171.html (accessed 2 November 2012).

Sheller, M. and Urry, J. (2004) 'Places to play, places in play', in M. Sheller and J. Urry (eds), *Tourism mobilities: Places to play, places in play*. London; New York: Routledge, 1–10.

Sheller, M. and Urry, J. (2006) 'The new mobilities paradigm', *Environment and Planning A*, 38(2): 207–26.

Simpson, K. (2004) '"Doing development": The gap year, volunteer tourists and a popular practice of development', *Journal of International Development*, 16(5): 681–92.

Smith, M. P. (2001) *Transnational urbanism: Locating globalization*. Oxford: Blackwell.

Stewart-Withers, R., Banks, G., McGregor, A. and Meo-Sewabu, L. (2014) 'Qualitative research', in R. Scheyvens (ed.), *Development fieldwork: A practical guide*, 2nd edn. Los Angeles: Sage, 59–80.

Telfer, D. J. and Sharpley, R. (2008) *Tourism and development in the developing world*. London and New York: Routledge.

Thulemark, M. M., Duncan, T. and Cohen, S. A. (2014) *Lifestyle mobilities: Intersections of travel, leisure and migration*. Aldershot: Ashgate.

Tomazos, K. and Butler, R. (2008) *Volunteer tourism: Tourism, serious leisure, altruism or self enhancement?* Gold Coast, Qld: Griffith University.

Tomazos, K. and Butler, R. (2010) 'The volunteer tourist as "hero"', *Current Issues in Tourism*, 13(4): 363–80.

Tomazos, K. and Butler, R. (2012) 'Volunteer tourists in the field: A question of balance?', *Tourism Management*, 33(1): 177–87.

UNICEF (2011) *With the best intentions …: A study of attitudes towards residential care in Cambodia*. Phnom Penh: UNICEF Cambodia.

Urry, J. (2007) *Mobilities*. Cambridge: Polity Press.

Urry, J. (2008) 'Moving on the mobility turn', in W. Canzler, V. Kaufmann and S. Kesselring (eds), *Tracing mobilities: Towards a cosmopolitan perspective*. Aldershot: Ashgate, 13–24.

Verstraete, J. (2014) 'The impact of orphanage tourism on residential care centres in Cambodia: A qualitative research', unpublished MSc thesis, Leeds Metropolitan University.

Vodopivec, B. and Jaffe, R. (2011) 'Save the world in a week: Volunteer tourism, development and difference', *European Journal of Development Research*, 23(1): 111–28.

Voelkl, H. T. (2012) 'Developing an understanding of the experience of children with international short-term volunteer tourists: A case study of an orphanage project in Ghana', unpublished MA thesis, Brunel University.

Vrasti, W. (2013) *Volunteer tourism in the Global South: Giving back in neoliberal times*. London and New York: Routledge.

Vrasti, W. and Montsion, J. M. (2014) 'No good deed goes unrewarded: The values/virtues of transnational volunteerism in neoliberal capital', *Global Society*, 28(3): 336–55.

Wearing, S. (2001) *Volunteer tourism: Experiences that make a difference*. Wallington and New York: CABI.

Willis, K. (2011) *Theories and practices of development*, 2nd edn. Abingdon: Routledge.

# 15 Mobility for all through English-language voluntourism

*Cori Jakubiak*

This chapter investigates the practices of mobility associated with English-language voluntourism, or short-term volunteer English-language teaching in the Global South.[1] English-language voluntourism involves various types of mobility: the movement of globally commodified, prestige-variety English language dialects around the globe; the affordance of professional teacher identities for short-term travelling volunteers; and imagined, future mobilities – both social and economic – for the recipients of volunteers' service. In these ways, English-language voluntourism creates new forms of relationality between people and places (cf. Sheller and Urry 2006). Paying attention to these new forms of relationality sheds light on the practice's ideological foundations and has implications for mobility studies more broadly.

I begin this chapter with a brief discussion of English-language voluntourism. Following this and a short account of my study methods, I share an analysis of data collected from English-language voluntourism promotional literature and interviews with in-service and former volunteers. Findings indicate that although English-language voluntourism is a growing and popular form of humanitarian travel (cf. McMillon *et al.* 2003), it does not fulfil its advertised purpose. Instead of reliably delivering high-quality prestige-variety English language skills to people in the Global South, English-language voluntourism fosters new forms of global connection. One of these forms of connection is the idea that all people, everywhere, should live highly mobile, cosmopolitan lifestyles – lifestyles congruent with the labour demands of late capitalism and modelled by short-term visiting volunteers.

## English-language voluntourism

As Allon, Anderson, and Bushell (2008: 76) observe about the last few decades: 'There has been a paradigmatic shift in global international migration patterns away from permanent migration and settlement towards the non-permanent, temporary movements of people across multiple destinations.' One of these forms of temporary mobility occurs through English-language voluntourism, a form of volunteer tourism in which well-intentioned, often young, people travel on a short-term basis to the Global South to teach basic or conversational English.

Volunteer tourism in general has been criticised for paying little attention to the structural causes of problems (Conran 2011). However, its popularity continues to grow, in large part because volunteer tourism fits well with contemporary, governmental rationalities about the importance of individual voluntary service (Butcher and Smith 2010). Also, participating in volunteer tourism allows people to claim adventurousness, generosity, and worldliness – traits that serve as cultural capital in an increasingly lean job market (Vrasti 2013).

Unlike other forms of volunteer tourism such as construction, nature trail maintenance, or even sea turtle preservation (cf. Gray and Campbell 2007), the ostensible benefits of English-language voluntourism to host communities are never realised in the present. If (and whether) host community residents learn any English from visiting volunteers, it is up to host community residents to find a use for these skills. Pennycook (1999) notes that English *for* development (a process in which English language skills help people to participate in existing development projects) is often confused with English *as* development (a process in which English language learning itself is the development goal). In the case of English-language voluntourism, it is unclear whether English language skills are *for* development, *as* development, or something else entirely. A mobilities lens suggests the third option. Volunteers in English-language voluntourism programmes do not reliably increase people's language capacities; however, these programmes undoubtedly foster new forms of global connection. I discuss this idea further following an explication of my study's methods.

## Research methods

Data for this chapter were drawn from a larger, multi-sited ethnographic study (Marcus 1995) of English-language voluntourism. In a multi-sited ethnographic project, a researcher pays close attention to the ways in which macro-level structures shape particular places, as well as to the permeability of the local/global binary itself. Multi-sited ethnography is thus well suited to a study of English-language voluntourism. The practice is influenced by numerous multi-scalar actors, including the United Nations through its Millennium Development Goals (Global Volunteers 2008: 6), public policy organisations through advocacy (e.g. Brookings Institution 2006); and numerous international NGOs through finance and governance. Yet, the specific sites in which English-language voluntourism projects take place are often small, seemingly spatially bounded communities. Indeed, the opportunity to experience life in one of these so-called 'remote' locales contributes to English-language voluntourism's allure (Keese 2011).

For two months in 2007, I conducted participant observation in Costa Rica under the auspices of an NGO-sponsored English-language voluntourism programme. For six weeks in 2008, I worked as a volunteer programme assistant in the north-eastern US home offices of the NGO that had sponsored by programme. I returned to the NGO's home offices for ten days in January 2009 to interview programme alumni and to conduct member checks with study participants.

In total, I conducted 53 open-ended, semi-structured interviews with numerous actors affiliated with English-language voluntourism. These actors included in-service and former programme participants; NGO programme directors and other staff members; and the English teacher at my Costa Rican school. I also conducted a content analysis of 21 commercial and NGO English-language voluntourism sponsors' websites and promotional materials. I used a process of purposeful sampling (Patton 2002) to identify organisations that run English language teaching programmes of one to ten weeks in the Global South, do not require programme participants to have prior teaching experience, are non-sectarian, and are based in the United States or United Kingdom.

While study participants' social locations reflected a broad variety of perspectives, related themes emerged in the data corpus. These themes became increasingly robust as I triangulated interview data with field-notes, promotional materials, and member checks. Data were analysed using a constructivist grounded theory approach (cf. Charmaz 2006). Following a recursive process that involved initial coding, writing analytical memos, and focused coding (Emerson *et al.* 1995), I identified three themes that tied to directly to mobility: English, the global commodity; English for (global) mobility; and English language teaching as modelling cosmopolitanism. I explicate each of these themes in the following section.

## Findings

### *English, the global commodity*

English-language voluntourism promotional literature continually stresses that volunteers need no expertise. Prior teaching experience, an understanding of second language (L2) acquisition, and knowledge of language pedagogy are all unnecessary. In the words of Projects Abroad (n.d.), a commercial English-language voluntourism sponsor, 'a lack of formal qualifications can be more than made up for with plenty of enthusiasm and commitment'. Similarly, the NGO, Global Volunteers (2008), states: 'You don't need specialized skills to make a real difference.' In other words, professional credentials and educator experience are irrelevant to volunteer teaching. However, these same organisational sponsors insist that there is one thing volunteers must possess: they must speak a prestige-variety dialect of English (e.g. Standard American English or British Received Pronunciation). For example, the NGO, Cross-Cultural Solutions (n.d.), states: 'You do not have to be a teacher to teach conversational English. The only requirement for this type of volunteer work is that you are fluent in English. International students learn a great deal simply from your pronunciation.' Similarly, Global Volunteers advertises that 'English has become the international language of technology, commerce, and opportunity. Hearing you speak the language helps local people train their "ear" for English, and practise pronunciation, thereby improving their chances to get a good job.' Jackie, the executive director of this study's focal NGO, offered a similar point of view. When asked to describe the main purpose of the NGO's work, she explained that host ministries of education 'want us to send native English speakers to teach primarily English – primarily spoken English – so their kids can communicate – can understand it – can hear it, understand it, and can speak it. And we can correct them so they do it right accent' (16 June 2008).

Among English-language voluntourism's organisational sponsors, then, volunteer English language teaching is tied to modelling prestige-variety dialect pronunciation. This pedagogical approach reflects what Friere (2000[1968]) calls the banking model of teaching: knowledge is transferred one way; the teacher is the sole classroom authority; and students are *tabula rasa* into which knowledge bits are deposited.

This banking model approach to English language teaching is problematic for numerous reasons. For one, L2 acquisition research contraindicates the idea that a particular variety of a language can be transferred by simply modelling its pronunciation. Speakers' phonological and phonetic inventories are developed in early childhood; they are based on the sounds and sound patterns of their primary home language(s), or L1s. For teenage and adult L2 learners, certain consonant blends, vowel sounds, or tones may difficult to distinguish aurally, let alone reproduce orally (Fromkin *et al.* 2014). This is why French L1 speakers, for example, are recognisable as French when they speak English. Their English accents are governed by (and follow predictable patterns based upon) the sound inventory of French. This is not to say that L2 accents cannot be reduced. Specific training in distinguishing between minimal pairs, for example, or practice with articulatory phonetics can mitigate L1 influence on L2 (see Rahman 2009 for an account of 'accent neutralisation' in call centres). These and related pedagogical strategies, however, demand linguistics knowledge and familiarity with language education. English-language voluntourism's insistence that volunteers need only 'enthusiasm and commitment' to be effective pronunciation teachers belies the technical knowledge that is required.

English-language voluntourism's fetishising of 'correct' English pronunciation, moreover, reflects intensifying commodification processes. English-language voluntourism sponsors frame prestige-variety English dialect speakers as in possession of a valuable, distributable product. It is not volunteers' pedagogical skills but rather their prestige-variety English-language dialects that volunteers bring to host communities. This idea resonates with Heller's (2010) observation that as languages become commodities rather than identity markers or repositories of culture, they move towards exogenous norms. Singapore's 'Speak Good English Movement' illustrates this point. Designed to discourage its citizens from speaking Singlish, a local variety of English, the Singaporean national government uses advertising campaigns and a 'Speak Good English' website (complete with a British Received Pronunciation guide) to stress the importance of English for transnational intelligibility. Although Singlish functions as a powerful identity marker among those who speak it, Singlish is ridiculed by the Singaporean government for being provincial and therefore useless in the global marketplace (Wee 2008).

Similar to Singapore's Speak Good English Movement, English-language voluntourism offers to remediate local varieties of English by converting them into globally useful, value-added, and widely identifiable products. Even if study of the English language is already occurring in a host community, English-language voluntourism sponsors insist that volunteers are needed nevertheless. Projects Abroad (n.d.) takes this stance in its description of volunteer teaching in India:

> despite the fact that you will find English speakers throughout the country [India], the standard of conversational English teaching in public schools is usually very poor. The students may know about English literature and are better at grammar than most native-speakers, but they find it hard to make themselves understood.

Although Projects Abroad does not clarify to whom, exactly, Indian English dialect speakers are unintelligible (presumably not one another), suggested here is that all varieties of English should reflect prestige-variety norms. Despite the fact that people worldwide study and use different varieties of English for numerous, often highly local, purposes (Pennycook 2007), English-language voluntourism insists that only certain English varieties are correct (see Fromkin *et al.* 2014 for more on linguistic prescriptivism).

English-language voluntourism is congruent, then, with intensifying commodification processes that increase the imagined, if not actual, exchange value of certain language varieties more than others (Tan and Rubdy 2008). It is under these conditions that prestige-variety English dialect speakers are licensed to travel as short-term language teachers to the Global South. The commodification of prestige-variety English dialects worldwide produces a social field in which Global North English-language speakers are cast as experts *sans* credentials. As Simpson (2005: 465) notes:

> Volunteer-tourism places travellers in the position of expert or at least as knowledgeable by locating them in placements as teachers, builders, medical workers etc. Often these are identities and positions not available to the same individuals 'at home'. The freedom from qualifications can be used as an enticing part of such programmes.

Indeed, in nation-states such as the US, the barriers to entry into many professions – including teaching – are becoming increasingly formidable. For example, all American public school teachers must now be 'highly qualified' in the subject area(s) they teach, as per the No Child Left Behind Act of 2002 (Spring 2008). English-language voluntourism, however, allows young people to bypass such restrictions. For those who can afford the often four-figure participation fees (in US dollars) (WorldTeach n.d.), participation in English-language voluntourism provides distinctive professional experience (Vrasti 2013). As Pooley *et al.* (2005: 15) note, 'mobility is more than the mechanism through which mundane tasks are carried out ... Movement can itself become a performance through which we make statements about ourselves and acquire status.'

The significance of new mobilities 'stems from their coordination of new kinds of transnational connections, new warpings of distance and proximity, time and space, and ultimately, from their fashioning of new linkages and relationships between peoples, places and cultures' (Allon *et al.* 2008: 77). English-language voluntourism, I argue, is one of these new linkages. Because the logic of late capitalism commodifies even languages (the yellow, Rosetta Stone boxes in international airports being a vivid example of this), prestige-variety English dialect speakers possess a valuable if not so easily distributable commodity (Niño-Murcia 2003). This instrumental view of language combines with Global North governmental rationalities about the importance of voluntary service (King 2006) to produce and laud English-language voluntourism. While this social practice opens up new mobilities for prestige-variety English dialect speakers – allowing them to assume temporary professional roles in the Global South – the mobilities it imagines for the recipients of volunteers' service are uneven and a bit more tentative.

### English for (global) mobility

As I have reported elsewhere, English-language voluntourism promotional literature suggests that prestige-variety English language skills will allow people instant access to a worldwide, global economic network (Jakubiak 2012). According to English-language voluntourism sponsors, possessing (a certain kind of) English language proficiency offers increased career and educational opportunities in the global imaginary, a spatial location that mandates English for entry. In illustration, Projects Abroad (n.d.) claims: 'Brazil is becoming a major player in the world economy and many Brazilians are discovering that learning English is an important way to improve their lives and gain access to this increasingly globalized world.' Similarly, Global Volunteers (2008) states: 'Our staff and project leaders at each work site enable you to help Chinese students and teachers prepare for work in the global arena, where English serves as the universal language of commerce, technology, and opportunity.' In this promotional literature, the 'global arena' is described as an actual place. It is a site in which all transactions and interactions occur exclusively in prestige-varieties of English.

Study participants expressed similar beliefs about the purpose of English-language voluntourism. Daniel, the director of admissions and recruitment at this study's focal NGO, used the discourse of 'global entry' when describing the NGO's goals. He explained:

Our goal is through education – specifically, through what we can offer in English language education – to be able to empower those in developing countries, to grant them access, as much as possible, to the global economy ... English is increasingly a critical asset within and a prerequisite for participation in the global economy.

(6 June 2008)

English-language voluntourism discourse links English language skills to increased and elevated job prospects, unparalleled economic opportunities, and entry into an elite, nearly physical, space. Although mobilities research suggests that nearly all people, worldwide, are already interconnected through the global marketplace – be it as consumers or bearers of risk (Hannam *et al.* 2006) – English-language voluntourism discourse asserts that those who do not speak English are set apart.

Following this line of logic, the settings in which English-language voluntourism take place (particularly through this study's focal NGO) are often small, rural communities in which English is rarely used or spoken. In fact, English-language voluntourism sponsors frame these communities as sites of need precisely *because* they lack English language resources and English educational programming. In illustration, Hands Up Holidays, a commercial English-language voluntourism sponsor, characterises its Thailand programme site as a place where 'there is a great demand for more knowledge, more contact with foreigners, learning English and getting in touch with the world'. Using nearly identical rhetoric, Projects Abroad (n.d.) claims: 'Deeply ingrained in the hearts of the young people of these communities [volunteer placement sites] is a desire to speak English, the language that can put them in touch with the rest of the world.'

Contra these discourses about the global demand and need for English, many in-service and former volunteers opined that English had been irrelevant in their host communities. Local residents, they explained, did not use English in their daily lives and often showed little interest in learning it. Josh, a former volunteer in Costa Rica, spoke to this issue as follows:

[The role of English in my town was] very, very minimal. I mean it's – it's, I guess, yeah, it did seem like there was a disconnect between the very rural setting [of the volunteer placement sites] where they're probably never going to use English.

(29 January 2009)

Many in-service and former volunteers specifically noted that physical relocation was required if local residents wanted to use English for employment. Audrey, a former volunteer in Costa Rica, shared this insight. When asked whether many jobs in her host site had demanded English language proficiency, she replied:

Not as many as in the capital, but the capital was only an hour away, so it was possible for [host community members] to live there during the week. But as you got closer to the capital, there were more English jobs. In the town, there weren't a lot of English jobs.

(28 January 2009)

Shrusti, another former volunteer in Costa Rica, observed this same phenomenon. Describing the uses of English in her host community, Shrusti explained:

> No one really spoke very much English. But it's also because people that – I think the people that learned and spoke English went, like, leave the town to go into Quepos/Manuel Antonio because it's so close, and there's such – there are so many tourists there that it's really lucrative if you can speak English.
>
> (28 January 2009)

The value of English in the employment marketplace, then, is tied to certain locations alone. Despite celebratory discourse tying English to 'global' opportunities, the economic benefits of knowing English may only be realisable in particular contexts.

With a clear eye as to how the commodity value of English is tied to specific places, some in-service and former volunteers saw their roles as facilitating others' movements abroad. These participants tied English language learning to international study, travel, or immigration. Edward, an in-service programme participant, offered this perspective:

> if the students of Costa Rica can become more proficient in English ... it would allow for great opportunities for those kids as they begin to move into both tourism in Costa Rica and world-wide business as a whole ... [Also], in talking to the most of the students, the vast majority want to continue to university – go to San Jose ... and take that and move to the United States.
>
> (9 July 2007)

Jim, another in-service volunteer in Costa Rica, spoke in comparable terms. He said: 'I think English will help basically improve the tourism industry and maybe allow students who study here to study abroad, if they want to, in English-speaking countries' (9 June 2007). As these study participants' comments reveal, the value of English for local residents is often tied to imagined, temporally and physically distant, futures. Particularly in communities in which little English is used or spoken – the very communities in which English-language voluntourism takes place – English has little currency in the present or in residents' immediate surroundings.

English-language voluntourism, then, *projects* economic, social, and physical mobility for English language learners while facilitating the movement and professional experiences of volunteers. It also suggests new forms of immobility. Because speaking a prestige-variety dialect of a dominant language increasingly marks one as cosmopolitan (Heller 2010), people who do not – or cannot – learn English (or relocate for jobs that require it) are ever more framed as out of touch. Gale (2008: 2–3) notes:

> the concept of mobilities presupposes its opposite, namely immobilities. It is easy to be seduced by the idea that everyone (and everything) is on the move, but, in practice, the very processes that have enhanced the mobility of some

people(s) have merely served to highlight, and sometimes to reinforce, the immobility of others.

English-language voluntourism discourse makes dramatic relocation seem natural. Because the sites in which English-language voluntourism takes place are by definition lacking English language resources and educational programming, it is unlikely that the jobs, opportunities, and social futures available to residents in these communities demand English language proficiency. The implied goal of English-language voluntourism is to equip people with the skills they need to leave.

Explaining the theoretical uses of the new mobilities paradigm, Sheller and Urry (2006: 214) write:

> A clear distinction is often drawn between places and those travelling to such places. Places are seen as pushing or pulling people to visit. Places are presumed to be relatively fixed, given, and separate from those visiting. The new mobility paradigm argues against this ontology of distinct 'places' and 'people'. Rather, there is a complex relationality of places and persons connected through performances.

English-language voluntourism affords short-term, visiting volunteers the opportunity to perform highly mobile, professional identities in rural Global South communities and extend the possibility of future mobility to others. In that sense, it exemplifies the relationality of people and place that is brought out by the new mobilities paradigm. Precisely because little English language learning occurs in a particular host community, English-language voluntourism frames that community as a site of need. These sites, then, become spaces in which English-language voluntourism 'needs' to be enacted. As Hannam *et al.* (2006: 13) note, 'activities are not separate from the places that happen contingently to be visited. Indeed, the places travelled to depend in part upon what is practiced within them.' For even if English language *learning* has little relevance to individuals in a particular community, perceptions of the global value of English cast all English language *teaching* as an appropriate and benevolent intervention.

Because English-language voluntourism occurs in places in which little English is spoken or used, however, there are few on-the-ground mechanisms for assuring quality English language instruction. Volunteer teachers are rarely accountable for whether their students learn or improve their English. As I discuss next, however, this lack of accountability may not be problematic. The imagined future mobilities that volunteers extend to host community residents may not in fact require English language proficiency. Rather, volunteers' cosmopolitan, hypermobile lifestyles are cast as models for others to follow.

### English teaching as modelling cosmopolitanism

More than half of the participants in this study reported that their on-the-ground English language teaching was weak and ineffective. Citing a lack of curricular knowledge, unfamiliarity with students and their backgrounds, and an inability to enforce even class attendance, in-service and former volunteers alike explained that their instructional impact was minimal. A main problem, articulated by Chris, a former volunteer in Ecuador, was that teaching in the English-language voluntourism context lacked focus. He said:

> It was just difficult because I couldn't see what they [the students] wanted to get out of the class. Especially with my morning class, which was beginners of all ages. Like, there was a mom there taking it to get better for business, and kids whose parents made them go. My afternoon class were older teenagers, and one of them was like, 'I'm going to be an accountant. Like, I need to learn this English to be better – to get a better job.' And I'm like, 'Okay, I can tailor lessons more specifically to that.' But, so, in terms of my mission, I don't know – I essentially felt I was play-schooling for them during the summer while they weren't in school.
>
> (30 January 2009)

Chris's description of his classroom resonates with other volunteers' accounts. In-service and former volunteers alike characterised their teaching as improvised. Josh, introduced above, reflected this position as follows:

> I had never thought about having to design my own curriculum. And, and, just sort of – I think it's – I guess I sort of anticipated we'd be teaching a standard curriculum; we wouldn't have to go in there and take a step back and think, 'Okay, if I were – you know, when I learned Spanish in school, they taught it through – they started with verbs, and then nouns, and then, you know, we did a unit on, you know, telling time, and we did a unit on ...' and then I tried to transport that into teaching that in English. So, I didn't feel prepared at all. I sort of felt like I was just making stuff up as I went along.
>
> (29 January 2009)

Akin to the way in which volunteers circumvent the need for professional credentialing by teaching in the Global South, volunteer teachers' lessons need not be aligned with any curricular goals, learning objectives, or accountability measures as mandated by Global North educational bodies (see Spring 2008 on the rise of scientific school management in the US). As Chris alludes to with his comment about 'play-schooling', teaching in the English-language voluntourism context is often more performative than substantive.

Many in-service and former volunteers assessed their students as having learned little. Whether due to pedagogical content knowledge gaps or broader structural constraints, study participants continually explained that their students' English progress was slow. Karen, a former volunteer in Poland, shared this opinion:

> I expected that my students would be better at English, I guess. So, I had sort of this idea of more complicated projects, I guess, that we would do, and

none of that was possible because their skill level was too low. I don't know.
I guess I also thought that there would be more direction of what we should
be teaching … Maybe they learned, like, a few words, you know, but I don't
think that they learned a lot.

(28 January 2009)

Josie, another former volunteer, also reflected that her instructional impact was
slight. Citing time limitations, Josie described her teaching in Ecuador as follows:

It was basic, basic level. You know, they [the students] didn't know 'hello'
before I came. Although I suspect that a volunteer might have, like – an
American or an English speaker of some sort came through before – but, for
some reason, all of the kids knew the word 'yellow'. I don't know. But they
knew the word, 'yellow', but they couldn't say 'hello'. So, you know, you're
basically – you're not going to teach them a whole lot in a summer.

(29 January 2009)

Short-term volunteer English language teaching may not deliver much English on
the ground. It is not a rigorous or organised enough teaching programme to
impact beginning students' English language repertoires.

English-language voluntourism contains innumerable contradictions. It promises to extend new forms of social and economic mobility to rural Global South
residents by providing them with a highly tradable commodity in the global
marketplace: prestige-variety English language skills. Yet – by design – the
communities in which English-language voluntourism takes place rarely have
employment opportunities for those with English language proficiency. Further,
little English gets taught through English-language voluntourism. How, then, can
we account for English-language voluntourism's rising and sustained popularity,
particularly as a federally endorsed development strategy (cf. Brookings
Institution 2006)?

Mobilities studies provide some explanatory power here. While English-
language voluntourism may not reliably deliver prestige-variety English language
skills, it generates new forms of global connectivity, merges a variety of life
paths, and inserts new, fetishised commodities – the least of which is the English
language – into the rural Global South communities in which these programmes
take place. New forms of psychic and material connection are not only made
possible but realised through English-language voluntourism even if no one's
English language skills improve. Despite study participants' insistence, for example, that 'no one really spoke much English' in their host communities, a volunteer's presence alone (as well as their English language classes, iPod imported
music, etc.) casually overrides this same observation.

To be sure, a close examination of English-language voluntourism promotional
literature and volunteers' talk reveals explicit attention not to the English
language but to cosmopolitan, hypermobile lifestyles. The NGO Cross-Cultural
Solutions (n.d.) puts it this way: 'Your personal and professional path offers local

people new insight into life, education, and *careers overseas*' (my emphasis). Similarly, Travel to Teach (n.d.) advertises that 'volunteers teach ... basic English ... while also diffusely contributing to children's creativity by offering perspectives that are "outside the box" of the rural Indian mindset'. In this promotional literature, volunteer teachers are not pedagogues *per se* but innovative subjects with creativity, worldliness and wisdom.

Danica, a former volunteer in Ecuador, used language reminiscent of this promotional literature when explaining English-language voluntourism's purposes. She said: 'At least with my host family, they learned a little bit about a different culture and that living in Costa Rica for your whole life is not the only possibility' (28 January 2009). Jim, introduced above, also saw his main role in Costa Rica as inspiring others' latent mobilities. Not primarily a language teacher, he saw himself as a model for host community residents for where and how to live. He said:

> I think people may look to me and see, you know, try to figure out why I'm here, like what I've done with my life – you know, is, is what he's doing a good way to approach life, you know? And how I want to live life? Or, do I want to – you know, I, I would like to show them that there are more options than they know. Like, if they want, they can just hang out in their town for the rest of their lives and they might be happy with that, but there might be others who want to, you know, come to San Jose to study and then go to live somewhere else maybe.
>
> (9 June 2007)

Through his personal example, Jim hoped to inspire others to live cosmopolitan, hybermobile lifestyles. Unruffled about his teaching abilities, Jim hoped that local residents could find inspiration and the will to relocate in his image.

Scott, another in-service volunteer in Costa Rica, also viewed English language teaching as secondary to his aspirational role. He saw himself as a cultural ambassador and a model of life's possibilities. Scott said:

> All I'm doing is teaching everyone a bit of English ... Other than that, I guess it's like, [having an English-language voluntourist] is a new experience for people in the town. They haven't met someone like me probably, just because I'm from another country ... I think that if you live in a place where, like, you're just sort of – all you know [is] this one way of life, you might, it might not occur to you to do other things that you'd otherwise want to do.
>
> (28 June 2007)

Although many of the communities that hosted summer volunteers did so on an annual basis, in-service and former volunteers alike often assumed that their presence was novel and life-changing for local residents. Less teachers than intrepid models of international travel, both in-service and former volunteers expressed the desire to help others be physically mobile.

Speaking to the importance of the new mobilities paradigm for understanding contemporary social formations, Hannam *et al.* (2006: 2) note:

> The global order is increasingly criss-crossed by tourists, workers, terrorists, students, migrants, asylum-seekers, scientists/scholars, family members, business people, soldiers, guest workers and so on. Such multiple and intersecting mobilities seem to produce a more 'networked' patterning of economic and social life, even for those who have not moved.

English-language voluntourism also puts numerous mobilities in collision. Although host community residents may not learn much English from visiting volunteers, they do receive input on what is required for 'success' in an increasingly networked world. Economic markets at every scale are precarious and volatile; job security is minimal; and lifelong learning and encountering cultural difference are now expected parts of life for most people. While short-term, uncredentialed volunteers may not always be effective English language teachers, they very aptly serve as role models for cosmopolitanism and hypermobility in an increasingly interconnected world.

## Conclusion

Discussing the theoretical shift in global tourism studies to one of mobilities more generally, Lyon and Wells (2012: 4) write: 'A focus on tourism mobilities moves us away from the preoccupation with the tourist and travels to distant lands and recognizes instead the interconnected movements of a range of individuals ... voluntarily on the move.' Using this idea of 'interconnected movements' to analyse English-language voluntourism, I have argued that the phenomenon's staying power comes from the physical and imagined mobilities it generates rather than its language teaching effectiveness. To the extent that English-language voluntourists see their roles as inspiring others to *move* – whether to the next town or abroad – volunteers' own cosmopolitan subjectivities are affirmed. Following Žižek, Vrasti (2013: 83) points out: 'Volunteerism has the advantage of producing a *kulturlos* subject, a subject that can be at home in any culture, unencumbered by a sovereign or cultural boundaries.' English-language voluntourists model this hypermobility for their students.

Yet, it is the global commodification of nationally bound, prestige-variety dialect English(es) that grease the wheels of volunteer teachers' movements. English that indexes Chicago or London, for example, has a higher exchange value in the global marketplace than does English that indexes Lagos or Mumbai – or, for that matter, inner-city Detroit. In that sense, the global movement opportunities that English-language voluntourism affords volunteers derive from *being from* and *speaking like* a person from a very specific place.

Scales, places, commodities, and performances interweave in English-language voluntourism. Regionally identifiable, highly commodified English language varieties allow young, uncredentialed volunteers the opportunity to be teachers in communities characterised as needy and remote. Yet, volunteer teaching in these same communities marks visiting volunteers as cosmopolitan and mobile – the very qualities that volunteers then model for their students. A tourism mobilities perspective thus allows for a more nuanced understanding of English-language voluntourism – one that brings its claims and theoretical underpinnings to greater light.

## Note

1   I use the terms Global North and Global South throughout this chapter in lieu of 'developed/developing world' or 'first/third world', which suggest that high standards of living, equal access to educational opportunity, and technological resources, among other benefits, are evenly distributed throughout Western Europe and countries such as the United States, the United Kingdom, and Australia. In many cases, elites in countries considered 'developing' have higher standards of living, greater access to services, and more employment security than certain groups living within 'developed' countries. Used frequently in anthropology and human geography, the terms Global North and Global South also index the ways in which certain countries' wealth and status has relied on the historical and contemporary extraction and exploitation of other countries' natural and human resources.

## References

Allon, F., Anderson, K. and Bushell, R. (2008) 'Mutant mobilities: Backpacker tourism in "global" Sydney', *Mobilities*, 3(1): 73–94.

Brookings Institution (2006) *International volunteering: Smart power*, Policy brief no. 155. Washington, DC: L. Rieffel and S. Zalud.

Butcher, J. and Smith, P. (2010) '"Making a difference": Volunteer tourism and development', *Tourism Recreation Research*, 35(1): 27–36.

Charmaz, K. (2006) *Constructing grounded theory: A practical guide through qualitative analysis*. Los Angeles: Sage.

Conran, M. (2011) 'They really love me! Intimacy in the volunteer tourism encounter', *Annals of Tourism Research*, 38(4): 1454–73.

Cross-Cultural Solutions (n.d.) Online at: www.crossculturalsolutions.org.

Emerson, R. M., Fretz, R. I. and Shaw, L. L. (1995) *Writing ethnographic fieldnotes*. Chicago: University of Chicago Press.

Friere, P. (2000 [1968]) *The pedagogy of the oppressed*, 30th anniversary edn (trs. M. B. Ramos). New York: Continuum.

Fromkin, V., Rodman, R. and Hyams, N. (2014) *An introduction to language*, 10th edn. Boston, MA: Wadsworth.

Gale, T. (2008) 'The end of tourism, or endings in tourism?', in P. M. Burns and M. Novelli (eds), *Tourism and mobilities: Local-global connections*. Cambridge, MA: CABI, 1–14.

Global Volunteers (2008) *Adventures in service* (brochure). St Paul, MN: Global Volunteers.

Gray, N. and Campbell, L. M. (2007) 'A decommodified experience? Exploring aesthetic, economic, and ethical values for volunteer ecotourism in Costa Rica', *Journal of Sustainable Tourism*, 15(2): 463–82.

Hands Up Holidays (n.d.). Online at: www.thai-experience.org/volunteer/teaching-english.html.

Hannam, K., Sheller, M. and Urry, J. (2006) 'Mobilities, immobilities, and moorings', *Mobilities*, 1(1): 1–22.

Heller, M. (2010) 'The commodification of language', *Annual Review of Anthropology*, 39(1): 101–14.

Jakubiak, C. (2012) '"English for the global": Discourses in/of English-language voluntourism', *International Journal of Qualitative Studies in Education*, 25(4): 435–51.

Keese, J. R. (2011) 'The geography of volunteer tourism: Place matters', *Tourism Geographies*, 13(2): 257–79.

King, S. (2006) *Pink ribbons, inc.: Breast cancer and the politics of philanthropy*. Minneapolis: University of Minnesota Press.

Lyon, S. and Wells, E. C. (eds) (2012) *Global tourism: Cultural heritage and economic encounters*. Lanham, MD: Rowman & Littlefield.

Marcus, G. (1995) 'Ethnography in/of the world system: The emergence of multi-sited ethnography', *Annual Review of Anthropology*, 24(1): 95–117.

McMillon, B., Cutchins, D. and Geissinger, A. (2003) *Volunteer vacations: Short-term adventures that will benefit you and others*, 8th edn. Chicago: Chicago Review Press.

Niño-Murcia, M. (2003) '"English is like the dollar": Hard currency ideology and the status of English in Peru', *World Englishes*, 22(2): 121–42.

Patton, M. Q. (2002) *Qualitative research and evaluation methods*, 3rd edn. Thousand Oaks, CA: Sage.

Pennycook, A. (1999) 'Development, culture and language: Ethical concerns in a postcolonial world', paper presented at the Fourth International Conference on Language and Development. Online at: www.clet.ait.ac.th/hanoi_proceedings/pennycook.htm.

Pennycook, A. (2007) *Global Englishes and transcultural flows*. New York: Routledge.

Pooley, C. G., Turnbull, J. and Adams, M. (2005) A mobile century: Changes in everyday mobility in Britain in the twentieth century. Aldershot: Ashgate.

Projects Abroad (n.d.) *Volunteer and intern abroad* (brochure). New York: Projects Abroad.

Rahman, T. (2009) 'Language ideology, identity and the commodification of language in the call centers of Pakistan', *Language in Society*, 38(2): 233–58.

Sheller, M. and Urry, J. (2006) 'The new mobilities paradigm', *Environment and Planning A*, 38(1): 207–26.

Simpson, K. (2005) 'Dropping out or signing up? The professionalization of youth travel', *Antipode*, 37(2): 448–69.

Spring, J. (2008) *The American school: A global context from the Puritans to the Obama era*, 8th edn. New York: McGraw Hill.

Tan, P. and Rubdy, R. (eds) (2008) *Language as commodity: Global structures, local marketplaces*. New York: Continuum.

Vrasti, W. (2013) *Volunteer tourism in the Global South: Giving back in neoliberal times*. New York: Routledge.

Wee, L. (2008) 'Linguistic instrumentalism in Singapore', in P. Tan and R. Rubdy (eds), *Language as commodity: Global structures, local marketplaces*. New York: Continuum, 31–43.

WorldTeach (n.d.). Online at: www.worldteach.org.

# 16 When *pesos* come at the expense of tourism proximity and moorings

*Matilde Córdoba Azcárate*

## Introduction

*(At the estuary, February 2004): It is Miguel's turn to show the pink flamingos to the group of German tourists, but he is not in. Tourists ask. They are ready. They have their sunscreen, swimming clothes, and orange life-vests on, and they are on board. Just a few steps from their boat there are at least eight other tour guides seemingly doing nothing, 'just sitting', looking and chatting. 'Why aren't those guides taking us on the tour?' 'What are they waiting for?' A couple of tourists from the group go to the office to complain about the situation. The officer from the Biosphere Reserve comes back to the boat with them and asks the rest of the guides to take the tour and 'to keep things smooth and moving'. But 'It is Miguel's turn,' they say. 'He must be at the cantina.' The guides send a kid on his bicycle to look for him. More than half an hour later Miguel's brother arrives. He jumps on the boat, which has not moved since, and leads the tour. Later on he will explain to me that Miguel was too drunk to take the tour. It is the low season and if Miguel's brother had not taken the boat it would have meant waiting at least three weeks for the next group of tourists. In taking his brother's tour at least the 'tourists' pesos will still go to our mother,' he says.*

*(At the beach, July 2012): Ángel frantically walks the 1 km stretch separating the main plaza from the beach where buses disembark tourists. He is trying 'to catch tourists' for the flamingo tours departing from the beach. He comes and goes on his bicycle from the plaza to the beach restaurants, from the restaurants to the hotels, and walking again from the stands of craftswomen to the tour guides' makeshift stand, and back again. He whistles and talks loudly, almost shouting, addressing tourists in a mixture of Spanglish and Italian. He moves pesos and dollars from pocket to pocket and distributes them among other guides when the tours are back. He counts them once, and then again. He wanders around. He is in charge of distributing tourists in the boats. When tourists arrive he must do all of this quickly since most of them are in Celestun just for a couple of hours and hardly anyone knows about boat tours departing from the beach before they arrive. 'These men*

*are so insidious,' one tourist tells me. 'They want to grab your arm and almost put you in the boat without further dialogue ... and I don't know if their rides are legal at all ... I mean ... where are the safety vests, why is there no information about them at all?!' Ángel will tell me later, 'we operate kind of on the margin ... we need to capture tourists quickly, otherwise they leave.'*

These two vignettes emerge from my field-notes during my ethnographic research on tourism and development at Celestun, a coastal Mexican community. This community became part of the Biosphere Reserve Ria Celestun and a major ecotourist destination because it is one of the few nesting and breeding sites of pink flamingos in the country. Both scenes evince the anxieties and conflictive social relations that typically precede tourists' encounters with pink flamingos as well as the way in which specific collectives of the local population actively engage and shape ecotourism development activities from below. The first vignette describes the tense waiting episodes and bitter encounters with hosts that often precede official ecotours at the estuary, a hyper-regulated conservationist and ecotourism spot. This episode captures the (im)mobilities informing the strategies to gain control of ecotours that have been developed by a group of ex-fishermen who have been transformed into tourist boatmen locally known as *los lancheros*. The second describes the frantic activity of capturing tourists for informal boat tours that have emerged to compete with the high prices of official ecotours. This example captures the intense motilities (walking, wandering, cycling, gazing) deployed to stay put in an unregulated tourism spot.

Stasis and movement are two dialectically and unevenly related processes conforming to the same reality: in Celestun, Mexican *pesos* and US dollars from ecotourism come after long hours of staying still in the estuary and at the beach, the only two sites where boats depart to show pink flamingos. Building on this contrast, this chapter discusses the politics of ecotourism development and (im)mobilities which structure contemporary host–guest encounters in natural protected areas. I understand (im)mobilities here extending Pellegrino's defini- tion (2012: 11–12) as 'a relation to the world which shapes our sense of closeness and distance to people, objects, ideas', which do not simply 'allow us to feel and perceive through permanence and instability in space, time and society', but actively shapes them politically. I will show how the transformation of Celestun from a fishing village into an international conservation and ecotourist site has re-engineered the community into a highly contested spaced governed by a new system of (im)mobilities. More specifically, I argue that in Celestun this system is organised through the production of mobilities for mooring (Adey 2006, 2010; Hannam *et al.* 2006) and corporeal proximity (Urry 2002, 2007; Pellegrino 2012). Mobilities for mooring and corporeal proximity inform the main motility practices through which different groups 'appropriate the field of possibilities relative to movement' (Kaufmann and Montulet 2008: 45) at the expense of others, generating in so doing new alignments of power and social stratification. As I demonstrate below, the production of mobilities for mooring and corporeal proximity requires the everyday mobilisation and control of the spaces of the estuary and the beach in which locals fight to stay still to be physically close to tourists. These practices deeply inform development and conservation policies on the ground and should be taken into account for more inclusive development planning. They ultimately serve to illustrate the politics of mobilities (Cresswell 2010), as well as the centrality of tourists and labourers' mobilities for tourism to take place, as Chapter 1 in this volume states.

In what follows I elaborate on how the production of stasis through movement and corporeal proximity in these ecotourist hotspots (Córdoba Azcárate 2010) works through both the informal reorganisation of tour guides' collectives beyond conservationist mandates and the re-spatialisation and control of everyday practices, such as walking, wandering, cycling, and gazing. The argument is organised in two sections. In the first section, I offer a brief description of the implementation of conservationist and ecotourist development frameworks in the area. I analyse how both frames have worked through the commodification and spectacularisation of pink flamingos and discuss effects that this has had on social and spatial relations in the community. Specifically I argue how these frames have required the immobilisation of the estuary and the beach as movement spaces (Thrift 2003) of tourists, fishermen, tour guides, expert knowledge, pink flamingos, and capital, and how this has reworked social stratification and hierarchies among locals. In the second section, I discuss the strategic appropriation and use of the movement spaces of the estuary and the beach by building on the chapter's opening ethnographic vignettes. In the conclusion, I reflect on the strengths of mobility studies for development and conservation research and planning, highlighting the political role of tourism informed mobilities and moorings in redefining everyday systems of exclusions and power relations (Olesen and Lassen 2012) and hence their leverage in mediating development and conservationism on the ground.

## Framing nature for ecotourism development in a natural protected area

Tourism is both an industry and a socio-cultural process. It is a primary form of contemporary mobility and is integral to economic globalisation processes as a major force in creating landscapes of power (Hannam *et al.* 2014: 172). When employed as a development strategy, tourism acts as a vehicle of modernisation, enfolding Western ideals of social and economic progress (Escobar 1995, 2001). Over the last decades, different models of sustainable tourism, such as ecotourism, have been heralded as useful ways of reconciling seemingly irreconcilable economic and ecological imperatives while at the same time offering to empower local populations (Hall and Lewe 1998). In practice, however, the development of these sustainable forms of tourism is often coupled with an aggressive faith in market solutions to environmental questions, giving rise to what some authors have defined as a new era of environmental managerialism and neoliberal conservation (Brockington and Duffy 2010: 470). The particular history of the Biosphere Reserve Ria Celestun, by the Gulf of Mexico coast, offers a good example of how this environmental managerialism takes root through the commodification and spectacularisation of particular animal species (Igoe *et al.* 2010).

The history of conservation of the area dates back to 1979, when it was declared a Wildlife Refuge for the 'Greater Flamingos'. In 2003, the Ramsar Convention declared the area a Wetland of International Importance and a year later, in 2004, the Mexican government reclassified this area as a Biosphere Reserve, which included it in the UN Man and the Biosphere (MAB) Program (García Frapolli *et al.* 2009). The conservation and development discourses contained in these plans framed nature, and in particular pink flamingos and wetlands, as 'international resources' and environments 'in need of conservation', and thus in need of global planning and management. These plans highlighted informal housing, the lack of urban planning, and overfishing as the main 'social' problems threatening pink flamingos and their ecosystems (SEMARNAT 2000).

The creation of this conservationist frame brought about three major changes in the community, which reworked the relationships between nature, space and society, as well as social relationships themselves. First, the designation of the area as a protected area implied a new spatial organisation to respond to Biosphere Reserve's zoning practices as defined in the MAB Program. Nuclear, buffer and recuperation zones were delineated according to their different levels of protection. The space of the estuary and the beach were redefined as nuclear and buffer zones respectively, which meant that no productive activities should take place in those areas; this has led to constant monitoring of both sites in the name of natural conservation.

Second, along with zoning, the protection of the area as a Biosphere Reserve meant the creation of a new system of conservationist regulations, which severely restricted the productive activities of the community, especially fishing at the estuary (García Frapolli *et al.* 2009). Prior to the establishment of the Biosphere Reserve, residents of Celestun used to fish shrimps and various other species in the estuary on a small-scale basis, providing the main source of livelihood for many residents. As a matter of fact, and despite this preservationist frame, Celestun is still today the second fishing port of the peninsula with almost 90 per cent of its population making a living from fishing activities (INEGI 2012).

Third, the creation of the Biosphere Reserve meant bringing in different forms of expert knowledge personified in NGO personnel and volunteers as well as Biosphere Reserve technicians. While these experts emerged as 'the guarantors' of the endangered resources of the area, the local population was described as 'environmental criminals', and traditional knowledge as unsustainable practices in relation to their own 'natural' resources. The lack of participation of the local population in any of these preservationist measures, together with the restrictive preservationist agenda of these experts, resulted in tense relationships between experts and locals, which have led to conflicts over fishing in the estuary (García Frapolli *et al.* 2009; Córdoba Azcárate 2010).

This preservationist frame has been supplemented since the late 1990s by a new ecotourism frame, which has emerged as a response of the Mexican federal and state governments to the global and national demands to make natural protected areas productive for the economy. The promotion of ecotourism as a development strategy was presented in Celestun as 'an opportunity to minimize conflicts between local population and conservation authorities' and 'an effort to diversify economic opportunities for the population' (SEMARNAT 2000), given the restrictions imposed on traditional activities like fishing.

Paradoxically enough, ecotourism in Celestun has been built upon the very same resources that conservationist legislation and practices have sought to protect: the pink flamingo and the habitat of the estuary. Ecotourism has strategically mobilised pink flamingos as a way of inserting Celestun as the 'nature destination' in the itineraries of package tours coming from all-inclusive resorts in Cancun and the Riviera Maya on the Caribbean coast. For these tours, the Biosphere Reserve represents the possibility of engaging in an environmental gaze to encounter pristine, untouched nature, a 'fragile ecosystem', 'refuge for wildlife' within the comfort of the familiar. The arrival of 'pink-packaged tourists', as they have been labelled in the community, has resulted in the massive flow of tourists in the community, which is estimated to be close to 50,000 per year since 2004 (Ramsar 2004). This flow of tourists has spatially reorganised Celestun around a system of highly choreographed tourism mobilities. Tourists circulate non-stop from the estuary, where buses stop for tourists to take the boat tours to admire the flamingos, to pre-booked restaurants in the beach where they eat fresh fish. This rigid circulation of tourists to and from the estuary and the beach bypasses the rest of the community, which is nonetheless spatially and politically shaped by the everyday pulses and rhythms, dictated by the presence or absence of the tourist buses (Córdoba Azcárate 2010). These ecotourist and tourist-related mobilities take place within the nuclear and buffer zones of the Biosphere Reserve – that is, on conservation spaces where human activities are regulated to be kept at a minimum and are closely monitored in the name of global conservation and sustainable development. This superimposition of conservationist and tourism activities and regulations has been particularly conflictive at the estuary, which has become a hyper-regulated conservationist space and tourism hub and a crucial knot in the community's socio-political organisation.

In the next section, I describe how the superimposition of these conservationist and ecotourist frames has created a new system of mobilities for mooring at the estuary and at the beach, and how closeness and distance from and to these spaces, as well as to tourists themselves, emerge as this community's new socio-political organising principle.

## Mobilities for mooring and corporeal proximity

Prior to the creation of the Biosphere Reserve, fishermen in Celestun used to offer boat rides to locals and regional holidaymakers in order to view pink flamingos at the estuary, an activity that contributed to household economies during high tourist seasons, such as Easter and summer vacations (SEMARNAT 2000). However, facing an increase in fishing restrictions resulting from the designation of the area as a natural protected space, a group of native fishermen, the so-called *lancheros*, strategically organised themselves into Societies of Social Solidarity in the mid-1990s. According to the Mexican law these societies have five main objectives: (1) to create jobs; (2) to preserve and help promote the ecology; (3) to rationally exploit natural resources; (4) to educate; and (5) to produce, industrialise and commercialise the goods and services needed in order to achieve the afore-mentioned goals (Cornelius *et al.* 1994). This legal category enabled *lancheros* to appropriate the geographical space of the estuary, the main fishing and tourism site of the community, as well as control principal access to pink flamingos.

By the late 1990s there were seven of these societies, offering what they called 'environmentally responsible ecotours'. Four of them were based at the estuary and three at the beach. However, as the increasing demands associated with ecotourism started to show the first negative impacts on the estuary and flamingo colonies, the practices of tourist boatmen became the object of increased attention and further regulation. As a result, the state and federal governments decided to reorganise activities in an effort to control the circulation of boats within the estuary. They fused all societies of social solidarity into a single collective, the Federación de Lancheros Unidos de Celestun, and constructed two major tourist infrastructures, or *paradores*, one at the estuary and one at the beach to centralise tours and provide tourists with basic services.

In addition to this, any fisherman wishing to receive institutional credits or subsidies for fuel, boat repairs, or life-vests had to use these infrastructures and comply with the Biosphere Reserve mandates on how to organise and conduct pink flamingo ecotours. The number of tourists in the boats was regulated to a maximum of eight persons, and two major itineraries with designated stops were created to navigate the estuary, a one-hour tour and a two-hour tour; this included regulations over the distances between boats and the pink flamingos. All tourists accessing the *paradores* had to pay a quota for using its services, which included toilets and showers, small eateries, souvenir shops, and a small educational biology museum. Turnstiles were installed to count the number of people accessing the facilities, and an office was created to be in charge of dispensing tickets for boat rides.

Today only 85 fishermen, the *lancheros*, of a population of more than 6,000, are legally allowed to take boat tours to see the pink flamingos at this natural protected area (Córdoba Azcárate 2010). However, divisions in this collective soon started to arise as a consequence of the unevenness of their geographical location and proximity to tourist flows and the pink flamingo. Fully conscious of their privileged position of being close to both tourist flows and the pink flamingo, the boatmen at the estuary established firm control over who could access this space. To secure their total control of the area, they have organised an informal system of mobilities for mooring that enable them to extend their control beyond the Biosphere Reserve regulations and institutional conservationist efforts to control their activity.

*Lancheros* at the estuary have erected a kiosk with makeshift benches and hammocks in front of the Biosphere Reserve main office. A rotation of shifts among the 45 members of the four societies working at the estuary enables them to control the number and distribution of tours beyond the quotas established by the Biosphere Reserve authorities. They control the number of tourists that go in each boat, which they distribute according to their particular interests, and control how long the tours last. In low seasons, when fewer tourist buses access the *parador*, boats take fewer tourists so more boats can depart and vice versa. When more tourist buses and hence more tourists access the *parador*, boats take the regulated number of tourists but tours are undertaken more frequently and don't last as long. As Miguel's vignette makes clear, *lancheros* regulate when other fishermen can access the estuary to take the tour and also when other boats, as happens in high tourist season's, may be granted occasional access.

The control over this system of tourism mobilities requires them to moor at the self-erected kiosk in the estuary but it has also enabled them to control the distribution of the benefits derived from tourism among the societies' members and their extended kin. As a way of ensuring the monopoly over these benefits, '*lancheros* from the estuary' have prohibited other licensed tourist boatmen from using the tourist infrastructure of the estuary, which effectively forces these other boatmen, locally known as the '*lancheros* from the beach', to start their tours from the beach. This has the effect of not only increasing the length of boat tours by more than one hour, making their trips much less profitable since they spend twice as much on fuel, but also making them more vulnerable to weather conditions, as they need to drive their boats through a stretch of 'rough water' in the Gulf of Mexico.

The spatial immobilisation of *lancheros* at the estuary has been crucial in establishing a new social stratification and patterns of exclusion in the community based upon who is close and who is distant from this space and its tourist flows. This fact perfectly illustrates the spatial interconnection of people's daily lives and the politics of mobilities that inform them as the mobilities paradigm states. In Celestun, the boatmen at the estuary, along with their families, are described as 'the wealthy ones', 'the privileged' and 'the chosen', while the rest of the community, including other boatmen, have been excluded from this space and the proximity to tourists and pink flamingos. One of those other boatmen is Ángel, the protagonist of the second opening vignette.

Ángel is part of the group of 40 boatmen operating from the beach. Although they are officially part of the Federation and thus allowed into the estuary to show pink flamingos to tourists, beach *lancheros* do not receive any government support or recognition, nor are their boat rides counted in conservation and ecotourism statistics. The main reason for this is their refusal to use the official beach *parador*, built by the government a few blocks away from the community's main access to the beach, by the plaza. The *parador* was destroyed by a fire the very same day it was finished and it has not been repaired since – something that, as these *lancheros* explain, did not seem to happen 'by accident'. According to the boatmen, the *parador* was poorly conceived since it was 'too far' from tourists arriving at the main plaza, which put them at a clear disadvantage from the boatmen at the estuary. As one of them put it in an interview, 'we were never consulted about where to put the *parador* ... if they had asked, we would have said here and not there ... it makes a difference ... from over there you don't see the buses coming; when you finally see them, you don't have enough time to get to them before they go into the restaurant.'

The lack of official support has forced boatmen from the beach to reorganize their activity in an attempt to create an alternative form of corporeal proximity to tourist flows, and in doing so to reappropriate indirect benefits derived from ecotourism in this natural protected area. The production of this alternative proximity has been made possible through their (im)mobilisation at the beach. The beach *lancheros* have built an alternative makeshift stand to receive tourists at the main entrance of the beach, right between the restaurants and the main plaza where the tour buses stop. In contrast to the spatial stillness of the tourist boatmen at the estuary, the beach *lancheros* have to be constantly moving to and fro while staying within a very well-defined one-kilometre stretch of the beach.

The stopover of tourists at the beach is a very short and unpredictable one. It depends on how saturated the estuary is with buses; tour guides have to decide whether or not to stop at the beach so that tourists from buses can grab something to eat at the restaurants or to stretch their legs before going to see the pink flamingos on the official tours at the estuary. This is also the main stop for tourists arriving to the natural protected area in rented cars, who normally miss the beginning to the estuary right at the entrance of the community. Beach boatmen have to be quick to harness these evanescent tourist flows. They come and go by bike from the plaza to the beach and by foot from their stand to the restaurants and boats. They shout and whistle to attract tourists' attention, they reach out to touch and even grab them, trying to attract them to their stand before they get to the beach restaurants or back to their buses and cars. They offer 'more real tours', they promise the desired flamingo photos that the 'mainstream' estuary experience cannot provide, and they 'charge less', or so they claim. Their success depends on their ability to control this 'proximal space' and make sure that no other fishing boats recruit tourists for the rides. They can do this thanks to the craftswomen – in most cases the wives and relatives of these boatmen – who have erected makeshift stands that run crosswise along this one-kilometre stretch of the beach. Together with the craftswomen, the *lancheros* have instituted a tight surveillance over this space, making sure that no other collective, such as other fishing boats or street vendors, can use it and profit from it.

These strategies to control the beach, like those employed to control the estuary, reveal the interconnected system of everyday mobilities and moorings that *lancheros* have developed to control these highly contested movement spaces. In this sense, they show how, in a place where the ability to earn some *pesos* and have a better life is determined by relative distance from tourist flows; the ability to produce and control proximity to these flows emerges as the key variable around which social relations and hierarchies are organised.

## Conclusion

In the dialectical understanding of mobilities advanced by the mobilities paradigm, the movement of some is enabled by others' staying put – be it infrastructures, peoples, objects, technological systems, or animal species (Adey 2010; Hannam *et al.* 2006; Sheller and Urry 2004; Tuvikene 2014). In this chapter I have focused on the political effects of these dialectics by exploring how the combined pressures of ecotourism development and conservation have transformed Celestun into a space of interconnected and contested (im)mobilities in which the production and control of corporeal proximity to tourists in core movement spaces has reorganised the spatial, social, and power relations in the community. The ethnographic attention to how locals construct and control this proximity has helped to understand how the *lancheros* fight to monopolize the movement spaces of the beach and the estuary through the development of different everyday (im)mobility practices, such as sitting, walking, wandering around, cycling, and boat riding, which have enabled them to create the forms of proximity required to access the benefits derived from ecotourism flows in this natural protected space. Importantly, the attention to these everyday mobilities and the moorings or spatial fixities informing them has also showed how they are capable of producing spaces of agency and power, which have enabled *lancheros* not only to shape their social stratification but also to appropriate global tourist flows and rework conservationist and development mandates. In this sense, the examples addressed show how the dictates of development, tourism, and conservation are not just imposed on populations but must 'work within and through local cultures' (Escobar 1995: 49), and how everyday practices of (im)mobilities play a crucial role in this process.

## References

Adey, P. (2006) 'If mobility is everything then it is nothing: Towards a relational politics of (im)mobilities', *Mobilities*, 1(1): 75–9.

Adey, P. (2010) *Mobility*. London: Routledge.

Brockington, D. and Duffy, R. (2010) 'Capitalism and conservation: The production and reproduction of biodiversity conservation', *Antipode*, 42(3): 469–84.

Brockington, D., Duffy, R. and Igoe, J. (2008) *Nature unbound: Conservation, capitalism and the future of protected areas.* London: Earthscan.

Córdoba Azcárate, M. (2010) 'Contentious hotspots: Ecotourism and the restructuring of place at the Biosphere Reserve Ria Celestun (Yucatan, Mexico)', *Tourist Studies*, 10(2): 99–116.

Cornelius, W., Craig, A. and Fox, J. (eds) (1994) *Transforming state-society relations in Mexico: The national solidarity strategy.* La Jolla: University of California San Diego, Center for US-Mexican Studies.

Cresswell, T. (2010) 'Towards a politics of mobility', *Environment and Planning D: Society and Space*, 28(1): 17–31.

Escobar, A. (1995) *Encountering development: The making and unmaking of the Third World.* Princeton, NJ: Princeton University Press.

Escobar, A. (2001) 'Culture sits in places: Reflections on globalism and subaltern strategies of localization', *Political Geography*, 20(1): 139–74.

Garcia Frapolli, E., Ramos Fernandez, G., Galicia, E. and Serrano, A. (2009) 'The complex reality of biodiversity conservation through Natural Protected Area policy: Three cases from the Yucatan Peninsula, Mexico', *Land Use Policy*, 26(3): 715–22.

Hall, M. and Lewe, A. (1998) *Sustainable tourism: A geographical perspective.* Edinburgh: Pearson Educational.

Hannam, K., Butler, G. and Paris, C. (2014) 'Developments and key issues in tourism mobilities', *Annals of Tourism Research*, 44(1): 171–85.

Hannam, K., Sheller, M. and Urry, J. (2006) 'Editorial: Mobilities, immobilities and moorings', *Mobilities*, 1(1): 1–22.

Igoe, J., Neves-Graca, K. and Brockington, D. (2010) 'A spectacular eco-tour around the historic bloc: Theorizing the convergence of biodiversity conservation and capitalist expansion', *Antipode*, 42(3): 486–512.

Inegi (Instituto Nacional de Estadistica Geografia e Informatica) (2012) *Anuario Estadistico de Yucatan.* Aguascalientes, Mexico: Inegi.

Kaufmann, V. and Montulet, B. (2008) 'Between social and spatial mobilities: The issue of social fluidity', in W. Canzler, V. Kaufmann and S. Kesselring (eds), *Tracing mobilities: Towards a cosmopolitan perspective.* Farnham and Burlington, VT: Ashgate, 37–56.

Olesen, M. and Lassen, C. (2012) 'Restricted mobilities: Access to, and activities in, public and private spaces', *International Planning Studies*, 17(3): 215–32.

Pellegrino, G. (ed.) (2012) *The politics of proximity: Mobility and immobility in practice.* London: Routledge.

Ramsar, The Convention on Wetlands (2004). Online at: http://ramsar.rgis.ch/cda/en/ramsar-about-introductory-ramsar/main/ramsar/1-36%5E16849_4000_0__ (accessed 16 June 2015).

SEMARNAT (2000) Programa de manejo de la Reserva de la Biosfera Ria Celestun. Comision Nacional de Areas Protegidas: Mexico, DF.

Sheller, M. and Urry, J. (eds) (2004) *Tourism mobilities: Places to play, places in play.* London: Routledge.

Thrift, N. (2003) 'Movement-space: The changing domain of thinking resulting from new kinds of spatial awareness', *Economy and Society*, 33(3): 582–604.

Tuvikene, T. (2014) 'Mooring in socialist automobility: Garage areas', in K. Burrell and K. Hörschelmann (eds), *Mobilities in socialist and post-socialist states: Societies on the move.* Basingstoke: Palgrave Macmillan, 105–21.

Urry, J. (2002) 'Mobility and proximity', *Sociology*, 36(2): 255–74.

Urry, J. (2007) *Mobilities.* London: Polity.

# 17 Making tracks in pursuit of the wild

## Mobilising nature and tourism on a (com)modified African Savannah

*William O'Brien and Wairimũ*
*Ngarũiya Njambi*

### Mobilising the safari destination

An Expedia.com advertisement depicts an adolescent girl who is fascinated by African wildlife. Her interest is evident in her attention to a collection of plush toy giraffes, elephants, zebras, and other animals that her father has brought as gifts from his many business trips. Sitting at his laptop, the father observes his daughter playing and then returns his attention to the computer screen where he sees a high number of accumulated Expedia rewards points. With a click of his mouse, the duo appear on an African savannah landscape, riding in an open-top Land Rover, and observing giraffes and other wildlife. The ad ends with an acacia tree in the frame as their vehicle drives towards the sunset. The landscape imagery is iconic, mobilising a desire for travel by presenting a common safari fantasy. This depiction of the apparently single father and his daughter highlights a marketing awareness of trends towards greater diversity in family structure, while in contrast with these social changes, the portrayal of the white, middle-class, suburbanite pair suggests common and durable ideas about 'wild nature' in Africa. In a changing world, the ad seems to suggest some places and things can be relied upon to represent the eternal and primeval. In this familiar tourist imaginary, as Igoe points out, the African wildlife park is 'portrayed as exotic and inhabiting an unspoiled world that no longer exists in the West' (Igoe 2004: 14).

While the specific wildlife park in the advertisement is unnamed, the location might well have been the Maasai Mara National Reserve, located in south-west Kenya and the focus of this chapter. With its abundance of animals, including its annual Great Migration of wildebeest and zebra and the presence of the 'Big Five' (lions, leopards, elephants, rhinos, buffalo), the park has long been the biggest tourist draw in East Africa, referred to as 'the jewel in the crown of Kenya's tourism industry' (Ole Seur 2003: 1). The park was established under British colonial rule in 1961 as a unit in an expanding system of national parks and reserves and today occupies an area of 1,510 square kilometres (Walpole *et al.* 2003: x). It is described as 'a rolling area of mixed open grassland interspersed with riverine forests and hilly bush or woodland areas, bounded on the west and north by the Isuria and Mau Escarpments and on the south by the Serengeti National Park of Tanzania' (Talbot and Olindo 1990: 67). The safari booking website MaasaiMara.com effuses that 'it forms Africa's most diverse, incredible and most spectacular eco-systems and possibly the world's top safari big game viewing eco-system' (ORD Group 2015).

As a major tourist attraction, the Maasai Mara National Reserve, along with Kenya's other wildlife parks, contributes significantly to both national and local development. In 2005 over two million visitors travelled to Kenya's national parks and reserves, the vast majority from wealthier world regions such as Europe and North America (while visitation from East Asia, particularly China, is currently on the rise). The revenue-generating park is thus a commodified landscape, tied closely to the global economy, although its (ironic) attraction to tourists is that it represents the 'wild nature' they've seen in television documentaries and on film, a natural ecosystem set apart from human economic transformation. From this common perspective, the Maasai Mara National Reserve, along with other wildlife parks, is viewed as a 'nature island', preserved as a fixed and bounded 'destina-tion' that moors the mobilities of safari tourists who are 'drawn by wildlife films, good airline connections, and package tours' (Honey 1999: 295).

This chapter scrutinises this 'island' imaginary, suggesting along with Hannam (2009) that the notion of fixed and separate places 'needs to be problematized', given the 'complex relationality of places and persons' (and also non-humans) that facilitate tourist mobilities (Hannam 2009: 109). The Maasai Mara National Reserve exists in a hybrid ecology that is not limited to its purported natural components (with tourists merely traversing the park as visitors), or even limited by its boundaries. By necessity the park is made from far-ranging interrelation-ships among both humans and non-humans, of material and semiotic actors. In this frame, the tourist-bearing safari vehicles that dot the landscape are as much a part of the park's ecology as the wildebeest, zebra, and the predators that hunt them. We hope to demonstrate Sheller's point that 'the making of places *to* play thus depends on particular ways of putting places *in* play' (Sheller 2004: 14, original emphasis), suggesting that 'global tourism mobilities take place through mobilizations of locality and rearrangements of the materiality of places' (Sheller 2004: 21). The 'destination' called the Maasai Mara National Reserve performs 'nature', fixity, and timelessness for tourists at the intersection of numerous factors that mobilise park space.

## Producing the timeless present

The idea of the wildlife park as a fixed and immobile place is reinforced in another advertisement. The 2015 list of 'Luxury Small Group Journeys' from the travel company Abercrombie & Kent includes an itinerary for 'The Great Migration Safari in Style: Luxury Lodge Edition': a 14-day six-park journey in Kenya and Tanzania that costs US$15,000 per person (Abercrombie & Kent 2015). The journey includes several days at the Maasai Mara National Reserve, described as a place where you can 'immerse yourself in the wild'. A brochure map reinforces the image of this and the other parks on the itinerary as fixed and immobile, represented as solid dots connected by arrows symbolising the movement and flow of potential tourists between the sites by air and by road. Photos display examples of the wildlife contained within those destinations, while the lone photo of humans indicates a wide view of a grassland/acacia land-scape with a small tour group observing elephants from an open-top Land Rover. The image highlights the relative solitude that tourists expect from the safari nature experience (particularly this 'luxury edition'), while a similar image of solitude is also promoted in the Expedia.com advertisement.

Sheller (2004: 13) contends that places come into play in part through imagina-tion and narration. In this sense, the Maasai Mara National Reserve occupies a story that is entangled with a physical space. Foregrounded in these advertise-ments is a combination of desire and place, a dreamscape entwined with the African safari landscape. One can trace the production of such imaginaries of the 'African wildlife park' through nineteenth- and twentieth-century US discourses of nature preservation, European presumptions of Africa's 'primitivity' that are traced back further in time (see Mudimbe 1994), and in twentieth-century wildlife conservation narratives represented on film. Romantic ideas about wilderness, rooted in literary and artistic movements in the nineteenth century in the US and UK, suggested that 'spiritual truth emerged most forcefully from the uninhabited landscape' (Nash 2001: 46). The presumed personal benefits of being alone in nature, evident in the advertising described above, is promoted in this durable travelling discourse, which shapes expectations of how a nature park should look. These imaginaries of a natural world are rehearsed and replicated in countless documentary films and television accounts of African wildlife. Inspired by films such as *Serengeti Shall Not Die* (1959), *Born Free* (1966), the American televi-sion show *Wild Kingdom* (1963–88), the BBC's *Big Cat Diary* (1996–2008), and many others, tourists over the years have developed a strong sentiment for protecting African wildlife and for experiencing the solitude with the protected nature that is depicted onscreen. As Neumann states, 'national park boundaries have long served as the physical and symbolic divide between nature and culture and as the geographic expression of humanity's moral commitment to biodiversity protection' (2004: 817).

The relevance of historical narrative and imaginations of nature and wildlife suggest that accounting for the Maasai Mara National Reserve benefits from, as the editors of this volume suggest, a diachronic analysis rethinks common views of tourism as a discrete activity, structured by present conditions. One can demon-strate that the past inhabits the present in significant and tangible ways, both in the physical form of the park and in tourist experience. As Latour puts it, 'the past is not surpassed but revisited, repeated, surrounded, protected, recombined, rein-terpreted, and reshuffled' (1993: 75). The imaginaries and narratives that link the past to the present mobilise and reinterpret myriad human and non-human elements, which give particular shape and character to the place.

Narratives of nature preservation shape tourist expectations of what to find at a 'nature park', while in turn the physical space embodies them through design in the visual style of park structures and landscapes. This globalised travelling narrative that helped to construct the Maasai Mara National Reserve was developed and promoted by a scenic park movement that emerged in the US by the late nineteenth century. It arose in reaction to concerns about resource depletion in the American West, prompting calls to preserve examples of monumental and spectacular scenery as remnants of 'unspoiled' nature. This effort led to the creation of national parks including Yellowstone, Yosemite, and Glacier. The scenic park idea was soon exported abroad, and particularly to the UK, which carried the idea to its colonies. The mobilisation of this desire to both preserve and visit remnant examples of 'nature' in both the US and UK is traced through what Nash calls an 'intellectual revolution that made unmodified nature per se a mecca for travelers' (Nash 2001: 347).

Having little wilderness at home to protect, wealthy and influential British tourists who had visited North American parks lobbied to bring these ideas to the African colonies to see them implemented. Tying these US park discourses to existing imaginaries of an Edenic Africa, Neumann suggests that 'the British were attempting to implement a mythical vision of Africa as an unspoiled wilderness, where nature existed undisturbed by destructive human intervention' (Neumann 1998: 128). Imaginations of African nature were tied closely to its wildlife, which formed the focal point of the parks constructed there during the twentieth century. The model for producing a natural setting was found in the policies and practices imported from Yellowstone National Park in the US. The Yellowstone model had attained global influence in the twentieth century, demarcating a clear conceptual boundary between people and nature. The model in a nutshell entailed 'setting aside pristine wilderness areas and banning all human uses therein, apart from tourism' (Marris 2011: 18).

The model also helped to establish a particularly US American national park design aesthetic that was exported abroad. The rustic style of the early US national parks was incorporated into African safari park design, evident in the architecture of, for instance, the Sekanani or Ololaimutia Gates at the Maasai Mara National Reserve. Their 'natural' appearance is achieved through the use of log rafters for roof support, stone facades, and wooden signs announcing entry to the park. Such elements today are part of a global semiotics of scenic parks which signal to tourists that they are at the threshold of a truly natural space. Also according to the model, the space inside the park is notable for its relative lack of built features. Other than the unpaved roadways that traverse the park space, deemed necessary to facilitate tourist movements, there are only a few lodges and a number of tented campsites within the park. Like the entry gates, the architecture of these accommodations, such as Keekerok Lodge, is rustic in character. The lodge employs rough-hewn wood, shake shingles, and stone supports to present the structures visually within a 'nature' imaginary. Most tourist accommodations for overnight stays are relegated to the periphery of the park space, outside of its boundary. The design attempts to suggest minimal human intrusiveness into the natural space beyond that which is needed for tourist access.

The recirculation and renewal of the Yellowstone model during much of the twentieth century has been achieved partly through the work of international conservation institutions such as the IUCN (International Union for the

Conservation of Nature) and WWF (Worldwide Fund for Nature), both created in the decade following World War Two. The US National Park Service also played a key role in maintaining this American park vision through a programme that invited park staff from other countries to travel to the US to learn the best practices of park management (Nash 2001). As an example of the mobile and global reiteration of park ideology, the First World Conference on National Parks, held in 1962 in Seattle, was organised by the IUCN and hosted by the National Park Service. In his keynote address, titled 'Nature Islands for the World', US Interior Secretary Stewart Udall declared that the establishment of parks 'strikes a wholesome note of sanity in a troubled world', arguing for the need to maintain 'nature-islands of solitude and repose' (Udall 1962: 3). His words rehearse those of the preservation icon John Muir in 1901, who famously declared that 'tired nerve-shaken, over-civilized people are beginning to find out that going to the mountains is going home' (1901: 1). This call to visit 'nature' for its spirit-renewing values has been effectively remobilised over generations, particularly in wealthier parts of the world. Its legacy is evident in the durable image of the relatively wealthy, white and Western safari tourist, which remains evident in Abercrombie & Kent's exclusive luxury tour package, but also in the middle-class father and daughter safari arranged through Expedia.com and assisted by rewards points.

Through such globalised discourses, tourist destinations such as the Maasai Mara National Reserve have solidified as places that exist simultaneously on the ground, on maps and film, and in tourist imaginations. The island metaphor testifies to the perception of radical difference between what lies inside and outside of the nature park. While durable, it is also important to remember that perceptions and policies change with time. For instance, the circulation of global discourses of biodiversity conservation eventually led away from hunting and gradually towards a focus on photographic safaris. Kenya in 1977 banned hunting in its parks to accommodate the mobilisation of this mainly Western turn in public opinion (Honey 1999).

As a colonial project, the existence of the Maasai Mara National Reserve is made up of additional narratives that are tied closely to that history. The park contains not only tangible legacies of the colonial power to confiscate lands for the Crown, evident in the park's physical existence, but also in a colonial motif that suffuses images of the 'African safari park' and what it means to 'go on safari'. A colonial nostalgia (see Rosaldo 1989) influences the architectural design and interior décor of accommodations in and around the park. Colonial-era luxury hotels in downtown Nairobi, such as the Stanley and Norfolk, promote their colonial histories through interior design, including the choices of historical photographs on their walls, as they serve as way stations for travellers on their way from the airport to their safari park destinations. This colonial nostalgia even influences the clothing choices of safari tourists, some of whom still choose to wear the classic khaki safari hats, shirts, and other items that evoke images of 'the great white hunter' of a distant past.

Honey (1999) describes a surge in safari tourism to Kenya after the 1985 release of the Academy Award-winning film *Out of Africa*, which circulated benevolent images of colonial rule, permitting a positive audience perception of colonial land confiscation and race relations. Contemporary safari advertisements, particularly for luxury tours, present images such as tented housing and outdoor fine dining that appear as scenes from a 'golden age' of colonial rule, including an implied promise of unquestioning hospitality from the service staff. One of the authors of this chapter, a Gĩkũyũ woman from Kenya, has, while on safari tours, been confused with service staff by other tourists who perhaps expected a clearer racial division of travel and labour. (On the other hand, more Africans are participating as tourists in recent years as the Kenyan middle class grows, potentially changing this dynamic.) Salazar (2010: 43) discusses the role of nostalgia in tourism in more general terms:

> the imagery surrounding tourism to developing countries is about fantasies, and often about an ambivalent nostalgia for the past – ambivalent because returning to the past is not what people actually desire. Modern myths – nature, the noble savage, art, individual freedom and self-realization, equality, and paradise – all have special significance for and are manifested in the practices of international tourism.

The Maasai Mara National Reserve and similar parks are occupied by colonial myths as much as they are by animals, grasslands, and acacia trees.

## Mobilising the Maasai Mara National Reserve

Hannam, Butler, and Paris (2014: 173) state that 'places are thus not so much fixed but are implicated within complex networks'. Those very cultural, historical, and economic factors that produce (and reproduce) the Maasai Mara National Reserve as a container for nature have mobilised the park as a place with a particular character and material features. The production of place as a savannah designed with amenities for tourist consumption requires massive globalised mobilisation of humans and non-humans alike. The purportedly fixed and natural site is thus actually a hybrid one, grounded in the perpetual mobilities of various features. Sheller and Urry (2006) urge attention to multiple mobilities, examining a 'fluid interdependence' among intersecting and overlapping movements. Citing John Law (2006), they state, 'we are not dealing with a single network, but with complex intersections of "endless regimes of flow", which move at different speeds, scales, and viscosities' (Sheller and Urry 2006: 213). This flow traverses time as well as space. While tourists often mobilise expectations of a fixed and bounded wildlife park, the atmosphere, wildlife, and livestock engage in mobilities of their own (see Philo and Wilbert 2000; Thompson 2002; Whatmore 2002; Kohn 2013).

The park space remains occupied in important ways by colonial practice. The space that became Maasai Mara National Reserve began to take shape near the start of the twentieth century at a time when the British government was attempting to consolidate control over its East Africa Protectorate. Steps towards park development took the form of game reserves that were aimed at preventing over-hunting. The Society for the Preservation of the Fauna of the Empire (SPFE), founded in the UK in 1903, mobilised much of this effort and was led by well-connected and titled English landowners who had such influence in the Colonial Office that they could 'virtually write colonial park and wildlife policies' (Neumann 1998:128). Early game protection in the Mara region did not restrict livestock grazing, given the colonial perception of the Maasai themselves as 'primitive man' and thus an element of 'nature'.

Nonetheless, the creation of this protected space was founded on limiting the movements of the Maasai and their livestock, who had lost more territory to colonial rule than perhaps any other ethnic group in Kenya (Hughes 2007). In 1904, many Maasai had been forced to move from their best northern grazing grounds in the Rift Valley to make way for white settlers. The reserve onto which they were moved was itself confiscated in 1911 to make way for more white settlers, displacing around 20,000 people and 2.5 million head of livestock towards an existing southern Maasai reserve in the drier Mara region (Hughes 2007: 310). Steps taken towards the eventual creation of the Maasai Mara National Reserve had to contend with the needs of the Maasai for pasture and were negotiated in a context of their ongoing resistance to colonial restrictions.

This hybrid effort, combining colonial policy, the Maasai, and more also included the circulation of park examples from other African colonies. Kenya's national parks drew inspiration and ideas from the example set by the first official national parks in Africa – Congo's Albert National Park (now Virunga, in 1924) and South Africa's Kruger National Park (in 1925). Additionally, the London Conference for the Protection of African Fauna and Flora in 1933 called for an increase in the number of national parks and reserves in the colonies (Nash 2001). Kenya's colonial government followed in 1945 with its National Parks Ordinance, and the establishment of a wildlife sanctuary at the Maasai Mara site occurred in 1948. The implementation of national parks in Kenya shifted the emphasis from hunting to wildlife protection, advocating, in accordance with the Yellowstone model, for the eviction of local people from within park boundaries (Honey 1999: 294). However, in part because of the large number of Maasai in the area, whose movements were notoriously difficult to control, the colonial government in 1961 decided that it was more prudent to create the Maasai Mara as a (more porous) reserve rather than a national park (Talbot and Olindo 1990).

But the choice of a specific location for the reserve was not simply grounded in the colonial ability to mobilise state power, the movements and displacement of Maasai herds, or in international discourse and practice of park preservation. The location stands at the intersection of various additional factors that have produced the place. It is obvious, for instance, that the mobilities of atmospheric forces on global, regional, and local scales have produced a site that is conducive to both wildlife and livestock. The idea of a fixed and bounded 'nature island' is rendered quite problematic when contemplating the scale of the mobile forces that shape the savannah landscape. The growth and distribution of grasses that drives the movements of ruminants, predators, and tourists alike is tied to the seasonality and distribution of rainfall. Mobilised quite literally by all of the Earth as it revolves around the sun, the intersecting flows of wildlife and tourists are linked in the network by the movements of the Inter-Tropical Convergence Zone (ITCZ), a band of low air pressure that encircles the tropics (Sinclair 1995). The ITCZ normally passes through the region twice in a year, and save for periodic drought, brings rains during April–May and again in October–November. The Great Migration into the Maasai Mara National Reserve takes place in the dry season between these rains, from July to October, making it the peak season for the arrival of tourists. This solar systemic movement, which mobilises grasses, live-stock, wildlife, and tourists, is a vital component of a boundless and hybrid park.

Insect and virus mobilities might also be acknowledged for their role in co-producing the Maasai Mara National Reserve. Contributing to the complex network of intersecting mobilities, the spread of the rinderpest virus and tsetse flies played a significant role in the choice of the particular location for the reserve. Pastoralism had co-existed with wildlife in the area for millennia, but the presence of tsetse flies displaced the Maasai from that site near the turn of the twentieth century (Broten and Said 1995). Rinderpest, a viral livestock disease imported from Asia, led to a decline in animal populations in the area. The reduction in grazing resulted in an increase in woody vegetation, which in turn fostered the spread of tsetse flies and thus trypanosomiasis. By the 1930s the flies spread into much of the best grazing land in western Narok, and by the time the Maasai Mara National Reserve was being considered in the following decade, around 2,330 square kilometres of grazing land was unusable by livestock. It was this space that was transformed into what officially in 1961 became the Maasai Mara National Reserve (Hughes 2007). Fires set by the Maasai had steadily reduced the vegeta-tion and thus the infestation in most of the Maasai Mara area (Talbot and Olindo 1990), making it habitable once again by the 1960s.

Perhaps the most famous display of mobility at the site is the Great Migration, in which over one million wildebeest and over 200,000 zebra and other animals move northwards between July and October from Serengeti National Park into the Maasai Mara National Reserve in search of dry season pasture (Walpole *et al.* 2003). The wildebeest act as a keystone species, driving ecological interactions among grasses, ruminants, predators, and other animals in an event that the American Broadcasting Corporation (ABC) once called 'one of the seven natural wonders of the world'. But the 'nature' that the migration represents is not contained by the park boundary. The wildebeest and others quite normally move well beyond it in search of pasture. The lack of a fence around the park facilitates the two-way flow of livestock and wildlife through the open border; the former regularly occupy parts of the reserve while the latter move into the Maasai communities that act as buffer zones (Serneels *et al.* 2001).

Over 70 per cent of wildlife migrates beyond the park boundaries, making the buffer zones in the Maasai communities crucial to the success of conservation efforts. An inventory of wildlife and livestock in the Mara ecosystem suggested that between 25 and 33 per cent of the cattle herd from neighbouring Maasai ranches could be found inside the reserve (Reid *et al.* 2003). This arrangement means that the park (the purported 'island') is in effect unbounded despite its nominal 1,510 square kilometres, allowing Maasai livestock and wildlife to flow into and out of the official reserve space. Such interactive movements of humans, livestock, and wildlife continues a long history of such cohabitation on the savannah. Pastoralism in the Mara region goes back at least 2,500 years, according to archaeological evidence (Reid *et al.* 2003: 14), although colonial rule and nature ideologies have conspired to disrupt that arrangement.

While tourist imaginaries maintain a 'nature island' expectation, its official 'reserve' status allows the Maasai access to parts of the protected space, although a core section of the park is allocated exclusively for tourist access and facilities. At the same time, as an accommodation to the local Maasai, the park since its creation has been managed by the Maasai themselves. Park fees are collected by the local Narok County Council rather than by the agency that runs the rest of the country's park and reserve system, the Kenya Wildlife Service. As Talbot and Olindo (1990: 69) state, 'in fairness to the Maasai inhabitants and in consideration of the potential for success in conserving the areas, it was felt that they should receive some status which protected them but which also provided benefits from that protection to the Maasai'. The flexible territorial arrangement and ability to distribute benefits locally are major reasons for the success of the park and its relations with the Maasai (which stands in contrast with the tensions that have persisted at Amboseli National Park, in another part of Maasailand, designed more strictly according to Yellowstone model principles – see Talbot and Olindo 1990). The revenue that accrues to Maasai communities helps maintain the supportive local political environment needed for park success. These arrangements, which ensure the flow of money through the local and international tourist economy, are central to the persistence of the park and its wildebeest and other wildlife populations. This political economy is part of the complex network that constitutes the place and puts it 'in play' (Sheller and Urry 2004).

In additional ways, the purported nature of the park is not as distinct as one might imagine from the society that surrounds it. Regarding the Great Migration, one might be surprised to learn that this 'natural wonder', a phrase that evokes a timeless stability, a remnant of an African Eden, is itself produced in a complex hybrid network. Walpole *et al.* (2003: x) note that this movement 'from the Serengeti in the south has occurred on a significant scale only since 1972, when wildebeest numbers increased as a result of the successful control of rinderpest'. The rinderpest virus travelled along with the colonial transfers of cattle to Africa from Asia in the 1880s, and had seriously impacted East African cattle and ruminant wildlife by around 1890. It was not until after 1960 that a cattle vaccination programme also led to its eradication among wildlife, resulting in 'a sixfold increase in the wildebeest population between 1963 and 1977' (Sinclair 1995: 8). Their numbers rose from around 200,000 in the late 1950s to nearly 1.5 million by 1977 (Mduma *et al.* 1999), suggesting that the 'timeless' natural wonder is a hybrid, mobilised through globalised cattle exchanges, viruses, ruminants both wild and domesticated, laboratory science, and veterinary medicine.

## Tensions in the tourist imaginary

A truism of nature park tourism is that the tourists themselves are merely temporary visitors in the preserved natural spaces. From this perspective, what is real and significant about wild and scenic places are the animals, plants, and other elements of the park's ecology that are being preserved and protected from human harm. As we have attempted to demonstrate, however, tourists ought to be viewed as an integral part of the ecosystem at the Maasai Mara National Reserve. Like the climatic forces that shape the park's grasslands, tourists are a perpetual presence in the park landscape; safari vehicles are as ubiquitous as Thompson's gazelles, while the global circulation of money, airplanes, hotel networks, websites, etc., traces the reserve outwards from its purported boundaries. It is clearly the case that tourists impact the park space profoundly. Without the continual circulation of tourists and the revenue they bring, it is very possible that other elements of the ecosystem – the lions, elephants, and giraffes they come to see – might not exist at all in a location that might otherwise be transformed into farms and ranches. In a sense, the tourist is the keystone species that shapes and maintains the Maasai Mara National Reserve.

For safari tourists, however, the Yellowstone model persists as a common-sense assumption that has been crafted and renewed for over a century, even though the model no longer guides park management in African contexts. The model's strict nature/society divide was supplanted by the early 1990s with an approach that emphasised community participation (for local cooperation) and the need for porous boundaries to facilitate wildlife (and even livestock) movements (see Adams and McShane 1992). In fact, the Maasai Mara National Reserve, with its original flexible boundaries and benefits-sharing with local communities, stands as the earliest example of what is now a more commonplace approach to park management. The perception in the tourist imaginary, however, remains tied to the Yellowstone model. Its legacy means that visitors persistently demand purity in their safari experience, separating the natural sanctuary inside from the degraded outside, even though their expectations often run counter to their experience.

Bilal Butt (2012) explains that parks in East Africa are fetishised for tourists in a manner that obscures the historical transformations that made them available as 'natural' places for visitors. These park spaces represent the final bastion of pristine, primeval nature, and tourists expect to experience it as such upon arrival. As Butt (2012: 109–10) points out, internationally 'the safari is created among a network of tour actors by enforcing a separation between "nature" and "culture". This is evident from the popular imagery describing the "anticipated" safari and from the narratives of the tourists themselves.' When tourists perceive violations of this arrangement, such as the presence of Maasai livestock in the park, they often speak out accordingly. Butt describes such tourist expectations as a problem for park staff: 'Tourists often become dissatisfied when they witness people and/ or cattle inside protected areas, as these experiences contrast with the safari experience marketed to them' (2012: 105).

Butt's interviews with tourists confirm their imagination of nature in a particularly pure form. The most common response heard regarding cattle inside the park is 'why are those cows inside the park? Isn't that illegal?' (Butt 2012: 108). A tourist from Boston declared: 'They should not allow cows into the park. They are damaging this precious ecosystem and *it is not natural*. They eat all the grass and scare away all the animals that we have traveled thousands of miles to see!' (Butt 2012: 108, emphasis in original). Hotel managers, front-desk clerks, and park rangers all testify to this common refrain, while they in turn often pressure park managers to take steps to keep cattle out of tourist view. The global circulation of safari tourism, with its connection to local and global economies, impacts the steps taken by park management to placate these demands.

The persistence of the Yellowstone model in the tourist imaginary perpetuates ideas about protecting 'nature' and reinforces assumptions about the temporary presence of the tourist. At the same time this imaginary can obscure awareness of the impacts that tourists themselves have on the landscape. In this sense transportation and communications technologies are important components of safari park ecology. The Land Rovers and pop-top minivans carry tourists on 'game drives', during which the drivers/guides seek out examples of the most glamorous of wildlife species – particularly the Big Five. The vehicles also serve to protect the tourists from the animals they observe, allowing drivers to stop within metres of a feeding lion or leopard without fear of harm. CB radios installed in each vehicle provide vital guidance to tourist movements, allowing guides to communicate with one another where animals can be viewed (speaking in languages, such as Kiswahili and Gĩkũyũ, the drivers also sometimes use the radios to poke fun at their tourist clients). Tour guides have a significant interest in pleasing their clients, in part to generate added income from tips, repeat business, and word of mouth for their employers. Towards this end, upon hearing radio communication about the location of a lion, leopard or rhino, it is quite common for drivers/guides to abandon the park roadways and drive (at a quickened pace) in a straight line to the location. In effect, the vehicles make their own tracks through the grasslands in the pursuit of wildlife, and repeatedly so, creating visible damage to the landscape along the way. Honey (1999: 312) points out that 'off-track driving is illegal but very common, and this causes deep ruts and destroys grasses and shrubs eaten by the animals'. This is a problem that has been discussed in Kenya for decades, with observers calling for more effective forms of management in park systems throughout East Africa. As far back as 1979, David Western, a key figure in Kenyan wildlife conservation and former director of the Kenya Wildlife Service, called for greater intervention in the control of park visitors, such as traffic controls, as a means of avoiding ecological degradation and deterioration of the scenic resource.

An additional dimension of these technological effects is the crowding of animals by safari vehicles. Once the location of a desirable wildlife specimen is known and communicated, multiple vehicles in the vicinity soon arrive, and drivers move in for the best photographic views. Viewers of the Expedia.com and Abercrombie & Kent advertisements described earlier in this chapter might be disappointed to learn that the promised solitude with wildlife is likely to be shared with half a dozen or so other vehicles packed into the same location. It is quite normal, if illegal, for a semi-circle of vehicles to park within just a few metres of a lion or leopard eating its prey. Igoe (2004: 14) points to the hybrid experience that disrupts tourist 'nature' expectations:

> This imaginary vision is difficult to resolve with the reality of a traffic jam of zebra-striped safari vans converging on a rhino that happens to be wearing a collar that allows authorities to monitor his movements with a high-tech satellite tracking system.

## Conclusion

The modern myths that encourage tourists to view the Maasai Mara National Reserve as a 'nature island', a place to glimpse a remnant of Eden, produce a park with an appearance of stability as a fixed destination for tourists. But as Sheller puts it, destinations are 'always fluid, relational, and unstable' (Sheller 2004: 21). Safari tourism in the Maasai Mara National Reserve is presented in this chapter as a hybrid of nature and culture that shapes the park over its history and exceeds its boundaries. Its status as a destination is complicated by intersecting networks of trade, race/class, predators, prey, and ecological relationships, and so much more. We follow Sheller and Urry (2004: 21) in saying that while 'mobility is always located and materialized', these '[p]laces to play are only contingently stabilized for purposes of tourist consumption'.

## References

Abercrombie & Kent (2015) *Abercrombie & Kent best of 2015: Luxury small group journeys.* Brochure, Lombard, Illinois, USA.
Adams, J. S. and McShane, T. O. (1992) *The myth of wild Africa: Conservation without illusion.* Berkeley: University of California Press.
Broten, M. D. and Said, M. (1995) 'Population trends of ungulates in and around Kenya's Masai Mara Reserve', in A. R. E. Sinclair and P. Arcese (eds), *Serengeti II: Dynamics, management, and conservation of an ecosystem.* Chicago and London: University of Chicago Press, 169–93.
Butt, B. (2012) 'Commoditizing the Safari and making space for conflict: Place, identity and parks in East Africa', *Political Geography*, 31(1): 104–13.
Hannam, K. (2009) 'The end of tourism? Nomadology and the mobilities paradigm', in J. Tribe (ed.), *Philosophical issues in tourism.* Bristol: Channel View, 101–13.
Hannam, K., Butler, G. and Paris, C. (2014) 'Developments and key concepts in tourism mobilities', *Annals of Tourism Research*, 44(1): 171–85.
Honey, M. (1999) *Ecotourism and sustainable development: Who owns paradise?* Washington, DC: Island Press.
Hughes, L. (2007) 'Rough time in paradise: Claims, blames and memory making around some protected areas in Kenya', *Conservation and Society*, 5(3): 307–30.
Igoe, J. (2004) *Conservation and globalization: A study of national parks and indigenous communities from East Africa to South Dakota.* Belmont, CA: Wadsworth/Thompson.

Kohn, E. (2013) *How forests think: Toward an anthropology beyond the human*. Berkeley: University of California Press.

Latour, B. (1993) *We have never been modern*. Cambridge, MA: Harvard University Press.

Law, J. (2006) 'Disaster in agriculture: Or foot and mouth mobilities', *Environment and Planning A*, 38(2): 227–39.

Marris, E. (2011) *Rambunctious garden: Saving nature in a post-wild world*. New York: Bloomsbury.

Mduma, S. A. R., Sinclair, A. R. E. and Hilborn, R. (1999) 'Food regulates the Serengeti wildebeest: A 40-year record', *Journal of Animal Ecology*, 68: 1101–122.

Mudimbe, V. Y. (1994) *The idea of Africa*. Bloomington: Indiana University Press.

Muir, J. (1901) *Our national parks*. Madison: University of Wisconsin Press.

Nash, R. F. (2001) *Wilderness and the American mind*, 4th edn. New Haven, CT and London: Yale University Press.

Neumann, R. P. (1998) *Imposing wilderness: Struggles over livelihood and nature preservation in Africa*. Berkeley: University of California Press.

Neumann, R. P. (2004) 'Moral and discursive geographies in the war for biodiversity in Africa', *Political Geography*, 23(3): 813–37.

Ole Seur, D. (2003) 'Opening address', in M. Walpole, G. Karanja, N.Sitati and N. Leader-Williams (eds), *Wildlife and people: Conflict and conservation in Maasai Mara, Kenya*, IIED Wildlife and Development Series No. 14. London: International Institute for Environment and Development, 1–2.

ORD Group (2015) *Maasai Mara National Reserve*. Online at: http://maasaimara.com (accessed 5 September 2015).

Philo, C. and Wilbert, C. (eds) (2000) *Animal spaces, beastly places: New geographies of human–animal relations*. New York: Routledge.

Reid, R. S., Rainy, M., Ogutu, J., Kruska, R. L., Kimani, K., Nyabenge, M., McCartney, M., Kshatriya, M., Worden., J., Nga'nga, L., Owuor, J., Kinoti., Njuguna, E., Wilson, C. J. and Lamprey, R. (2003) *People, wildlife and livestock in the Mara ecosystem: The Mara count 2002*. Nairobi: International Livestock Research Institute.

Rosaldo, R. (1989) *Culture and truth: The remaking of social analysis*. Boston, MA: Beacon Press.

Salazar, N. B. (2010) *Envisioning Eden: Mobilizing imaginaries in tourism and beyond*. New York: Berghahn.

Serneels, S., Said, M. Y. and Lambin, E. F. (2001) 'Land cover changes around a major East African wildlife reserve: The Mara ecosystem (Kenya)', *International Journal of Remote Sensing*, 22(17): 3397–420.

Sheller, M. (2004) 'Demobilizing and remobilizing Caribbean paradise', in M. Sheller and J. Urry (eds), *Tourism mobilities: Places to play, places in play*. London: Routledge, 13–21.

Sheller, M. and Urry, J. (2004) 'Places to play, places in play', in M. Sheller and J. Urry (eds), *Tourism mobilities: Places to play, places in play*. London: Routledge, 1–10.

Sheller, M. and Urry, J. (2006) 'The new mobilities paradigm', *Environment and Planning A*, 38(1): 207–26.

Sinclair, A. R. E. (1995) 'Serengeti past and present', in A. R. E. Sinclair and P. Arcese (eds), *Serengeti II: Dynamics, management, and conservation of an ecosystem*. Chicago and London: University of Chicago Press, 3–30.

Talbot, L. and Olindo, P. (1990) 'The Maasai Mara and Amboseli reserves', in A. Kiss (ed.), *Living with wildlife: Wildlife resource management with local participation in Africa*, World Bank Technical Paper No. 130. Washington, DC: World Bank, 67–74.

Thompson, C. (2002) 'When elephants stand for competing philosophies of nature: Amboseli National Park, Kenya, in J. Law and A. Mol (eds), *Complexities: Social studies of knowledge practices*. Durham, NC: Duke University Press, 166–90.

Udall, S. L. (1962) 'Nature islands for the world', in A. B. Adams (ed.), *First world conference on national parks*. Washington, DC: United States Department of the Interior, 1–10.

Walpole, M., Karanja, G., Sitati, N. and Leader-Williams, N. (2003) 'Introduction', in M. Walpole, G. Karanja, N. Sitati and N. Leader-Williams (eds), *Wildlife and people: Conflict and conservation in Maasai Mara, Kenya*, IIED Wildlife and Development Series No. 14. London: International Institute for Environment and Development, ix–xi.

Whatmore, S. (2002) *Hybrid geographies: Natures, cultures, spaces*. Thousand Oaks, CA: Sage.

# 18 Decolonising tourism mobilities?

## Planning research within a First Nations community in Northern Canada

*Bryan S. R. Grimwood, Lauren J. King, Allison P. Holmes, and the Lutsel K'e Dene First Nation*

## Introduction

The tundra thunders underfoot when muskoxen bolt across the terrain. Clad in thick wool coats, a strong musky odour during rut, and long curved horns, these large ancient-looking members of the *Bovidae* family have adapted and evolved in habitat primarily located in Arctic Canada and Greenland. Like other herd species, muskoxen's primary defence mechanism when they sense danger is to run. They are unique, however, in that after a few hundred metres they stop and circle up, the bulkier males stationed on the outside to protect the smaller females and calves on the inside. Against wolves and other historic predators, this response has proven successful in terms of maintaining herd health and integrity. But against humans with guns, muskoxen are, emblematically, sitting ducks.

Near the turn of the twentieth century, as settler exploration of the central Canadian sub-Arctic intensified, hunters and adventurers took full advantage of modern weaponry to decimate muskoxen populations. A principal purpose was to procure woollen hides cherished by distant markets. John Hornby was one of a handful of Euro-settler explorers who wrote vehemently to centralised authorities in Ottawa (Canada's capital city) about the possibility of muskoxen extinction and the drastic need for wildlife management measures to be taken (Pelly 1996). In 1927, officials at the now defunct Ministry of the Interior designated initial boundaries of a protected area of 15,000 square kilometres called the Thelon Game Sanctuary. Straddling boreal forest and tundra ecozones, the Sanctuary's stated mandate was to conserve and manage natural resources, with muskoxen being one particularly valuable asset to protect. As detailed by environmental historian John Sandlos (2007), all hunting and trapping was formally outlawed within the Sanctuary's borders. This included the subsistence and culturally entrenched harvesting practices of Denesoline (Chipewyan Dene) and Caribou Inuit – peoples who, over generations, had sustained nomadic and semi-nomadic livelihoods within the region and relied heavily on areas within the Sanctuary. Indigenous mobility within this space was explicitly displaced by colonial command.

While state legislation and policy aimed to move indigenous practices out, the Sanctuary – along with its namesake, the Thelon River – was becoming conceived and performed as a space for other corporeal mobilities. In addition to explorations of scientific and resource extraction personnel, recreational canoe travellers, with gazes fixed upon the Thelon's emblematic 'wilderness' and 'northern frontier' qualities, began passing through as early as 1962 (Morse 1987). As a destination for independent and guided multi-day canoe expeditions, the Thelon entered into the circulation of a particular 'nature narrative', one that views travel as an escape from the everyday, environmentally benign, and fundamental to a particular Canadian nationalistic identity (Erickson 2013; Grimwood 2011). As Grimwood *et al.* (2015) have shown, contemporary enactments of such touristic mobilities within the Thelon Wildlife Sanctuary, now 52,000 square kilometres, help perpetuate colonial tendencies that marginalise, in both overt and subtle ways, the livelihoods of Indigenous peoples. Drawing on critical discourse analysis of touristic texts, Grimwood *et al.* show how tourists' emplacement of Indigeneity within certain spatial (pristine nature) and temporal (historic) registers works to obscure and deem out-of-place contemporary Indigenous practices, meanings and mobilities within the landscape. That existing livelihoods of Denesoline and Caribou Inuit are 'othered', if not concealed, in discursive representations of touring the Thelon mirrors effects observed elsewhere in Canada (e.g. Braun 2002) and beyond (e.g. Hall and Tucker 2004).

The aim of this chapter is to profile research activities designed to elevate Indigenous uses, narratives, and mobilities associated with the Thelon as a counterbalance to the colonial silencings often perpetuated through tourism. Focus is placed on reviewing the development and planning of collaborative research between university researchers and the Lutsel K'e Dene First Nations (LKDFN) in Canada's Northwest Territories. In the wake of postcolonial critiques of tourism and other leisure mobilities (Hall and Tucker 2004; Fox 2007), and the recognition that touring the Thelon (or any other place for that matter) does not exist in a cultural vacuum but comprises multiple flows of corporeal mobility and values (Grimwood 2015), the chapter seeks to augment emerging literature that engages with decolonising and Indigenous perspectives. More specifically, our task herein is to build off related theoretical, reflexive, and empirical work (see e.g. Peters and Higgins-Desbiolles 2012; Russell-Mundine 2012; Chambers and Buzinde 2015) by reporting research partnership and planning processes that may contribute to decolonising tourism mobilities. These intentions will be clarified as we situate our research activities within related literatures.

## Decolonising perspectives for tourism mobilities

One upshot of the turn to mobilities in tourism studies is that theoretical and empirical insights have been greatly enhanced by engaging the blurred boundaries between tourism and other categories and scales of corporeal movement (Coles *et al.* 2006; Hannam 2009; Cohen and Cohen 2014, 2015). Cohen and Cohen (2015), for instance, argued that situating tourism within a broader mobilities paradigm provides opportunities for better understanding expanding tourist flows from emerging world regions, and thus serves as a response to the limits of modernist Eurocentric theoretical frameworks in widespread use in tourism (see e.g. Aleng 2002). To further marshal the move beyond Eurocentrism proffered by mobilities requires that our field also learn to value and equitably engage non-Eurocentric epistemologies and methodologies (Chambers and Buzinde 2015). Such engagement will create spaces for knowing tourism as a dimension within broader contexts and relations of (im)mobility (Hannam 2009), and provide tools for fostering social justice via research (Johnson and Parry 2015).

Tourism researchers increasingly acknowledge that the Eurocentric nature of knowledge and its production tends to obscure, if not ignore, the knowledges of other cultures and historically marginalised groups (Cater 2006; Chambers and Buzinde 2015). Prompted by the 'critical turn' in tourism studies (Ateljevic *et al.* 2007), the field has done well to embrace postcolonial, post-structural, critical realist, and other theoretical perspectives to challenge conventional ways of knowing tourism, doing tourism research and relating to indigenous tourism stakeholders (Peters and Higgins-Desbiolles 2012). Yet, as several scholars have observed, much more must be done to realise any true sense of equity and respect within knowledge production processes. A case in point is the study of indigenous tourism (Butler and Hinch 2007). For example, as Nielsen and Wilson (2012) observed, despite being a topic of academic interest for over three decades, there is a dearth of Indigenous tourism literature that discusses the role of Indigenous people themselves within the research process. Moreover, seldom have non-indigenous researchers approached indigenous peoples as tourists themselves, opting instead to reinscribe Indigenous subjectivities as 'host' or touristic 'other'. In effect, Indigenous tourism research remains predominantly driven by the needs and priorities of non-Indigenous people (Nielsen and Wilson 2012).

Chambers and Buzinde (2015) provide important conceptual and reflexive footing for 'de-linking' research from such ethnocentrism and hegemony. These authors focus on decolonial theory, which they indicate 'urges scholars to think of the possibility of another way of knowing about and being in tourism that does not privilege Western epistemologies' (Chambers and Buzinde 2015: 5). In turn, decolonial research reflects a process that continuously critiques imperialism and colonialism while implementing 'indigenous epistemologies and critical interpretive practices that are shaped by indigenous agendas' (Smith 1999: 20). It falls within the broader project of decolonisation that aims 'to create space in everyday life, research, academia, and society for an indigenous perspective without it being neglected, shunted aside, mocked, or dismissed' (Kovach 2009: 85). All aspects of decolonial research processes thus aim to foreground, value, and reclaim Indigenous voices and knowledges, and to forge cross-cultural partnerships with, between and among Indigenous researchers and allied others (Chambers and Buzinde 2015). Collaborative projects that draw on common goals, reflect anticolonial sensibilities in action and ensure reciprocity with respect to benefits of research are other aspects of decolonial research (Chambers and Buzinde 2015).

Indigenous scholars have raised concern that the language of 'decolonial' research helps to enclose Indigenous identities and cultures within a totalising discourse of colonialism (Smith 1999; Kovach 2009). Scholars have thus aimed instead to articulate and apply Indigenous methodologies (Louis 2007; Wilson 2008; Kovach 2009; Chilisa 2012). Characterized by Louis (2007) to include relational accountability, respectful representation, reciprocal appropriation, and endorsement of Indigenous rights and regulations, Indigenous methodologies emphasise cyclical and dynamic research styles with the central intent of performing sympathetic, respectful, and ethical research from an Indigenous perspective (Smith 1999; Wilson 2008). The methodological politics here include instilling axiology across disciplines and fields of study in order to challenge objectivity, universal abstractions and generalised understandings (Panelli 2008). Indigenous methodologies advocate styles of knowing and producing knowledge that are responsive to place and strive for balanced power relationships between the researcher and researched (Wilson 2008; Johnson 2010).

Looking across the scope of tourism and mobilities research, the literature describing specific decolonising and/or Indigenous methodological processes is rather scarce. Lacking in particular are reports on how research partnerships might be forged between Indigenous and non-Indigenous allies. These gaps are not surprising given Nielsen and Wilson's (2012) analysis of the role, presence and engagement of Indigenous peoples in research in our field. Drawing on a review of literature, these authors identify and describe four 'types' of Indigenous tourism research – invisible, identified, stakeholder, and Indigenous-driven – which are differentiated based on the role of Indigenous peoples in the research process (e.g. their degree of participation and control) and the overall research focus or objectives (e.g. from descriptive ethnographies to prompting Indigenous self-determination). The main argument underpinning this typology 'is that the voices of Indigenous people, and their engagement in the industry, are still rarely heard beneath that of (White/western) academics' (Nielsen and Wilson 2012: 3). Wearing and Wearing (2014) echo this perspective, albeit within an ecotourism context and on the premise that greater attention to a 'bottom up' community development and participation approach to moral encounters in tourism is necessary.

Accordingly, by reporting on aspects of developing and planning collaborative research between university researchers and the LKDFN, this chapter contributes to specific methodological opportunities for realising the potential of a decolonising research paradigm within tourism and mobility studies. In what follows, we report on research within Lutsel K'e that mirrors what Nielson and Wilson (2012: 5–6) describe as the Indigenous-driven 'type' of research:

> Within the *Indigenous-driven* phase, Indigenous people often drive the tourism research process. In this phase, there is considerably more Indigenous authorship and co-authorship of papers. Further, in many cases, Indigenous people are the end users of the research, with findings and outcomes directly geared towards their needs. In the small but growing Indigenous-driven position,

a range of topics has been investigated, including Indigenous tourism development, cultural information protection and cross-cultural/reconciliation activities. Indigenous self-determination is also an overt goal throughout the entire research process.

Importantly, and especially in the case of our research, as Nielsen and Wilson (2012: 6) indicate: 'Indigenous-driven research does not dictate that only Indigenous people might conduct it.' We are encouraged by Kovach's words, that 'non-Indigenous critical theorists are strong allies for Indigenous methodologies. They can assist in making space for Indigenous methods (protocols, ethics, data collection processes), but also for the epistemic shift from a Western paradigm that Indigenous methodologies bring' (2009: 86).

## Developing and planning collaborative research

### Case study background

The Thelon River is a main artery in the Hudson Bay watershed in sub-Arctic Canada. From its headwaters east of Great Slave Lake in the Northwest Territories, the Thelon flows roughly 900 kilometres out of the boreal biome and into the tundra, emptying at Baker Lake in Nunavut. Raffan (1993: 46) has described the Thelon as 'a place of edges', an area of cultural and biological transition with a 'compelling combination of wildlife, wild water, history, scenery, and sense of isolation'. Indeed, the Thelon traverses some of the most undeveloped terrain remaining on the planet: an emblematic wilderness for adventurers (Pelly 1997) and ideal habitat for large mammals such as migratory herds of barren-ground caribou (Kelsall 1968). For generations of Indigenous inhabitants, including the Denesoline and Caribou Inuit, caribou have been primary subsistence and cultural livelihood resources (Gordon 1996). Significant harvesting activity continues at various caribou crossing sites along the Thelon River. The contemporary reality of the watershed, however, is not limited to perceptions of 'wilderness' and 'homeland'. The Thelon is also a place characterised by both rapid and gradual social, ecological, economic, and cultural changes. These changes are associated with climate, colonial regimes of wildlife management, treaty negotiations and land claims, competing sovereignties, protected areas, resource extraction, and Indigenous peoples' transition from nomadic societies to wage economy and settlement lifestyles (Sandlos 2007; Parlee 2012; Grimwood and Doubleday 2013a).

*Picturing the Thelon River* is an extended case study that engages different knowledges of the Thelon River watershed in Arctic Canada to cultivate enhanced understanding of, and responsible relationships to, a significant place within the context of social-ecological change. More specifically, the project involves diverse Thelon River stakeholders, primarily Indigenous inhabitants and non-Indigenous river tourists, in documenting and dialoguing knowledges with the intention of mobilising collective place-based and values-centred visions for

*Table 18.1* Multiple phases of *Picturing the Thelon River*

| Research phases | Research activities |
| --- | --- |
| Phase 1 (2008–11) | • Research with Caribou Inuit residents of Baker Lake, NU and river canoe tourists<br>• Photo-interviews, experiential river journeys, community workshops |
| Phase 2 (2012) | • Outreach activities in Lutsel K'e, NWT<br>• Community workshops |
| Phase 3 (2013–16) | • Research with Lutsel K'e Dene First Nation<br>• Narrative interviews, community workshops, knowledge exchange land camp |

positive nature–society transformations. Oriented by principles of community-based and participatory research (Castleden *et al.* 2012), the study emphasises collaborative research relationships between northern Indigenous and non-Indigenous communities and decolonising methodologies. As highlighted in Table 18.1, the project has evolved in three phases. Activities associated with the current third phase are the primary focus below.

### *Initiating new research relationships*

Between 2008 and 2011, research was carried out with Caribou Inuit residents of Baker Lake, Nunavut, and Thelon River canoe tourists, which gleaned insight into the multiple relationships, perceptions, and experiences of the Thelon. Methods included participant photography and interviews, followed by work-shops with Caribou Inuit in which research materials were shared with and inter-preted by elders, youth, and land users. These methods prompted dialogue concerning observations of change, cultural norms and practices, different types of river experiences, and the significance of the Thelon to individual and cultural constructions of identity (Grimwood and Doubleday 2013b). In effect, centring interviews and workshops with participant photographs created safe social spaces for knowledge exchange, which in turn enabled relational metaphors of shared values and responsibilities to surface (Grimwood 2015).

Sharing these research outcomes with Denesoline inhabitants of the Thelon was Grimwood's primary objective for visiting Lutsel K'e, Northwest Territories in November 2012. Lutsel K'e is a Denesoline community of roughly 300 people situated on the east arm of Great Slave Lake, which maintains strong cultural ties to the Thelon's headwater and upper river regions. The LKDFN has a history of capacity for collaborating with university researchers. For example, projects with Parlee have led to increased understanding of traditional caribou monitoring strategies, Indigenous perspectives on health, and the role of traditional knowl-edge in resource management (Parlee *et al.* 2007; Parlee 2012). Other collabora-tive studies have documented Denesoline knowledge of barren ground caribou (Kendrick *et al.* 2005) and explored community perceptions of conservation benefits (Bennett *et al.* 2010).

Grimwood's November 2012 outreach visit was arranged following initial telephone and email communications with band representatives. The LKDFN Chief at the time appointed the Lutsel K'e Wildlife, Lands, and Environment Committee (WLEC) to oversee communications and research partnerships. The WLEC agreed to host a meeting at their community office and wished to learn more about Phase 1 research with Caribou Inuit and canoeists. They also expressed interest in building on previous community-sanctioned research noted above, as well as recent conservation-oriented events that afforded opportunities for Lutsel K'e youth to reconnect with the Thelon as sacred ancestral territory (Petermann 2000; Sanjayan 2011).

During the meeting, Phase 1 research materials such as photographs, excerpts from interview transcripts, and maps were circulated for inspection and discussion. Emphasis was very much on dialogue, storytelling, and co-learning. Midway through the workshop, the WLEC requested that Grimwood leave the meeting so that they could deliberate in confidence and determine the path forward. The decision to include Denesoline participation in the Thelon River study was very much in the hands of these community representatives. When Grimwood was invited back to the meeting, the WLEC Manager summarised committee deliberations and shared expectations, rationale, and possible processes for adapting the study to their local context. Grimwood and the WLEC agreed to work together to translate these ideas into a research funding application. The WLEC also made arrangements for project information and future research plans to be shared with Elders and youth prior to Grimwood's departure from Lutsel K'e.

Over the next two months, Grimwood worked with the WLEC Manager and a university colleague to develop a grant proposal based on outcomes from the Phase 2 outreach workshops. The substance and scope of the grant evolved based on feedback from the WLEC via their manager. It ultimately focused on three objectives:

1   *Documenting local and traditional knowledge* – to foster and celebrate Denesoline cultural livelihoods by recording, experiencing, and exchanging local and traditional knowledge associated with the Thelon River watershed.
2   *Decoding Thelon representations* – to synthesise, critically analyse, and interpret Thelon River watershed policy documents, archives, and conservation-driven media productions for meaningful use within the community context of Lutsel K'e.
3   *Research planning and development* – to mobilise knowledge outcomes to plan and pilot a knowledge exchange land camp that would provide a context for (a) Denesoline land users, Denesoline youth, and university researchers to interpret research while experiencing or *doing* Denesoline traditional knowledge; and (b) future collaborative research between Denesoline, Inuit, and university researchers.

In June 2013, this third phase of the Thelon River study was awarded two years of funding from Canada's Social Sciences and Humanities Research Council (www.sshrc-crsh.gc.ca/).

### *Planning community-based and participatory research with Denesoline*

After funding was obtained, an important next step was for university researchers and community representatives to clarify research priorities and plan activities that would address these aims. In December 2013, Grimwood, King, and Holmes visited Lutsel K'e for five days. The main purpose of this second preliminary fieldwork visit was to participate in and facilitate a two-day planning workshop with the WLEC and other interested LKDFN representatives. The goals of the workshop, which occurred in the Lutsel K'e Council Chambers, were to:

- develop a solid foundation for future work together by building relationships between the community of Lutsel K'e and university researchers;
- collaborate on clarifying expectations, priorities, and timelines about the research project and associated land camp, including the various roles to be played by community and university researchers; and
- generate feelings of excitement about the *Picturing the Thelon River* research project.

As people arrived to the workshop, introductions were made over coffee, tea, and morning snacks. The workshop commenced following an opening prayer offered by an Elder member of the WLEC. To prompt some initial dialogue and shared understandings, attendees were invited to describe a personal experience or tell a story associated with the Thelon River or with research more generally. Next, we discussed the broader *Picturing the Thelon River* study, which involved revisiting information and photographs from work carried out with canoeists and Caribou Inuit, as well as details on the evolution of the newly funded project. In this overview, emphasis was placed on the collaborative dimensions of the research and how the substance and processes of the project could be adapted based on input received during the workshop.

The balance of the two-day meeting consisted of a series of interactive, brainstorming, and discussion-generating activities aimed at specifying research priorities and best practices from a community perspective. Some of these activities were adapted collaborative social-engagement methods (Chevalier and Buckles 2008) and talking circles (Wilson 2008), while others evolved more organically or in consultation with the WLEC Manager. With the consent of all attendees, the workshop activities, discussions, and outcomes were recorded through field-notes and photographs. These records were instrumental to preparing a thorough and accurate workshop report for the WLEC and broader LKDFN community. They have also been integrated in the following overview of workshop outcomes, which is organised around the key questions or topics of the workshop.

### *Research planning outcomes*

In response to the question, 'What would you like people to know about the Thelon River?', workshop participants emphasised that Denesoline stories about the Thelon must be communicated within and beyond Lutsel K'e. These stories involve both historical and contemporary relationships to the Thelon, and relate to the following: ancestors; sacred animals like caribou, muskoxen, and white fox; how the Thelon Wildlife Sanctuary came to be; place names and traditional uses; respecting the land while travelling; and the historic and contemporary role of Denesoline and Caribou Inuit as primary stewards of the river system. Telling Denesoline stories of the Thelon was identified as a way to teach young Denesoline and visitors about protecting the river environment – inclusive of animals, caribou calving grounds and migration routes, ancestors, drinking water, cultural artefacts like spearheads and caches – from resource exploration and exploitation.

Workshop participants were then asked, 'What does "good" or "respectful" research look like?' This question aimed to distinguish community understandings of and preferences for research processes and practices that could be deemed responsible. Workshop participants were first tasked with recording individual responses in the form of single words or short phrases on cue cards. Each workshop participant then reported their ideas and helped arrange these into initial themes on a white board. Group discussion was prompted and additional notes and linkages between ideas were represented. Group discussions continued following individual reports and led to more refined groupings of cue cards based on content. Figure 18.1 depicts how ideas were ultimately synthesised. They show that, according to workshop participants, 'good' and 'respectful' research is about doing research that can contribute towards 'being a Dene on the land'. This process consists of seven components, the meanings and details of which are summarised in Table 18.2 and reflect verbatim content contained on cue cards.

The next question WLEC and other Lutsel K'e community members were asked was, 'What are the main priorities for the Thelon River research project?' Workshop participants engaged in a second cue card activity to identify and rank research priorities and desired learning outcomes. Similar to the previous activity, individuals identified and reported initial ideas and then grouped cue cards into related themes. The next step, however, was for participants to rank cue card themes using coloured stickers. Each participant was allocated an equal number of stickers and instructed to place these on cue card themes they perceived as most important. Accordingly, the more stickers a cue card theme received, the higher the priority. In the end, seven priority themes resulted:

- *Future orientations: youth connections.* The study must be future-oriented. It can help to inform and teach young people about the sacred significance and national recognition of the Thelon, and how to mitigate real and potential impacts.
- *Play a leading role in Thelon governance and management.* The study should promote local understanding of management issues (e.g. user information, monitoring) and support Lutsel K'e's involvement in Thelon River and Sanctuary governance.
- *Land camp experience.* The study should encourage Dene of all ages to return to the Thelon with their families. It can promote trips to different sites and in different seasons.

*Figure 18.1* Framework for research that can help 'being a Dene on the land'.

- *Denesoline connections with Inuit.* The study, and specifically the land camp experience, can be a bridge between Denesoline and Inuit, and their respective representatives and governments.
- *Changes observed and responses to them.* The study can enable enhanced knowledge of changes that have occurred, or are occurring, within the Thelon (e.g. with respect to impacts of climate change and mining on water, wildlife or plants), and how Lutsel K'e has responded, or is responding, to these changes.
- *Thelon stories.* The study should emphasise stories about Denesoline relationships to the Thelon River and encourage these stories to be told and heard within Lutsel K'e.
- *Identifying and understanding different ways of using the Thelon.* The study can enable enhanced knowledge of different uses, and potential uses, of the Thelon River.

The next activity was entitled 'Imagining the headwaters land camp'. Complementary to emerging interest in arts-based methodologies (Rydzik *et al.*

*Table 18.2* Components of research that can help 'being a Dene on the land'

| Framework components | Verbatim content of cue cards |
| --- | --- |
| Collaboration | Team work; communication; working with elders, youth, WLEC; traditional knowledge; become friends; collaborate in data collection, analysis, publication. |
| Learning together | Learning from each other; learning (youth, elders, community, researchers, students); teaching and learning traditional knowledge; return T.K. back to schools for our young ones for next generation. |
| Review and reporting | Transparency (e.g. open communication); ongoing reporting; intensive review and reporting (different ways of reporting – radio station, going to schools, feasts – not just public meetings); review everything before published; accurately convey LKDFN relationship, meaning, activities and stories, and to protect them. |
| Respect | Respect different knowledges; respect all caribou movement (pathways and migration); good researchers are allowed back; community-driven outcomes reflect a positive relationship between the researchers and the community; listening to stories and listening for stories; honesty. |
| Local protocols and ownership | Follow local research protocols; local ownership of research and knowledge outcomes. |
| On-the-land observations; being there | Animals – what type roam in the area during different seasons?; what type of vegetation grows in the Thelon area?; balancing scientific knowledge and traditional knowledge; understanding landscape features (trees, wildlife, terrain). |
| Benefits to the community | Tangible, possibly long-term benefits; meaningful partnerships with knowledge holders; useful data or information for LKDFN; using local knowledge; help protect the Thelon; training for community members – taking advantage of knowledge and capacity that comes from the community. |

2013), a drawing exercise proved to be a highly interactive and creative way for participants to express their ideas and expectations about a future land camp experience. Working in small groups and using chart paper, markers, and pencil crayons, the workshop generated four illustrative maps. These are shown in Figure 18.2. Upon completion, each group explained the substance of their map to other workshop participants, spurring dialogue and debate about this capstone research activity. Overall, a number of expectations for the land camp were identified. Consensus determined that the land camp would involve six to eight participants, including youth and land users from Lutsel K'e, and members of the research team. The group would travel in early spring (March or April) along Denesoline trails to one of the Thelon's headwater lakes via snowmobile, carrying food, camping equipment, and other supplies upon towed sleds. The WLEC envisioned this as an opportunity for Denesoline youth to directly experience local and traditional knowledge under the guidance of Denesoline land users and to be involved in research activities. The camp would serve as a base for sharing and co-interpreting

*Figure 18.2*  Visions of a research land camp on Denesoline lands.

knowledge derived from other research activities in Lutsel K'e, and from previous Thelon River research with Inuit and tourists. Knowledge could also be integrated into action items for designing future collaborative research bringing together Denesoline and Caribou Inuit to celebrate and maintain distinctive cultural livelihoods within the Thelon watershed. Thus, the WLEC viewed the land camp as an ideal environment for learning about Denesoline relationships to the Thelon, and for communicating knowledge between generations and across cultures.

### *'Moving forward'*

A final discussion focused on identifying specific action items and desired research outcomes. Regarding the former, the WLEC requested that university researchers prepare a detailed workshop report and a concise plan of research activities that aligned with the expectations, priorities, and visions expressed during the workshop. The WLEC Manager was designated to support and facilitate open lines of communication between university researchers and the LKDFN.

Other action items that were identified included preparing applications to the University of Waterloo research ethics board and to the Aurora Research Institute for an academic research licence, and developing a formal research agreement to be signed by university and LKDFN officials. The WLEC also advised that data collection should begin during April and May 2014 so as to avoid the summer months when people are often unavailable and travelling on the land. A Lutsel K'e research coordinator would be identified to facilitate this work. It was agreed that the knowledge exchange land camp was best suited for later on in the project, in 2015 or 2016, once data had been collected and some preliminary analysis completed.

The desired research outcomes represent the types of reciprocal research benefits that advocates of Indigenous, community-based and participatory methodologies have called for (Castleden *et al.* 2012). For example, ownership of information collected during the study would be retained by the LKDFN and all data would be permanently stored in the community's traditional knowledge digital archives. University researchers would be granted access to this data for analysis and interpretation. Workshop participants identified that dissemination strategies should include not only academic papers reviewed by LKDFN representatives prior to publication, but also outputs designed specifically for community use or development. Ideas included ongoing plain-language research reports, school curriculum resources like children or youth story books, community events to celebrate knowledge contributions and Denesoline connections to the Thelon, and information pamphlets or websites that would circulate information within and beyond Lutsel K'e. It was agreed that the definitive outcome of the study – the knowledge exchange land camp – would focus on teaching and learning, telling stories, and respecting the land and water.

## Conclusion

This chapter has reported on research development and planning methodologies underpinning Indigenous-driven research on relationships between tourism and Indigenous cultural livelihoods. More specifically, the chapter highlights aspects of *Picturing the Thelon River*, a multi-phased study oriented by principles of community-based, participatory, and Indigenous methodologies. Emphasis has been placed on processes that enabled university researchers and representatives of the LKDFN to engage as equal partners in research from the outset of our current project. From this allied approach emerged study objectives and priorities, ground rules for 'good' and 'respectful' research relationships, desirable and mutually beneficial study outcomes, and guideposts for future research activities. Although we recognise that justice, power, and equity are always in the making during research, we argue that this chapter informs and advances dialogue on emerging decolonising perspectives in the study of tourism and mobilities. This applies not only to the decolonisation of research methodologies – our focus above, to be sure – but also to the potential and promise of attending to Indigenous mobilities – what Prout (2009) might refer to as the spatial practices used by

Indigenous peoples to procure, contest, and cultivate security and belonging (e.g. our anticipated research land camp) – as a means for decolonising touristic spaces. In consideration of both circumstances, our study aims to support the maintenance and resurgence of Denesoline knowledge, values, voices, and contemporary occupancy associated with the Thelon River watershed (cf. Simpson 2008) and put into research praxis the ethical principles of respect, relevance, reciprocity, and responsibility (Kirkness and Bernhardt 1991). An intention with this chapter has been to set the stage for others to consider the opportunities and implications of engaging decolonising perspectives in their own research.

## References

Aleng, V. (2002) 'The modern does not care for natives: Travel ethnography and the conventions of form', *Tourist Studies*, 2(2): 119–42.

Ateljevic, I., Pritchard, A. and Morgan, N. (2007) *The critical turn in tourism studies: Innovative research methodologies*. Amsterdam: Elsevier.

Bennett, N., Lemelin, R. H., Johnston, M. E. and Lutsel K'e Dene First Nation (2010) 'Using the social economy in tourism: A study of National Park creation and community development in the Northwest Territories, Canada', *Journal of Rural and Community Development*, 5(1/2): 200–20.

Braun, B. (2002) *The intemperate rainforest: Nature, culture and power on Canada's west coast*. Minneapolis: University of Minnesota Press.

Butler, R. and Hinch, T. (2007) *Tourism and Indigenous peoples: Issues and implications*. New York: Routledge.

Castleden, H., Garvin, T. and Huu-ay-aht First Nation (2008) 'Modifying photovoice for community-based participatory Indigenous research', *Social Science and Medicine*, 66: 1393–405.

Castleden, H., Mulrennan, M. and Godlewska, A. (2012) 'Community-based participatory research involving Indigenous peoples in Canadian geography: Progress? An editorial introduction', *The Canadian Geographer*, 56(2): 155–9.

Cater, E. (2006) 'Ecotourism as a western construct', *Journal of Ecotourism*, 5(1&2): 23–39.

Chambers, D. and Buzinde, C. (2015) 'Tourism and decolonisation: Locating research and self', *Annals of Tourism Research*, 51(1): 1–16.

Chevalier, J. M. and Buckles, D. J. (2008) *SAS²: A guide to collaborative inquiry and social engagement*. London: Sage.

Chilisa, B. (2012) *Indigenous research methodologies*. Thousand Oaks, CA: Sage.

Cohen, E. and Cohen, S. (2014) 'A mobilities approach to tourism from emerging world regions', *Current Issues in Tourism*, 18(1): 11–43.

Cohen, E. and Cohen, S. (2015) 'Beyond eurocentrism in tourism: A paradigm shift to mobilities', *Tourism Recreation Research*, 40(2): 157–68.

Coles, T., Hall, C. M. and Duval, D. T. (2006) 'Tourism and post-disciplinary enquiry', *Current Issues in Tourism*, 9(4–5): 293–319.

Erickson, B. (2013) *Canoe nation: Nature, race, and the making of a Canadian icon*. Vancouver: University of British Columbia Press.

Fox, K. (2007) 'Aboriginal peoples in North American and euro-north American leisure', *Leisure/Loisir*, 31(1): 217–43.

Gordon, B. H. C. (1996) *People of sunlight, people of starlight: Barrenland archaeology in the Northwest Territories of Canada*. Hull, QC: Canadian Museum of Civilization.

Grimwood, B. S. R. (2011) '"Thinking outside the gunnels": Considering natures and the moral terrains of recreational canoe travel', *Leisure/Loisir*, 35(1): 49–69.

Grimwood, B. S. R. (2015) 'Advancing tourism's moral morphology: Relational metaphors for just and sustainable Arctic tourism', *Tourist Studies*, 15(1): 3–26.

Grimwood, B. S. R. and Doubleday, N. C. (2013a) 'From river trails to adaptive co-management: Learning and relating with Inuit inhabitants of the Thelon River, Canada', *Indigenous Policy Journal*, 23(4): 1–18.

Grimwood, B. S. R. and Doubleday, N. C. (2013b) 'Illuminating traces: Enactments of responsibility in practices of Arctic river tourists and inhabitants', *Journal of Ecotourism*, 12(2): 53–74.

Grimwood, B. S. R., Yudina, O., Muldoon, M. and Qiu, J. (2015) 'Responsibility in tourism: A discourse analysis', *Annals of Tourism Research*, 50(1): 22–38.

Hall, C. M. and Tucker, H. (2004) *Tourism and postcolonialism: Contested discourses, identities, and representations*. New York: Routledge.

Hannam, K. (2009) 'The end of tourism? Nomadology and the mobilities paradigm', in J. Tribe (ed.), *Philosophical issues in tourism*. Toronto, ON: Channel View, 101–13.

Johnson, C. W. and Parry, D. C. (2015) *Fostering social justice through qualitative inquiry: A methodological guide*. Walnut Creek, CA: Left Coast Press.

Johnson, J. T. (2010) 'Place-based learning and knowing: Critical pedagogies grounded in indigeneity', *Geojournal*, 77(3): 829–36.

Kelsall, J. P. (1968) *The migratory barren-ground caribou of Canada*. Ottawa, ON: Canadian Wildlife Service.

Kendrick, A., Lyver, P. O'B. and Lutsel K'e Dene First Nation (2005) 'Denésǫłiné (Chipewyan) knowledge of barren-ground caribou (*rangifer tarandus groenlandicus*) movements', *Arctic*, 58(2): 175–91.

Kirkness, V. J. and Bernhardt, R. (1991) 'First nations and higher education: The four Rs – respect, relevance, reciprocity, responsibility', *Journal of American Indian Education*, 30(3): 1–15.

Kovach, M. (2009) *Indigenous methodologies: Characteristics, conversations, and contexts*. Toronto: University of Toronto Press.

Louis, R. P. (2007) 'Can you hear us now? Voices from the margin: Using Indigenous methodologies in geographic research', *Geographical Research*, 45(2): 130–9.

Morse, E. (1987) *Freshwater saga: Memoirs of a lifetime of wilderness canoeing in Canada*. Toronto: University of Toronto Press.

Nielsen, N. and Wilson, E. (2012) 'From invisible to Indigenous-driven: A critical typology of research in Indigenous-tourism', *Journal of Hospitality and Tourism Management*, 19(5): 1–9.

Panelli, R. (2008) 'Social geographies: Encounters with Indigenous and more-than-White/ Anglo geographies', *Progress in Human Geography*, 32(1): 1–11.

Parlee, B. (2012) 'Finding voice in a changing ecological and political landscape: Traditional knowledge and resource management in settled and unsettled claim areas of the Northwest Territories, Canada', *Aboriginal Policy Studies*, 2(1): 56–87.

Parlee, B., O'Neil, J. and Lutsel K'e Dene First Nation (2007) '"The Dene way of life": Perspectives on health from Canada's north', *Journal of Canadian Studies*, 41(3): 112–33.

Pelly, D. F. (1996) *Thelon: A river sanctuary*. Hyde Park, ON: Canadian Recreational Canoe Association.

Pelly, D. F. (1997) *Arctic cairn notes: Canoeists' reflections on the Hanbury-Thelon and Kazan rivers*. Toronto: Betelgeuse Books.

Petermann, H. (2000) *Spirit of the Thelon: By canoe across the Canadian north.* Detmold: Alouette.

Peters, A. and Higgins-Desbiolles, F. (2012) 'De-marginalising tourism research: Indigenous Australians as tourists', *Journal of Hospitality and Tourism Management,* 19(6): 1–9.

Prout, S. (2009) 'Security and belonging: Reconceptualising aboriginal spatial mobilities in Yamatji Country, Western Australia', *Mobilities,* 4(2): 177–202.

Raffan, J. (1993) 'Where God began', *Equinox,* 12: 44–57.

Russell-Mundine, G. (2012) 'Reflexivity in Indigenous research: Reframing and decolonising research?', *Journal of Hospitality and Tourism Management,* 19(7): 1–6.

Rydzik, A., Pritchard, A., Morgan, N. and Sedgley, D. (2013) 'The potential of arts-based transformative research', *Annals of Tourism Research,* 40(2): 283–305.

Sandlos, J. (2007) *Hunters at the margin: Native people and wildlife conservation in the Northwest Territories.* Vancouver: UBC Press.

Sanjayan (2011) 'Thelon expedition: Life at camp', *Huffington Post.* Online at: www. huffingtonpost.ca/m-sanjayan/thelon-expedition-life-at_b_917629.html.

Simpson, L. (2008) *Lighting the eighth fire: The liberation, resurgence, and protection of Indigenous Nations.* Winnipeg: Arbeiter Ring.

Smith, L. T. (1999) *Decolonizing methodologies: Research and Indigenous peoples.* London: Zed Books.

Wearing, S. and Wearing, M. (2014) 'On decommodifying ecotourism's social value: Neoliberal reformism or the new environmental morality?', in M. Mostafanezhad and K. Hannam (eds), *Moral encounters in tourism.* Burlington: Ashgate, 123–37.

Wilson, S. (2008) *Research is ceremony: Indigenous research methods.* Halifax, NS: Fernwood.

# 19 Afterword

*Noel B. Salazar*

Mobility entails much more than mere physical motion (Marzloff 2005). After all, every form of mobility is movement infused with both self-ascribed and attributed meanings (Frello 2008). Mobility studies, then, call attention to the myriad ways in which people, objects, and ideas become part, in highly unequal ways, of multiple translocal networks and linkages, variously located in time and space. We have come a long way since the first formulations of transdisciplinary mobility studies over a decade ago (Hannam *et al.* 2006). Judging from the number of conference presentations and publications, mobilities have become a mainstream focus of attention in most of the social sciences and humanities. However, this popularity also contains an imminent danger. When reading the various chapters that constitute this volume, the reader may be confused as to what mobility actually refers to in each of the cases. As Peter Adey (2006) warned us a long time ago, 'if mobility is everything then it is nothing'.

It is useful, therefore, to clearly distinguish between two different uses of the term. First, mobility is an analytical lens, a focused perspective to look at the world, both mobile and immobile and everything in between (Salazar and Jayaram 2016). The 'new mobilities paradigm', for instance, incorporates novel ways of theorising how people, objects, and ideas travel by looking at social phenomena through the lens of movement (Hannam *et al.* 2006). This can be seen as a critique of both epistemologies of sedentism and deterritorialisation, trends in social science research that confine both researchers and their object(s) of study. However, considering mobility as a natural tendency in society naturalises it as a fact of life and as a general principle that rarely needs further justification. Peter Merriman (2014) has warned us about some of the methodological pitfalls of mobility studies, questioning, for example, the underlying assumption that mobilities research is necessarily a branch of social science research, and highlighting the production of overanimated mobile subjects and objects such research tends to produce, its inherent prioritisation of certain kinds of research methods and practices over others, and the overreliance on specific kinds of technology.

Second, there is mobility as an object of study – a complex assemblage of movement, imaginaries, and experience (cf. Cresswell 2006). This volume gives just a taster of the many types of mobilities that can be studied, even when limiting the scope to the domain of leisure and tourism. Important in this respect is the question of methodology because the traditional social science research methods were not developed to study people, things, and ideas in motion (Büscher *et al.* 2011; Fincham *et al.* 2010). Mobility scholars have called for novel research methods that are concomitantly 'on the move' and 'simulate intermittent mobility' (Sheller and Urry 2006: 217). Various contributions in this volume illustrate that the study of mobilities does not necessarily require a mobile researcher. Studying mobility by remaining in place, so to speak, 'offers a type of perspective that is concerned more with the social organisation of mobility than with particular circuits, more with a system than a place of origin or a specific destination' (Lindquist 2009: 10).

Critical analyses of mobility focus attention on the political-economic processes by which people are bounded, emplaced, allowed, or forced to move (Cunningham and Heyman 2004; De Genova and Peutz 2010). Such studies show how mobility is always materially grounded. The physical movement of people entails not only a measure of economic, social, and cultural mobility, but also a corresponding evolution of institutions and well-determined 'circuits of human mobility' (Lindquist 2009: 7). Importantly, the substance of such circuits is 'the movement of people (and money, goods, and news, but primarily people) as well as the relative immobility of people who do not travel the circuit' (Rockefeller 2010: 222). To assess the extent or nature of movement, or indeed even 'observe' it sometimes, one needs to spend a lot of time studying things that stand still (or change at a much slower pace). Equally important are the entangled histories that inform contemporary mobilities and help us to make sense of them (Salazar 2016).

What remains somewhat understudied are mobilities as embodied practices and experiences, the emotion in motion (Conradson and McKay 2007; Svasek 2012). What do various types of movement (differing across time and space) do to people? The chapter by Mike Collier on 'meandering' (moving slowly) gives us some insights. At the same time, his work makes us aware of the fact that there's more than one way to understand mobility. Academics clearly have a lot to learn from how artists tackle the same issues they are grappling with. Perhaps the most productive way to increase our knowledge of mobility is through cross-disciplinary and cross-sectoral efforts. However, attempts in this direction also show the limits of our methodological toolbox. Many elements are lost, for instance, when we try to translate multi-sensorial experiences into verbal accounts. What would the horse perspective be like of the human–equine leisure mobilities described by Paula Danby and Kevin Hannam? What are the 'mobilities' about in their case, and would there be any difference with work-related human–equine relations?

The chapter by Jonas Larsen on bicycle mobilities shows us the importance of context. Not only does it just matter where one cycles (in terms of traffic regulations, bicycle culture and climatic circumstances), but with whom one cycles (in this case the presence of the researcher's eight-year-old son). This reminds us of the importance of age as a determining factor in the experience of (im)mobility. Kevin Hannam's piece on female Pakistani migrants driving in Saudi Arabia similarly points to how a particular context can be very limiting in terms of mobility, creating differences between groups of people that in similar circumstances elsewhere are largely absent. Jillian Rickly's work on the subculture of rock climbers illustrates the relationality of movement, namely the ways that tourism or leisure-related movements encourage (and are encouraged by) other movements and the ways travel is put to use in, as well as extends, other aspects of life.

Jacqueline Salmond's chapter on the Perhentian Islands made me think of the ground-breaking work of Johan Lindquist (2009) on Batam Island. Both use a mobility lens to show how in the context of tourism the lines between leisure and work become blurred. Salmond argues that engaging with (international) tourism work is a lifestyle pursuit. The same has been said about expatriatism, which is explored in Roger Norum's contribution. What is telling here is that the imaginaries that people have about expat lifestyles do not always change as quickly as these lifestyles themselves (cf. Salazar 2014). In other words, the way we look at the (im)mobilities of others sometimes says more about our own positionality than anything else (cf. Franquesa 2011). Gergina Pavlova-Hannam discusses how not only imaginaries but also EU policy regimes shape the ambivalent mobilities of Bulgarians in terms of their work experiences in the tourism and hospitality industries.

Mobility regimes play a key role in William Terry's chapter on the mobility inequalities within the cruise industry. Ironically, while cruise workers are mobile at the scale of the global economy, they are relatively immobile while working on board. Many of these case studies illustrate that people are only as mobile as their governments and economies allow them to be (Salazar and Glick Schiller 2014). Meghann Ormond and Mika Toyota find remarkably similar trends in contemporary German and Japanese international retirement migration, namely the elderly not migrating out of necessity but rather because of economic precariousness. This shows, once again, how a broader context – in this case, an economic one – can enforce a certain type of mobility (moving overseas) while limiting other options (such as lifestyle mobility). Antonio Paolo Russo and Alan Quaglieri Domínguez analyse home swapping. This appears to be very much a Western phenomenon of 'mobile' cosmopolitan middle classes and destinations. Such findings confirm the importance of culture and cultural boundaries in the mobility choices people make (Salazar 2010).

The last set of contributions in this volume are grouped under the heading 'development'. Lauren Wagner talks about diasporic development and mobilities through the transient encounters at beauty salons of women of Moroccan descent during their holidays in their 'home' country, Morocco. Tess Guiney discusses orphanage tourism in Cambodia, raising the question whether tourism (principally enjoyment) and development (conceptualised as helping others/communities or for sustainability projects) are compatible at all. Cori Jakubiak analyses volunteer English language teaching abroad and describes the common confusion between English *for* development (a process in which English language skills help people to participate in existing development projects) and English *as* development (a process in which English language learning itself is the development goal).

Matilde Córdoba Azcárate reports about the everyday practices of (im)mobilities informing the strategies to gain control of ecotours in Mexico by a group of ex-fishermen who have been transformed into tourist boatmen. It raises interesting questions about how previous forms of mobility inform newer ones (Salazar 2016). William O'Brien and Wairimũ Ngarũiya Njambi discuss how nature is being (im)mobilised at the Maasai Mara National Reserve (cf. Salazar, in press). It brings us back to the structure-agency debate within the social sciences and social theory, the primacy of social forces versus free will in shaping behaviour (e.g. Giddens 1984). In the context of mobility studies, it would be a big mistake to equate structure with immobility and agency with mobility (as is often done). Talking about agency, the last chapter showcases a Canadian collaboration between Bryan S. R. Grimwood, Lauren J. King, Allison P. Holmes and the Lutsel K'e Dene First Nation. With this approach, the group hopes to contribute to specific methodological opportunities for realising the potential of a decolonising research paradigm within tourism and mobility studies. A lofty ideal, of which we would like to see much more in the future.

In sum, this volume give us much food for thought. It raises many issues, giving us a full agenda for future research on leisure and tourism mobilities. One of the biggest challenges ahead of us is the rising share of non-Western participants in global leisure and tourism (both as 'clients' and as service providers) and the fact that our predominantly Western explanatory models are highly insufficient to understand the mobility phenomena at hand (Cohen and Cohen 2015). In other words, we will need some ground-breaking mobilities within academia as well in order to keep up to date with the mobile world around us …

## References

Adey, P. (2006) 'If mobility is everything then it is nothing: Towards a relational politics of (im)mobilities', *Mobilities*, 1(1): 75–94.

Büscher, M., Urry, J. and Witchger, K. (eds) (2011) *Mobile methods*. London: Routledge.

Cohen, E. and Cohen, S. A. (2015) 'A mobilities approach to tourism from emerging world regions', *Current Issues in Tourism*, 18(1): 11–43.

Conradson, D. and McKay, D. (2007) 'Translocal subjectivities: Mobility, connection, emotion', *Mobilities*, 2(2): 167–74.

Cresswell, T. (2006) *On the move: Mobility in the modern Western world*. London: Routledge.

Cunningham, H. and Heyman, J. (2004) 'Introduction: Mobilities and enclosures at borders', *Identities*, 11(3): 289–302.

De Genova, N. and Peutz, N. M. (eds) (2010) *The deportation regime: Sovereignty, space, and the freedom of movement*. Durham, NC: Duke University Press.

Fincham, B., McGuinness, M. and Murray, L. (eds) (2010) *Mobile methodologies*. New York: Palgrave Macmillan.

Franquesa, J. (2011) '"We've lost our bearings": Place, tourism, and the limits of the "mobility turn"', *Antipode*, 43(4): 1012–33.

Frello, B. (2008) 'Towards a discursive analytics of movement: On the making and unmaking of movement as an object of knowledge', *Mobilities*, 3(1): 25–50.

Giddens, A. (1984) *The constitution of society: Outline of the theory of structuration.* Cambridge: Polity Press.

Hannam, K., Sheller, M. and Urry, J. (2006) 'Editorial: Mobilities, immobilities and moorings', *Mobilities*, 1(1): 1–22.

Lindquist, J. A. (2009) *The anxieties of mobility: Migration and tourism in the Indonesian borderlands.* Honolulu: University of Hawai'i Press.

Marzloff, B. (2005) *Mobilités, trajectoires fluides.* La Tour d'Aigues: Editions de l'Aube.

Merriman, P. (2014) 'Rethinking mobile methods', *Mobilities*, 9(2): 167–87.

Rockefeller, S. A. (2010) *Starting from Quirpini: The travels and places of a Bolivian people.* Bloomington: Indiana University Press.

Salazar, N. B. (2010) 'Towards an anthropology of cultural mobilities', *Crossings*, 1(1): 53–68.

Salazar, N. B. (2014) 'Migrating imaginaries of a better life … until paradise finds you', in M. Benson and N. Osbaldiston (eds), *Understanding lifestyle migration: Theoretical approaches to migration and the quest for a better way of life.* Basingstoke: Palgrave, 119–38.

Salazar, N. B. (2016) 'The (im)mobility of *merantau* as a sociocultural practice in Indonesia', in N. G. Bon and J. Repič (eds), *Moving places: Spatial relationality and the meanings of return, rootedness and belonging.* Oxford: Berghahn.

Salazar, N. B. (in press) 'The Maasai as paradoxical icons of tourism (im)mobility', in A. C. Bunten and N. H. H. Graburn (eds), *Cultural tourism movements: New articulations of indigenous identity.* Toronto: Toronto University Press.

Salazar, N. B. and Glick Schiller, N. (eds) (2014) *Regimes of mobility: Imaginaries and relationalities of power.* London: Routledge.

Salazar, N. B. and Jayaram, K. (eds) (2016) *Keywords of mobility: Critical engagements.* Oxford: Berghahn.

Sheller, M. and Urry, J. (2006) 'The new mobilities paradigm', *Environment and Planning A*, 38(2): 207–26.

Svasek, M. (ed.) (2012) *Emotions and human mobility: Ethnographies of movement.* London: Routledge.

# Index